LEONA ROSTENBERG

THE MINORITY PRESS
&
THE ENGLISH CROWN

A Study in Repression
1558 - 1625

With 18 illustrations

NIEUWKOOP · B. DE GRAAF
1971

By LEONA ROSTENBERG

English Publishers in the Graphic Arts 1599-1700 (New York, 1963)

Literary, Political, Scientific, Religious & Legal Publishing, Printing & Bookselling in England, 1551-1700: Twelve Studies (New York, 1965)

The Minority Press & The English Crown: A Study in Repression 1558-1625 (Nieuwkoop, 1971)

ISBN 90 6004 271 9
LC 71-145401
© Leona Rostenberg, New York, 1971

Printed in the Netherlands by N.V. Drukkerij Trio, The Hague

THE MINORITY PRESS & THE ENGLISH CROWN

For Madeleine

*"Friendship, like the immortality of the soul,
is too good to be believed."*

ACKNOWLEDGMENTS

I wish to express my particular indebtedness to the following who placed at my disposal the resources of their libraries: Mary Isabel Fry, The Henry E. Huntington Library; Maud Cole, Philomena Houlihan, and Lewis M. Stark, Rare Book Division, The New York Public Library; Carolyn E. Jakeman, The Houghton Library, Harvard University; Elizabeth Niemyer, The Folger Shakespeare Library; Richard H. Pachella, Union Theological Seminary Library; Dr. Dennis Rhodes, The British Museum Library. Above all I thank Madeleine B. Stern who gave tirelessly of her scholarship and time.

CONTENTS

	List of Illustrations	XII
	Introduction	3
I	Elizabeth the Great: Reign of the Queen	7
II	An Explication of the True Catholique Fayth: The English Catholic Press at Home and Abroad	18
III	Fardels of Popishe Trashe: The Circulation of Orthodox Books in England	31
IV	Spyings Abroade and Inquisitions at Home: Official Reprisal	43
V	Sharp Pointed Tongues & Slanderous Books: The Archpriest Controversy	53
VI	Overlord of the Whole Land: Reign of James I	67
VII	Careful and Diligent Search: Censorship	78
VIII	Audacious Pernicious Fellowes: The Underground Catholic Stationer	93
IX	Chests of Books at St. Omers: The Seminary Presses	111
X	Hartie Wel Wishers: John Heigham & Lawrence Kellam	123
XI	An Honest man sent to Lie Abroad for the Good of his Country: The English Ambassador	135
XII	The Foreign Circulation of Royal Texts: James I, Author	149
XIII	An Admonition to the Parliament: Puritan Reform	161
XIV	Printing in Corners: The Domestic Puritan Press	170
XV	A Liberty of Printing: The Puritan Press in the Netherlands	190
	Conclusions	202
	Notes	213
	Works cited	237
	Index	245

LIST OF ILLUSTRATIONS
(Illustrations between pages 209 and 213)

I   Engraving of Queen Elizabeth I from Henry Holland, *Herwologia Anglica* [1620].

II   Engraving of William, Cardinal Allen from Isaac Bullart, *Academie des Sciences et des Arts*. 1682.

III   Title-page of *The Life and end of Thomas Awfeeld a Seminary Preest and Thomas Webley a Dyers seruant*. 1585.

IV   Engraving of William Cecil, Lord Burleigh from Henry Holland, *Herwologia Anglica*. [1620].

V   Title-page of John Mush, *A Dialogve Betwixt A Secvlar Priest, and a Lay Gentleman*. 1601.

VI   Engraving of King James I from Thomas Milles, *The treasurie of aunicent and moderne times*. 1613.

VII   Manuscript List of Intercepted Catholic Books Submitted to Sir Julius Caesar. 1609.

VIII   Title-page of *Prvrit-Anvs*. 1609.

IX   James I, *A Proclamation for the search and apprehension of Iohn Cotton Esquire*. 1613.

X   Titles of "Popishe trashe" listed by John Gee in *The Foote out of the snare*. 1624.

XI   Title-page of John Wilson, *The English Martyrologe*. 1608.

XII   Title-page of John Heigham, *A Devovt Exposition of the Holie Masse*. 1614.

XIII   Manuscript List of Catholic Books shipped to the Venetian Embassy in London. 1609.

XIV   James I, *A Proclamation for Ambassadours and forreigne Ministers*. 1623.

XV   Elizabeth I, *A Proclamation* [confiscating Thomas Cartwright's *Second Admonition to the Parliament*]. 1573.

XVI   Elizabeth I, *A Proclamation* [forbidding the importation of the writings of Robert Browne and Robert Harrison into England]. 1573.

XVII   James I, *A Proclamation against Seditious, Popish, and Puritanicall Bookes and Pamphlets*. 1624.

XVIII   Title-page of William Ames, *Rescriptio*. 1617.

INTRODUCTION

The Catholic and Puritan emerge as the principal minority faiths in England under Elizabeth I and James I. To them the existing governments were unacceptable spiritually; to many Catholics they were also inadmissible politically.

The official attitude of England toward its religious extremists belies the concept of a harmonious nation exercising a philosophy of political latitude. A country whose queen had outwitted threats to her royal succession could ill afford dissension within. A state religion which was comparatively young could not countenance the restoration of the powerful orthodoxy it had rejected or the innovations of radical spiritual leftists. The ideologies of the minorities were little tolerated by a state insistent upon conformity in faith and the absolute authority of the Crown and Parliament. Disloyalty was to be chastised; treason excised.

Cognizant of that relentless authority, the religious minorities relied upon their own devices and inner strength. The Catholic nonconformist, the recusant, falls into two groups. The militant Catholic refused to take the Oath of Allegiance to the monarch and sought aid from abroad – even contemplating the overthrow of the kingdom. The pacifist Catholic retained his loyalty to the government and pursued his faith secretly. The Puritan never overtly bellicose stressed a spiritual regeneration. Divergent in religious issues – abhorrent to each other – both camps, however, found a bulwark in sermon and homily, controversial and devotional literature. To spread the word, Catholic and Puritan chose the powerful medium of the press. To their aid came the devoted, courageous Catholic and Puritan stationer.

In the shadowy world of agents and spies, zealots and prophets the stationer of the minority commingles, advances and recedes, a constant factor to indoctrinate, to propagandize. Fanatic or reasonably pious, quixotic or to a degree mercenary, he emerges as a vital ancillary to the missionary crusade of the Catholic and Puritan minorities. A force which gave the times a spate of literature, he demands an inquiry into his person, his career, his publications and achievements.*

The influence of the Catholic press had by 1560 alarmed the government which considered it to be "derogatorie to the soveraigne state of her Maieste ... impugning the rites established by law for Christian religion." Such "deroga-

---

* A study of the minority printer is based upon the sources of the age: letters and diaries, dispatches, confessions, official reports. They reveal the general background of the age, and despite their obvious bias, help create a valid portrait of the minority stationer and his implacable enemy, the English Crown.

INTRODUCTION

torie" literature had been issued by the Catholic printer whose Puritan counterpart was to experience similar hazards and difficulties in daily existence. Chased by the "lynx-eyed" pursuivants, members of a ruffian gang of official hirelings, and Messengers of the Press employed by the august Company of Stationers ever ready to placate the government – the minority printer was compelled to work in obscure areas of London and its suburbs. Driven from the Capital by agent or personal fear, he sought the semi-security of the provinces: Lancashire, Staffordshire, Warwickshire, Northamptonshire and the havens of wealthy patrons, "the house of a widow named Stonor which stood in the middle of a wood, twenty miles from London," the precincts of the Spanish Embassy in London and the manor of Sir Richard Knightley in Fawsley.

Aware of no respite in persecution, the minority printer occasionally departed England to pursue his profession abroad, hopeful for security and tranquillity. In the Netherlands the Catholic and Puritan found toleration and a haven to publish their particular religious political dogma which in turn was sent or brought by scouts and missionaries to the homeland. Despite the apparent safety of exile, the refugee printer could not completely elude the authority of the Crown whose diplomatic servant, alerted to subversive or critical publication, impounded the text and seized the offender.

In a program of reprisal aimed at national conformity the government had found it imperative to silence its opponents among them the minority printer. His premises were infested by an army of spies; he was fettered and arrested, thrown into a loathsome jail, the Clink, Newgate or the Poultry, served sentence in cells of "little ease" and upon occasion climbed the gallows at Tyburn.

The official attempt to stifle the minorities in England failed. Long after the defeat of the Armada the orthodox movement persisted in England. The "Puritannicall spirits" so abhorred by James I triumphed completely and mastered the realm bequeathed by him to his son.

In their search for recognition the Catholic and Puritan faiths were abetted by the printer-publisher whose texts provided political exemplars and spiritual nutriment. Theirs has been a history unexplored – a service neglected. Their lives ephemeral and skeletal will be reanimated, their contributions and productivity estimated.* In the great missionary crusade of the sixteenth and seventeenth centuries the participation of the Catholic and Puritan stationer must be assessed and placed in its rightful position.

---

* A discussion of the books published by the minority press is limited to works in English designed for an English speaking community. The author expresses her deep indebtedness to the excellent bibliographical monograph, *A Catalogue of Catholic Books In English Printed Abroad Or Secretly in England 1558-1640* by A.F. Allison & D.M. Rogers.

I

ELIZABETH THE GREAT

Reign of the Queen

The throne won by Elizabeth of England in November 1588 had often appeared to her illusive and remote. She was to assume her royal inheritance despite the connivance and intrigue of adversaries who would have denied her the Crown and rule of England. Matured in a world of cold, distrusting ambition, she determined to safeguard her realm for its well-being and her own security. She was to pursue an authoritarian policy, to impose her will upon the government and people. She was to become "the life, the head and authority of all things that be done in England." Her prerogative, declared Bacon, was never to be discussed. "The Queen hath both enlarging and restraining power. She may set at liberty things restrained by statute and may restrain things which be at liberty."[1]

Ever sensitive to criticism and to any threat to her Crown, Elizabeth demanded a conciliatory council and realm, loving and passive. Allegiance to the state and the established religion was arbitrary. Not fanatical in matters of religion, she regarded theological wrangling as stifling and tedious. Yet she believed in one faith and her official religious policy demanded an absolute observance of the tenets of the Established Church of England.

The Acts of Supremacy and Uniformity of 1559 required all holding or taking public office to subscribe to an oath forswearing Catholicism and denying Papal authority. By these Acts the Queen became the supreme ecclesiastical arbiter in the realm. Any deviation incurred official chastisement – her servants prosecuting the dissident. The severe legislation levelled against the Catholic minority casts a baleful shadow upon the splendid achievements of the age. The difficulties which beset the Catholic resulted from his affirmation of his ancient faith; his refusal to take the Oath of Allegiance; his study abroad at Catholic seminaries; his return to the motherland to preach and to convert. He became the outcast, the subject of the Roman pontiff, cohort of the King of Spain, enemy of the state.

Yet not all Catholics pledged an absolute obedience to the Pope. The question of papal supremacy in religious and temporal matters divided the English Catholic minority into two groups: the pacifist and the militant. The former retained his loyalty to the Crown and pursued his faith secretly. He balked at the idea of foreign invasion or leadership and accepted the Roman Pope only as his spiritual master. The Queen remained his temporal mistress. Her government was his, to be obeyed and to be defended. The militant, on the other hand, refused to take the Oath of Supremacy; he encouraged sedition from within and promoted invasion from without – even contemplating the assassination of his monarch – to achieve a Catholic victory, a Catholic England.[2]

It would be utterly fatuous to believe that the majority of English Catholics were involved in intrigue and cabal, the accomplices of Jesuits and foreign missionaries, prepared to subvert the Kingdom for the Vicar of Rome and the King of Spain. The average Catholic longed merely to practise his faith undisturbed – and for this desire – many suffered persecution and imprisonment. Although within the recesses of his conscience the pacifist English Catholic acknowledged the Pope as supreme religious arbiter, he took the Oath of Allegiance only to salvage his earthly existence. The more tractable Catholic wished to enjoy the largesse of his country: its political lustre, its expanding wealth, the benefits of trade, the advantage of guild participation, the security of a profession. He sought to live unmolested; to provide sustenance for himself and his children – to rest secure – without enmity, without fear.

England was not to tolerate her Catholic subjects who dwelt in a ruthless, arbitrary society, where liberty of conscience was still-born. Theirs was a struggle against harsh, repressive laws. The loyal Catholic suffered abuse and persecution along with the militant, the subversive, the recalcitrant. The glorious image of Elizabethan England is shattered by the cruelty inflicted upon a religious minority.

During the late 'sixties the home government was fully aware of the infiltration of missionaries and books printed abroad "contayning matters derogatorie to the soveraigne state of her Maiestie... impugning the rites established by law for Christian religion." Catholic and other offensive literature was circulating in England, having been imported by Catholic agents and militants. Such books were to be yielded to the authorities within twenty-eight days. They were "neither to be read or imported under severer penalty than hitherto inflicted in the Star Chamber."[3]

The publication of the papal Bull, "Regnans in Excelsis," issued against Elizabeth on February 25, 1570 by Pope Pius V, excommunicating the Queen of England, widened the breach between the state and its Catholic subjects. The Pontiff's sentence "against Elizabeth the Pretended Queen of England and those heretics loyal to her person," declared that her subjects were severed from all allegiance to her, "all manner of duty, fidelity and obedience." The Roman Vicar had denied her authority as head of the English Church. She had been accused of refusing bishops their sees, endorsing legislation against His Holiness and approving heresy. The Bull forcibly brought home the issue to the English pacifist. Practising his faith, he became a traitor to the state; asserting his devotion to the Crown, he became an outlaw of the church. While the pacifist chose to take the Oath of Allegiance, the militant remained obdurate and resolute.[4]

The outburst of unprecedented patriotism that resulted from the publication of the Bull was most disappointing to His Holiness. The papal "bulla" compared with the muscular English bull became the subject of parody and derision.

Popery was scorned in a variety of ballads: *Ye braynless blessynge of the bull; The begynninge and endynge of all popery; A manyfest or a playne Dyscourse of a hole packefull of popysshe knavery.* Public indignation continued to be fanned by anti-Catholic rhymes and ephemera: *A gentle Jyrke for the Jesuite; All shall be well the pope is now proued vicar of hell; A defence of the old and true Christianitie against the newe and counterfaite secte of the Jesuits or feloship of Jesus.*[5]

Burleigh, incensed, demanded harsher Catholic legislation. On July 1, 1570 a proclamation referred to the circulation of papal bulls in the country, emphasizing "certen wicked and malicious persons [who] by secret manner . . . bring in trayterous bookes and Bulles, as it were from Rome . . . not sparyng . . . to vtter hygh Treasons against the estate and Royall dignitie of her Maiestie to engender in the heades of the simple ignoraunt mvltitude a mislykyng or murmering agaynst the quiet gouernement of the Realme." Books and "bulles" were to be immediately surrendered to the Lieutenant of a shire or his deputy; their vendors to be arrested.[6]

In his retort to the Bull, Bishop Jewel denounced its author and expressed his poignant devotion to the Queen: "God gave us Queen Elizabeth and with her gave us peace, and so long a peace as England hath seldom seen before." Despite the Bishop's expression of loyalty and the fulminations against Rome, seditious books continued to enter the country. Reference is made in September 1573 to "obstinate and irrepentant traytours [who] fledde out of the country [and] . . . remayned in forraigne partes, with a continual and wylful determination . . . to contriue al the mischiefe that they can imagine . . . hauing a trade in pennyng of infamous libelles, not only in the Englishe, but also in Latine and strange languages. By these meanes they haue lately caused certain seditious bookes and libelles to be compiled and printed in diuers languages, wherein theyr final intention appeareth to be to blaspheme . . . theyr natiue Countrey." Such texts were condemned as "the workes of despisers of gods true religion, of obstinate traytours against her maiesties person." These books were forbidden to enter the country and if found were to be destroyed immediately.[7]

England by the late 'seventies was totally committed to the Protestant cause. The new legislation of 1581 increased the penalty for non-attendance at the Established Church to twenty pounds per month. All who attempted to win Englishmen from allegiance to their monarch or to proselytize for the orthodox faith were condemned as traitors. Elizabeth's popularity and influence were strongly resented by Pope Gregory XIII who believed that her demise – even by an assassin's hand – would prove a boon to the Catholic world. "She is the cause of so much injury to the Catholic faith. There is no doubt that whosoever sends her out of the world with the pious intention of doing God's service, not only does not sin but gains merit."[8]

Despite relentless legislative measures executed and misinterpreted by government agents, the English Catholics persevered in the tenets of their faith. "Infinite numbers [ran] into the church and [were] reconciled to their faith. Good men, making no account of losing their lives, hazard themselves to save their souls."

It was announced that masses were said even in the Court daily "as in any other Country abroad." The distinguished Jesuit, Father Robert Persons, active in England during the 1580's, noted the abounding Catholic fervor. "At Mass," he declared, the people were "so overpowered by a sense of awe and reverence that when they hear the name of the Pope pronounced in the Office they beat their breast and when the Lord's body is elevated, they weep so abundantly that they draw tears even voluntarily from my dry and parched eyes." Notwithstanding "the heat of the persecution waging against the Catholics throughout the whole realm ... most fiery, such as has never been heard of since the conversion of England," Persons estimated in 1580 that the number of converts had increased by twenty thousand since the preceding year. According to a statement issued in 1584, five hundred seminary priests roamed the Kingdom; the Pope was rumored to have given the English Catholics five thousand pounds, while the King of Spain, Philip II, spent much more "to maintain papists and seminaries."[9]

Reports received by the government referred to the steady infiltration of Jesuits and priests from the Continent. Some arrived in "French boats that come ... for coals who do land the said priests either at Newcastle or in some creek near the place." The informer, Richard Verstegan, acknowledged a regular route from the Continent via Middleburg or Amsterdam. Using a variety of pseudonyms and disguised as merchants, soldiers, tumblers or even galley slaves, the Catholics entered England, frequently eluding the port and customs officers. James Lessman, a Franciscan friar, revealed in 1582 that he had "lately returned from beyond the seas apparelled in a cloak of rats colour lined with green baize the cape of tuffed taffeta, red and blue, his girkin and gascoyne of the colour of the cloak, his doublet white and stockings of his hose of a bluishe or murrey colour."[10]

It was no secret to the government by July 1580 that plots were being hatched abroad for the invasion of England by mercenaries of the Pope and the King of Spain. Native-born Englishmen were skilfully trained abroad as missionaries and teachers to penetrate the country. Hence subjects were cautioned "to be in good readiness" and "murmerers were to be apprehended and chastised." A system of espionage, employing a rabble group of spies and informers, was relied upon. Often the guile and efficiency of the Catholic zealot outwitted English expertise. Despite the fact that the government had been informed of the pending arrival of Fathers Campion and Persons and had even supplied the port officials with woodcut portraits of the two most prominent English Jesuits, both men slipped through their hands and eluded arrest.

Indifferent to the chilling prospect of Newgate, Marshalsea, the Clink and even the gallows on Tyburn Hill, Jesuits and priests pushed on to English soil. Although Cardinal Allen had hoped to provide every missionary with a new suit and six or seven pounds for his journey, he often entered the country penniless. It was with great difficulty that the Jesuit could obtain money since people "refused to endanger themselves for them and be at charge also."

The arrival of Fathers Campion and Persons posed a grave threat to the country.

Their appearance 'midst their co-religionists was inspirational, inducing more conversion and hope. A new enactment was issued which denounced all Jesuits and priests who entered the country "to stir up rebellion and deprive [depose] her Majesty." Not only were all Jesuits and priests considered traitors but all persons who harbored them. The Continental seminaries were condemned as centers of propaganda and sedition. According to the Catholic agitator, Nicholas Faunt, "the young gentlemen go over by heaps from thence, but of all places and most by creeks and in fisher boats carrying them with great provisions of all necessaries." Scotland was declared to be "a common passage for all English caterpillars into foreign parts." Oxford and Cambridge were reported "full of popish rogues."[11]

Pope Gregory XIII had become extremely impatient with the offensive conduct of Elizabeth toward his Catholic flock. In November 1583 he renewed the excommunication of the Queen, reminding her subjects that their monarch had not yet repented but had heaped new infamies on the old. Therefore he had decided to re-issue the Bull of his predecessor, Pius V, against "that Elizabeth or rather that Jezebel." Elizabeth was deposed and Mary Stuart recognized as the lawful Queen of England. No subject was to consider himself bound to the reigning monarch. The Bull was not published, but copies were to have been brought to England by Cardinal Allen after the successful invasion of the Armada.[12]

Incensed by the Pope's attitude and the continued circulation of "slanderous, wicked, seditious and trayterous bookes and libelles," a proclamation of October 12, 1584 decreed that all such texts – if detected – were to be delivered immediately to a county sheriff or his deputy. It was further declared that "all marchantes, masters of shippes, officers of ports, or any other that shalbe bringer into this Realme of any the sayde seditious bookes or libelles, or a dispenser of the same . . . shall be committed . . . to prison."[13]

The following year all Jesuits and seminary priests were banished from England on pain of death. All Englishmen educated abroad were compelled to return to the motherland within six months and required to take the Oath of Allegiance. Shortly thereafter Walsingham was instructed to have a list drawn up of all wealthy recusants in every shire that "there be such an order taken with them as they may do no harm nor be any comfort to the enemy."[14]

Although stricter watch was demanded at the English ports, the venality of the harbor agents was berated by the Catholic leaders who asserted that many priests had been arrested upon their arrival in England, since "they do not have the money to bribe officials who never accuse any one with money." The Jesuit, Thomas Fitzherbert, was to write of the dishonor brought to the state by the "persons, messengers and others which are employed by warrant from the High Commission, sell[ing] such priests and Jesuitts for great sommes of money." Father Gerard declared that "an army of spies and informers was prowling about the length and breadth of the land, living by their wits and feeding partly upon the terror of others and partly upon the letter of the law as laid down by recent acts." The "gentle" poet, Robert Southwell, contemptuously referred to the "lynx-eyed pursuivant" whose business it was to arrest Catholics. "They ransack homes, and they rob those who lay hands on of their money, horses and belongings. Some Catholics have died in Newgate overcome by the stench of the prisons; others in the same place suffer greatly from their confinement and the filth."[15]

English antipathy toward Rome and Spain was further inflamed in May 1588 by a broadside purportedly issued by Pope Sixtus IV. Its authorship has been attributed to Cardinal Allen. *A Declaration of the sentence and deposition of the vsvrped and pretensed qvene of England* reiterates Elizabeth's excommunication and deposition. The broadside further endorsed the political ambitions of Philip of Spain. The time had arrived for all loyal Englishmen to accept the Pope's authority and to assist the liberators of their harassed island. A proclamation forbade Englishmen to circulate this malicious Bull. Dispersers were to be tried by martial law. According to Lord Burleigh, twelve thousand copies of this "hellish bull" had been printed at Antwerp. He believed that the publication should be "impeached" and "all men of judgment not corrupted with Romish poison would be rather stirred to defend the Queen's person and the country than to offend." The Lord Secretary was further incensed by the content of an Antwerp dispatch, stating that thousands of bulls and libels had been printed there, "discharging her Majesty's subjects of their obedience."[16]

To rouse the religious enthusiasm of the pacifist English Catholic, Cardinal Allen issued *An Admonition to the Nobility and People of England* in which the highest ecclesiast of the realm referred to his rightful queen as "an incestuous bastard, begotten and born in sinne." He glorified the projected invasion of Philip II as a holy crusade to drive Elizabeth, "that monster of impiety and unchastity" from the throne. His was a mission to further the welfare of God and Christendom and to relieve the Cardinal's long suffering brethren "from the yoke of heresie and thralldom of [their] enemies." Allen's excoriation had been published anonymously at Antwerp and, like the *Declaration* of Sixtus IV, was to be circulated throughout England by the Duke of Parma after the triumphant invasion. Lord Burleigh had been able to secure copies of the "Bull" and the *Admonition* through Sir Henry Killigrew, English Ambassador to the Low Countries; the printer's devil having brought him sheets concealed within the folds of his shirt. Once the *Admonition* was secretly distributed in England, Burleigh demanded its prohibition "upon the pain of treason." He referred to the "booke . . . so violently, sharply and bitterly written . . . so arrogantly falsely and sclaunderously against the person of the Queene . . . as so many good men of our own religion offended therewith."[17]

The omnipresent fear of Catholic intrigue and combat is betrayed in a note from William Giffard to Walsingham: "We cannot deny the existence of certaine intemperate and seditious spirits among the English Catholics who seeke unnaturalie to disturbe and chaunge the estate by bringinge or consentinge to forrayners to the subversion of hir majesties estate." The loyal subjects of Elizabeth were in "good readiness," as the "forrayners" aboard His Spanish Majesty's Armada failed their monarch in his most Christian mission. The Spanish fleet in the midsummer of 1588 was soundly trounced by the sea-dogs of Elizabeth, among them many of her faithful Catholic subjects, including her Lord High Admiral, Lord Howard of Effingham. The nation rejoiced at its deliverance. The people wept and gave thanks for their great and glorious victory. They gathered to pay homage to their queen, the saviour of their realm. The august Company of Stationers assembled its "fflages and other necessaryes pertayning to the Companyes attendance at her Maiesties repaire to Paules to gyve thancks for her victory over the Spaniardes and for twooe seuerall Dynners for the Companie at the same tyme at twooe dayes." The members of this selfsame Company proclaimed their gratification in the various publications which lampooned the Spaniard and hailed English success: *A ballad of the obteyning of the galeazzo wherein Don Pedro de Val[d]ez was chief; A Joyfull sonnet of the Rediness of the shires and nobilitie of England to her Maiesties service; The late wonderful dys[a]stres whiche the Spanishe navye sustayned yn the late fighte in the sea; A ballad of thankes gyveinge vnto God, for his mercy toward his Maiestie; A new ballad of the glorious victory of Christ Jesus, as was seene by the overthrowe of the Spanyardes* and *The ioyfull Tryumphes performed . . . beyond the seas for the happines of England and the overthrowe of the Spanishe barge.*[18]

Neither chauvinistic tracts nor hours in prayer and thanksgiving permitted any official relaxation toward the Spanish spectre. To discourage further invasion Lord Burleigh issued a pamphlet, *The Copy of a Letter sent out of England to Don Bernardino Mendoza, Ambassador to France for the King of Spain declaring the State of England.* The *Letter* presented a harmonious English front in which Catholic had joined with Protestant in defense of their beloved country. To emphasize his argument, Burleigh had cleverly employed a ruse, ascribing the work to one Richard Leigh, a seminary priest, who had been hanged at Tyburn.[19]

The presumed Catholic author refers to the wavering policy of his co-religionists in the recent period of national crisis: "For I do find and know that many good, and wise men, which of long time have secretly continued in most earnest devotion to the Pope's authorities, begin now to stagger in their mindes, and to conceaue that this way of reformation, intended by the Popes holines is not allowable in the sight of God, by leauing the ancient course of the Church by Excommunication, which was the exercise of the spirituall sword, and in place thereof to take the temporal sword, and put it into a monarches hand and to inuade this realme with forces and armes, yea to destroy the Quene thereof, and all the people addicted to her: which are in very truth now seene by great proofe this yeare to be in a sort infinite and inuincible." Burleigh deplored the "sundry things written and put into print, and sent into this realme, their object to hearten the people for invasion and the annihilation of the Queen . . . things so odiously taken, as the hearts of all people were inflamed."[20]

Although Elizabeth's loyal servant had described a strong, consolidated state, the nation was actually torn by religious strife. Burleigh had never relaxed his anti-Catholic policy harshened by the threat of recent invasion. His implacable attitude aroused criticism from his own immediate circle. His agent, John Snowden, wryly observed that in place of one Catholic put to death another ten stole into England from the Continental seminaries. "Their martyrdom is the greatest service to opponents abroad, for accounts are printed, painted and published and princes are moved to compassion." Yet Burleigh's obduracy persisted. Father John Gerard wrote that "the Spanish attempt had exasperated the public mind against Catholics; most rigid serches and domiciliary visits had been set on foot, [that] the guards were posted in every village along the roads and streets." In 1591 a new Edict insisted that Jesuits and priests depart the realm. New commissioners, "men of honesty, fidelity and good reputation," were appointed in every shire, city and port-town "to enquire ... what persons by their behauiours or otherwise [were suspected] to be any such persons ... to acknowledge any kind of obedience to the Pope or to the King of Spain." Verstegan remarked that persecution had never been so vigorous, while Father Southwell declared that "all evil publikely done" was always attributed to Catholic machination.[21]

The ever-pervasive threats of larger Armadas, looming on the coastal horizon, alarmed the stout-hearted. Stories circulated and multiplied. A released Spanish prisoner declared that Englishmen of all conditions had assured him of their high hopes for a Spanish invasion and of their zeal for the Catholic faith. "If they do not openly avow their sympathy it is that they may not lose their home and possessions." In 1593 rumors spread abroad of imminent landings in the country of a force under the leadership of the expatriate William Stanley backed by Spanish power. "As soon as the arrival is reported, the whole Spanish fleet is to be ready; Persons present and Cardinal Allen is to come to Rome."[22]

The threat of the Spaniard conjured up the image of the Jesuit, cadaverous and lean, in his black habit, scurrying about with his breviary into dark recesses, where tapers burned and crucifixes hung.[23] His cunning and astuteness were carefully drawn to Lord Burleigh's attention: "He is a most dangerous person, continually whispering and busy in secret devices ... very dangerous to the prince and state where they liue. [They] put forth infamous libels, howsoever disguised under forms of petitions, etc. printed and dispersed in all places slandering her Maiesties Council, Government and subjects. Their opposition and hatred as you know is very deep and vehement." Bacon expressed his concern at the recurrent attacks upon the Crown and state. "What a nomber of libellous and defamatory books and writings and in what variety, and with what art and cunning handled, haue been allowed to pass through this world in all languages against her Majesty and her government."[24]

Aware of Elizabeth's declining health, the militant Catholic at home and his colleague abroad strove through nimble action and word to win the country as a papal fiefdom. Had not a proclamation been drawn up by the great "Adelantado of Castilla, Earle of Sant Badea and of Bundia, Commendador of Salmea,

Captayne General of the galleyes and army of the Ocean Sea and of the Catholike camp" that the new planned invasion of England was a crusade to restore Catholicism? Had not His Spanish Majesty promised all good Catholics of England protection and the rightful sequestration of heretics' property? Had not the most shrewd of Jesuits, Father Persons, suggested the Spanish Infanta as Elizabeth's rightful successor? Was she not a direct descendant of John of Gaunt, a Lancastrian? Using the pseudonym, R. Doleman, Persons published *A Conference about the next Succession to the Crown of Englande* which appeared at Antwerp in 1594. The choice of Father Persons' Spanish princess – despite her direct descent from John of Gaunt – was completely ignored by Elizabeth Tudor. Persons' book was denounced as treasonable and seditious and its circulation forbidden in the country.[25]

The appointment of a successor to the Crown of England was the responsibility of a much beloved queen whose life span had now entered its last decade.

Fired by the loyalty of some English Catholics and Spanish ambition, Father Persons impatiently awaited the Queen's demise. In a communiqué of July 3, 1600 to Philip III of Spain he stated that Elizabeth had but little time to live. "The English Catholics beg your Majesty to declare yourself in the matter of the succession. Your Majesty's decision may be conveyed in confidence to the Archpriest and General of the Jesuits in England so that it can be published at the proper time. It is agreed that the first thing is to exclude utterly from the succession the Kings of Scotland and France. The forces of Flanders and the Fleet should be made ready, so that on the very day the Queen dies a movement be made from both sides simultaneously in favor of the object aimed at."[26]

A dispatch from Pope Clement VIII to the Papal Nuncio in Flanders advised of the current state of affairs in England and of the country's glorious Catholic future. "It is likely that there will soon be a great change by the death of her, who, by the secret judgment of God, has so long afflicted that noble kingdom." The Nuncio was advised that English Catholics had been instructed to unite and refuse support to anyone who was not of their faith. As soon as His apostolic envoy received word of the demise of "the miserable woman," he was to inform the English faithful who, in the name of the Pope, were "to stand ready" and to work for a Catholic king who "will give you and your successors true obedience."[27]

Elizabeth died on March 24, 1603, her demise inspiring a barrister of the Middle Temple to write: "Shee now [dwells] among the royall saints in Heaven in eternall joyes." Five days later James VI of Scotland was advised of his succession to the English throne.[28]

II

AN EXPLICATION OF THE TRUE CATHOLIQUE FAYTH

The English Catholic Press at Home and Abroad

Throughout the years of persecution under Elizabeth – despite the harsh legislation, the search of the pursuivant, the stench of Newgate and Marshalsea, the spectre of Tyburn, the zeal of the orthodox remained constant. From several sources he derived his strength, his courage. His personal conviction bolstered his moral fiber. From the missionary and priest he received the succor of prayer and the promise of life everlasting, transcending the drudgery and oppression of a harsh, daily existence. From the printed text he derived a more tangible assurance. Indelible, the written proof of religious experience and triumph, of ultimate reward and ecstasy unfolded before him.

    The literature which nourished the Catholic faith in England was supplied to some small extent by the underground English printer. His was a hazardous role subject to the relentless pursuit of a determined and outraged state. His office demanded the conviction and talents of the most resolute, the intrepid, the fearless. The majority of the controversial and devotional English Catholic treatises, which permeated England during the reign of Elizabeth, were printed abroad either by the English Catholic in exile or by foreign craftsmen motivated by religious background, sympathy and economic incentive. The hazards which beset the refugee English Catholic publisher can scarcely be compared with those confronting the domestic underground craftsman. As the printer of Catholic texts, the latter emerges a subversive agent whose publications challenged the authority of the Queen, the supreme head of the Church of England. The role assumed by the English domestic Catholic printer branded him a renegade, a traitor to the state. To support his conviction and his career, he defied edict and search, arrest and imprisonment, torture and death. With the priest, he became a stalwart missionary, his press a stout bulwark for the faithful, a rampart against the fulminations of the adversary.

Although the predecessors of Elizabeth had been fully aware of the growing influence of the press, it was not to become a serious political menace until her reign. Measures had been taken by her father's government to curb this powerful propaganda medium. The 1538 Proclamation of Henry VIII which sought "to expell and auoyd the occasion of errours and opinions opined" was the first attempt to establish a regular censorship and licensing over all kinds of printing. The threatening nature of the press was evident during the early years of Mary's reign. Alarmed by an increasing number of unauthorized printers and the circulation of books disrespectful to the regime and the Queen's person, the state insisted that none be permitted to print or sell "false" books, ballads and rhymes without the queen's license. Almost at the advent of her reign the press became the object of Elizabeth's "restraining" power. The steady increase in the number of printers and booksellers had naturally produced a far greater production of books and pamphlets.[1]

Although the royal controls upon the printing trade were presumably designed to protect the small and destitute craftsman, the rigid Elizabethan legislation of 1559 reflects the government's awareness of the political danger implicit in an unbridled press. The so-called paternalism of the English Crown appears to be rather dubious. Because of "a great abuse in the printers of bookes which for covetousness chiefly regard not what they print so they may haue gain, whereby ariseth great disorder by publication of unfruitful vayne and infamous bookes and papers," the state declared that all new books, before publication, were to be submitted for scrutiny to six members of the Privy Council. Any person who printed in violation of any statute was compelled to forfeit all copies of books illegally executed. In addition, such material was to be burned and the offender fined one hundred shillings. Reference was made to the importation of books from abroad and others secretly printed at home "filled with heresy and treason." Any distributor of such books "shall be taken for a rebel and executed by martial law."[2]

An apprehensive state found an ally and bulwark in the recently established Company of Stationers. The charter of the Company provided against politically unruly members: "It shall be lawful for the Master and Keepers or Wardens ... to make search whenever it shall please them in any place, shop, house, chamber, or building of any printer, binder or bookseller whatever within our Kingdom of England ... for any bookes or things printed ... and to seize, take, hold, burn ... all and several those books and things which are or shall be printed contrary to the form of any statute, act or proclamation made or to be made."[3]

Hence armed with searchers of the Company of Stationers and official pursuivants, the government strove to curb the press, to stifle any publication critical of the Crown and the established religion. Citizens were advised in 1569 of "certain persons [who] scatter seditious bills and books [which] slander the Queen and nobility. Any person finding such a booke is to take it to the Lieutenant of the shire ... or at least [to] some Justice of the Peace who shall send it sealed to the Privy Council. Any persons suspected of being authors of such are to be strictly examined." Informers were promised rich bounties – concealers warned of severe reprisals. In March 1576 a reward of one hundred forty pounds was promised to anyone below the rank of gentleman and one hundred pounds to any gentleman who would divulge the names of the authors of seditious libels "set up in sundry places about the City and Court invented for the ruin of some of good estimation with her Majesty."[4]

The Edict of 1586 limited printing to London, Oxford and Cambridge. The Archbishop of Canterbury and the Bishop of London were to decide the number of presses and to authorize the licensing of all publications. The government's directives were levelled primarily against persons suspected of authoring, harboring, publishing and distributing seditious and libellous writings. Its principal target was the Catholic whose religion branded him hostile, an enemy of the state. He was the traitor, guilty of lèse-majesté. His person, his family, his utterances were suspect. The struggle between the government and the Catholic minority, which voiced its tenets and its grievances through the press, evolved into a ruthless campaign. Faith and courage became the defense of the minority; intolerance and suppression the weapons of the state!

Robert Caly set the precedent for the publication of Catholic books in England. Obviously he was most active during the reign of Mary. His beginnings and end coincide with the religious transition of the nation. During Edward's reign he left England to return under the rule of his Catholic half-sister and to depart once again upon the accession of Elizabeth.

Caly may have begun as a stationer, with other English craftsmen, in the publishers' row of London, St. Paul's Churchyard. His strong Catholic leanings took him abroad, since the first known work to bear his imprint was issued from the subsequent hot-bed of Anglo-Catholic printing, Rouen. Here in 1551 he published *An explication and assertion of the true Catholique fayth touching the most blessed sacrament of the aulter* by Stephen Gardiner. It was "imprinted at Roan by Robert Calye and are to be solde in Paules Churchyarde at the Signe of the Bysshopes Head." It appears that Caly retained a London factor – his identity unknown – who imported Catholic publications for domestic distribution. With the accession of the Catholic Mary, Caly returned to London and on April 30, 1558 he received a royal license from the Queen. From his London premises, "within the precincte of the late house of the Grey Friars" Caly issued an approximate thirty-three books by Catholic authors, including the *Sermons* of James Brooks, Bishop of Gloucester, "a zealous maintainer of the Roman Catholic religion"; the homilies and sermons of John Feckenham, last Abbot of Westminster, *The Holsome and Catholyke doctryne concerning the seven Sacraments* by Thomas Watson, Bishop of Lincoln and one of the principal Catholic controversialists, the writings of St. John Fisher and Vincent of Lerins, in addition to breviaries and primers. Caly, alarmed by Elizabeth's antipathy toward Catholics and the more stringent press regulations, was not active after 1558.[5]

Caly confronted no political hazard. As a printer of Catholic texts under a Catholic queen, he pursued his profession under favorable auspices. The career of William Carter compares little with that of his Catholic colleague. Upon him was bestowed no royal favor. Rather he suffered persecution and destruction by the state in its obdurate campaign to extirpate Catholic practise and expression.

William Carter, the son of a London draper, had served his apprenticeship with the distinguished London stationer, John Cawood, indentured to him on February 2, 1563 for a period of ten years. Later he became amanuensis to the Catholic divine, Nicholas Harpsfield, until the latter's death in 1575. Bishop Aylmer described Harpsfield as an "evil fellow and very pigheaded," and declared that Carter not only "wrote" [copied] the books which he published [circulated] for him while he was alive but took the greatest pains to scatter them abroad after his master's death. Carter's secretly printed "papistical books" were issued from his press on Hart Street which circulated approximately eleven titles largely devotional in content. These include among others, *The godlie garden of Gethsemanie, Instructions and advertisements how to meditate the misteries of the rosarie of the most holy virgin*, Henry Suso's *Certain sweet prayers of the glorious name of Jesus*, the *Catechisme* of St. Peter Canisius, the *Jesus Psalter*. To avoid detection Carter not only employed imprints of well-known Douai presses, but also occasionally attributed the place of publication to Antwerp and Bruges. Several books bear only the date of issue.[6]

Bishop Aylmer, who had become suspicious of the activities in Hart Street, in 1579 sent pursuivants to inspect the premises. He reported gleefully that they had "found out a presse or pryntinge with one Carter ... who hath byne divers tymes before in prison for the printinge of lewd pamphlettes." Now the Bishop's men detected "among other naughtye papysticall Bookes ... one written in ffrenche intytled the innosency of the Scottish Quene a very Dangerous Book wherein he calleth her the heire apparent of this Crowne." Obviously a Stuart sympathizer – and not only a printer but as well a stationer, stocking Catholic Continental texts – Carter had imported copies of François de Belleforest's *L'Innocence de Marie, royne d'Escosse* which had been printed anonymously in 1572. The presence of Belleforest's treatise betrayed Carter's allegiance to the cause of Mary Stuart. He was hauled before the Court of High Commission, where he was booked as "William Carter bokebinder de civitate London." Lacking sufficient evidence to convict him of the crime of high treason, the Court nevertheless regarded him as a firebrand and sentenced him to a term in the Gatehouse.[7]

The searchers, dissatisfied with their original evidence, returned to Hart Street. A more zealous investigation produced proof of guilt, the notorious *Treatise of Schisme* by Gregory Martin – printed by Carter – a work fraught with treason, suggesting to Elizabeth's attendants the assassination of their royal mistress. Reporting the search, Aylmer stated that Carter had refused to admit his guilt "vppon his othe." He referred to "newe formes of letters [types] made by Carter and another book offensive to the Queen." Carter, incarcerated in the Gatehouse, was informed that he could not leave prison unless he posted a bond of one hundred marks. There is considerable confusion of facts regarding the printer's prison stay. There is some evidence that he was at large, since, according to the Recusant Rolls, he was indicted in late May 1581 for not attending church. He apparently had been temporarily released but was dispatched to the Tower where he almost succumbed to the torture of the wrack. His meagre existence within the Tower walls is reported by the Keeper who itemized the cost of his prisoner's light and food ration, having spent thirteen shillings, four pence for his diet and "chardges including fuel, wicks and candles." According to Carter's wife Agnes, a former servant to Lady Carew, the final search of her husband's premises not only revealed Martin's treatise but had proved to be so violent that "all in our house has been taken away [and] certen roomes shutt vp."[8]

The appeal of Agnes Carter for her husband's life proved to be in vain. Walsingham's agent reported that "there is neither Jesuite, prieste nor Papyste of any accompte within England but he [Carter] knowethe them [and] is acquainted with the secret dealings of the Papists." His wife was considered likewise to be extremely dangerous and the government encouraged her imprisonment as well. "She knoweth as much as her housbande, not onelie in this, but in all other affayres and causes concernyng the dealinge of the Papists." Carter admitted at his trial in Old Bailey that he had printed 1,250 copies of the ill-fated treatise of Gregory Martin. He was condemned upon the charge of high treason. The state's action was deeply deplored by the Catholic historian, John Bridgewater, who wrote: " . . . id crimini datur quod 1583 in necem Reginae conuerauit, religionisque mutationem cogitarit: quod vt facilius pro arbitratu executioni mandaret eu[m] typis mandasse, & in luce[m] edisse libru[m] quendam seditiosum hoc nomine Tractatus quidem de schismate . . ." On January 11, 1583, after a lengthy imprisonment Carter was taken to Tyburn where he was hanged, disemboweled and quartered. In a short note written during the following summer Agnes Carter requested the release of certain "goodes and books" the property of her late husband, a martyr to his faith.[9]

While Carter pondered his fate, Richard Rowlande, a printer who was to assume future importance in the English Catholic movement abroad as a spy and news-agent, operated a secret press in Smithfield. This venture was exceedingly short-lived since only one book is known to have appeared from this press. The execution of the gentle Campion on December 1, 1581 aroused Catholic consternation and public curiosity. Among the witnesses of his death were the Dolman brothers, two young Catholic students and the priest, Thomas Alfield. The Dolmans took note of the "wordes and manner of executyon and deliuered the same to Rowland the prynter in Smythfield." *A true reporte of the death and martyrdome of M. Campion Iesuite and priest M. Sherwin and M. Bryan priests* published by Rowlande in 1582 and long attributed to Alfield was actually written by Stephen Vallenger, a Norfolk Catholic divine who was to become a prisoner for life in the Fleet.[10]

Shortly after publication of *A true reporte* Rowlande's press was discovered by searchers and, according to a letter from William Fleetwood, serjeant-at-law, April 14, 1582: "It fell owt the first weke of lent that there was a booke cast abroode com[m]endinge of Campian and of his fellowes, and of their deathe. I pursued the matter so nere that I found the presse, the l[ette]res the figures and a nosmber of bookes." Rowlande, however, had made a quick getaway, settling temporarily in Paris, where he issued two books in 1583, *A treatyse of Christian peregrination* by Gregory Martin and *A refutation of sundry apprehensions* of William Rainolds.[11]

Shortly after the nimble Rowlande made his escape from England a few religious manuals by the Welsh grammarian Griffith Robert were printed to the far west of London – in Wales. Educated in Italy, Robert had written in 1567 a Welsh grammar which was printed by the Milanese stationer, Vincentio Girardoni. There is some evidence that Robert's books were issued by a secret press in Wales. His *Christianogawl*, a religious manual, appeared with the fictitious imprint, "Rothomagi apud Iathroni Favonis," having actually been printed at Rhiwledyn in Wales. Robert's *Ynglynion ar y Pader y Credo*, the author's interpretation of the Credo, is tentatively ascribed to a Welsh press of one Thackwell whose very existence is based upon some deprecatory remarks in the Marprelate tract, *The Epistle*. The writer waxes indignant about the "knave Thackwell the printer [which printed popishe and traiterous Welshe bookes in Wales]. [He] is at liberty to walk where he will and permitted to make the most he could of his press and letters whereas Robert Waldegrave [printer of the Marprelate tracts] does not show his face for the printing of books which toucheth the Bishops Myter. Though he [Thackwell] printed Popishe and trayterous bookes, [he] may have the fauour to make money of his presse and letters."[12]

A press – which may have belonged to Thackwell – was found in a cave near the shore of Creuddyn in Carnarvonshire. According to a resident Justice of Peace, metal printing types had been found there which – it was assumed – had been hastily thrown into the sea by a rapidly departing printer upon the approach of the pursuivant. It is of course conjectural whether the master of the Creuddyn cave is identical with Thackwell.[13]

Before the Welsh printer set up his secret press in Wales, the most astute of English Jesuits, Father Robert Persons, had arrived in Dover in June 1580. Attired as a soldier, wearing a "suit of buff laid with gold lace, with hat and feathers suited to the same," he eluded detection and proceeded to London. By the following October Father Persons had established his first secret English press.

During his London stay Persons had become acquainted with an active Catholic, Francis Browne, brother of Lord Montague, who permitted him the use of his residence for the installation of a press – "a large and fair house near a place they call Greenstreet, East Ham." Persons engaged an able printer, Stephen Brinkley, who employed seven assistants. Hopes for the East Ham Press were high. Brinkley's men were given rich apparel to disguise themselves to allay any suspicion. Despite this considerable personnel only six books were issued by the Greenstreet Press, the first by Father Persons: *A Brief discours contayning certayne reasons why Catholiques refuse to goe to church*. Others include controversial treatises by Richard Bristow, Thomas Hide, Persons and two editions of *A Manual or Meditation*. To elude detection the majority of the Greenstreet publications bear the imprint "Louvaine John Lion."[14]

Thomas Alfield, who was later to assist Master Rowlande in Smithfield, was one of Persons' most able supporters and is primarily known as Persons' "man." Educated at Eton and later abroad where he had been "nusseled up among many the old caterpillars of the churche," he helped with the distribution of the East Ham Press publications and probably took some to Gloucester, the city of his birth. He appears to have been frequently on hand advising his master of intruders and possible government agents.[15]

The East Ham Press caused a disturbance sufficient to convoke Parliament in 1581 when that body issued a resolution "to find a remedy for the poison of the Jesuits." Official wrath produced results. Spies observed the comings and goings of Brinkley's men. Despite his elegant hose and doublet one of the staff, who had been dispatched to London for the purchase of paper, failed to dupe the pursuivants. He was arrested; brought to the Tower and put to torture. Shortly thereafter the house was invaded and the press broken up.[16]

Father Persons, undiscouraged, sought a new location for his second press. For this purpose he employed the services of an "experienced priest," William Maurice, who was to find "fresh facilities for a printing press." Maurice searched "very diligently" and "with great difficulty found the house of a widow named Stonor which stood in the middle of a wood, twenty miles from London." Here Persons had his type, presses and paper transported and "this not without many dangers." His East Ham Press manager, Brinkley, was called upon for the direction of the Stonor Park Press, assisted by William Maurice, "procurator of paper." The new press issued only two books: Persons' *Discouerie of I. Nichols minister* and Father Campion's *Rationes decem*. According to Persons, Campion had earlier arrived in London with a revised version of his book. He went "at once to stay at the said house in the wood where the book was published and printed." Campion's text enjoyed an unusual distinction, since at the Oxford Commencement of 1581 copies were to be found on the benches of St. Mary's.[17]

In August 1581, Sir Henry Neville and an assistant were advised "to repair unto Lady Stonor's house and to search for some Latin books dispersed already in Oxford at the last commencement which Campion confessed to have been printed in a wood and also for such English books as of late have been published for the maintenance of popery printed also there, as is thought, by one Parsons Jesuit and others. And further for the press and other instruments of printing thought also to be there remaining." The Stonor Park Press was seized August 8, 1581. Brinkley and four of his assistants were arrested. Brinkley was to remain a prisoner in the Tower for two years until his release, when he abandoned England to rejoin his old master, Father Robert Persons, who had returned to Rouen.[18]

Father Persons, priests and missionaries had found in the Catholic cities of France, Italy, Flanders and Germany a refuge where they could undisturbed draft their proselytizing campaign. The Netherlands because of its policy of toleration and proximity to England proved particularly attractive to the burdened orthodox Englishman. As early as 1569 the States General had agreed that liberty of conscience be permitted both Roman Catholic and disciple of the Reformed Church. Among those who sought the tolerance of the Lowlands was the English born printer, John Fowler.

John Fowler ranks as the first important English printer in exile who issued books for the English Catholic community and the orthodox congregation in the homeland – his influence far overshadowing that of Robert Caly.

The difficulties which were to confront the printer of Catholic books in England had been early apparent to the cultivated Bristol born John Fowler. Educated at Winchester and New College, Oxford, Fowler obtained a Master's degree in 1560. The progressively repressive anti-Catholic legislation of Elizabeth had disturbed him sufficiently to leave England for Flanders.[19]

Fowler's first Continental stop appears to have been Louvain. From letters of examination tendered him later in life by the Douai magistracy Fowler's scholarship is evident, revealing a fluency in "Latin, French, Italian and a smattering of Greek and Flemish." Fowler's linguistic proficiency proved of great advantage in his academic pursuits and profession. He translated in 1566 from Latin into English Pietro Frarini's *Oration against the vnlawfull insurrections of the Protestants of our time, vnder pretence to refourme religion*. The translation was doubtless inspired by personal outrage against current Protestant indignities. Fowler was later to edit and publish St. Thomas More's *Dialogue of cumfort against tribulation*, translating and printing in 1576 *A brief fourme of confession*. Late in his career he edited the *Dicta et facta* of the Dalmatian monk, Marko Marulic. Wood describes Fowler as "a tolerable poet and orator and a theologian not to be contemned."[20]

Fowler probably decided upon a publishing career as the best possible profession to satisfy his personal, financial and spiritual needs. In addition he fulfilled a commitment to his refugee co-religionists and the Catholic community at home. Both groups could derive from his publications powerful religious sustenance.

Fowler was active in Louvain and Antwerp from 1565 to 1577, during which time he issued an approximate fifty titles. His first publication appeared in Louvain in 1565, *The Supper of our Lord set Foorth . . . According to the Truth of the Gospell and Catholic Faith* by the English Catholic historian, Nicholas Sander. The book was printed anonymously – Fowler apparently somewhat wary of the antagonism of the Flemish dealers. His concern appears to have been groundless, since the book was reprinted the following year bearing the publisher's name. During 1566 he opened a second office in Antwerp where he published five books. By 1567 he had abandoned his Antwerp premises probably because of the outrageous religious incidents provoked by the Protestants who had not only pillaged the great Cathedral but also indulged in a violent iconoclastic rampage.[21]

When Henry Simpson, the Catholic divine, gave evidence at York in 1575, he stated that "Mr. Fowler an Englishman prints all the English books at Louvaine by Mr. Hardinge and others." The Fowler imprints from 1567 through the following ten years represent the writings of outstanding Catholic leaders. Referred to by Cardinal Allen as "Catholicissimus et doctissimus librorum impressor," he circulated the treatises of his admirer Allen, Thomas Harding, Thomas Stapleton, Cardinal Pole and the contumelious attacks upon the English Crown by John Leslie, Bishop of Ross, including his notorious *Treatise of*

Treasons against Q. Elizabeth in 1572. Fowler issued only one book in Dutch, *Hortulus anime*, bearing the imprint "I. Foulaert: Tanwerpen 1574." In apparently only one instance does Fowler refer to his English origin. The colophon of Richard Bristow's *Demaundes to be proponed of Catholiques to the heretikes* reads "Antwerpiae Iohanni Foulero Anglo." Issued fairly late in his career, the imprint betrays some possible nostalgia for the homeland.[22]

In 1573 Fowler seems to have relinquished his office in Louvain, where during that year, he had printed one known book. He returned to his old Antwerp retreat, where until his retirement in 1577, he issued thirteen Catholic books. His press may have been destroyed in the Spanish Fury of 1576, when seven thousand citizens perished. The last known work associated with Fowler's name is the *Dictorum factorumque memorabilium libri sex* of the Dalmatian Marulic which was printed by the Antwerp publisher, Gerard Smits. Possibly in the hopelessness which followed the torment of Antwerp, Fowler consoled himself in reading and editing the spiritual nutriment of a distant Catholic religious. Disassociating himself from his publishing career, he eventually settled in Namur where he died in February 1578/79.[23]

Upon Fowler's death, his wife Alice continued as a stationer, supplying books printed at Douai to the great Plantin house at Antwerp, apparently having become associated with members of the firm during her husband's Antwerp residence. The Fowlers had a son, John, Jr., who travelled back and forth from the Continent, bringing Catholic texts to London colleagues. According to the Recusant Rolls which frequently confuse Christian names, the younger Fowler's wife is referred to either as Ann or Mary. Mrs. Fowler, Jr. enjoyed an important Catholic contact. Her brother was Dr. Robert Taylor, at one time secretary of the Spanish Ambassador to England, Diego Sarmiento de Acuña, Count Gondomar, a favorite of James I. Hence it is quite possible that the Fowlers were somewhat *au courant* with Spanish intrigue. According to the venomous pen of the vituperative Catholic critic, John Gee, who inveighed against orthodox writers and stationers, a "Mrs. Fowler of Fetter Lane tradeth much to St. Omer." John Fowler, the Younger, apparently deceased, had left a widow knowledgeable in the Continental Catholic book trade and competent to negotiate with foreign stationers, the heirs of those publishers known to her parents-in-law.[24]

The elder Fowler had died before the establishment of the secret presses set up at East Ham and Stonor Park by Father Robert Persons. He had probably known the great Jesuit crusader who, alarmed by the detection of his second press, had resolved to pursue his printing propaganda in a safer climate on the Continent, where he might work unmolested by English officialdom. After a brief stay in Sussex, Persons had proceeded to Rouen in 1582 where he established his third press. Here he was "to have Catholic books he was writing printed which could no longer be done in England since the press in Stonor Park had been discovered." He engaged as its manager a "very pious zealous merchant named George Flinton."

Little is known of Flinton. He had been active in business in England and, as an enthusiastic Catholic, had thrown in his lot with Persons. He appears to have been a man of some education and deep spirituality, having translated and edited a *Manual of Prayers* which he described as "gathered out of many and divers famous authors as well aunciont as of the present tyme." The work enjoyed enormous popularity since twenty-seven editions appeared from Rouen, St. Omer and unknown English printing houses. Later editions included the "Jesus Psalter" and the "Golden Litany."[25]

Flinton was succeeded by Father Persons' former East Ham associate, Stephen Brinkley, who was to remain with the Rouen Press until his death several years later. Persons declared that not only his own books but numerous others were printed "in many cities as well in Flanders as in France, and good books apt to purpose and in sufficient numbers." He regarded them as "a most efficacious means for helping the Catholic cause abroad and at home whither many copies were exported." The Persons-Rouen Press issued three of its patron's most important works: *A defence of the censure, gyuen vpon two bookes of William Clarke and Meredith Hamner mynysters, whiche they wrote against M. Edmond Campion; An epistle of the persecution of Catholickes in England* and *The first booke of the Christian exercise appartayning to resolution*. In addition the press imprint is to be found in the devotional treatises of Gaspare Loarte, Diego de Estella and Cardinal Allen's *True sincere and modest defence of English Catholiques*. The Persons-Rouen Press was discontinued in 1585 possibly the year of Brinkley's death. Its distinguished founder was now deeply involved in urgent religious and political matters preceding the preparation of the Armada and the anticipated Catholic conquest of England.[26]

Father Persons' press director, Flinton, had engaged the native printer, Georges L'Oyselet, to set his texts. L'Oyselet himself had been and was to continue an independent publisher of English Catholic writings. He was assuredly in contact with the clique of French and Flemish stationers, several of whose professional forbears had issued English orthodox texts. Aegidius Coppenius Diesthensis, known as Aegidius or Gilles Diest, and Jan Laet nad been extremely active at Antwerp during the 'thirties and 'forties. Their trade lists had included miscellaneous works by Gemma Frisius, Petrus Apianus, Sebastian Serlio, André Thevet, Leonhart Fuchs, and other general writers. However, with the increase of English Catholic refugees in Flanders, they attracted an additional audience – and income – through the publication of appropriate English orthodox texts. Each firm printed ten works by English Catholic authors: the treatises of Cardinal Allen, Thomas Stapleton, Lewis Evans, Thomas Harding, William Rastell and others. At Louvain, where the Elder Fowler had established himself, he had met Jean Bogard who, as early as 1556, had issued *Pro Catholicae fidei antiquitate et veritate adversus prophanas omnium haereson nouatione liber* of St. Vincent Lerins, an English version of which was to be published by Diest.[27]

From the presses of Paris, Louvain, Rheims and adjacent Flanders a total of one hundred and eleven known English Catholic treatises reached their readers. The anonymously published fulmination of the Scottish divine, Adam Blackwood, in defense of Mary of Scotland was purportedly issued at "Edimburg chez Jean Nafield;" John Leslie's *Defense of Mary Quene of Scotland* is attributed to a London printer of "Flete Strete, at the signe of Iustice Royall against the Blacke bell." Cardinal Allen's *Apologie and true declaration of the institution and endeavours of the two English colleges* published by Foigny at Rheims was presumably issued at "Mounts in Henault." It is evident that even the foreign stationers sought some security in the safety of fictitious imprints. Although they endorsed the sentiment of their Catholic authors, nonetheless, they strove to insure their personal welfare against the long arm of English law which, upon occasion, extended itself across Channel waters to ensnare author and printer.[28]

Of the approximate two hundred and twenty-three English books printed abroad and secretly in England from 1565 to 1603 there is almost an equal division between controversial and devotional writings. The former strove to demonstrate the tenets of Catholicism and to refute the attacks of opponents. They represent the opinions of Cardinal Allen, Father Persons, Thomas Harding, Thomas Dorman, John Rastell and others. Three authors, representing militant Catholicism, challenged the authority of the English Crown. Their crime was treason! In their attempt to spread sedition through the dissemination of literature designed to achieve a Catholic victory, they must be branded traitors to the state. Father Persons' *Conference about the next succession to the crowne of England* advocated a Catholic heiress to the throne of Elizabeth; John Leslie's *Treatise of treasons against Q. Elizabeth, and the croune of England* denied the royal power. His *Defence of the honour of the right highe, mightye and noble princesse Marie quene of Scotland . . . with a declaration aswell of her right . . . to the succession of the crowne of Englande* supported the claims of Mary Stuart. The *Martyre de la royne d'Escosse* of Blackwood, championing the Scottish monarch, attempted to expose the guile of Elizabeth.[29]

Devotional treatises were represented by the ever popular writings of St. Peter Canisius, Gaspare Loarte, Luis de Granada, Laurence Vaux, the Psalters and Manuals of Prayer.[30]

According to William Fulke's "Catalogue of all such Popish Bookes either answered or to be answered, which haue been written in the English tongue from beyond the Seas, or secretly dispersed here in England . . . since the beginning of the Queenes Majesties reign," numerous titles, issued by Fowler and his Flemish colleagues, had been imported into England for distribution among Catholic readers. These were circulated by underground agents, who had obtained them from priests and missionaries to whom a sacred oath had been administered to return to England "for the salvation of souls whenever it shall be seen good." Theirs was a goal to disseminate in the motherland a rich literary bounty for the intellectual and spiritual elevation of their fellow Catholic.

III

FARDELS OF POPISHE TRASHE

The Circulation of Orthodox Books in England

Through the exportation of Anglo-Catholic literature to England the English Catholic printer in exile and his Continental colleague furnished their fellow believers those texts denied them at home. Such books were designed, not merely to bolster the faith, but also to influence and convert the Protestant heretic. There is no detailed record of the relationship between the foreign stationer and his English associate. The State Papers and reports of informers and pursuivants afford an occasional glimpse into the dangers of the illicit traffic in Catholic literature: the hazards of the exporter and recipient; the devious Channel routes employed for shipment; the port search, the transport of the "maunds" and "fardels" along little-trod bypaths to London; the activity of the English factors of Fetter Lane and St. Andrews, Holborn.

The Catholic books sent from the Continent to England confirm Cardinal Allen's conviction that the circulation of foreign printed texts opened the way for the great Catholic revival of the fifteen-eighties. Persons wrote to Aquaviva, General of the Jesuit Company, in September 1582, that he had arranged to send books to Scotland as well as to England, "that is to say books in the vulgar tongue as well as for devotion, of which there are few in Scotland, as there is no press, and even the heretics have to send into England to get their books printed." [The good Father was in gross error, since in 1508 Andrew Myllar of Edinburgh had set up with Walter Chepman the first printing press in Scotland.] As early as April 1565 Guzman de Silva, the Spanish Ambassador to England, writing to Philip II, stated that books shipped from Louvain had done incalculable service in spreading the faith. The Jesuit, Creswell, referred to the great variety of books both "in English and Latyn and other languages already come forthe." During his travels in the Netherlands he observed "diuers kindes of answers to Elizabeth's proclamation of 1591 against the Jesuits printed in English without names of authors ... others coming foorth though I could not learne by whome." Four thousand copies of Father Persons' *Newes from Spayne and Holland* were printed in 1593, so that they might be shipped to England for Easter of that year.[1]

It has been affirmed that, prior to 1580, not less than 20,000 Catholic texts had been imported into England and there secretly sold. It is not an unreasonable estimate, but it must be remembered that editions varied in size – the average ranging from one thousand to 1,500 copies. There were of course exceptions. The Antwerp Press of Arnout Conincx printed 4,000 copies of Persons' *Newes from Spayne and Holland*, while a work of such singular significance as the first edition of the *New Testament*, printed by Foigny at Rheims, consisted of an edition of 5,000 copies. Father Persons had hoped to place copies of the work shortly into the hands of his "beloved countrymen." Not all of the foreign publications were intended for export. A large number were retained at the Continental seminaries for courses in theology and philosophy. The reading of devotional texts was a custom at dinner and supper – designed not merely as a spiritual, but also as a physical catharsis – to help digest the bare, frugal meal. Books were stocked by foreign dealers for consumption by English exiles or dispatched to other Continental cities harboring religious sympathizers.[2]

The circulation of foreign printed Catholic books in England was accomplished through the media of orthodox groups. Dependent upon passenger and cargo vessels or the bark of an ambassador, the traveler, concealing his wares, ultimately reached the motherland. Foreign and English intelligencers, through a network of spies, helped diminish the hazards of the journey and arranged the contact between the visitor and English agent. Jesuits, priests and laymen arrived in England with new publications concealed in cloaks and capes, buried in trunks within miscellaneous merchandise. A seaman might be induced to hide the forbidden cargo in "fardels" or "maunds." The newly landed visitor, presenting himself as a scholar, merchant or "swaggering trauailer," trod neglected paths; crossed estuaries and inlets at night to attain his destination, usually London. With zeal, hope and unfailing courage the missionary worked to convert and redeem the heresy-ridden land.

To abet him in his task, the Catholic missionary service availed itself of paid intelligencers who provided the departing crusader with letters, information and advice. Richard Rowlande, the former "prynter of Smithfield" was one of the best known agents for Anglo-Catholic affairs. Having fled England after the seizure of his press, he settled in Paris, where he printed for a brief period. Eventually he moved to Antwerp, where he remained as a spy and news-agent. Master Rowlande, now adopting a new career, also assumed a new name, Richard Verstegan. His talents were many. He was the master of several languages, English, Latin, French and Dutch. He was the author, editor, engraver, translator and publisher of thirty-two books. Practising his original vocation as goldsmith, he engraved the plates for several of his books, the best known, his *Theatrum Crudelitatum haereticorum nostri temporis*, which ran through several editions. He was also the author of several violent anti-English tracts and broadsides.[3]

Verstegan's virtuosity is revealed in his role as intelligencer or spy for the Anglo-Catholic cause. He enjoyed the confidence of the influential and eventually became a pensioner in the pay of Philip II of Spain, receiving an annual stipend of thirty escudos. According to an entry in the Spanish Archives, he had been recommended to the Spanish service by Cardinal Allen and Don Bernardino da Mendoza. The Jesuit, Henry Holt, upon interrogation, admitted that Cardinal Allen, Father Persons and he himself "receaved all their intelligences that I know by Verstegan," while Peter Knowles, a priest, referred to a certain

Lawrence, a bookbinder of Antwerp, who "speaks good French and comes over often with intelligences being sent by Mr. Verstegham a printer."[4]

The correspondence of "Mr. Verstegham" reveals his knowledge of English affairs and literature. In a letter to Father Persons he refers to the circulation of recent anti-Catholic tracts in the homeland, including *The trial of trueth* "wherein I could wish that the vntrue trial of this vaine pamphlet were confuted because the foolish thing carieth some credit among the Protestants." A letter of March 1595 refers to the recent arrival of a copy of Lewis Lewkenor's *Discourse of the vsage of the English fugitiues, by the Spaniard,* "a new English pamphlet very lately printed in London."[5]

Verstegan, on the payroll of Philip II, naturally reported to Spain the movements of the English in Flanders, their spies and counterspies. His dispatches to Spain were sent via Richard Hopkins, his "ligger in Paris." He supplied the English Seminary at Seville with books of a controversial nature including even some Puritan polemical material: *A treatise of ecclesiastical discipline* by Matthew Sutcliffe, Dean of Exeter; *A treatise conteyning the true Catholike and apostolike faith of the holy sacrifice and sacrament ordeyned by Christ* by William Rainolds; as well as *The last acts of Parliament* [intended for Father Persons' use]; a copy of Holinshed's *Chronicles;* 12 copies of *The folowing of Christ* of Thomas a Kempis; 2 copies of his own composition, *Speculum pro Christianis seductis;* the anti-Marprelate tract, *A Myrror for Martynistes;* music and some English "grammers." He received a most heartfelt reply from the priest, Richard Walpole, stationed at Seville: "Wee thanke you for all your diligence in bringinge more books sent for by Father Peralta and hereafter shall have occasion to trouble you for more in that kinde for this colledge in Civill [Seville] which yet is unfinished of a librarie."[6]

Although Father Persons referred somewhat contemptuously to Verstegan and the Welsh exile, Hugh Owen, as "very unfitting persons if money be given them for it [information]," he apparently was grateful to receive Verstegan's communiqué that he had intercepted at Antwerp the confession of Anthony Tyrell, the renegade priest and spy, and "the interrogation practises of Walsingham."[7]

Other undercover agents were Humphrey Shelton in Rouen, the Benedictine monk, Edward Barlow, and Francis Ridgely stationed at Bruges who "informed from thence." Anthony Ralston is named as intelligencer from Spain. Creswell stated that a certain Jacques Ghibbes of Antwerp had carried people and letters to England for years and had sent to the Continental Catholic authorities reports of all the secret activities of the English. William Wollaston, an English agent employed by Cecil, advised his master that an Irishman, Dones, had been living in Rouen for many years. He reported that he had become "an obstinate Catholic" and acted as a broker, sending mass books from Newhaven to Ireland. Mention is made of "certain common carriers of papisticall bookes and letters from one papist to another . . . Godshall, Moore and Marsham." Allen described Moore as a Master of Arts from Cambridge and a recent student in the

Seminary at Rheims. The "unfitting" Hugh Owen accepted the "employment of Scotland," bringing "priests and Catholic books to the ill-affected nobles there."[7]

Experienced informers, like Verstegan, naturally eased the trip of a missionary to England. Confronting an ever-increasing official vigilance, the visitor was compelled to seek less known routes to the homeland. The regular run from France to England was via Calais, Dieppe and Boulogne. The missionary could ill afford to risk such public passages. Catholics, en route to England from Spain, were advised to stop first at Flanders or Denmark, while others journeyed from Bilboa to Nantes, where one Hilles, an Englishman, also reputed to be in the pay of the King of Spain, was known to convey travelers across the Channel. By 1606 Hilles had apparently settled in England. According to a complaint lodged by the Constable of Petworth, Hilles had desired a carrier, Henry Paine, who "had liued almost 7 years in Spain to bring him certain books from the College of Jesuits in Spain." Paine was known to have brought out from Antwerp "certain books bound and unbound" by the Polish prelate, Cardinal Hosius.[8]

For convenience, agents attempted to establish themselves near ports. A Catholic spy reported in 1584 that he had been obliged "to maintain a modest establishment in Rouen which is a most convenient city on account of its nearness to the sea, so that from there some can take trips to the coast to arrange for boats to convey people across (for they cannot use the public boats or the ordinary ports that are well known) whilst others take charge of the preparation and introduction into the country of books written in English and both on spiritual and devotional subjects and on matters of controversy and in answer to the calumnies with which the heretics assail us. Then, too, there are the holy oil, the chalices, vestments and Bibles to be sent over."[9]

Ingenuity opened new paths across the Channel to England where the wary traveler might elude arrest. Father Persons usually journeyed from Antwerp via Gravesend, taking a circuitous route to London. With an enthusiasm, which was subsequently to be dampened, the distinguished Jesuit discussed the successful return of Brother Emerson from England. He had "come back from the sea where he had done wonder having arranged new routes along which he sent four priests and 810 books." Alas, Father Emerson's good fortune was to change. Upon a later trip he shipped from Dieppe in the company of Father Weston, the latter disembarking between "two ports" on the English coast. Emerson remained aboard the vessel with the luggage since the two missionaries had agreed that "in dead of night we would send him [Emerson] a horse for the conveyance of our goods and likewise the books, of which [we] had brought over no small number for distribution in England." Once the packages had been brought ashore, Emerson met Weston at an inn where he was promptly arrested. The searchers pounced upon the suspect packages; found forbidden Catholic texts and took Emerson into custody. This unfortunate missionary was to linger many years in the Poultry for having brought into England "sartyn books."[10]

William Carr was likewise arrested at Berwick after having slipped into

England at Leith. He had with him "a great cloak bag in Tweedmouth wherein was found a great sort of English books with English litanies." After his return to France from England, Cardinal Allen related the hazards of his recent voyage: "in the night [we proceeded] with a pair of oars to Tillbury where one Nicholas de Hew a french man of Callais" took him to Dieppe. Father Southwell reached England at a lonely stretch of the Downs between Dover and Folkestone. At the same time Mallory Conyers traveled from Hull to Rouen and on to Paris "with books, catechisms and testaments." Anthony Skinner, a Jesuit, was apprehended upon his return from Calais, "going up a small river," while Father Walpole had been seized at North Flamborough, his arrest reported with great glee by Topcliffe, the notorious high-priest of torture. A report sent from the Mayor of Boulogne to Essex in 1598 advised that three or four Spanish Jesuits had passed through Flanders. "Take care of your havens," he remarked, "'tis there the danger lies."[11]

New arrivals aroused the suspicion of port and inland authorities. They were empowered to examine with the utmost care baggage and person. The harbor officials were instructed to be on constant alert for "traiterous persons" who entered the country "disguised both in names and persons. Some come in as gentlemen, with contrary names, in comely apparel, as though they travelled in foreign countries for knowledge: and generally all for the most part are clothed like gentlemen in apparel and many as gallants, yea in all colours, and with feathers and such like disguising themselves, and many of them in their behaviour as ruffians, far off to be thought or suspected to be friars, priests, jesuits or popish scholars."[12]

Contemporary records are copious in their reference to books brought into England by Catholics. A memorandum of December 1582 refers to a "fardell" opened in the presence of several respectable citizens of Lewes which contained manuscript pictures in silk of the greater and lesser sort, Agnus Dei, beads and a "piece of the bone of Mary Magdalene." Peter Roper and a friend Peter Lanson were detained at Dulwich for having conveyed "popish trashe from Rouen . . . in diuers packs." Roper and Lanson appear to have been active carriers of Catholic texts between Rouen and Newhaven. Lanson on one occasion transported five hundred *Catechisms* of Laurence Vaux, forty copies of Latin primers, fifteen copies of the Rheims *New Testament* and fourteen copies of the *Meditations* of St. Bonaventure. An advice to Burleigh of February 1597/98 stated that "very bad books" had been concealed in a shipment of cochineal and indigo sent from Dartmouth to London. A deponent, Bryan Tracy, admitted that he had left some parcels at the home of Anthony Bourne concealed "in a cloake bagge with bookes . . . come from beyond the seas since Hollow Masse." South Shields on the mouth of the Tyne near Newcastle has been described as a favorite landing place for papists, where "Popish traiterous books were sent from Rheims in barrels and fardels," and "hence transported across the water to Newcastle in baskets covered with fresh fish."[13]

The Governor of Dover Castle, Sir Thomas Fane, received word from an

English under-cover agent of Calais, William Gelke in November 1599, that books and primers were destined for England. Gelke advised Fane that he had carefully prepared a trap for the carrier, a sailor, Martin Audin, to whom he was offering a bribe of forty pounds if he would take over and disperse for him in England Catholic books. Gelke promised that he would introduce him to some prominent Jesuits of Saint Omer and Douai. The unsuspecting Audin played into Gelke's hands. He arrived at Dover with passengers and books. The texts were immediately confiscated and the passengers with their captain arrested.[14]

Not all Catholic visitors were apprehended. The venality of the customs officers was well known. Attractive bribes produced results. Papists slipped through at a price. A justice of peace readily accepted ten pounds from a willing victim; a tithing man could extract only twenty shillings. It was reported in 1584 that Randall, a searcher at Gravesend, "receaveth money of passengers suffering them to pass without searching."[15]

Hans Wowtenel, a Fleming, dwelling at St. Faith's, Farringdon, traveled back and forth from Antwerp bringing with him Catholic texts. He was in close contact with Verstegan who supplied him with the latest orthodox work printed abroad. According to a dispatch sent to Burleigh in March 1599, Wowtenel had recently received "a great number of books printed at Antwerp in the year '99 under the title of the primer of office of the Blessed Virgin Mary in Latin and English." Further mention is made of "some store [of books] in town in a burgher's hands," which were to be brought to the attention of the Council of State "to procure them to be stayed." These and others, it was stated, had come to England via Breda, "the provider and sender thereof [being] presently in England."[16]

The infiltration of England by English and foreign Catholic agents bore fruit. The missionaries with their message, their enthusiasm, and their books traversed the realm. The hazards which beset them are aptly expressed by Father Persons, who himself was in frequent danger. "In generall every man can imagine by hym selfe how difficult a thyng yt is in Englande at this day for a Catholique man to write any book, where neither libertie nor rest, nor libraries, nor conference, nor beinge is permitted hym."[17]

The successful Catholic exportation program is well attested by the list drawn up by the Puritan divine, William Fulke, noted as "accerimus Papastamix." His "Catalogue of all such Popish Bookes either answered or to be answered which have been written in the English tongue from beyond the Seas or secretly dispersed in England" appeared in 1579. It was reprinted three times, revised and supplemented. The 1580 version includes forty-one titles of Catholic books printed abroad and at a secret English press.

An analysis of Fulke's "Catalogue" reveals that the majority of the books by Catholic English authors were printed abroad. It is of interest to note that fifteen of the texts cited include vituperative retorts by Fulke himself. Thus in compiling his short-title catalogue of foreign Catholica, Fulke sought to bring to the attention of the scrutineer of English religious conformity not only the danger of orthodox propaganda but also his own role as a zealous *defensor fidei*. Posing as the St. George of the Established Faith, he had plunged his sword into the Roman dragon. His "Catalogue" may have been compiled for his own self-advancement, but whatever the author's motives, it remains an excellent index to the circulation of Anglo-Catholic books of the period.

Of the thirty-three titles identified, two had been published by Caly during Mary's reign. Twenty-eight had been imported from abroad. Eleven bore the Antwerp and Louvain imprints of John Fowler, while an additional thirteen were issued by the Antwerp presses of Jan Laet and Gilles Diest. Four were printed by Beller, Silvius and Bogard at Antwerp, Louvain and Douai. The omniscient Master Fulke was quite unaware that three titles had been published in London not too distant from his Cambridge incumbency. The texts of Gregory Martin, Jean Albin de Valsergues and St. Peter Canisius had been printed on the Hart Street Press of the martyr, William Carter. Master Fulke had not glanced into his own backyard.[18]

The titles mentioned by Fulke, and many unknown to him, were familiar to the English Catholic minority. Father Persons had outlined to Father Alphonso Agazzari, Rector of the English College at Rome, the English missionary book program: "With no lesse peril on the part of the priests [the books] are circulated, even at the cost of danger, in order that what is written may reach the hands of all. Their method is as follows: All the books are brought together in London without being issued [circulated] and after being distributed into the hands of priests in parcels of a hundred and fifty, are issued exactly the same time to all parts of the kingdom. Now on the next day when according to their wont the officials begin to search the houses of Catholics because these books have been distributed, there are plenty of young men of birth to introduce these books by night into the dwellings of the heretics, into workshops as well as palaces, to scatter them in the Court also, and about the streets, so that it may not be Catholics who are accused in this matter."[19]

Catholic books were found not only in workshops and palaces, but even in Anglican houses of worship – probably placed there as a suggestion for conversion. In July 1582, Dr. Hammond submitted a note to Chief Justice Popham that a "seditious pamphlet" had been found in the church porch of St. Giles, Cripplegate. It had been picked up by the sexton "coming to ring the bell for the morning lecture at six o'clock."[20]

Confessions and inventories reveal a variety of Catholic material circulating throughout England. Had not the infuriated Burleigh referred to twelve thousand copies of the "roaring hellish bull" against Elizabeth which had been printed at Antwerp, "some having entered the country"? The first edition of Father Persons' *Christian directory* had been sold out, since in the preface to the second edition, he remarks: "I perceaued many moneths before that al the first copies of the said former booke were wholy dispersed and none remaining to be had." Walsingham's agent, William Berden, informed him that William Hartly "the late banyshed prieste" had brought over "some store" of the *Directory* for

English consumption, adding that there still remained ninety unsold copies of the Rheims *New Testament*. A letter from Rome of January 1599 declared that no books were to be exported to England which offended the government politically as "The booke of succession . . . D. Bristow's Motives . . . Father Allen's Booke contra iustitiam Britannicam, D. Stapleton's Didimus and others."[21]

The demand for foreign printed Catholic literature remained constant. John Vincent, stationed in Brazil, wrote in 1593 to his confrère, Richard Gibbon of the College of Madrid, to send him "certain new books made by the English touching the persecution of the Catholics in England." He added that he had already received two in Latin as well as copies of Persons' *De persecutione anglicana*, the *Rationes decem* of the glorious martyr, P. Campion, "with another in English about 12 martyrs that suffered there."[22]

The distributors of Catholic books were often "young men of birth" alluded to by Father Persons. One of the best known was Persons' "man," who had assisted Richard Verstegan, the former Richard Rowlande, "prynter of Smithfield."[23]

Thomas Alfield, "a person of mean stature," was born in Gloucester ca. 1545, the son of a schoolmaster, who "brought him up in good literature." He attended Eton and Cambridge and in 1576 left England for Douai. Returning to the homeland for a brief stay, he again departed for Rheims, where he attended the Seminary, having become a Catholic convert.

Alfield was considered sufficiently competent to be sent on an English mission. According to his detractors, he attempted "to insence and seduce the people against their prince and their cuntrie." He lived during this time "about London," where he presumably assisted with the circulation of Catholic literature. He plied his route between London and Gloucester, having engaged an assistant, John Davis, who admitted that he had taken all of Alfield's books to the west country. He later agreed that they were "very evil and seditious." During his London residence Alfield, with the Dolman brothers, had witnessed Campion's execution and possibly pondered his own fate for having embraced this "develish doctrine."

As the representative of the Continental mission, Alfield in London apparently also directed the schedules and routes of his agents. He is reported to have stayed at the home of one "Mynnarley in Aldersgate Street" and is described as "one of the most traiterous Papists of that Seminary of Satan."[24]

Alfield was arrested during his London residence; dispatched to the Tower, but apparently released upon his "hypocritical submission." He returned to France, only to depart again for England "with about 300 books and upward containing nothing but treason, heresie and blasphemie and detestable doctrine written by an archpriest called Dr. Allen which bookes he commended and did cause them to be dispearsed by his fauorers [agents] Thomas Webly and William Crab both notorious priests."

Alfield had brought into England more than five hundred copies of Cardinal Allen's *True sincere and modest defence of English Catholiques that suffer for their faith*, printed at the Persons-Rouen Press in 1584 and had engaged as his agents for the book's circulation Thomas Webley of Gloucester, apprentice to a dyer, and William Crab, the "sonne of Webleis mistresse."

The government, outraged by Cardinal Allen's pernicious treatise, swiftly pursued its dispersers and arrested Alfield and Webley in May 1585. Alfield was dispatched to the Tower on the charge of "dispersing of slaunderous bookes against the execution of justice," to be transferred to Newgate on May 27, 1585. William Fleetwood, zealous persecutor of papists, presided at Alfield's trial held July 5, 1585. He condemned in particular the defendant's "beastlie behaviour," stating that he "was become the first that ever was arraynd of felonye of any that ever passed Cambridge during the last fifty years."[25]

Alfield admitted that he had brought over "ffyve or syx hundred" of Allen's *Defence* into the realm and "dispearced them, as he sawe occasion." He insisted that the Cardinal's treatise was "a loyal book tending to seduce English Catholics to remain loyal to England." He stated it had been printed in Paris and declared that the Pope had authority to deprive "any Kynge yf he sawe cause." The state scarcely agreed with the political concepts of Thomas Alfield. He and Webley were condemned "for bringing over seditious bookes into England contrary to the lawes of the Realme, the penalty whereof is to dye as a felon." Advising Lord Burleigh of the trial, Fleetwood denounced the arch-culprit who "did most trayterously maynteyne the boke, with longe, tedious and friuolous woordes and speeches." Once sentenced, he stated, Alfield "behaved hymselfe moore arrogantlie than any they ever the Commissioners had hard or seene in their tymes."[26]

Alfield and Webley were hanged at Tyburn the day following their trial, when they proclaimed even with "ye Rops about theyr necks that they which did not beleeve as they beleeved were damned to the bottomless pit of hell fire." They refused "to haue any to pray with them but desyring Catholikes to say one Credo for them in the midst of their agony." Alfield deprived of life was denied a decent burial. "He was brought to St. Pulchers to be buryed but the parishioners would not suffer a traytors corpse . . . and so the carcasse was retourned to the buryall grounds neer Tybourn and there [left]."[27]

The execution of Alfield and Webley was to set an example "to all such secret lurkers in corners" who were to "speedily be converted . . . or end their daies in ye like or more sharper sorte."

England had now exacted the supreme penalty from a Catholic printer and two Catholic dispersers of orthodox texts. The state's efforts for conformity in religion were not to relax. Having stalked its "traiterous offenders," the Crown was to pursue a program of relentless persecution against its obdurate heretical minority.

IV

SPYINGS ABROADE AND INQUISITIONS AT HOME

Official Reprisal

Alfield and Webley had been, according to the state, guilty of treason. Their crime was an effort to subvert the religion and government of England through the circulation of seditious works. The Crown, its agents "lurking in corners" had carefully observed their "detestable course." The government's hierarchy of officials was constantly alert to the cabal and intrigue of the Catholic who strove "to ensnare and seduce the ignorant and simple people to be pertakers [of] the Rhemish and antichristian sinagoge."

In a four-fold program the government attempted to extirpate the Catholic faith. It intensified its harbor patrol, its system of search, arrest and imprisonment. Walsingham had by 1572 become the Grand Master of espionage. "He was," says Camden, "a most subtle searcher of secrets, nothing been contrived anywhere that he knew not by intelligence." To him "intelligence [was] never too dear." He strove to clamp down upon Catholic subversive writings through a network of spies and counterspies. In particular he labored to safeguard the harbors against the entry of offensive books. The Bishop of Winchester, who insisted that a "diligent watch" be kept at all landing places, believed by 1584 that the English harbors were so thoroughly guarded "there was no way either to enter or leave the country." Agents reported to the Privy Council that books were being immediately seized upon their arrival in England "either bound or unbound as they come into port."[1]

The Plymouth town officials were instructed in their particular responsibilities: "Whereas we understand that diuers tymes there are broughte into the porte of Plymouth and other westerne portes lewde and seditious bookes and other reliques daungerous and unfitt to be dispersed, both in regarde of the state and commonpeace of the churche . . . we do authorize you . . . to view all kinde of bookes and reliques or whatsoever you finde tending to idolatrie or superstition or contrary to her majestys laws . . . which you shall staye and safely keepe in your custodie until further dirrecion from us."[2]

To stem further the importation of offensive texts, the government appointed special customs officers at the Port of London to examine all books that came into the customs house. The Wardens of the Stationers' Company were authorized to inspect all incoming cargoes, "packs, dryfatts [barrels], maunds [wicker baskets] and other things wherein books or paper shall be contained." All stationers selling foreign books in England were to supply the authorities with a list of such items before any sale was consummated.[3]

The network of the English spy system, with its under-cover men, its counter-agents, its pursuivants and hooligans, was ever ready to obtain information. Agents lived abroad in disguise, adopted foreign mannerisms and cultivated friends to probe and extract information. They assumed the nostalgia of the exile, the languor of the ill, the desolation of the banished, the religious mania of the most devout. English spies settled in Spain posed as pilgrims bound for Compostella; others in France sought the path to Lourdes. An involved plan, conceived by the indefatigable Cecil, reveals numerous under-cover agents stationed in Continental cities. His Lisbon man was given a roster of aides, all of whom could be called upon to forward directives to London: "Samuel Robinson merchant" in the capital, with a cover directed to "Diego Gardia de Paredes, mercador en Roan." At Calais, the agent might send his communiqués to Jean van Dale superscribed to Giles Snode. His Scottish addressee Andro Hart, Bookseller at Edinburgh, was to further information to Alexander Johnson, "actually Mr. Johnson the Queen's agent." News for Ireland was to be forwarded to Robert Meagh with an endorsement for "William Meagh or Robert Copinger at the Starr in Cheapside." By including several participants as the recipients of information, Cecil guaranteed the state against the possible loss of a team man who might have been "mussed up" by the enemy or even have defected through bribe, influence or fear.[4]

The foreign agents at their stations dispatched reports of the Catholic movements to the home office, sending word of leaders, travel, books, factors. Nicholas Berden associated himself with Richard, the servant of Cardinal Allen, to enable him to ascertain "what books are in pryntinge, who is the printer and who did write them."[5]

Father Southwell informed Verstegan that the government spies "as namely Berden, Bakel and Vachel," pretended to be Catholics, hearing Mass to apprehend their prey. Ruyvot, an agent, active in Spain, posed as a Bordeaux wine merchant to ascertain the activity of the English Jesuit Seminaries at Madrid and Valladolid. Lord Burleigh was informed in August 1592 that a servant of the Bishop of Glasgow had been persuaded "to observe practices in Spain and Flanders" and had shipped from Calais as damaging evidence "17 little books touching the religion of their neighbors." He referred at the same time to "Bad books" that he had received from a servant of the Jesuit, James Gordon.[6]

John Blount, Cecil's man at Hamburg, indignantly advised his master that a new book had just been published "slaunderous against the Queen and those about her and the late Lord Burghley." He had purchased all available copies "at his cost rather than have them viewed by the world," assuring Cecil that other copies had been bought up by indignant Englishmen. Henry Mirkell, either an English agent or visitor to Spain, advised the government that "pernicious books [had been] compiled in English at the College of Valladolid by Persons entitled a 'Letter of State' and another a continuation of the Venerable Bede and of the 'History of the Church of England' at the present time." In his opinion the latter "would prove to be the most pestilential book ever published by them."[7]

Cecil might well have pondered over a rather involved dispatch relayed to him by Lord Hertford that one Bass, an English merchant in Spain, had been the recipient of a suspicious book. Hertford identified the work as Bede's *History of the Churche of England*, which had been referred to earlier by Mirkell. The revised text, edited by the Catholic priest, Thomas Stapleton, enjoyed considerable popularity. Bass had notified Lord Hertford that copies of the *History* had been sent to Bristol from Cadiz "by a mariner who did not understand it and sold the book to a bookbinder in Bristol for little or nothing." The latter, "little esteeming it, used diuers leaves as forrels [parchment for the binding] for the books." The scrupulous Fleetwood submitted to Cecil "a box of such stuffe as these libellers use for their printe. There be certain Yrishmen," he continued, "that are utterers of the last lewde book." He implicated one Dowdaly, a merchant of Wexford who "doth use to sell them."[8]

The government by 1587 was fully aware of the insidious practises of the Continental English seminaries. To protect itself against the penetration of disguised Catholic students, it attempted to ascertain the "names of all such English scholars as be in the English seminary in Rome, Rheims, Paris and Douay and those departing from Rome on the first of April in the company of Edmond Campion and Persons." Had not the portraits of the Jesuits Campion and Persons been submitted for scrutiny to the port authorities? Had not both men cleverly eluded the selfsame officials? John Sledd, in all likelihood an English agent in Spain, submitted to the home office a dossier of two hundred eighty-five resident Englishmen, students, priests, soldiers and merchants whose movements he had observed. Questions were put to all foreigners and suspects visiting the country, whether they had been "in Rome, Rheims or Spain during the last five years" or whether they had been – like the students – at any of the colleges or elsewhere.[9]

Subversive literature brought into the country eventually became state property. As early as March 1568 an edict had been issued against foreign publications "contayning matters derogatorie to the soveraigne estate of her Maiestie or impugning the orders and rites estalished by the lawe for Christian religion and deuine seruice within the Realme." All such books were to be surrendered to a bishop within four weeks. Offensive material was not to be imported "under pain of severer penalty than hitherto inflicted in the Star Chamber at Westminster." The royal proclamation was doubtless directed against Cardinal Allen's recently published *Treatise made in defence of the lawful power and authoritie of the priesthod [sic] to remitte sinnes* issued by Fowler at Louvain in 1567. The work was subversive in character since it questioned the authority of the ruler in the resolution of spiritual matters.[10]

Similar legislation was formulated "against certain seditious and slanderous books slandering the government with cruelty and reproaching Henry VIII ... and their bringing obloquy to the Queen and her government." All persons dispersing them were to be punished and no shipmaster was to allow them in his ships.[11]

If books distasteful to the Crown were not yielded to the authorities, the government was prepared to wield one its most ruthless weapons, the right of search. Abetted by the power of the Stationers' Company over its recalcitrant members, the law with little mercy assailed the spreading opposition. The Charter of the Stationers' Company had deemed it "lawful for the Masters and Keepers or Wardens to make search whenever it shall please them in any place, shop, house . . . or building or any printer, binder or bookseller within our Kingdome of England." The right to search was renewed in 1576 when the Company resolved that a surveillance of London printing houses be maintained once a week by two searchers. Twenty-four members were delegated to this task, rotating in their inquisitorial duties. They were to inquire into "what euery prynter prynteth and how many he prynteth of euery impression . . . and for whom they are printed." They were further to report the number of apprentices, journeymen and presses. By 1586 searchers made their odious visits in groups of three, anticipating indignation and possible physical resistance.[12]

Catholic England was made aware of the intensified official program of harassment and arrest. "Every corner of the realme was searched for bookes," declared the divine, William Rainolds. "The portes were layed for them, Paules Crosse is witness of burning of many of them . . . colleges, chambers, studies, closets, coffers and deskes were ransackt for them . . . aunciet men and students of Diuinitie were imprisoned for having them." Campion had earlier declared that he could not long escape the "hands of the heretics; the enemies have so many eyes, so many tongues, so many scouts and crafts."[13]

The English search system is described in a detailed letter sent by an English priest to Agazzari: "Their serches are many and severe. The chief time for them are when the Catholikes are most busie to serue God, as on Sondaies, holie daies, Easter, Christmasse, Whitsontide and such very good feastes. They come either in the night or early in the morninge, or much about dinner time. They willingliest come when few are at home to resist them, that they might riffle coffers and do what they list. They locke the servants and mistress of the howse and the whole familie up into a roome by themselves while they, like young princes, goe rifling the house at their wil. The maner of serching is to com with a troupe of men to the howse as though they came to fight a field. They beset the howse on every side, and when they rush in and ransacke euery corner euen womens beds and bosomes – with such insolent behauiour that their villanies in this kind are half a Martyrdome. When they find any bookes, church stuffe, chalices or other thinges they take them away."[14]

Father Creswell referred to the "English spyings abroad and inquisitions at home: searchinge of houses at midnight then at noone dayes, apprehensions, examinations . . . practice of the racke." Prior to his arrest, Father Southwell stated that the pursuivants had been "raging all around. I heard them threatening and breaking wood work and sounding the wall to find hiding places."[15]

Father Gerard was to recall the horror of a Catholic gentleman "to have his house suddenly beset on all sides with a number of men in arms both horse and foot, and not only his house and gardens . . . but all highways laid for miles near unto him that none shall pass but only shall be examined. Then are these searchers thieves so rude and barbarous that, if doors be not opened in the instant when they enter, they break open the doors with such violence, as if they were to sack a town of enemies won by the sword. They go presently to search for secret places, and that they do most cunningly and strictly sounding the floors and walls to see if they can find any hollow places . . . they measured the walls with long rods, so that if they did not tally they might peerce the part not accounted for. Thus they sounded the walls and all the boards to find out and break into any hollow places that there might be. They got into the chimney by a ladder to sound with their hammer. They break down the walls wholly and enter themselves to search with candles and torches in all such dark places and housetops where some times nothing but mice and birds come of many yeares." John Ferne, the authority on heraldry, referred to the roughshod treatment of Catholics in a letter to Cecil from York, July 3, 1599. He announced a recent raid of Groman Abbey at two in the morning, stating that "the recusants have so many eyes . . . that I could not take men enough to compass the house and resist their violence." Hence it was necessary to call upon the aid of a neighbor Lord Sheffield, who arrived with thirty-six servants leaving their horses at a distance of a half a mile to surprise their victims. Having tried "doors, ceilings, pavement and double walls and vaults of a strange conveyance," they found "things for furnishing a mass . . . and diuers Popish books."[16]

When the Catholic was apprehended he was usually sent to Bridewell Prison which is described as "a slaughter-house where the cruelties inflicted are scarcely credible. The tasks imposed are continuous and beyond ordinary strength and even the sick are driven to them under the lash. It is the one purgatory that all we Catholics dread," wrote Father Gerard, "where Topcliffe and Young butchers have compleat license to torture." Other notorious jails were the Gatehouse, Westminster, the Compter in the Poultry, the Tower, the Clink, the Queen's Bench and the White Lion. At Fleet Prison it was reported that inmates succumbed "like dogs in their corner, mouldy straw beneath them, and foul rags spread over their emaciated forms surrounded by brawling, filth and vermin; many laden with chains and braces." Prisoners were occasionally confined to cells of "little ease," a unit of such small dimensions that the occupant could never stand, sit or lie at length and was compelled to remain in a squatting posture for days "inhaling the rank putrid air, surrounded by filth, lice and rodents." The Separatist leader, Francis Johnson, described Newgate as "filthy and unclean, more unwholesome than dunghills, more stinking than swine sties." [17]

Confined at Marshalsea, Father Gerard recalled a strict search had been made for "churche stuffe, Agnus Dei and relics." On one occasion he stated quantities of Catholic books and sacred objects had been seized "enough to fill a cart." Solace was offered to him and his co-religionists through the "consecrated crucifixes hallowed by His Holiness, with books" which had been smuggled into their dank, dark, moldering cells.[18]

The *Records* of the Stationers' Company allude to the expenses incurred by messengers for stalking their prey and their books. The Company's clerk was allotted ten shillings for filling out a search warrant. Company agents in 1586 received a total of twenty-eight pounds, four shillings, eleven pence for their labor. Twelve shillings had been allocated for the apprehension of a "popishe booke which was impryntinge." Entries refer to the quest for "extraordynarye presses" [secret presses], charges "for serche for twooe dayes" by the Master of the Company; "for boat hyer about the causes viis;" for the "pursuyvant attending them for a secret press." The repulsive nature of the work seems scarcely to have bothered the Company agents. There are frequent references to "breakfastes for serchers;" the costs of "going to and from Lambeth;" "serch dynners, Master Harrison and others vi s., 8d." – award banquets "at the Bell in Holbourne, the Constable or Master of the Company being present." Carried away by their holy zeal, the pursuivants often outdid themselves, and apparently uncertain of their destination, not infrequently sacked the home of an innocent citizen. In one instance the unfortunate victim was indemnified since the Company in October 1587 allotted two shillings "to a poore woman whose house was serched at Kingston."[19]

The relentless pursuit of the heretic by the government and Company officials led their agents from a cave in Wales to the retreats of the nation's scholars. The stupidity and bigotry of the official program are clearly reflected in a raid of February 21, 1569, of the home of the country's eminent antiquary, John Stowe, who had acquired a considerable library which he consulted for research: chronicles, copies of chancery records, cartularies, documents and a variety of printed books. Stowe was reported to have spent as much as two hundred pounds annually upon his collection.

Stowe's religious convictions had been suspect, for he had previously been questioned for having in his possession a copy of the Duke of Alva's "Manifesto against Elizabeth," copies of which had been circulated in London by agents of the Spanish Ambassador. During the morning of February 21, 1569, Watts, the chamberlain of Bishop Grindal, visited the scholar's home. There he examined his library, subsequently reporting to his master books of a suspicious content. Grindal submitted Watt's report to Cecil: "He hath a great sorte of foolishe fabulous bookes of oldye printe ... also touching bookes printed in the old tyme. We have taken a note of such bookes as haue been lately putt forth in this realme or beyond the seas for the Defense of Papistrye. His bokes declare him to be a great fav[oure]r of Papistrye."[20]

"The Cataloguy of svch vnlawfulle bookes ... in the study of Stowe of London" reveals thirty-eight items, some of which are strongly Catholic in content. Three are manuscripts, including the author's revised copy of *The summarie of Englyshe chronicles* which is referred to in the "Cataloguy" as "corrected by hym." Twenty-four titles have been identified. Stowe's Catholic leanings – if not allegiance – are reflected in his copies of books by Thomas Heskyns, Cardinal Hosius, Robert Pointz, John Rastell, Thomas Dorman and others. An analysis of the imprints in the Stowe Library indicates that seven had been issued by

Caly, while several bear the colophons of Diest and Laet. Two originate from Fowler's Antwerp Press. The Stowe Collection further reveals the circulation of Continental Catholic books among the English orthodox.[21]

The raiders' descent upon the Borstall lodgings and "studie" of George Brome and his sisters Elizabeth and Bridget produced thirty books and relics, the latter including "a droppe of bloode wrapped in a paper in a basket" owned by his sister Elizabeth and a crucifix of "perle and silver." Among the books identified were a *Catechisme et sommaire de la religion chrestienne*, *Le cabinet de l'âme fidele*, *La pollicie chrestien* of Jean Talpin, the *Exercise of a Christian life* of Gaspare Loarte, Dante's *Inferno, purgatorio e paradiso*, a treatise by "Louis de genado principall of the holy order at Portugall;" a *Manual of Prayers* and a Latin Psalter. Four of the books can be attributed to the presses of Father Persons and L'Oyselet at Rouen. The Brome Collection, like that of Stowe, is further evidence of the distribution of Catholic texts in England.[22]

Apparently the historian and cartographer, John Speed, shared the religious convictions of his colleague, Stowe. When Thomas Banks, a deputy of Alderman Richard Martin, searched London for suspicious persons and material, he found in August 1584 in the "howse of John Spede in Powles Churchyarde . . . 7 bokes tending unto papistrye." A hunt by the pursuivants on the same day led to the residence of Sir Thomas Tresham, who had been confined in the Fleet for harboring Campion and other noted Jesuits. There the searchers found "popishe relics and printed bookes."[23]

A list of "Trayterous and popish bookes" intercepted by agents was submitted to the Master of the Stationers' Company in 1584. This report is a document of unusual bibliographical interest since it cites the number of copies of each book listed. The dossier itemizes four hundred thirty copies of six printed books and seven hundred loose printed sheets. Four titles had been issued by Fowler at Antwerp; three hundred sixty-seven copies of Bristow's *Demaundes to be proponed of Catholiques to the heretiques;* twenty copies of the seditious *Treatise of treasons against Q. Elizabeth* by John Leslie, Bishop of Ross; twenty-eight copies of St. Thomas More's *Dialogue of cumfort against tribulation;* nine copies of Possevino's *Treatise of the holy sacrifice of the altar called the masse*. Other titles include five copies of a *Latin Primer*, one copy of Bede's *History of the church of Englande* translated by Thomas Stapleton and published by Laet at Antwerp. In addition, the searchers confiscated "700 sheetes printed, conteyning a miracle wrought upon an English woman at Bruxelles."[24]

Earlier successful raids of June and August 1581 by Masters George Bishop and Ralph Newberry of the Stationers' Company, assisted by a pursuivant Cole, yielded a cache of one hundred books which included fifty copies of the Psalms (possibly printed by Fowler) and "three dozen of testamentes in 32 . . . 2 more testamentes in 32."[25]

"A commaundement from [his] Lordes Grace of Canterbury" on August 15, 1592 ordered the burning of books in the hall of the Stationers' Company. This directive does not specify the number of books to be destroyed but vaguely alludes to their titles: "Thesaurus principum Ministromachum . . . Rossaeus de re publica . . . little French books in 8 . . . Surius Chronicle." Two of the books identified were imports from the Netherlands, although neither had been printed by prominent Anglo-Catholic firms. William Rainolds, the noted Catholic divine, had issued his *De iusta reip. Christianae in reges impios* in 1592, adopting the pseudonym William Ross, while Laurentius Surius, the Flemish hagiographer, had published twenty years earlier *A History of the Dominican Order*.[26]

The command to burn "popishe bookes and thinges," the search, the midnight raids, the assignation of pursuivants, the patrol of the English ports, the spies and counter-spies in Madrid and Rouen, Hamburg and Calais – like all subsequent efforts to stifle the thought and faith of man – proved senseless and futile. The zeal of the devout was not to be crushed. The books, expounding his tenets, continued to be printed on the Continent and within the homeland. Neither persecution, conflagration, search nor sequestration could diminish the dedication of the Catholic – his conviction, a burning taper held aloft, a votive candle to his God, a soaring flame of faith! His was the true religion not to be vanquished by the state and its instruments of destruction.

V

SHARP POINTED TONGUES & SLANDEROUS BOOKS

The Archpriest Controversy

During the last years of Elizabeth's reign rebellion and insubordination developed within the ranks of the English Catholic priesthood. The Archpriest Controversy was to cleave Catholicism and to incite the struggle between members of the Jesuit Order and the old English priesthood loyal to the Crown of England.

The general English antipathy toward the Roman pontiff is familiar. Rumblings of further resentment were heard in England in 1595 when English students at the Jesuit College in Rome complained of Jesuits aspiring to dominance over the English mission. Agazzari had advised Father Persons of the enmity felt toward him by English scholars who "speak frequently and cuttingly against [your] book on the succession to the English throne and against its author . . . and they can hardly hear [your] name mentioned." The patriotism of the English students abroad had been aroused at the suggestion of a fellow-religious to seat a foreigner on the throne of England.[1]

At home Catholic priests and Jesuits had been imprisoned in Wisbeach Castle where even there the Jesuits strove to assume leadership. In his *True relation of the faction begun at Wisbich*, the Catholic divine, Christopher Bagshaw, berated the Jesuits' overbearing behavior "as if Catholicke faith had never been trulie preached, nor any good order rightlie established by us poore secular priests."[2]

To settle the growing rift between the priesthood loyal to the government and the more radical religious, Pope Clement VIII on March 7, 1597/98 appointed an Archpriest of England, Robert Blackwell. He was known to be one of the unqualified admirers and panegyrists of the Company of Jesus and of the opinion that "they that discommend them, know neither themselves nor them." The Archpriest was to exercise full authority over the secular clergy of England and Scotland. No decisions were to be made by him and his immediate advisers without the approval of the Superior of the English Jesuit Order. The loyal English clergymen found Blackwell's appointment intolerable. Representing the power of the Jesuit Order, the will of Rome, he was dubbed by his critics "an archpriest of clouts . . . a Jesuitical idiot." His opponents, known as the Appellants, sent four of their members to Rome to appeal Blackwell's appointment. Their petition was denied. Blackwell remained Archpriest of England![3]

The patriotism of the loyal English priesthood is reflected in their books and appeals. Thomas Bluet, representing the moderate group, sought an audience before the Queen, assuring her Majesty of the devotion of his fellow religious to her. William Gifford, English appointee to the See of Rheims, deplored the

Jesuit attitude toward England: "Ffor I am a Catholike . . . so I have ever detested these violent and b[l]oody spiritts who continually and unnaturallie practise against theyr prince and country and seeke to expose the spoyle of forayners by inivst invasion and conqueste of all sorts of people of what religion whatsoever." He denounced Father Persons' intrigue and particularly his *Conference about the next succession to the crowne of Englande* – "those that negotiate abroad for forraigne invasion and conquest from all their foolishe bookes of titles and right to the Crowne." *A letter of expostulation to Blackwell* by William Clarke alludes to the general dislike of the Jesuit Order, stating that not only Cardinal Allen, but "all these gentlemen who were with him can testify that he mvch disliked theyr dealinges towardes vs, and the Jesuits cannot withowt great impudence deny it, whomsoever they do shuffle of the blame."[4]

A Proclamation of November 5, 1601 indicates the government's cognizance of the Order's propaganda and hold upon the priesthood. It refers to the Jesuits as "Receivers, Relievers and Informands. Their own books show that most of the seminary Priests are in the hands of the Jesuits and are ready to fight against us." All Jesuits and secular priests were cautioned to leave the country and "not to return."[5]

The Controversy produced a flyting literature between the Jesuits and the Appellants. As Camden states, "With sharp pointed tongues and slanderous books did Jesuits and seculars fight with one another." It was complained that Jesuit spies abounded everywhere, even in the booksellers' quarters. "There is no place where men doe meete or walke in either Pauls, Westminster, the Temple Church, the Exchange or like places, but they [Jesuits] have an insinuating fellow . . . to listen and hearken to every man's discourse and learn what he can."[6]

The cause of the Appellant priests was espoused by several of the leading London stationers who saw in their plight a national issue. Although they lent their presses to the service of the loyal priesthood, they risked neither their position nor their security. The tracts issued by them bear no genuine imprint. Their origin is veiled in anonymity – occasionally attributed to Rouen and Rheims, cities espousing Catholicism.

Twenty-one tracts are associated with the Archpriest Controversy of which seventeen represent the sentiment of the Appellant group. These have been identified as the publications of seven English stationers, six of whom were prominent in the trade. Each apparently, in issuing four works or less relating to the Controversy, may have hoped to conceal such titles among general publications. It is of interest to note that Richard Field, Thomas Creede, James Roberts and Adam Islip, the principal publishers of the Archpriest tracts, had two points in common. All were non-conforming members of the Stationers' Company and all – with the exception of Islip – published the plays and sonnets of Shakespeare. Their contribution to the Catholic cause was small – veiled by anonymous and disguised imprints. They desired no publicity, for their aid to a movement – although patently patriotic – was, nonetheless, linked with the faith and aspirations of the detested Catholic minority.

Richard Field of the Splayed Eagle, Great Wood Street doubtless knew William Shakespeare. They probably played together as children in Stratford, their fathers having been close friends. John Shakespeare evaluated the property of Richard's father Henry upon his death in 1592.[7]

Upon his arrival in London, young Richard was apprenticed to the Huguenot dealer, Thomas Vautrollier, who imported books from France and Flanders. In London he used as his agent one Jean Desserans who assisted him in the distribution of books imported from the great publishing house of Plantin at Antwerp. While Vautrollier was abroad on business trips, young Field represented his master at the shop. He conducted the concern's affairs with the help of "Ffrenchmen or Dutchmen or such lyke." Hence he had the opportunity of meeting many foreigners and probably men of diverse faiths – if not some Catholics who slipped into the metropolis. Field married either Vautrollier's widow or daughter Jacqueline in 1588, when he succeeded to the ownership of the business at the Black Friars near Ludgate. Married to a Huguenot, Richard Field can scarcely be identified as a Catholic.[8]

Field's religious affiliation, however, did not preclude his interest in the flyting warfare promoted by the Archpriest Controversy. To his press have been attributed the treatises of John Colleton, Thomas Bluet, William Watson and Anthony Copley. Of the four authors Bluet and Watson are best known for their outspoken opinions which caused much indignation among the Jesuits and some criticism within the Appellant group itself.

In 1601 Field issued Bluet's *Important considerations, which ought to moue all true and sound Catholikes ... to acknowledge ... that the proceedings of her Maiesty ... haue bene both mild and mercifull*. A contemporary observed that Bluet had attempted "to move all true and sound Catholics who are not wholly jesuited to acknowledge without equivocations, ambiguities or shiftings, that the proceedings of her Majesty and of the state with them since the beginning of her reign have been both mild and merciful." If Bluet found some compassion in Elizabeth's attitude toward her minority subjects, he failed to recognize much virtue in the connivance of an eminent fellow Catholic, Father Persons, who, he believed was "the cause of all the conspiracies of the late years directed against the Queene." Colleton's *Iust defence of the slandered priestes: wherein the reasons of their bearing off to recieue maister Blackwell to their superior before the arriuall of his Holines breue, are layed downe* has been assigned to Field's press. When the book reached Rome, Persons, incensed by the author's attitude, had the work placed on the Index.[9]

A decacordon of ten quodlibeticall questions, concerning religion and state by the radical divine, William Watson, appeared in 1602. The book was harshly criticized by the Appellant priest, William Bishop, for its "sharpnes of stile regarding some assertions perillous." Watson's treatise was levelled principally against the Jesuits' high-handed dictatorship. The author asserted, "yf toleration [were] introduced then there should be no collor to publishe bookes how tyrannical the persecution of Catholikes is." Anthony Copley's *Answere to a letter of a Iesuited gentleman . . . Concerning the appeale; state, Iesuits* was also issued by Field in 1602. The fervor and loyalty of the poet and conspirator, Copley, are revealed in his denunciation of "the folly and spirit of the Jesuits."[10]

Field had thus associated himself, albeit anonymously, with those who attacked the Jesuits. His large trade-list included, in addition to the four writings relating to the Controversy, two works by the English priest, Thomas Preston. He issued his *Apologia* and *Responsio*, both of which appeared under the author's pseudonym, Roger Widdrington, and bore the fictitious imprint "Cosmopoli apud Theophilum Pratum" – a rather thin disguise.[11]

Field, the publisher of four editions of *Venus and Adonis,* was in business for a short time with the disreputable printer, Roger Ward, whose press and type, concealed in a "henhouse near St. Sepulchres Church," were seized by the government agents. Ward was accused of conducting secret printing at Southwark and Hammersmith. Field, with Adam Islip, is listed among fourteen stationers summoned early in the century before Archbishop Whitgift and Bishop Bancroft for having printed books distasteful to the Crown.[12]

Islip, like Field, had been briefly associated with the offensive Ward. He had also provided him with type which, as an apprentice, he had stolen from his master, Thomas Purfoote. Islip's interest in the Archpriest struggle is reflected by his publication of two or three Appellant tracts. *A dialogue betwixt a secular priest, and a lay gentleman* by Dr. John Mush was issued by Islip in 1601, bearing the fictitious imprint "Rhemes." In all likelihood he also printed his *Declaratio motuum ac turbationum quae ex controversiis inter Iesuitas . . . et sacerdotes seminariorum in Anglia*. The book appeared with the Rouen colophon "Rhotomagi apud Iacobum Molaeum 1601." If Islip assumed responsibility for its publication, he was certainly not over-familiar with its content. A two-page errata list at the end admits the printer's ignorance of Latin – naturally the mistakes can be attributed to the compositor. The author of both treatises, John Mush, was one of the most outspoken Jesuit critics. He was one of the leading Appellants, an enemy of Blackwell, and one of the four divines sent to Rome to appeal the Archpriest's appointment. He keenly resented the Machiavellian deviltry of Persons whom he considered "an incendiary guilty of causing all sorts of external and internal disturbances. We have to do penance at home for his sinning abroad."[13]

Further criticism of Jesuit ambition is expressed in Robert Charnock's *Answere made by one of our brethren . . . to a fraudulent letter of M. George Blackwels, written to Cardinal Caietane*. The work was issued anonymously by Islip in 1602. As late as 1613, long after Master Blackwell had been deprived of his high office, Islip printed Preston's *Theologicall disputation concerning the oath of allegiance*, a work of politico-religious significance during the reign of James I.[14]

Thomas Creede of the Old Exchange printed between 1598 and 1602, in addition to ballads and broadsides, several plays of Shakespeare: the second editions of *The tragedy of King Richard the third, The most excellent and lamentable tragedie of Romeo and Juliet*, the first edition of *The cronicle history of*

Henry the fift and the first edition of *A most pleasaunt and excellent conceited comedie, of Syr Iohn Falstaffe, and the merrie wives of Windsor.* Three works of a less diverting nature emerged from his press during this period. Dr. Christopher Bagshaw had spent some time in Wisbeach Castle where he had earned the enmity of several inmates as "a man of no worth, unruly, disordered and a disobedient fellow not to be favoured or respected by any." Bagshaw was apparently unconcerned by this unflattering estimate. He proceeded to relate the disturbances incited by the Jesuits and their high priest Blackwell in his *Relatio compendiosa turbarum quas Iesuitae Angli, vna cum D. Georgio Blackwello archipresbytero, sacerdotibus seminariorum populoq; Catholico co[n]ciuere. The hope of peace* by John Bennett, who is castigated by Father Persons as the "greatest dissembler and most perilous fellow," appeared in 1601. In its preface the author refers to two recently published books "by the priestes in the necessary defence of their good name and fame." Creede had assigned to the publication the fictitious imprint "Franckford heires of D. Turner." Bennett later admitted that the book had been printed at London. Creede employed the colophon "heires of Ia. Walker at Roane" for his publication of *The copies of certaine discourses, which were extorted from diuers, as their friends desired them, or their aduersaries driue them to purge them selues of the most greeuous crimes of schisme, sedition, rebellion.*[15]

James Roberts, active at the Love and Death, Fleet Street, like his colleagues, Creede and Field, printed several Shakespeare quartos: the second editions of *The tragicall historie of Hamlet, Prince of Denmark* and *A midsomer nights dream*, the first edition of *The most excellent historie of the Merchant of Venice*, and others.[16]

There is some indication that Roberts had Catholic leanings. He married Alice Charlewood, widow of John Charlewood, known as J.C., the Earl of Arundel's man. According to recent scholarship, the Catholic benefactress, the Countess of Arundel, had persuaded Charlewood, her printer, to permit his press to be brought to Acton for the use of Father Robert Southwell. His willingness to please his patroness does not however necessarily brand him as a Catholic. Charlewood was a large-scale printer-publisher and several of his imprints represent the radical Puritan point of view. He was a somewhat irresponsible person, occasionally at odds with the Company for printing "priviledged copies" – who, indifferent to divergent religious issues, – sought profit from his profession.[17]

Roberts had come into conflict with the Stationers' Company in September 1598 for his printing of a *Brief Catechism*. The Court of Assistants ordered that "clerely from hensforth [he must] surcease to deale wth the printinge of the brief catechisme wth the A.B.C. letany and other things inserted whiche he hath lately printed . . . contrary to her maiesties prohibic[i]on and thorders of this Company." He was compelled to deliver to the Company all sheets of the book. In 1596 Roberts was fined for "com[m]ittinge twoo seu[er]all offences in a printinge a booke called newe tydings contrary to the honorable decrees of the starre chamber, and the laudable Ordinances of this Company."[18]

Three books emanating from the Archpriest Controversy have been linked to Roberts' press. He published in 1601 Bagshaw's *Sparing discouerie of our English Iesuits*. In the opinion of a contemporary critic, the author had spoken "very bitterly against Parsons" and his fellow Jesuits. "Of late years the Jesuits no longer live[d] according to their first institution of their order, for of late years they take such a course as if religion were nothing else but a mere political device . . . and they were the men that by Machiavels rulers are raised up to maintain it by equivocations, detractions, dissimulation . . . for superiority, a stirring to strife."[19]

Two years later Roberts issued another treatise against Persons by the Appellant critic, William Clarke, *A replie vnto a certaine libell*. Other works, representing the anti-Jesuitical point of view published by Roberts, are English translations of the writings of the French publicists, Antoine Arnauld and Estienne Pasquier. The latter's *Iesuites Catechism*, translated into English by William Watson, falls within the category of Appellant literature. Both writer and translator were avowed opponents of the Order. Rumor circulated that Pasquier hated a Jesuit even more than a Huguenot.[20]

Roberts' Catholic leanings are further indicated by his semi-official association with a small printer and bookseller, Edward or Walter Venge of Bishop's Hall, Stepney. Only three books bear Venge's imprint, all of which reflect contemporary literary and social interests. His Catholic predisposition emerges from the *Records* of the Stationers' Company.

Venge was associated with Roberts in the printing of the *Brief Catechism*. He was summoned before the Court of Assistants the same day as Roberts and advised to bring into the hall "all suche leaves as are printed of the second Impression of the Catechisme." He was "never hereafter to meddle wth the printinge sellinge byndinge or stitchinge of the same or any p[ar]te thereof." Venge chose not to heed the Company's injunctions, but used his press at Bishop's Hall for the printing of "prymers, Catechismes and Almanacks." The Company searchers found on the premises "a presse with certen pica and Romayne, Englishe and other letters, and certen prynted leaves of the prym[m]ers to the quantitie of 4 or 5 Reames." The press and type were promptly taken to the Company hall, where they were "sawed in peeces melted and defaced and made vnserviceable for pryntinge." Venge's enthusiasm had been somewhat cooled after the dissolution of his press. He emerges as a bookseller in 1599 and after another brief wrangle with the Company in 1601 he sinks into obscurity. He apparently had died by 1606, since in October of that year the Stationers' Company allotted to the Widow Venge "toward her relief 13s., 4d."[21]

In 1601, while Venge confronted the wrath of his guild, the distinguished firm of Felix Kingston issued two important treatises relating to the Archpriest Controversy: Bagshaw's *True relation of the faction begun at Wisbeach* and Copley's *Answere to a letter of a Iesuite gentleman*. Kingston's rival, Robert Barker, printed two years later Robert Charnock's *Reply to a notorious libell intituled a briefe apologie or defence of the ecclesiastical hierarchie.* As a publisher Barker was not greatly influenced by the religious schism. In 1601 he had issued Father Persons' *Briefe apologie, or defence of the Catholike ecclesiastical hierarchie & subordination in England, erected these later yeares by our holy father Pope Clement the eyght.*[22]

The anatomie of popishe tyrannie by the seminary priest Thomas Bell appear in 1603. The title suggests the fairly comprehensive scope of the work: "wherin is conteyned a plaine declaration and Christian censure of all the principall parts of the Libelles, Letters, Edictes, Pamphletes and Bookes lately published by the secular priestes and English hispanized Jesuits." The publisher, Richard Bankworth, a former draper, had often defied the Company, having pirated several works, among them, Sidney's *Arcadia.*[23]

Two months before Elizabeth's death, the Appellant priests drew up their Protestation of Allegiance in which they acknowledged the sovereign power of the Queen. They swore to defend her and the state against conspiracy and attempted invasion. They refused to obey the Pope in any command which required them to abandon their monarch. The Pontiff was recognized only as their "spiritual chief pastor."[24]

This was their last act of defiance. The Appellant group had laid down their arms. Although the Archpriest Controversy was now bereft of its initial vigor, the cause of Catholicism would be supported by other members of the Honorable Company of Stationers.

Edward Allde found himself frequently at odds with his country and his guild. The son of the printer John Allde, Edward at his shop in Cripplegate published ballads, the writings of Thomas Churchyard, Thomas Dekker, Christopher Marlowe and other contemporary literati. In 1597 he antagonized the officials of the Stationers' Company. His "booke ... being a popishe Confession, Called a brief fourme of Confession" was seized by the searchers and his press was made "vnserviceable for printinge."[25]

Two years later he again offended the authorities by printing certain distasteful books which were condemned and ordered to be burned. At the very outset of James' reign Allde made his submission before the Archbishop of Canterbury for his "disorders in pryntinge," having outraged the Company by publishing fifteen hundred copies of the monarch's *Basilicon Doron* "contrarie to the decrees of the most hon'able Courte of Starrechamber and the ordynances of [his] Companie." He was sentenced to prison for this misdemeanor. Apparently Richard Bancroft, Bishop of London, the friend and patron of several headstrong stationers, intervened. Allde got off fairly lightly. His press and type were "to be defaced and broken in peeces and hys ymprysonment deferred."[26]

It was apparently not until 1613 that Allde issued another Catholic text, the *Disputatio theologica* of Thomas Preston which bore the fictitious imprint "Albinopoli ex officina Theophili Fabri." The work was obviously successful since it was reprinted the following year.[27]

Allde was a highly fractious individual, constantly in trouble, either maltreating his apprentices or publishing books without license. He was chided by the Wardens of the Stationers' Company several times for using abusive language, "vttering verie vnfitting wordes and scandalous speeches." Richard Field, upon occasion, was the victim of his venomous tongue.[28]

As late as August 1621, Allde, in company with the news-printer, Thomas Archer, was sentenced to imprisonment for having disregarded the international libel agreement between the English King and the rulers of the Continent. Together they had printed *A breife description of the declaration of the Ban made against the King of Bohemia ... of no value*. The tract appeared with a fictitious imprint "The Hayf, A. Meuris, 1621." It was ordered that "the barres of [Allde's] presse shalbe taken downe." Edward Allde contritely bowed before the Masters of his Company on July 5, 1623, admitting that he had "at divers times ... giuen occasion of much offence to the Company ... behauing turbulently and disorderly towards them and vsing vnseemly and vnfitting words."[29]

Like Allde, John Danter was a lively and contentious member of the trade active at Duck Lane and Holborn Conduit. The son of an Eynsham weaver, Danter came to London in 1582, when he was apprenticed to the well-known printer, John Day. His master was to die two years later – Danter being transferred to the printer Robert Robinson, with whom he was to remain "vntill the feast of Sainct Michaelmas in 1588." Danter was admitted a freeman of the Stationers' Company on September 30, 1589.

His future as a somewhat fractious member of the Stationers' guild had already been observed during his service with Robinson. A secret press was detected in 1586 in Middlesex operated by young Danter and several associates. The sentence of the Company for this infraction was severe. Danter was to be denied the privilege of becoming a master printer and to remain a journeyman throughout his career. The sentence was, however, revoked upon his gaining his freedom, when he entered upon a short-lived partnership with William Hoskins and Henry Chettle. Danter set up for himself in 1591.[30]

Between that year and 1598, Danter's trade-list comprises a delightful variety of plays and interludes by Thomas Lodge, Robert Greene, Thomas Nashe and George Peele. In 1594 and 1597 he published *The most lamentable Romaine tragedie of Titus Andronicus* and *An excellent conceited tragedie of Romeo and Juliet* of Shakespeare. His list was supplemented by numerous ballads and popular news-tales, relations to startle the timid and stir the stout-hearted: *Strange sightes seene in the ayre, strange monsters beheild on the land ... in and about the cittye of Rosenberghe; Whites lamentacion made in the dungeon of Newgate the night before his death* and *A most horrible murther committed at Mayfield in Sussex*.[31]

Danter had apparently encountered some official opposition in 1593, since at the time a warrant for his arrest was issued by the Company. The nature of his offence is not stated. Three years later the searchers found in the house of John Danter "twoo printinge presses and certen letters pica, and pica Roman, and other sorts of letters in fourmes and cases, wch were employed in printinge of a booke called Iesus psalter and other things without aucthoritie." The press and type were promptly brought to Stationers Hall, where they were to be broken up against any future use. The *Records* of the Company list 3s. 6d. payment to the porter for having brought the press to the Hall. The Danter version of the *Jesus Psalter* was the eighth edition to be issued by an Anglo-Catholic press. Fowler had printed two editions in 1575 to be followed by that of Carter. The work enjoyed great popularity among the Catholic minority and in sponsoring its publication Danter followed not only his own sympathies but also those of a Catholic clientele.[32]

After this affront Danter's activity declined. He was dead by 1600 since in July of that year, his wife, apparently destitute, appealed to the benevolence of the Stationers' Company. The subversive behavior of her late husband had not affected the philanthropic instincts of the guild members. Upon her application, the Widow Danter was voted five shillings. It was decided that she would receive from the Company funds an annual stipend of twelve shillings.[33]

Gabriel Cawood at the Holy Ghost, St. Paul's Churchyard, had engaged James Roberts to print for him several editions of the most popular contemporary prose work, John Lyly's *Euphues*. While Lyly's romance in no way could be frowned upon by the authorities of the Stationers' Company, they regarded with less favor several texts printed by him for Cawood.[34]

Gabriel Cawood had entered the trade "per patrimonium." His father John had been not only Master of the Company upon three occasions, but also official printer to Elizabeth's half-sister, Mary. There is reason to believe that Cawood, high in the Queen's favor, was a Catholic. As an apprentice at his father's press, young Gabriel met William Carter, the future martyr, indentured to the Elder Cawood. Cawood had thus been intimate with a rabid Catholic and once established for himself, he engaged as an apprentice Peter Bulloch who was later not only to be indicted but also to be executed for his religion. Gabriel Cawood, like his father, was to enjoy great distinction as a member of his guild, becoming Warden and Master in 1597 and 1599. His publication list was small, comprising an approximate thirty-six books. The poet Robert Southwell was known as "the chief dealer in the affairs of the papists for England." In publishing two lyrical works of Southwell, Cawood may have attempted to vindicate Catholicism from the constant violent barbs of its detractors. *Mary Magdalene's Teares* and *Saint Peter's Complaint* were printed by Roberts for Cawood in several editions from 1591 to 1602.[35]

Cawood not only published the Catholic verse and prose of Father Southwell but also stocked Catholic texts. Upon examination in March 1594/95, the priest William Fitch, who frequently used the pseudonym, William Wiseman, denied any knowledge of "a book entitled Breviarum Romanum." He admitted that he had purchased a work "intituled Hieronymi Plati de Societate Jesu de bono statu religionis . . . and that he caused the same to be bought at Cawood's shop in Paul's Churchyard and saith that the book containeth nothing but true doctrine and that he translated it through with his own hand." He continued that he had lent the book to Father Edmonds and other priests at Wisbeach Castle. A Trier edition of this work had been published in 1593 by Heinrich Bock, copies of which were imported by Cawood or brought surreptitiously to his shop. John Bolt, interrogated along with Wiseman, stated that he had borrowed from the latter a copy of *St. Peter's Complaint* "and another on Campion's matters." Since Cawood did not publish *Saint Peter's Complaint* until April 1595, Wiseman had in all likelihood obtained either an advance copy, the proofs, or one of the many garbled and erroneous manuscript versions which were, to Southwell's annoyance, being circulated.[36]

When Cawood's apprentice, Peter Bulloch, completed his term of indenture in 1598, he became a bookbinder for a brief period. He was shortly thereafter arrested for selling popish books and in order to gain his freedom, he turned state's evidence against a professional colleague.

As a bookbinder, Bulloch was probably acquainted with William Wrench, who also had been a London bookbinder. Wrench was to become one of the most active Catholic underground printers in Staffordshire where in 1599 he issued Richard Bristow's *Demaundes to be proponed of Catholiques to the heretikes*. Copies of this work were distributed by the Catholic bookseller James Duckett who was presumably associated, from 1595 to 1601, with Henry Owen, a colleague of Wrench in the Staffordshire underground movement. Bulloch, aware of Duckett's involvement, betrayed him for an illusory promise of freedom. According to Gillow, James Duckett had been named after his grandfather James Leyburne, Lord of the Manor of Skelsmergh, who had been executed at Lancaster in 1583 for denying the Queen's supremacy. His grandson had been educated as a Protestant in London, where he had been bound over to a printer. His conversion to Catholicism was a result of reading Jean de Caumont's *Foundation of the Catholic Religion* and of his marriage to a Catholic widow. He presumably devoted twelve years to the publication and sale of Catholic texts, suffering periodic terms of imprisonment. There is evidence that James Duckett and his wife Ann of Chancery Lane, London, were practising Catholics since they were presented for non-attendance at church in May and October 1594. Duckett's fate was sealed by Bulloch, who, after a year's incarceration, hoped for his release by betraying the grandson of the Lord of Skelsmergh.[37]

Bulloch informed Chief Justice Popham that Duckett had in his possession twenty-five copies of Southwell's heinous *Humble supplication to her maiestie*. The searchers promptly pounced upon Duckett's quarters at the preferred hour of midnight. There they found no copies of Southwell's work, but instead an entire impression of *Mount Calvary* and other Catholic books. James Duckett, taken to Newgate, admitted upon further accusation by Bulloch, that he had in his possession some copies of Bristow's *Demaundes*.

Duckett's trial of April 17, 1601 is a travesty of English justice. It besmirches the name of one of the country's great jurists, Sir John Popham, Chief Justice of the King's Bench, and reflects further the hopeless position of the Catholic minority. Legally, Duckett was guilty – he had circulated a subversive book. Morally, English justice was culpable, since it begrudged James Duckett a fair trial.

A letter of the Jesuit Francis Rivers to Father Persons describes the atmosphere which pervaded Duckett's trial. He reported the presence of "one Bulloch a stationer [who had been] reprieved and promised pardon if he would accuse others. Whereunto having now consented, albeit this Ducket [sic] pleaded effectually by himself, so the jury coming in delivered their verdict not guilty." The Chief Justice of the King's Bench was apparently indignant at this "miscarriage" of English justice which had pronounced a Catholic heretic innocent! He immediately advised the jury "to go together again and at the second return" – fearful for their own safety – "they were of another mind and the poor man had judgment accordingly."

The turncoat Bulloch had not been too clever. His accusations boomeranged. In his betrayal of Duckett he had trapped himself since he admitted that he had bound copies of Bristow's *Demaundes*. The state had used Bulloch for its purpose. He was guilty by deed and association. His information was no longer required and on the same day, April 19, 1601, he and Duckett were hanged at Tyburn. Unlike his colleague, he died a traitor to his faith.[38]

Father Persons declared that Duckett "dyed exceeding well, disclaimed the malcontents ... and spake to his wyfe to burne all such books of theirs as were in his house and asked pardon of all the Societie for indeed he had been an instrument of the discontented for printing and publishing some of their books." Father Garnet assured Persons that all efforts to save Duckett had been in vain. Referring to Southwell's *Supplication*, he remarked, "The book I will gett if I can for they were all taken almost."[29]

The dissemination of Catholic literature by these eight printers and publishers, members of the Stationers' Company, although not widespread, does indicate the presence of an orthodox book-buying clientele in England. It is obvious that not all Catholic printing emerged from the underground presses or was furtively imported into England from abroad. The character of the Catholic books issued by these firms – with the exceptions of Allde, Venge and Cawood – is controversial. The participation of these stationers in the circulation of books by the Appellant priests may be condoned as a gesture of patriotism. They exposed the Jesuit conspirator – traitor to the English Crown. Although their motive has been interpreted altruistically, a more realistic economic incentive must be explored. The Archpriest Controversy attracted the attention of the thoughtful Englishman concerned with the well-being of his country. Readers were drawn to a literature exposing the struggle within the confines of a minority religion. Criticism of Catholic by Catholic was a *cause célèbre*, a struggle of sufficient rancor to attract attention. Despite the loyalty of the Appellant group, the printers and publishers, members of a venerable guild, sought no public identification with their authors. They issued their texts anonymously or with fictitious imprints. These stationers desired no government prosecution at a time when the Crown sought to drive from the land the Jesuits and seminary priests "whose books lately published show how wickedly they combined themselves together in the Realme for the advancement of enemies, the persecuting of subjects and the subversion of the state."

The realm conferred by Elizabeth upon her heir, James of Scotland, was to continue a nation torn by religious strife, a country besmirched by intolerance and the suppression of an ancient faith.

VI

OVERLORD OF THE WHOLE LAND

Reign of James I

Shortly after the accession of James I to the English throne, the London newscorrespondent, John Chamberlain, reported his impression of the new sovereign. He "uses all very graciously. These beautiful beginnings raise all men's spirits and put them in great hopes, insomuch that not only Protestants, but papists and puritans and the very poets with their idle pamphlets promise themselves great part in his favor." Joyfully the distinguished Father Henry Garnet imparted to Father Persons his high expectations of Mary Stuart's son, referring to "a great alteration by the death of the Queen. Great fears were; but all turned into greater security and a golden time we have of freedom abroad. Great hope is of toleration and so general a consent of Catholicks lies in his proclaiming as it seemeth God will work much. All sorts of religions live in hope and suspense; yet Catholicks have great cause to hope for great respect, in that the nobility, all almost labour for it and have great promise thereof from his Majesty."[1]

The hopes of all – particularly those of "Catholicks" were not to endure long. Through a streak of obstinacy and contempt James had almost completely shorn the halo from the despotic though beloved crown bequeathed him by Elizabeth. His subjects, deprived of the regal authority of their late queen, found to their growing dismay a monarch – with short bandied legs and an unattractive Scottish manner of speech – totally addicted to the principle of his own inviolate position, ruling a nation beset with increasing religious friction and financial insecurity.[2]

Elizabeth had sustained her hold upon England through her will, her understanding, her empathy for her people, her own particular political genius. Although she esteemed her subjects' love "far above earthly treasure," she left to her cherished England a successor who knew nothing of the particular laws and liberties of her subjects. James cared little about the history or the political institutions of his new realm. He neither comprehended its political tenets nor wished to compromise his autocratic principles. He was unable "to adopt his political theories to the realities of the delicate relationship built up between Elizabeth and her Parliaments." The new royal master was completely out of touch with his common-sensical subjects. He insisted upon the relevancy of the classical precept: "Quod principi placuit vigorem legis habet."[3]

In addition, James' fears and suspicions brand him as one of the most complicated neurotics ever to have ascended the English throne. He had spent much of his childhood in Scotland in fear of physical violence and assassination. As King of England, he could chillingly recall the attempts upon the life of his predecessor as well as upon his own. His mother had been beheaded, his two regents, Lennox and Moray, suffered murder and execution on the scaffold. Like the majority of his contemporaries, he contemplated a world of malevolent, supernatural powers and in his *Demonologie* he described the nature and influence of witches. He was erratic, restless, inconsistent in mood, at times generous, at other times avaricious, ranging from gloom to frivolity. He was gluttonous and extravagant, capable of love, but often alone and denied any real affection. Always convinced of his God-given authority, he was ever conscious of the prerogatives of his exalted position. Self-indulgent, he moved his court about constantly – visiting and hunting, drinking and carousing – arriving at Hatfield, Knole or St. Albans with three hundred carts of luggage. He created numerous titles; he lavished gifts upon favorites; he exercised his royal authority and shifted his position toward religious factions from indulgence to persecution.

James' political instability was engendered partly by his own neuroses and partly by the spectre of the Spanish invasion abetted by the English Catholics. The fear of orthodoxy and the phantom of foreign troops on English soil subverted James' better instincts. To destroy this threat he swayed from hostility to friendship, from tolerance to suppression. He embraced the dictates of the Spanish Ambassador to England; he negotiated a marriage alliance between Prince Charles and the Spanish Infanta which, failing, thrust him into a position of neutrality in the European conflict. His refusal to participate immediately in a war which involved his daughter Elizabeth and her popular husband, Frederick the Winter King of Bohemia, incensed the country confronted by a growing division between the religious groups.

James' personal rule was dictated by his political philosophy. Selected by divine ordinance to govern the English, James became the most eloquent interpreter of his predestined role. To insure his position, it was imperative for him to justify the concept of divine right. His claim to the throne had been disputed by the Roman controversialists since, according to them, it was based upon descent alone. To quash the objections of Papist and Presbyterian, the monarch argued that every individual is subject to royal authority and that the secular power is ordained by God alone and cannot be limited by Pope or ecclesiast. "No foreign king or state could or did ever set on as the King of England," declared Judge Whitelocke, while a conscientious critic stated that "the most religious could wish that His Highness would be more sparing in using the name of God and in comparing the Deity with the prince's sovereignty."[4]

James' political concepts are expressed in his treatise, *The Trew Law of Free Monarchies* in which he asserts that the "king is the overlord of the whole land, so he is master over every person that inhabiteth the same, having power over the life and death of every one of them." In his Speech to Parliament, delivered March 1610, he elaborated upon his position: "Kings are justly called gods for that they exercise a manner or resemblance of Divine power on earth; for if you will consider the attributes to God you shall see how they agree in person of a king. [They] have power to exalt low things and abuse high things, and make of their subjects like men at chess. And to the king is due both the affection of the soul and the service of the body of his subjects." To James his judgment was absolute, never to be questioned. Criticism implied wilfulness. "It should become you," he wrote to the Bishop Abbot, "to have a kind of faith implicit in my judgment as well as respect of some skill I have in divinity." In the hope of consolidating his realm, he remarked in his opening speech to Parliament: "I am the husband and the whole island is my wife. I am the shepherd and it is my flock."[5]

James' flock was divided among Anglicans, Puritans and Catholics, the latter splintered by the Archpriest Controversy. Although James, reared in a gloomy Calvinistic atmosphere, "speiking latin ar [he] could speik Scottis," little liked Bible-reading Puritans, he and his advisers never regarded them as a political threat. Their members formed a critical hegemony rather than a hostile, menacing force prompt to abet the potential invader. The Puritan was not the tool of the Pope and his princely agent, the King of Spain. The Catholic would always remain a stranger in the land, aloof and contemptuous, owing allegiance to a foreign power. He was in the pay of a Continental monarch and would unite with the advance guard of a foreign foe. The Roman Catholic problem remained as it had been – urgent and immediate. It required solution.

James had described the Jesuits as "venomed wasps and firebrands of sedition." The practises pursued by Elizabeth were to be continued. The bright promise that "Jesuits, seminaries and friars would come abroad in open bringing forth ... stones of images" was promptly forgotten. James' renewal of recusancy fines and his prompt dismissal from the country of Jesuits and priests endorsed Cecil's philosophy that the law of the land must be obeyed. "The object of these laws is to extinguish the Catholic religion in this kingdom." Father Gerard succinctly appraised the situation: "They make it death to receive the absolution of a priest, yea, death to harbour a priest in your house or to give him a cup of drink or any assistance in this need; death to persuade any to embrace the Catholic religion."[6]

Ever suspicious of the Catholic Spanish cabal, the new regime arrested, proscribed and hanged priests and Jesuits. The government constantly feared the approach of larger, more threatening armadas. The great Coke's ear was ever alert to the arrival of the detested Spaniard. He believed in military preparedness and warned the Crown of possible landing places in case of invasion. "If the King of Spain's army were great, Essex and Kent were judged fittest. If the army were small and trusted upon help in England," then Milford Haven was regarded as more accessible. To the distinguished jurist, treason was abetted in England by the Roman cleric.[7]

Coke's surmise proved to be partly correct. In November 1605 a conspiracy of preposterous enormity and ignominy, concocted by English Catholics, stunned the realm of James Stuart. The Gunpowder Plot has been described as the result of anti-Catholic legislation. Five hundred and sixty persons had been convicted of recusancy in 1605. The French Ambassador declared that "the king treats the Catholics with greater rigour than ever. I forsee that their condition will become daily worse." Father Garnet deplored the unfortunate situation of his co-religionists. "The courses taken are more severe than in Queen Elizabeth's time. Every six weeks in a general court, juries appointed to indict, present, find the goods of Catholics, prize them, yea in many places drive away whatsoever they find contra ordinem juris." Father Persons was informed that "all are desperate here, diuers Catholics are offended, with Jesuits."[8]

Fourteen miles from London, at Enfield Chace, "a low built half-timbered dwelling" known as White Webbs, originally the gift of Elizabeth to her personal physician Robert Huicke, housed a desperate band of plotters, devising the end of Catholic persecution in England. Their design involved the blowing up of King and Parliament. White Webbs was an appropriate selection for a Catholic rendezvous of such importance. Used by the Jesuits for their meetings, conferences and retreats, it had been described by Father Garnet as "a spacious house fit to receive so great a company that should resort thither." It was attractively furnished with its own chapel and even boasted relics, including a hair shirt worn by the sainted Thomas à Becket. For hasty departure it provided trap doors and passages on all sides, a house "very convenient for persons of evill affection to the state."

It was at White Webbs that Catesby, Tresham and Winter had met in 1601. Father Garnet had been encouraged to urge the invasion of England by Spain, whose monarch had promised one hundred thousand crowns for that cause. To the Catholic militant the destruction of King and Parliament was essential for the restoration of orthodoxy. The upheaval which would naturally follow the holocaust offered him the perfect opportunity to assume the reins of office.[9]

The Gunpowder Plot of November 4, 1605 failed. The touchwood and fuse, the tinder box and powder planted by Guy Fawkes and his collaborators were discovered in time. The fires which were to consume James and Parliament became bonfires of celebration – marking the deliverance of the nation from Catholic cabal and outrage. The plotters suffered torture and death. Their ill-starred venture brought upon the Catholic cause further opprobrium, restriction and harassment. The Plot intensified English hatred of all Catholics and Jesuits, "those reverend cheaters, prowling fathers and caterpillars of Christianity."

Despite its enormous impact upon the country, normalcy was restored by the third week of November 1605. The ports were reopened; "carriers from the ambassadors and merchants, and any honest known merchant or his factor" were allowed to trade freely, but others were stopped unless they could show a passport issued by the Council.[10]

The stern legislation of 1606 reflects the vindictive reaction of the state to Catholic machination. Every attempt was made to exclude Catholics from public life and professional careers. They were forbidden to come to Court or within ten miles of London without a warrant from the King or Council. A new Oath of Allegiance was to be taken acknowledging "Our Sovereign Lord King James... lawful rightful King of this Realm. The Pope neither himselfe nor by any authority of the Church or See of Rome... hath any power or authoritie to depose the King... or to discharge any of his Subjects of their allegiance and obedience to his Majesty." Subjects were compelled to swear absolute obedience to James, avowing that neither the Pope nor any other had power to absolve him from this oath. Pope Paul V did not countenance James Stuart's Oath of Allegiance but counterbalanced it with a Breve of October 1606 which advised English Catholics of the peril to their souls if they took this oath to the king.[11]

The Acts of 1606 were considered "good and prudent laws" against the priests, "corrupters of the people in religion and loyalty." Animosity against the "corrupters of the people" was further inflamed by the publication of pamphlets reflecting the Roman cabal. Stationers, aware of national indignation and certainly economic gain, printed and stocked a flurry of patriotic protestations and anti-Catholic fulminations. Loyal citizens might select a variety of works castigating the popish plotters: *An exact discouerie of Romish doctrine in the case of conspiracie and rebellion by pregnant observacons collected ... out of the expresse dogmaticall principles of popish priestes and doctors* was printed in December 1605 by Burbie and Weaver at the express command of "my Lords Grace of Canterbury." Tracts, appearing between January and May 1606, included *The vnmaskinge of murder of an extemporall Declaracon of the Cacolyke [sic] complotted treason lately discovered; The Ploughman's tale shewing by the doctrine and lyves of the Popishe clergie that the Pope is antichrist ... written by Sir Geffrey Chaucer amongst his Canterbury Tales; Great Brytayns great Delyuerance from the great danger of popish powder proponed by the hand of God; A Ballet called Garnettes arraignement or the popes looking glasse* and others.[12]

Whether or not he had purchased such works at the shops of Nathaniel Butter, William Stafford or Geffrey Charlton, the traveler to London was advised not to linger in the Capital but to return home "for the peace of the country which is disturbed either by papists or sectaries. These usurpations and anarchies are dangerous and the magistrates must have care that the people be not idle nor stir up discontent by prophecies or pamphlets. They must therefore look to all seminaries and their followers and to their conventicles and to all vagrants strong to labour, yet idle and gentlemanlike in approach, yet without means, libellers and devisers of plots." New persecution, following upon the assassination of Henry IV of France in 1610, was levelled against the Catholics and the Jesuit leaders. Had not Ravaillac, the assassin of the popular French King, been a member of the Company of Jesus?[13]

The nation was now suspicious of all strangers and vagrants who, without work or profession, were regarded as potential assassins, priests and Spanish agents intent upon intrigue. Wotton had informed Salisbury that an English merchant of Lucca, Stephen Stock, "a factor for divers London merchants in Italy," enjoyed great familiarity with the Pope and "hath undertaken to furnish [him] with powder and other munition."[14]

By 1611 the condition of the English Catholic had vastly deteriorated and his woeful status was bemoaned by Father Edward Coffin, who declared that the King planned the extermination of all Catholics. "The prisons are everywhere crammed. The Catholics hide themselves in caves and in holes of the earth and others fly before the faces of persecutors. An infinite number of pursuivants riotously passes through every county of England and it is incredible to tell how they harass and afflict the innocent man. The times of Elizabeth although most cruel were the mildest and happiest in comparison with those of James." A Letter of the English Mission of 1614 describes the harshness of anti-Catholic legislation. "The laws, as we have observed are more severe and cunningly planned to bring about the ruin of the Catholics, and lest they should prove a dead letter, informers are encouraged by the prospect of ample rewards." The writer refers to the pursuivants as "men of damaged reputation, thieves [who] ply their trade not only in London but have the country parcelled among them, with full license to act as if in enemy's territory." The Puritans protested any indulgence granted the Catholic condemned to London prisons which, they declared, had become recusant conventicles. The keepers of the metropolitan jails were summoned and "very severely castigated and one of them . . . also imprisoned for allowing two imprisoned priests to talk together."[15]

A policy of toleration was not to be suffered for several years. Priests who had been banished twice and "refused to heed warnings" were hanged at Tyburn, many of them "dying confidently." To avert uprisings and personal danger, the government forbade the carrying of "pocket dagges" while the shire officers were instructed to disarm priests. "What secret cause may be I know not," wrote Chamberlain, "but the world grows suspicious."[16]

James remained ever suspicious of the Catholics within his domain. At his Opening Speech to Parliament in 1612 he reiterated his intention to uproot Catholicism: "I know not how it is that despite so many laws enacted against them, the Papists increase in number. Let the laws already in force be so clearly construed in all their terms and clauses by Parliament as to leave no loophole of escape." The will of the monarch and his advisers failed to exorcise orthodoxy from the Kingdom. The Papal Nuncio stated at Brussels in 1613 that, according to information supplied him by English Catholics, six hundred priests had entered England. Swarms of Jesuits and religious, sufficiently wily to elude the harbor patrol, "arrived and crept in." A more stringent port search was introduced in 1615. Coke assailed the forging of passports, reporting that six had been fabricated by a minister and a justice of peace. Individuals were restrained from carrying letters abroad, a practise considered dangerous. Matthew de Questor, the Foreign Port Master, was to search for them and to apprehend any delinquent, who was to be brought before the Privy Council. In an overcharged bureaucratic system all Crown servants were suspect. Betrayal was common, each employee but a cog in the service, eager to curry the favor of a superior. In 1613 a certain Bostock, an Under-Customer of Rochester, with one Waller, was fined in the Court of Star Chamber five thousand marks. Both were to stand in the pillory, lose their ears and be whipped. Their crime had been the dissemination of false news.[17]

Disturbed by the unresolved state of religious differences within the Kingdom, James issued in 1614 his religious treatise, *God and the King: or a Dialogue Shewing that King James Being under God doth rightfully Claime whatsoever is Refused by the Oath of Allegiance*. James proposed to acquaint young and old with the divinely given authority of their liege lord. The archbishops were instructed to demand "the teaching of this booke." All persons were ordered to obey "upon the paine of ecclesiastical censure and princely indignation."[18]

Antonio Foscarini stated in 1618 that twelve parties existed in England: "One of the Catholics dependent on the Jesuits and Spain, two of Catholics who swear fealty to the King and obey his Majesty in temporal power, three of the indifferent, four of the religion of his Majesty and two Puritan parties." At the same time the Venetian Ambassador to England, Pietro Contarini, gauged the status of the English Catholic who, in his opinion, suffered continual persecution. "Many in order to escape extermination remain secretly good Catholics but accomodate themselves to necessity. The number of these is much larger than those who openly declare themselves. Those who are recusants are in the worst conditon of all."[19]

Despite this woeful picture of English Catholicism, official policy toward the minority had begun to relax. As early as 1617, rumors of a more liberal attitude toward the Catholics had reached Venice. Writing to Carleton, Sir Henry Wotton, English Ambassador to the Republic, declared that all the "gazettani here of this week in their idle leaves scattered a report that the King hath much enlarged the liberties of the Papists in England." Contarini noted in his *Relation* that not a year passed but the Spaniards had contributed large sums of money "to win over and bind men, not only among the leading people but even in the masses. They are very popular among the Catholics and their corruption has gone so far that no remedy however great could touch it unless too late."[20]

James I was governed to some extent by Spanish influence as well as by personal ambition. He decided that his eldest son, Prince Charles, should win the hand of the Spanish Infanta, and at Spain's request, James remained neutral in the Continental conflict which involved the safety of his daughter Elizabeth and her husband, Frederick of the Palatinate. James now delighted in the person of the Spanish Ambassador to England, Diego Sarmiento de Acuña, Count Gondomar, whose influence led to a kindlier policy toward the monarch's Catholic subjects. At his request, Jesuits were released from jail, while, according to the Venetian Ambassador, priests who paid their jailers "a trifling fee" were able to go in and out of prison at their own pleasure, "officiating privily in one house and then in another by which means they maintain themselves and make considerable profit." Priests attended Gondomar's residence, where they "were visited by many men of the Court of the Spanish faction, including some Catholics of whom there are many in the Kingdom and in London."[21]

If Gondomar failed to secure the liberty of all the Jesuits and priests confined within the Clink and Bridewell, he surely rejoiced at the improved conditions in the English jails, where "new altars were permitted to be erected at which in one morning thirty and more masses were celebrated with special prayers to God for the success of the Emperor and Spinola's army" and for the defeat of James' son-in-law, Frederick, Prince Palatine and his followers. The House of Commons apparently regarded with little favor the more relaxed policy of the King toward his Catholic subjects. It deplored the increase of popery which, according to the Remonstrance of December 1621, was to be attributed to the "vigilance of the Pope and his adherents." It referred to the distress of Protestantism abroad, the increase of recusants, "the printing of popish books and swarming Jesuits."[22]

Nonetheless, by August 1622, "all priests and Papists imprisoned were set at liberty and were no longer to be troubled for saying Mass or refusing the oath of allegiance or supremacy and the like." A few months later Chamberlain reported that "our papists begin to hold up their heads again for whereas writs were gone out to inquire o'er their lands and charges for not paying according to their stature, letters are gone downe to suppress that course."[23]

The English courtship of Spain ended in 1625. The Spanish marriage had not been consummated. Charles and Buckingham returned joyfully to the arms of James. The hopes of Count Gondomar had been in vain. He had never understood the English and their deep-seated hatred of Spain. He had overrated the number of belligerent English Catholics and underestimated the aversion of Protestant England toward a Catholic marriage. Parliament, freed of the Spanish nightmare, now entered the Continental war, eager to rescue Puritan souls and to spare an English princess further degradation. The domestic and foreign policies of a rapidly aging monarch had failed and in the popular jests of Tom-Tell-Troth the former "wisest fool in Christendom" had become the synonym for a knave and a dolt.

The English renunciation of a pro-Spanish policy reanimated the old laws and instigated new legislation against the Catholics. The hunt for the orthodox was resumed with new fervor and vigor. John Tendring, Provost Marshal of Middlesex, was empowered "to make a diligent search for all Jesuits, seminaries and popish priests and all suspected persons in that kind as also all such as harbor them." He was assigned a constable and "such other assistants as he thought meete." All copes, vestments and "massing stuffe and other relicts" were to be seized and brought to one of his Majesty's secretaries of state. The altars in the London jails were removed and the thirty masses – now celebrated in fear and secrecy – were radically reduced.[24]

When Charles I succeeded his father in March 1625, England was embroiled in a foreign conflict. At home a domestic clash had ensued between the Crown and Parliament. Pym's polemics thundered in the Commons. Puritan leadership, in fast ascendancy, was itself to become a demagoguery which tolerated no other faith.

VII

CAREFUL AND DILIGENT SEARCH

Censorship

As the personification of a divinely appointed kingship, James could scarcely tolerate any criticism of his royal authority. Hence his government outlawed more books of a political rather than a religious nature. To safeguard itself against seditious and libellous texts, printed secretly in England or imported from abroad, the Crown relied on procedures similar to those practised under Elizabeth: port control and espionage, search and arrest, burning and censorship of unsavory writings.

A royal Proclamation of 1603 demanded that Parliament exercise a tighter control of "Bookes of all sortes before they come to the presse." James exhorted the House "to looke more narrowlie into the nature of all those thinges that shalbe putt to the presse either concerning our authoritie royall or concerning our government." Accordingly, a motion was made in the House of Commons on June 11, 1604 "for the reformation of abuses bringing into the land, Printing, Buying and Selling of Seditious Popish Bookes."[1]

Although the Crown sought to control the press, its efforts were balked to some extent by the venality pervading official positions. At the advent of James' reign the offices of customs collector and of port searcher had become lucrative posts. There is evidence, as in the administration of Elizabeth, that such authorities continued to resort to bribery and extortion. A bill was sent to the House of Lords in 1606 to inquire into the "Extortions, Exactions of Customers, Comptrollers, Collectors, Searchers . . . or other officers . . . employed in or about the Customs of our Sovereign Lord the King." A second attempt was made in 1614 "to auoid the Extortions and Exactions of Custom[er]s and Comptrollers of the Port Towns."[2]

Mention is made at a later period of the fees paid to collectors and searchers at the Port of London; payment to the head searcher and his staff of five under-searchers on "the cargo and bottom"; fees to the under-searchers at Gravesend on ships and passengers. The iniquities practised by port officials is referred to by Chamberlain in a note to Dudley Carleton in which he alludes to the recent visit of a Milanese gentleman, Tomasso Cerronio: "He had 100 pounds in gold which the searchers at [the] seas took from him, a thing that should not have been done." The dishonesty of the pursuivants attached to the Court of High Commission was common knowledge. "They practise most dishonourable courses, for which they will buy and sell Jesuits for money. The bribes they take overpass[ing] books, church stuffe and letters are infinite."The informer Udall advised Salisbury in 1609 that he could name "a dosen Jesuits bought and sold."[3]

The officials at Gravesend and London were often tipped off by government spies. There is reference to the English agent, Turner who, prior to 1606, had been active in observing the movements of the English Jesuits at the Court of the Archduke Ferdinand. Later he spent some time at Calais to familiarize himself with Catholic students at this strategic port.[4]

The information of "intelligencers" did not prevent the infiltration of subversive texts into England. The pursuivants' search ranged from Lancashire and Staffordshire to Ely House where there were found "sundry conveyances by doors out of one chamber into another, with passages from the leads for escaping, all very convenient for persons of evil affection to the state." Here the searchers found "diuers great chests and coffers full of printed books of that seminary faction." A more intensive hunt revealed "a press itself with all things appertaining to printing, with letters set upon the press and paper for proceeding in the business." Father Gerard describes the house where he sought refuge after the Gunpowder Plot as "very suitable and convenient [having] private entrances on both sides . . . I had contrived in it some excellent hiding places."[5]

The role of the pursuivant and informer is reflected in the ingratiating, obsequious correspondence of the unctious William Udall, ever blaring his unselfish devotion to the Crown, ever ready to betray a colleague, ever eager to sell a victim at a price. The braggadocio of Udall, alas, has some element of truth: he did indeed assist in the detection of priests and presses, the apprehension of "bringers and receavers of bokes . . . from beyonde the seas;" the pursuit of the infirm, the devout. The odious nature of his profession bred depravity. In time Udall became the victim of his own brand of corruption and was betrayed by a fellow informer. His patriotic vaunting and protests became shrill echoes within the dank walls of the Gatehouse.

Udall's letters refer to the interception of at least "ten thousand bokes" through his efforts; his sequestration of seditious literature valued at more than four hundred pounds; the wait for subversive texts "readye to come from abroade" – some "now in hand as well in Englande as beyonde the seas;" the detection of eight hundred copies of "a most vile boke," the raid of a cache of "viii hundred pounds of Catholic bokes." Despite his protestation of loyalty to the government, he complained that never had he "receaued the benefite of one peny."

Udall is the prototype of the opportunist, the betrayer, the hoodlum, eager to harass and to destroy for his personal advancement. An altruistic motive to rid England of the heretic and achieve conformity scarcely preoccupied this vaunting, boastful mediocrity. A revolting individual, he was considered loathsome even to the Crown authorities who engaged him as one of their ruffian hirelings to spot the Catholic, the subversive, the nonconformist. The statesman, Sir Geoffrey Fenton, describes Udall as "a person hatefull to the better sort and not trusted with the worser."[6]

In the pursuit of his profession and in the desire to ingratiate himself with his superiors Udall was ever ready to inform upon his own colleagues. He advised Sir Julius Caesar in November 1608 of the foul play of two agents, Francis Atee and one Dowse, who had arrested priests and upon their payment of a bribe had permitted them to escape. A later memorandum refers to "the most dishonorable cosoning, irreligious and barbarous courses commonly practised by two messengers Humfrey Crosse and William Atkinson "agents of the Court of High Commission, sellers of priests." An obsequious note of March 1610 alludes to the dishonor done to the state by persons and messengers "which are employed by warrant from the [Court of] High Commission, who sell priests and Jesuitts for great summes of money which they do take in recusants houses."[7]

Like the potential victims of Udall and his gang, who for the most part were aware of their peril and possible arrest, the searchers themselves occasionally encountered some personal risk. Seldom earning the esteem of the State, they always evoked the contempt and detestation of the hunted. The searcher Henry Sanderson revealed the hazards of his occupation in a letter of April 1605 in which he advised Cecil that "diuers followers and special friends of our principal recusants publish openly that it will not be long before an end be made of me for apprehending their priests and some of themselves, and for burning certain mass books and other traiterous books; I have been commanded by his Majesty to make a great fire to burn them publicly in Newcastle."[8]

The city on the Tyne was to remain a Catholic stronghold. In 1616 the Archbishop of Canterbury referred to a recent report stating that "Jesuitts, semynaries, secular priestes and other popish recusantes, with their agentes and factors, are receiued and harbored by some ill-affected persons in the country of Northumberland and neere unto the towne of Newcastle upon Tyne, to the great perill and daunger of the Kinge and of the State and for the further breachinge forth of their damnable designes doe, in manifest contempt of his Majesty's lawes, passe beyonde the seas and repasse without lawful warrant, as alsoe bringe in diuers Popish seditious and prohibited books." The distinguished prelate offered "a diligent and privy search in all houses and places within the county of Northumberland and partes neere Newcastle." All "dangerous persons and their ayders and harbourers together with their letters, bookes and massing stuffe within the sayd county or near the town of Newcastle" were to be apprehended.[9]

The pursuivants frequently allude, during the first decade of the reign of James I, to Popish books; some seized and detained at the Customs House; a load of orthodox texts and relics shipped to Ireland, the consignment of a Dublin agent, Michael Hamlyn. Reference is made to the many seditious books "nowadays landed in secret places;" copies brought in from France "for which a great search is made;" the discovery of "two hundreth pounds worth of Popish books taken about Southampton House and burned in Paules Crosse." The agent William Waad was informed by alert fishermen that packets of books had reached England from St. Omer which, according to him, were destined for "Lord Monteagles, the disorders in whose house are an offence to the country."[10]

The officer of the Dover Customs, John Prettyman, prepared in November 1616 a memorandum of books brought illegally into the country. He had wrested a confession from a sailor, George Christopher, that he had brought the merchandise into England at the request of a certain Louis Dandine of the Calais post. Forbidden books were smuggled from the port towns to London, where they were distributed by Catholic agents. Udall stated that the books which were surreptitiously imported from the Continent were never circulated before Michaelmas, "the priestes of greatest note about London cannot gett a boke till towards the tearme." A wealthy vintner of London was reported to have concealed a great mass of Popish books under a church porch, while the rumor was circulated that "diuers stationers" as soon as they heard of forbidden books "get copies and hire some young fellowes to transcribe them when they are eagerly bought up."[11]

The Stationers' Company was requested not only to control the circulation of these "forbidden books," but also to seize and deliver them to the appointed authorities. The Company had at no time relaxed its vigilance. The right "to make search whenever it shall please them in any place, shop, house ... or building of any printer, binder or bookseller within our Kingdome of England" was observed by the Master and Wardens. They strove to coöperate with the ecclesiastical body represented by the hierarchy from the episcopal chaplains, burdened with the regulation of the press, to the Archbishop of Canterbury. The Courts of Star Chamber and High Commission were the highest tribunals to hear cases involving seditious books and heretical opinions.

None the less, the licensing system had become less effective under James I. In 1610 the King fulminated against "the itching in the tongues and pennes of most men, as nothing is searched to the bottome ... from the very highest mysteries in the Godhead and the most inscrutable Councels in the Trinitie, to the very lowest in the pit in Hell." Vexed by the indifference to printing regulations, James on September 25, 1623 re-issued the Printing Injunctions formulated by Elizabeth in 1586."The Masters and Keepers ... of the Mysterie of the Art of Stationers [were] to make carefull and diligent search for such scandalous and offensive Bookes or Pamphlets as are, or shall be imported into this Realme, or here imprinted contrary to our Royal Commandement and seize the same." No person was "to print any Book or Pamphlet, touching or concerning matters of Religion, Church Government or State which was not to be read, corrected and allowed by the Archbishop of Canterbury, the Bishop of York, the Vice-Chancellors of the Universities of Oxford and Cambridge. And no Booke Binder, or Bookeseller or other person whatsoeuer shall from henceforth presume to sell or offer to sell any such Booke or Pamphlet not so perused and allowed, vpon pain of our High Displeasure." A new edict was published the following year declaring its contravention would be met with punishment and imprisonment decreed by the Courts of Star Chamber and High Commission.[12]

In its attempt to preserve religious and political conformity, the state maintained a fairly rigid censorship, a power exercised by the inquisitorial arm of the Roman Catholic Church. The censorship of books pursued during Elizabeth's reign was to burgeon under James whose divinely appointed authority and dictates became the targets of outspoken attacks.

The royal person had been protected against libel and slander by the decree of "Scandalum Magnatum" of 1275 which declared that any one who published false news or scandal tending to prove discord between the king and his people or the magnates was to be imprisoned. By the advent of Elizabeth's reign the Council and the Court of Star Chamber concerned themselves with the slander of peers. The latter body ruled that "libelling and calumniation [were] an offence against the law of God."[13]

The publication in 1579 of *The discouerie of a gaping gulf whereinto England is like to be swallowed* by the high-minded Puritan John Stubbs was considered by the state as a work critical of the Queen's person. For several years the protracted marriage between Elizabeth and the Duke of Anjou, brother of the French King, had been the subject of speculation. Stubbs in his *Gaping gulf* had viewed Anjou's union with the Queen an impenetrable "gulf" for the country. The author's objections were based upon the pervasive fear of Catholic influence and his loathing of the French. He alluded to the physical and moral defects of the Valois family: "These needie spent Frenchmen of Monsieurs traine, being of the contrarie religion, the scomme of the King's court, which is the scomme of Europe, like horseleeches, by sucking upon vs, to fill their beggarly purses to the satisfying of theyr bottomlesse expence." His affection for the Queen is in contrast to his intolerance toward the French. He begs her Majesty "to view and surview" the problem and "to fetch her heart up to her eyes and carry her eyes down to her heart."[14]

The royal heart failed to appreciate her subject's loyalty. Elizabeth had been extremely piqued by Stubbs' implied criticism that she was perhaps too old to bear an heir to the throne. The premises of Stubbs' printer, Hugh Singleton, were searched in September 1579 where copies of the offending work were discovered. The printer, the publisher, William Page, an agent, Francis Chamberlain, and the author were arrested and brought to trial at the Queen's Bench. Singleton was charged with "maliciously and seditiously printing and causing to be imprinted a thousand of the aforesaid false and feigned books." The agent Francis Chamberlain was accused of knowing Stubbs' book to be "false, opprobrious and seditious." He had, none the less, ordered Singleton to print for Page an edition of one thousand copies. The latter's guilt was based upon his circulation of this venomous book, he having sent fifty copies to Sir Richard Greenfield of Cornwall with the request that he disperse them among his friends. Singleton and Chamberlain were exonerated by the Court. The author and publisher fared less well, having been condemned to lose their right hands. Stubbs after the execution of this barbarous act politely doffed his hat in salute to the Queen with his left hand fortunately intact. On September 27, 1589 a royal proclamation had referred to "a lewde and seditious book ... rashly compiled, and secretly printed ... seditiously dispersed diswading her Maiestie from marriage with the Duke of Anjou." The falsity of charges against Monsieur and his ambassadors is stated at length. It had therefore been necessary for her Majesty to charge "that both the foresaide booke or libel, wheresoever they, or any the like may be founde, shall be destroyed in open sight of some publike officer: and the fauourers ... thereof, to be attached to answere concerning to their demerites."[15]

An Edict of 1600 forbade the "engravings in brass" of "the pictures of noblemen" which were sold and "set forth often times with verses and other circumstances not fit to be used." The Queen, however, permitted the sale of engravings of her royal person "yf the same be wel done." The prohibition levelled against the growing sale of the engravings of noblemen, distributed largely by the firm of Sudbury and Humble, reflects the Queen's desire to enhance her public image only, since she readily consented to the circulation of engravings of herself executed by William Rogers, Renold Elstrack and other popular artists. The royal limitation of engravings elicits the conjecture that Elizabeth, stung by the recent behavior of her favorite Essex in Ireland, had become wary of the hold of the courtiers upon the popular imagination which could be heightened through the purchase of noble likenesses sold at a nominal rate.[16]

A year earlier the printer John Wolfe had been questioned regarding his publication of John Hayward's *The first parte of the life and raigne of King Henrie IIII* which had been dedicated to the Earl of Essex whom Wolfe considered "a martial man." The publisher stated that three weeks after the book's appearance not only the Wardens of the Stationers' Company but the Queen herself had vehemently objected to the dedication to Essex. Elizabeth had been greatly "incensed against Mr. Hayward's book, thinking it a seditious prelude to put into the people's head boldness and faction." She demanded that Bacon find in it "any place that might be drawn within case of treason."[17]

Wolfe declared upon interrogation that he had already sold either five hundred or six hundred copies of his edition before he had received official word to suppress the dedication to Essex. The printer stated that no book had ever sold better, the demand for it having greatly increased during the Easter season. Despite the suppression of the first issue – copies of which were burned at the Episcopal Palace – the second edition, which lacked the offensive epistle dedicatory, proved to be in ever popular demand since, according to Wolfe: "many had been at his shop for it."[18] He forlornly added that he had received "no recompence for printing the other save a few copies of the work." He resented the humiliation he had endured having been sentenced to a two-week prison term and having suffered the loss of the copies of the first issue. The licenser John Harsnett defended his innocent role, stating that Hayward had begged him for official approbation of the History "in the name of a cantel of our English chronicles, phrased and flourished over, only to show the author's pretty wit." He avowed that the dedication had been inserted only after he had licensed the book, adding that his approbation was but an "inducement for his master my Lord of London, to allow it but not a sufficient warrant to publish."[19]

Books by and about Essex, the late favorite of the Queen and a traitor to the state, were scarcely tolerated by the Crown he had betrayed. Essex had composed his *Apologie* in 1598. His Lordship, according to the evidence of his servant, Mr. Cuffe, had not desired its publication. An unauthorized version appeared which Essex affirmed had been based upon a manuscript draft "stolen from his chamber by the corruption of some of his servants . . . who might take and copy out his loose papers which lay sheet by sheet under the bed's head till he had leisure to finish the whole." He declared he had never sent any manuscript "copy" to a stationer's shop. Despite the Earl's testimony, the printer John Dawson had received "copy" of the *Apologie*. Dawson and his two assistants were taken by the Wardens of the Stationers' Company and put into close custody. Dawson admitted that he had already circulated two hundred and ninety-two copies of the work of which two hundred and ten had been confiscated.[20]

Essex's *Apologie* is not to be confused with the official version of the Earl's conspiracy, *A declaration of the practises and treasons committed by Robert late Earle of Essex*, written at the Queen's command by Francis Bacon. It appeared with the imprint of Robert Barker official printer in 1601. The duplicity of her late favorite had never been forgiven or forgotten by Elizabeth. The manuscript had been subjected to the scrutiny of the Lords of the Council, "weighed, censured, altered and made almost a new writing." It was perused by the Queen herself and after it had been set in type, Elizabeth, noting that "Mr. Bacon could not forget his ancient respect to the Earl of Essex, but termed him 'My Lord of Essex, my Lord of Essex' on almost every page of the book which she thought not fit, . . . would have it 'Essex' or the 'late Earl of Essex.'" The Queen insisted that Barker suppress all copies of the first issue and print it "de novo." Bacon's work was to demonstrate to the Queen's loyal and true subjects "the ambitious nature of the late Earl to make himself the first person in the kingdome."[21]

William Woodhouse, a prognosticator, had attributed the unfortunate Essex rebellion to the appearance of an eclipse. His *Almanac*, demonstrating the celestial causes of this calamity, was published in 1601 by James Roberts. The work considered to be "but a frey" was none the less condemned, since it predicted "the unfortunate estate of sundry great ones, great destruction of many men over . . . death to ecclesiastical persons, lawyers, rulers and the lusty."[22]

The Stationers' Company proscribed nine titles in addition to all of "Nasshes bookes and Doctor Harveys books wheresoever they may be found." On June 1, 1599 seven of the titles listed were "burnte in the hall:" John Marston's *Metamorphosis of Pigmalion's image* and *The scourge of villanie;* Edward Guilpin's *Skialetheia or a shadow of truth;* John Davies' *Epigrammes and elegies; Micro-*

cynicon. Sixe snarlinge satyres; The booke againste woemen and Antoine de La Sale's *Fyftene joyes of maryage*.²³

William Ferebrand issued in the Autumn of 1600 *The letting of humours blood on the head-vaine* of the miscellaneous writer Samuel Rowlands. The work was frowned upon by the government since it contained political allusions. It was ordered to be burned twice, once publicly and again "to be burned in the Hall kitchen of the Stationers Company along with other Popish Books and things that were lately taken upon its condemnation by the Stationers Company." *A true narration of the Strange and Grevous Vexation by the Devil of Seven Persons in Lancashire* by the exorcist, John Darrell, was consigned to the flames at the same time. Darrell's "pestiferous opinions," according to a contemporary report, had been "lately broached abroad in pamphlets and printed apologies pass[ed] underhand in the public view of rag and tag."²⁴

Elizabeth's program of censorship was to be continued by James I. The reaction of the Crown to several publications critical of official policy and ideology reflects the intolerance and rigidity of the government. The appearance of Dr. John Cowell's *The interpreter: or book containing the signification of words*, issued by John Legate in 1607, preoccupied the minds of His Majesty and His Parliament. A legal dictionary by a distinguished jurist, Regius Professor of Civil Law and Vice-Chancellor of Cambridge, *The interpreter*, had in its definition of certain legal expressions, implied some criticism of royal authority. The book was brought to the attention of the House of Commons and described by Sir Edwin Sandys – whose *Relation of the World* had been condemned shortly before – as "very inadvised and indiscreet, tending to the disreputation of the House and power of the common laws." After the Doctor's texts had been analyzed during several sessions of Parliament, a committee was formed on February 27, 1609 to submit a report on the book to the House of Lords. A decision rendered a month later declared that "when men goe out of their element and meddle with things aboue their capacities, themselues shall not onlie goe astray and tumble in darknes but will misleade alsoe divers others with themselues into many mistakes and errors." The Committee decided that Dr. Cowell "onlie a civilian had meddled in matters aboue his reach." The House therefore not only prohibited the buying, "uttering" or reading of the work, but also demanded that all copies be surrendered to the Lord Mayor of London.²⁵

The King himself read *The interpreter* which he believed had been "too bold with the Common law of the land holding it a great presumption in any subject to speak or write against those under which he must live." Was not Dr. Cowell's misbegotten text an instrument to stimulate "the insatiable curiosity in many men's minds to pry into the deepest mysteries of kings that are gods upon earth?" Had His Majesty been familiar with its contents before the opening of Parliament, he would have taken steps for its earlier suppression. James issued a decree on March 25, 1610 calling in all copies of *The interpreter*, informing his subjects of his "great dislike of this book [and] all others of like nature."²⁶

If James had been rankled by Dr. Cowell's text, he was horrified at the circulation of an anonymous libel levelled against himself and his royal forbears. The publication of that scurrilous pamphlet reflects the struggle between the supporters of the orthodox church and their foe, the English government. *Prvrit-Anvs . . . vel nec omne, nec ex omni, svr Apologia Pvritanis & Novatoribvs Vniversis* was purportedly printed by François Bellet at St. Omer in 1609. The imprint is fictitious as well as the name of the author, Horatio Dolabella. According to the controversialist, Lewis Owen, the work "was stuffed with such horrible blasphemies" that the authors had refrained from "subscribing their own names thereunto but borrowed a fained name of one Horatio Dolabella, a Neapolitan."[27]

Prvrit-Anvs, a slashing polemic against the Puritans, vehemently indicts their monarch, James Stuart. The King is castigated as the ruler who has confounded all Europe and incited the Turk against the Pope. It is further described as a nefarious pamphlet touching "upon the most secret affections of the English sovereigns" and especially Queen Elizabeth and Henry VIII who is depicted as anti-Christ for he "usurped the authority of the Pope." Nine of its paragraphs denounce the person and policy of James I.

Opinions differ regarding the origin of *Prvrit-Anvs*. The foreword states that the printer had received his "copy" of the manuscript from an Oxford student, adding that several noblemen had distributed copies, all of which had brought pleasure and applause. After consulting men of sound judgment, the printer had determined to issue it for the gratification of readers.[28]

Publication of the libel has been assigned by some to England – by others to the Continent. Lewis Owen ascribes its authorship to several hands, while one source asserts that the nucleus of the book had been written in France, finished in England by the Jesuit brothers, Thomas and William Wright, and the completed text printed in Staffordshire at the premises of Sir Francis Lacon by the Catholic underground printer William Wrench in collaboration with Lawrence Warren. Udall states that "the letter which printed *[Prvrit-Anvs]* is known to be Englishe." He boasted to Sir Julius Caesar that he was "in playne and direct course for the discoverye and apprehension of the printers."[29]

On the other hand, Lewis Owen also averred that the work had been written by John Wilson, director of the St. Omer English College Press "in collaboration with other Jesuits and there printed." Since by the summer of 1609 "many copies" of *Prvrit-Anvs* had slipped into England "in spite of the danger of those who sell it," there seems to be some validity to Owen's hypothesis. Two agents, active in the dissemination of Continental Catholic texts, admitted to the importation of copies of the work. Henry Parish acknowledged that he had brought over six bales, including other Catholic writings destined for Lord Monteagle's residence, while John and Joan Dabscot confessed that they had arranged for the shipment of four bales of *Prvrit-Anvs* from Calais.[30] James, very much "put out and little pleased" with a work assailing not only his person but also his illustrious ancestors, exhorted Cecil to employ greater diligence in detecting its origin and its distributors. The Archbishop of Canterbury ordered that all copies of this notorious libel be burned. It is obvious that scarcely the entire edition of *Prvrit-Anvs* was consumed by flames at "Paules Crosse after Sermon time," since a searcher found in the premises of the stationer, Ferdinand Ely of Little Britaine, copies of the "vile boke of Queres."[31]

The "vile boke" known as *Prvrit-Anvs* or *Queres* may have been familiar to a West county gentleman and recusant, John Cotton, whose Catholic proclivities had been observed by the authorities as early as 1607. Cotton's son George complained that the searchers had broken into his father's study, where they had rifled chests and taken away books "for bounty that are to be bought in every bookbinder's shop as Mercurius Gallo-Belgicus, Osorius and such like." It seems that Master John Cotton of "Warblington known as Subberton in the county of Southampton" had prior to 1613 written a "very scandalous and railing book" against the government. This work appears to have remained in manuscript. Its contents, however, were apparently known to the authorities, since in June 1613, the author was accused of treason and *A Proclamation for the search and apprehension of John Cotton Esquire* was issued. This insurgent resident of Warblington is described as a man of approximately 48 years "of a reasonable tall stature, slender of bodie, the haire of his head and beard flaxen, but now inclining to white, well complexioned, with somewhat a long and leane visage."[32]

Cotton strove to elude his pursuers. He was known to have fled from his home presumably "lurk[ing] or wand[ering] in unknown places." The Proclamation averred that English justice would never condemn "any man unheard," but since the "presumptions and proofes appear to bee so forcible against [him] if . . . he shall not forthwith come in and render himselfe," the state would find him guilty. A reward of one hundred pounds was offered for his apprehension. Cotton's planned escape was via the Thames, crossing to Lambeth Fields and farther south. Obviously apprehensive, he inquired the latest news of a bargeman who mentioned the recent Proclamation against him. Once landed, Cotton "muffled himself in his cloak thinking merely to pass unknown to any of his acquaintances that he might haply meet." He almost immediately encountered one who advised the "muffled" gentleman to surrender himself to Lord Southampton. Cotton apparently followed his friend's suggestion.[33]

Once in custody, the accused denied his authorship of the "railing tract." Thereupon his study was again searched and "diuers papers found, containing many several pieces of the said book (and which renders the man more odious), certain relics of the late saints of the gunpowder treason, as one of Digby's fingers, Percy's toe . . . with the addition of a piece of one of Peter Lambert's ribs, to make up the full mess of them." It was believed that the evidence against Cotton was so incriminating that it would cost him his life or "surely a sufficiency of misery and affliction." His misery was sufficient, since he was condemned to the Tower, where he languished for six years until 1619 "upon suspicion of being the author of a scandalous and traiterous book." He was released in May of that year on the bonds of his son and Sir Anthony Hungerford, upon the condition that he remain confined to his home and "not goe any way from thence beyond his garden and orchard."[34]

John Cotton of Warblington was not a national hero. Unlike the late Sir Walter Raleigh he had discovered no Eldorado, no great western realm. The celebrated explorer and courtier had begun his *History of the World* during his confinement in the Tower between 1607 and 1614. The first edition was printed by William Stansby for Walter Burre in 1614. The book which the author hoped would please the King scarcely gratified Raleigh's disenchanted monarch. James had disavowed Raleigh who, he believed, had been involved in a plot upon his life. A directive to the Stationers' Company of December 1614 concerned itself with the suppression of *The History of the World*. The Company's agents were "to repair vnto the printer namely William Stansby as alsoe vnto other stationers and booksellers which haue any of them in their custodie." Copies were to be immediately surrendered either to the Archbishop of Canterbury or the Bishop of London. Chamberlain observed in January 1615 that "Sir Walter Raleigh's book [has been] called in by the king's commandement for diverse exceptions, but specially for being too saucy in censuring princes." James in a note of September 1616 advised the Company of Stationers that all copies of the book still available were to be immediately yielded to his agent James Ramsey, informing the Master and Wardens that they were "to be disposed of. And this shal be yo[u]r sufficient warrant and discharge in that behalf. And hereof see you faile not as you will answer the contrary at yo[u]r vttermost perills."[35]

The "perills" confronting an author critical of the government were also experienced by the poet George Wither who in 1621 issued his poem *Withers Motto*. The "Wither Affair" reflects to some extent the uneasy position of some members of the administration and the economic corruption within the Company of Stationers. The poem is a series of reflections on current society sprinkled with barbed allusions to Stuart officials who found themselves extremely sensitive to the poet's remarks. Wither was arrested and confined to Marshalsea Prison. Upon his apprehension the Biblical scholar, Joseph Mead, wrote to Sir Martin Stuteville that "Withers for his Motto [is] in the Marshalsea, the King threatening to pare his whelp's claws."[36]

Five editions of *Withers Motto* appeared in 1621; the first issued by John Marriott with John Grismond; the second anonymously; the third by Marriott and Nicholas Okes; the fourth by Marriott and Grismond and the fifth by Grismond alone. Wither avers that thirty thousand copies of the *Motto* had been printed – no idle boast– since Okes in his deposition stated that he alone had sold six thousand copies. The first edition of the poem had been printed without the approval of the licenser of the press and hence this and subsequent editions aroused the Company's ire. Wither, upon examination, admitted that the licenser John Taverner, Secretary of the Bishop of London, had refused to permit the poem's publication unless it were revised according to his suggestions. Despite his refusal to coöperate, Wither stated he had received offers of others "to print it [and] sold them the copy for five pieces." The author insisted that there was nothing in his poem contrary to the proclamation restraining opinions relating to state matter, and added that the book had not been called into question until the first impression had been exhausted and the second was in preparation for publication.[37]

Upon examination the somewhat fractious publisher Nicholas Okes pleaded complete innocence, asserting he had never known that the book had not been licensed. He admitted that he had purchased the title-page from Marriott with the latter's imprint and had used it without his consent. He insisted he did not know the names of the purchasers of the poem. Wither supported Okes' testimony, declaring that the third edition had been licensed by Taverner who had expunged certain passages. Grismond the co-publisher of the first and fourth editions announced that he had sold copies of the poem even to the Master of the Stationers' Company, Matthew Lowndes, who "early sent for them" after he had accused him and Marriott of printing the work. Okes remarked that he and Marriott had printed an additional six thousand after they had been found guilty.[38]

Wither in 1624, still smarting from the Company's high-handed procedure, engaged the irresponsible printer George Wood to print his *Schollers Purgatory*. Wood had been frequently charged by the Company for contempt. His press at Stepney had been seized and destroyed in 1621 for issuing almanacs and primers contrary to the decree of Star Chamber. Undiscouraged Wood set up a second press in Grub Street which met a similar fate. At odds with his guild, he probably was flattered to be courted by a well-known poet, who made him one of his assignees for the printing of his *Hymnes and Songs*. Wood may have been the printer lampooned by Ben Jonson in his satire upon Wither entitled *Time Ridiculed:*

"His press in a hollow tree, where to conceale him
He workes by glow-worme light, the moone's too open."

Wood's press near Holborn Bridge, from which the *Schollers Purgatory* was issued, was raided by the Company's agents on September 9, 1624. It was condemned as "sett vp Contrarye to order ... ymployed in printing an vnlicensed book. Therefore the said wardens by vertue of the [said] Decree and proclamacon sett forth against disorderly printing &c have taken downe the said presse and Caused the same together w[th] the let[te]rs and other Instrum[ents] printing thervnto belonging to be brought to Station[e]rs hall to be defaced and made vnseruiceable."[39]

Wither, compelled to stand trial before the Court of High Commission, confessed that Wood had planned to print an edition of three thousand copies, adding the press had been seized after a small number had been printed. Incensed by the arrogant attitude of the Company, the poet wrote his *Letter ... in answere to a late Pamphlet partly Imp[rin]ted by George Wood* in which he sets forth the qualifications of a publisher. He must buy and sell and "gaine if he can." The poet's remarks reflect his understanding of the professional's position and need for business acumen. "Theire case is worse than other trades, for if sometimes they light upon a uendible Booke, their gaine is counted, talk't off and envied. But theire Charge, their huge piles of waist paper, and theire losses are neuer once thought vpon or considered, and oftentimes they are enjoyned to printe bookes that lie on their handes and are a general hinderance vnto them." Wither strove to exonerate his former publishers, Marriott, Okes and Grismond, assailing the high-handed attitude of the Stationers' Company whose very Master had purchased copies of an unlicensed book.[40]

Perhaps familiar with Withers' predicament, Joseph Mead referred to the general temper of the time when he remarked: "there is much talk of libel and dangerous books." A motion was made in the House of Commons in May 1624 for action to be taken against the sale of Popish texts. A "Catalogue of seven or eight score of Catholic books printed within the past two years" was to be examined by Pym and his colleague Ravenscroft. Although the House aimed as always at the ban of orthodox texts, the state had outlawed during James' reign more books of political context. Their fate reflects the determination of the government to stifle any deviation from political conformity, any criticism or independent thought. The repressive nature of censorship could not possibly be grasped by an autocratic monarch whose son perchance might later read that "Bookes are not absolutely dead things, but doe containe a potencie of life in them to be as active as that soule whose progeny they are ... [for] hee who destroyes a goode Booke, kills reason it selfe, kills the image of God, as it were in the eye." Punishment and censorship stemmed from the authority of power which at the very most could destroy the body of man but never fetter his soul. Undeterred by the force of the state, the Catholic minority and its champion, the underground press, remained courageous, steadfast and strong.[41]

VIII

AUDACIOUS PERNICIOUS FELLOWES

The Underground Catholic Stationer

In his vituperative anti-Catholic treatise, *The Foote out of the snare* the Catholic renegade, John Gee offers considerable, albeit prejudiced information about the activity of the English underground press during the reign of James I. Despite the garbled and slanderous presentation of his findings no investigation of secret English Catholic printing and bookselling as well as the importation program can be pursued without a study of Gee's work. He lists the titles (often scarcely intelligible) of 154 books available in England during the period, the majority of which were printed abroad. He occasionally cites the author; offers his sarcastic price evaluation and personal memoranda. Gee's survey cannot be lightly dismissed. It presents a microcosm of the underground Catholic publishing world, providing a dossier of 22 Catholic printers and agents active in the publishing and dissemination of orthodox literature in England. *The Foote out of the snare* remains a prime source for the knowledge of Catholic books printed in England and those imported from abroad.[1]

Although Gee cites 22 Englishmen as Catholic stationers and agents, a distinction must be made between the underground printer and his factor, the distributor of his books and the handler of Continental imports. His listing is scarcely definitive – limited in its allusion to printers and agents. Research has unearthed several unknown to the omniscient Gee – printers and scouts dwelling in a world of pseudonymity and obscurity.[2]

In an outburst of venom Gee refers to the "swarme of their [Catholic] bookes which you may heare hvmming vp and downe, in euery corner both of city and countrey. I uerily believe they [Catholics] have uented more of their pamphlets within the Twelve months then they did in many yeares before. They haue printing presses and Book-sellers almost in every corner."[3]

Gee's allegation is exaggerated. His "swarme of bookes" refers not to the imprints of the English underground press but rather to the foreign Catholic books imported by the agent-scout. In contrast to his sweeping statement, Horatio Busino, Chaplain of the Venetian Ambassador to England, declared in January 1618, that in "one particular quarter of [London] entirely inhabited by Booksellers not a single missal was to be found." The London stationer could hardly stock Catholic literature! His shop was a rendezvous for the literati, the clergymen, the statesmen, the diplomatic corps; his shelves reflected the talent of English virtuosi, the great names of English drama, verse and religious prose, Shakespeare, Dekker, Chapman, Jonson, Herbert, Wither, Fletcher, Hooker, Rogers and others. The majority of London booksellers and publishers, following the precepts or their Country and Company, pursued their profession unwilling to encounter inquiry and hazard.[4]

The underground printer – the friend of the minority and of the minority – confronted constant danger. Threatened by the prospect of arrest, he could scarcely tarry at any place for any length of time. He was ever apprehensive, moving about incessantly, hoping to enjoy some respite from possible persecution. Reëstablished, the itinerant Catholic printer set up his press and unpacked his type which could be quickly reloaded at the approach of the hot-footed pursuivant.

The cunning of the underground printer drove the state to despair and caused Richard Bancroft, Bishop of London, a friend of so delinquent a craftsman as William Wrench, to exclaim: "The printers do trouble me more than I will write of!" Udall's reports refer to the underground activity in Staffordshire and Worcestershire, where he had intercepted or was about to intercept presses. Sir William Waad declared in 1604 that the Bishop of London had received books seized in the two counties, as well as two printing presses. "The books are fit only for the fire and the sooner they are burnt the better." Udall alluded in 1610 to a secret press recently established between Staffordshire and Warwickshire. Earlier he had requested Salisbury's permission to visit the "contreys of Worcestershire, Staffordshire and Warwickshire" which he considered to be the most dangerous. Since he had passed most of his youth in these areas, he believed "his going into these contreys to [his] nearest friends being without all suspition" would prove most advantageous to the state. There he could personally observe underground activity as one who had "caused all prints that in England were offensive to be discovered."[5]

It is not known whether Udall visited Staffordshire, where William Wrench, the alleged printer of *Prvrit-Anvs*, was extremely active. Wrench had been briefly associated with Edward Jarrett of White Friars in 1597. There the authorities uncovered a printing press which had been used in "pryntinge papisticall bookes." It was ordered that the press be "destroied and made vnserviceable according to the decrees of the starchamber." It is quite possible that after the condemnation of Jarrett's press, Wrench sought a haven in Staffordshire. He was a skilled binder and in this capacity became acquainted with the turncoat Peter Bulloch. It has been affirmed that as a printer he issued Richard Bristow's *Demaundes to be proponed of Catholiques to the heretikes* which provided the evidence to condemn Bulloch and James Duckett.[6]

Wrench appears on the Staffordshire scene in 1602 when he met John Boulter who served as an apprentice to the suspect Catholic publisher John Danter. Boulter had been active in the area prior to Wrench's arrival. An entry in the *Records* of the Stationers' Company states that the Wardens had spent three shillings for "bolters charge about the presses in Staffordshire." This outlay leads to some speculation. Had Boulter's Staffordshire Press been seized or was its master an undercover man for the Company supplying it with information? The latter hypothesis is extremely attractive, but highly speculative.[7]

Boulter and Wrench apparently formed some partnership, separating after two years over financial difficulties. According to Allison and Rogers, the definitive bibliographers of recusant literature, Wrench, in association with the unidentified printer of John Brereley's *Apologie*, published between 1604 and 1605 an approximate thirteen books of Catholic content. These include controversial and devotional treatises by Thomas Wright, William Bishop, Miguel de Comalada, Robert Southwell and others. All were issued anonymously or with fictitious imprints: "Doway by John Mogar" or "Roane 1604."[8]

According to the deposition of the London printer, William Jones, Wrench was arrested. It appears that only through the timely intervention of Bancroft his life was spared. If Wrench did receive a prison sentence it was for a brief term. He was in London in March 1604/1605 since at that time he was indicted for not having attended church services. He is listed as a resident of the Parish of St. Bartholomew the Great in Farringdon Ward where his occupation is given as "Bokebinder." Two months later, Wrench and his wife Margaret – having moved to the area of St. Martin-in-the-Fields where he is again listed as a bookbinder – were indicted for the same misdemeanor. Mrs. Wrench and her husband's servant – probably an apprentice – are to be found among those who were sent to Newgate as recusants in 1610. It is quite possible that at the time William was in the provinces engaged in Catholic printing, binding or acting as an agent for the circulation of Catholic foreign texts.[9]

Wrench is named in 1609 by Udall as the printer of the venomous *Prvrit-Anvs*. In a letter addressed to Sir Julius Caesar, Udall insisted the tract had been printed by Wrench in association with a certain Warren "who hathe a share in the printing presse. Their aequivocating oathes and protestations are not to be trusted." He added that "these bokes *[Prvrit-Anvs]* are commen in Lancashire and Staffordshire and the countreys adjoyning them." Wrench and Warren appear to have been arrested, but having denied any association with the work, were released.[10]

According to Udall, Wrench was in London in 1609, since he was then active as agent for foreign printed books. The informer's letter of November 5, 1610 is most perplexing, since it refers to Wrench's Catholic activity which, according to Udall, was not censured by Parliament but rather condoned. It is true that at the time Udall was losing face with the government, but nevertheless it is difficult to comprehend the official attitude toward Wrench who on several occasions had been reported as an active underground publisher. "I was a sutor for the libertye of a printer called Wrench whose printing presse and himselfe I had caused to be apprehended but at Easter last the sute was denied because the printer was reported to be so dangerous but presently after the ende of Parliament this printer was not only discharged without performing any service but further made one of the prince his boke binders."[11]

This freakish turn of events is surely ironical. Prince Henry, Wrench's new master, was a devout Anglican who certainly was unaware of his bookbinder's secret activity and religious affiliation. Prince Henry had purchased in 1609 the library of his tutor, Lord Lumley, one of the finest private collections in England. Eager to enhance the appearance of the library, many of whose volumes were in worn and shabby bindings, Henry, after he was created Prince of Wales in 1610, engaged in addition to Wrench, a staff of binders who were to rebind the books and to stamp the covers with the royal arms. One can only conjecture whether the bindings of calf impressed in gold and silver with the lion rampant and the crowned double roses were executed for the son of James I by the alleged printer of the notorious *Prvrit-Anvs*. Prince Henry was to live but three years to enjoy his superb collection. His binder William Wrench was to dwell in obscurity for three and a half years following the demise of his royal master.[12]

In February 1616/1617 William Wrench and John Lichfield were appointed Printers to the University of Oxford. Wrench must have been gratified not only for the honor of this singular distinction but also for the opportunity it afforded him to live in Oxford, a town known for its Catholic sympathies. As Printer to the University, he certainly concealed his previous activity. His recommendation doubtless sprang from his former association with the royal family. With Lichfield he issued during the course of his year's appointment about seven books, none of which bears any resemblance to those printed by him during his Staffordshire retreat. After the termination of his appointment Wrench either remained at Oxford as a Catholic agent or moved to London. He was eventually designated by Gee as one of the dispersers of Catholic books within "these two yeeres last past."[13]

Udall stated that Wrench printed *Prvrit-Anvs* in association with a certain Warren also known as Waring. According to the informer, Warren had been arrested and had been confined to the Tower in 1606. In addition to his Staffordshire activity Laurence Warren had printed papist books at Brentford and Bethnal Green in the northeastern part of London. Udall asserts that Warren occasionally used the name of John Wilson, thereby hoping to confuse the officials since the latter was the director of the English College Press at St. Omer. Little is known of Warren's publications. Udall hoped to seize him in 1609, advising Sir Julius Caesar that "this printer I doubte not to finde very shortly." He also revealed that Warren worked with the Catholic stationer Henry Owen.[14]

Warren's colleague, Henry Owen of the Parish of St. Bartholomew The Great, was indicted with Wrench in March 1604/1605 for not attending church services. Henry Owen hailed from a prominent Welsh family. His brother Nicholas, known as "Little John," active in Catholic cabal and arrested for his participation in the Gunpowder Plot, committed suicide in the Tower where, according to Gee, he "ript out his own bowelles." He had served the orthodox cause through his particular talent as a builder of various artifices for escape: cupboards, trapdoors and secret passages. He assisted in the construction of Hindlip Hall in Worcestershire which concealed many priests, among them Father Garnet. "His chief employment," wrote Father Gerard, "was to hide priestes and churche stuffe from the fury of the searcher."[15]

It has been asserted that Henry Owen was associated with the unfortunate James Duckett from ca. 1595 to 1601, the time of the latter's betrayal by Bulloch. Their publications include the standard devotional treatises of Luca Pinelli, Lorenzo Scupoli, Luis de Granada and Laurence Vaux as well as the controversial writings of Thomas Wright, Father Persons, Thomas Hill, Father Southwell and others. These texts appeared either anonymously or with fictitious imprints of Antwerp, "Calice," Douai and Rouen. According to the deposition of the printer, William Jones, Henry Owen had been often imprisoned for selling "popish books." He apparently was little discouraged. After one release from jail "being imbouldened [he] fell to printinge again, and was taken and put into the Clinke and there had a presse and printed diuerse popish bookes til at last he was espied." After several arrests he was confined to the White Lion where he again broke loose and fled to Northamptonshire. In May 1600 Sir William Waad informed Cecil of Owen's escape and remarked that he had sought refuge in Northamptonshire where he printed a seditious pamphlet. He attributed to his press Thomas Wright's *Certaine articles of forcible reasons, Discouering the palpable absurdities, and most notorious errors of the Protestant religion*. Owen apparently departed Northamptonshire for Staffordshire where he printed alone or for a short period with Warren. He is qualified by Udall as "one of the three several printers" in the county, who occasionally used the pseudonym James Waterson. The informer asserted that after Wrench's arrest Owen was befriended by a gentleman who planned to take him "with his presse and letters towardes Ireland."[16]

During his proposed flight to Ireland Owen was arrested by William Chetwyn, member of a prominent Staffordshire family. Chetwyn advised Secretary Herbert that he had caught "certain suspicious persons that were travelling through the countrie towards Ireland, namelie one Henry Oven a printer, John Vincent, Richard Davies and John Birde, men that have practised in the printing and publishing of certain seditious bookes." Chetwyn notified Herbert of "bookes printed and published by them," but failed to submit specific titles. He continued that he had seized three presses at the time of arrest, which he proposed to sell. Udall encouraged the government to accept Chetwyn's offer since he believed it would be more advisable "to dispose of the matter heare acordingly to prevent what might happen." The trial of Henry Owen and his colleagues does not appear to have been recorded. If imprisoned, the agile Owen again escaped or was released since he is described by Gee as one who "did disperse, binde or sell popishe books about London."[17]

During their Staffordshire residence, Wrench, Warren and Owen had doubtless met the London dealer, Simon Pauley who, according to the later Puritan printer Michael Sparke, Pauley's apprentice, "had dealt much in Popish books." Sparke asserted that Pauley had spent considerable time in Staffordshire in 1603 engaged at Worly Hall in "binding, vending and putting to sale Popish Books, Pictures, Beads and such Trashe." Here the Puritan fanatic Sparke declared he had learned "to abhore Popery by seeing the grosse ignorance of many amongest them."[18]

Of the Staffordshire clique John Boulter, the erstwhile partner of William Wrench and possibly a Company agent, had scarcely fared as well as the future binder to Prince Henry or the elusive Owen. His name appears on a petition to Chancellor Ellesmere in 1613 in which the then destitute Boulter, with other craftsmen, declared himself to be one of "the miserable estate of a greate number of poore men [who] by reason of manifold disorders in our corporacon . . . are vtterly impoverished." Wrench's former associate – or the Company's undercover man – appealed to his "dread So[vraigne]" for sustenance and help.[19]

In his allusion to underground country printers, Gee refers to the activity of John Brereley of Lancashire whose press was "suppressed about some three yeares since in Lancashire where all Brereley his own works, with many other Popish pamphlets were printed." The participation of James Anderton, known as Brereley, in the Catholic underground printing movement has been the subject of several excellent monographs. Using the pseudonym John Brereley, the priest and author, James Anderton, published an approximate seventeen books at the family residence Birchley Hall. The estate has been described as an ideal center for the printing and traffic in recusant literature. Like Ely House, the Anderton mansion, built with several trap doors and secret passages, lay in a secluded area. The vestry of its chapel concealed a trap door disguised by a hollow wall, access to which was gained only through a secret panel. With its printing press, its winding passages, its secret doors, Birchley Hall became the center of Roman Catholic activity in Lancashire.[20]

Gee was familiar not only with the printers and sellers of Catholic books at Birchley Hall, Staffordshire and Lancashire but as well with a clique of London stationers who dwelt in close proximity to one another in the area of Gunpowder Alley within the City, Turnmill and St. John's Streets joined together by Clerkenwell Green, St. Martins-in-the-Fields to the west; St. Andrew's, Shoe Lane near St. Sepulchre's, Farringdon Street through to Fetter Lane and Little Britain. As neighbors and conspirators trafficking in forbidden literature, they could help and abet one another. They could supply a recent Catholic import; they might conceal the wares of a colleague warned of an imminent raid. There is little doubt that they coöperated in the dissemination of Catholic books either printed at their premises or brought to them from the provinces or from Flanders and France. For the most part the members of the London group were distributors of orthodox texts although a few emerge as printers of Catholica. Referring to the current traffic in recusant texts, Udall declared in June 1606 that "all the marchants of these wares are by no meanes either crossed or imprisoned. There are now 11 which begin the practise of the transporting of those bokes."[21]

Peter Smith of Turnmill Street may be counted among the "transporters" of books from the Continent and the printers of Catholic texts. Gee describes Smith and his son as "verye audacious pernicious fellowes." Peter Smith "prynter" was indicted on September 20, 1614 for non-attendance at church and is mentioned on the Recusant Roll of 1615 for the same misdemeanor. By June 1616 Smith had apparently moved to new quarters in St. James's, Clerkenwell.[22]

Smith does not appear to have been a member of the Stationers' Company. He is described in 1621 as "a foraynor" who at the time was ordered by the Company to leave London. Enjoying the good will of the well-known publisher, William Stansby, Smith remained in the city until the following November during which time Stansby at the Cross Keys had offered him refuge. Two years later Smith was arrested as the operator of a secret press at Bunhill. Here he was engaged in reprinting the Rheims *New Testament* and John Percy's *Answer to a Pamphlet intituled The Fisher . . . catch'd in his owne net.* Smith's premises were raided; the press and type brought to the Company Hall where they were battered and defaced. The friendship or business relationship between Smith and Stansby had endured, since after the dissolution of the press Smith again sought asylum at Stansby's premises. Smith was not easily discouraged. Deprived of his press, he apparently engaged in the sale of Catholic books. According to Gee, he had "a greate store of Worthington's bookes." The majority of the writings of this well-known Catholic divine were printed abroad and thence imported by Smith with other orthodox texts.[23]

At St. Paul's no great distance from Turnmill Street, Thomas Gubbins – mentioned by Gee – sold Catholic works. Gubbins' association with the Catholic program is highly ambiguous. His support is peripheral, motivated probably by the opportunity of profit. Indifferent to religious association, he printed a text which would bring him immediate profit. Gubbins had completed his apprenticeship to John Walley in 1585/1586, entering into partnership with Thomas Newman the following year. Their first publication was Boccaccio's *Amorous Fiametta* "translated out of the Italian." During a lengthy haphazard career, in association with Newman and others, Gubbins issued an approximate forty books. His trade-list is varied and even includes treatises by the Puritan divine, John Udall. None of his publications overtly identifies him with the Catholic program. Upon the defeat of the Armada he entered for publication a work celebrating the great victory and castigating popish influence: *Elizabetha triumphans wherein is conteyned the hellish subteltie the damnable devises and develishe practyses that the Popes have vsed ever sithence ye Queenes maiestie firste camme to the Crowne.* Of Gubbins' several partners Thomas Orwin alone can be associated with Catholicism, since he is alleged to have printed in 1591 the *Jesus Psalter* and *Ladies Psalter*.[24]

Despite no patent connection with orthodoxy, there is evidence of Gubbins' tie with the corps of Catholic stationers. In 1595 he took as apprentice "William Fysher sonne of John Fysher of Bryneton in the county of Northamptonshire." William Fisher emerges as a prosperous Catholic book dealer. It can be concluded that young Fisher had been apprenticed by his father to a master of his own religious persuasion.[25]

From 1598 to 1614 the name of Fisher's master, Gubbins, is not associated with any known publication. He appears briefly as an agent or underground bookseller. A letter of Sir William Waad of 1609 refers to his distribution of subversive literature. Waad assures his correspondent, Sir Julius Caesar, that "other pestiferus bookes . . . were done by one Gyggins and Alablaster." From Waad's note it can be inferred that "Gyggins" or Gubbins printed little but rather acted as an importer since Waad assured Sir Julius that the books associated with "Gyggins" had been "printed beyond the seas."[26]

Although Gubbins was made a freeman of York in 1603, he later returned to London. There in 1614 and 1615 he issued two books: Richard Brathwaite's *Prodigals teares* and Robert Greene's *Disputation between a hee conny-catcher and a shee conny-catcher*. No imprint can be assigned to Gubbins after 1615. Since he is indicted by Gee as a Catholic stationer there is the possibility that after his withdrawal from active publishing he lived on his wits and engaged in the distribution of forbidden books.[27]

A group of six active in the Holborn district are mentioned by Gee as either printers or individuals associated with the Catholic press: William Mann, Master Lovett in Holborn, Thomas Andrews "Bookebinder," Ferdinand Ely of Little Britain, John Browne and Michael Francklyn. William Mann, described as "Fisher's man" – the selfsame Fisher who had been indentured to Gubbins – was indicted for recusancy in December 1622. He gave his address at the time as the Parish of St. Andrew, Holborn. Fisher, who apparently engaged in large-scale bookselling, employed six apprentices, among them the future bookbinder Thomas Andrewes mentioned by Gee. Andrewes had come from Wiltshire and began his apprenticeship with Fisher in June 1612. He was to become a bookbinder and perhaps a close associate of the Catholic goldsmith, Drugo Lovett, referred to by Gee.[28]

Master Lovett, like Fisher, practised his trade in Holborn. He was fined in October 1603, January 1608 and May 1624 for non-attendance at church services. As a goldsmith, Lovett could easily have been acquainted with members of the book trade, notably the bookbinder. He may have supplied the stones and gold filigree for a particularly sumptuous binding executed for a missal or breviary of a prominent Catholic. He may have designed and set the jewels encrusted in handsome Jacobean embroidered covers.[29]

Quite possibly some choice bindings but more surely a variety of stolen goods were sold by Ferdinand Ely of Little Britain. Ely emerges as an unsavory character who appears to have depended for his livelihood upon merchandise confiscated or stolen by the pursuivants. Udall declared that a messenger, William Bray, had during the search of the "house of one Elye a stationer in Little Brittayne . . . found the vile booke of Queres *[Prvrit-Anvs]* coppied out. The stationer buyeth and selleth all prohibited bokes and stolen bokes. He dealeth with them who have warrant from the High Commission and what bokes most of them take in search they sell to this stacioner." Hence Ely's premises in Little Britain proved to be a ready outlet for many of the books taken from Catholics which he, in all likelihood, sold to other Catholic stationers and customers. The printer Bernard Alsop was to admit in 1626 that he had purchased the manuscript of Robert Cotton's *Short History of Henry III* from Ely. Because of this transaction, he was hailed, in company with Ely and others, before the Court of High Commission in 1628.[30]

John Browne, cited by Gee, also dwelt in Little Britain. The Elder Browne, active from 1598 to 1622, was succeeded by his son, John, Jr. Specialists in music publishing, the Brownes issued "ayres," madrigals, "anthemes," and musical miscellanies of Corkine, Lichfield, Pilkington, Bateson, East, Dowland and Ravenscroft. Other of their publications included the popular *Poly-Olbion* of Michael Drayton and the splendid fine arts manual, *Graphice* of Henry Peacham. The Brownes circulated the plays of Jonson, Chapman and Middleton. Only one Catholic devotional work, Granada's *Treatise of Consideration and Prayer*, bears the imprint of the younger Browne. On the other hand, *The Christians apparelling Christ* by the ardent Puritan divine, Robert Jenison, was published by Browne in 1625. The Brownes' attractive trade-list may have concealed some traffic in Catholic literature. Their circulation of books in the so-called "arts" and their association with musicians and musical writers may have introduced them to a non-conformist milieu. Either the unfortunate publicity given them by Gee or a clandestine relationship with the Catholic minority made John Browne, Jr. an official suspect, since in 1628 he was also ordered to submit a list of his publications to the scrutiny of the Archbishop of Canterbury.[31]

Michael Francklyn, a resident of the parish of St. Martin Ludgate – mentioned by Gee – was indicted for recusancy in February 1612/1613. He was apparently a fairly large-scale bookseller active from 1616 through 1648, engaging during these three decades at least five apprentices. No publication appears to be associated with his name.[32]

Gee alludes to an additional seven printers and agents engaged in the circulation of Catholic writings. The existence of Richard Avery of "Woode Streete," Jeremiah Jackson "neere Moorfields," Henry Barber "in Holbourne" and the ladies, "May in Shoe Lane" and "Mother Tuck" emerge skeletally without body or fiber. Gee states that "Henry Barber in Holbourne [was] once imprisoned on this occasion," implying that he had been arrested by agents for his involvement in the circulation of Catholic books. Richard Baily and Robert Bulmer, also alluded to by Gee, have been identified as apprentices to booksellers between 1607 and 1615. No positive evidence to date has identified any of the seven with the Catholic printing program. However since fourteen of the twenty-one dealers charged by Gee have been linked with Catholic printing and bookselling, it may be deduced that these seven were likewise involved.[33]

Gee indicts a quartet of ladies as purveyors of Catholic books: the previously mentioned Mrs. Fowler of Fetter Lane who "tradeth much to St. Omers;" a neighbor, Mrs. Bulloch, the Widow Douce, "a famous dealer, and Vdell of Gunpowder Alley." The participation of women in the book world was common.

Intermarriage among members of the trade was frequent, thus establishing an alliance of families and helpmates. A wife frequently assisted her husband at the shop. Widowed, she often continued the business, either adopting the firm name or, anticipating some adverse reaction to her role in business from an unenlightened customer, using only the first initial of her Christian name in an imprint. Economic necessity frequently compelled widows to remain in business. Often aided by a capable assistant who occasionally became her new husband, she was enabled to enhance her trade through his help and ability. Less fortunate ladies, unskilled in business techniques, unfamiliar with the mystique of the craft, or burdened with an impoverished estate – like the Widows Danter and Venge – were compelled to rely on the benevolence of the Stationers' Company.[34]

Religious motivation certainly inspired the four ladies censured by Gee to assist in the distribution of Catholic books. During their married lives, if not engaged at their husbands' shops, they had enjoyed greater opportunity to indulge their religious zeal through church attendance and pious acts. Once widowed, they perchance sought solace from prayer and faith. There is also the conjecture that a forlorn widow could escape official attention in a business world all but monopolized by a masculine society.

Mrs. Fowler was doubtless the widow of John Fowler, Jr. She had shared with her late husband the role of trader and seller of Catholic texts. In January 1604/1605 John Fowler and his wife Anne were fined for not attending church services. The following year Salisbury was advised that the Fowlers maintained a secret press in Staffordshire. She is described by Lewis Owen as a distributor of Catholic texts. In April 1606 Sir Julius Caesar received word that Fowler was dispatching to his wife "fowr cases of books from Paris" which he had just conveyed to St. Omer with "great secresy." They were to be sold by her in England "for the relief of her and her children not having other means to support them." Upon interrogation, Anne Fowler admitted that she had received "a portmanteau" which belonged to her husband containing Catholic texts, among them, the *Manual of Prayers*, Fulvio Androzzi's *Certaine deuout considerations*, St. Thomas More's *Dialogue of cumfort against tribulation*, Leslie's *Defence of the honour of . . . Marie quene of Scotland*, John Percy's *A Treatise conteyning the true catholike faith and holy sacrifice*, and Father Persons' *Christian Directory*. An analysis of Fowler's shipment indicates that he acted as a jobber sending to England not only several titles printed by his father but also the publications of other Flemish and Parisian dealers. Fowler was still active in 1609 since Udall affirms that he was "the same party that brought the pestiferus bookes from Sant Omers to Dunkerke."[35]

There is little doubt that by the time of Gee's research the Younger Fowler had died. His traffic in Catholic books was to be continued by his wife, herself an experienced dealer who continued to enjoy a well-established relationship with Continental suppliers, English underground printers and agents. She apparently not only retained her own Catholic book-buying clientele, but offered lodging to itinerant missionaries in her Fetter Lane residence. The steadfast support given to the orthodox cause by a member of the distaff side was assuredly appreciated by the Catholic minority.

Mrs. Bulloch also plied her trade in Fetter Lane. She was in all likelihood the widow of the turncoat Peter Bulloch who had betrayed James Duckett and had been executed at Tyburn with him. Many years had passed since her husband's defection and death. She had doubtless been left penniless, the legatee merely of a shameful estate. As a binder, Bulloch had bequeathed his wife few real assets: his tools and his materials. His skill had died with him. Nevertheless, reared in an orthodox atmosphere, familiar with country and local Catholic booksellers and agents, Mrs. Bulloch in time became involved as a factor in the distribution of books, some smuggled from abroad, others brought to her from the underground county presses or from the warrens and back alleys of Farringdon Ward.[36]

The Widow Douce is characterized by Gee as "a famous dealer." Her reputation is assuredly based upon her numerous indictments and her known zeal as a resolute Catholic. Her name appears constantly on the recusant rolls from 1608 through 1620. In 1607, when admitted to Newgate Prison, she is described as "a widow of Farringdon Ward." A report of the following year, submitted by Udall, refers to "Anne Dowse a widow in High Holbourne against the turning stile into Lincolnes Inn Fields. She selleth Popish Books." Udall alludes to the "Widow Douce" in 1609 as the recipient of subversive books which had been brought into England from overseas. Despite several sojourns within the unsavory confines of Newgate and the almost annual references to her nonattendance at Church, Anne Douce was able to carry on her trade in the sale of Catholic books. Like the ladies Fowler and Bulloch, she had developed a Catholic clientele among the devout and cemented a sound relationship with underground printers, scouts and importers.[37]

Perhaps the most surprising of names to be found on Gee's list is that of "Vdell of Gunpowder Alley." Gee probably referred to the clandestine activity of the widow of the informer Udall. Matured in an atmosphere of guile and deception, married to a man of no principle, familiar with Catholic agents and the rendezvous of underground printers, the Widow Udall was in an excellent position to deal in forbidden books. Her residence was not distant from the premises of the ladies Fowler, Bulloch and Douce and in close proximity to May of Shoe Lane since Gunpowder Alley ran west from the latter's abode. Having been dismissed from his post, despite his protestations of loyalty to an unappreciative government, Udall sank into oblivion, but, doubtless, before his death passed on much of his useful information to his second wife. She is referred to by Sir Julius Caesar as a dealer in Catholic books. Her orthodoxy is well attested by her untimely demise in the "Fatal Vespers" of November 5, 1623 during a Catholic rally at Hunsdon House, the residence of the French Ambassador, when the floor collapsed killing many in the audience.[38]

From the reports of informers and officials, figures emerge and recede as agents for the distribution of Catholic literature. Although Gee's information is an essential key to the world of underground printers and factors active in the sale of foreign texts, the names of several agents eluded him. One of the principal thoroughfares of Holborn was St. John Street, where Thomas Sleeps, a stationer, greeted at his home "a wondrous resort" of conspirators gathered to discuss plans for the Gunpowder Plot. Thomas Sleeps and his wife Catherine appear on the recusant rolls almost annually from 1591 through 1616. He is described in 1591 as a yeoman of Clerkenwell and in 1615 as a gentleman of St. James's. The latter abode surely proved more attractive to Master Sleeps than his more recent residence in Newgate, where he had been confined as a persistent recusant. Imprisoned with his wife in 1608 and 1612, he had been denied bail. Thomas Sleeps belongs to the shadowy world of agents who bought and sold Catholic texts.[39]

Active at the same time were John Coe "stacioner" and his wife Helen of St. Andrews, Holborn, both of whose names appear on the recusant rolls from 1610 through 1623. In 1610 the Coes spent some time in Newgate and were to be fined almost annually for non-attendance at Church. Like Sleeps, Coe obviously dealt in Catholic literature.[40]

Udall refers to the stationer Francis Bowin of the Parish of St. Dunstan in the West who was indicted for recusancy in February 1604/1605. As an Englishman, Bowin was fully aware of the principles of English law and demanded a trial by jury to judge his espousal of orthodoxy. Although Stuart justice found the strong-minded stationer guilty of heresy, Bowin apparently received a fairly light sentence since he was pursuing his profession in 1609 when he admitted that he had purchased copies of *Prvrit-Anvs* from Ferdinand Ely of Little Britain, specialist in stolen merchandise.[41]

John and Joan Dabscot, of French origin, their name being occasionally spelled D'Abridgecourt, were better known to the Crown messengers than Master Bowin. Their premises in St. Bartholomew Parish had been searched in 1603 for seditious books which the government declared had been brought "out of France or the Low Countries especially from Roane." The Dabscots appear to have been extremely active agents for books exported from the Spanish Netherlands. Udall described Joan Dabscot as "one of the two most dangerous women for thees causes" he had ever confronted. He informed Sir Julius Caesar in 1609 that Mrs. Dabscot had not only received literary contraband but also handled texts sent to her by "one Wilson." Udall recognized the existence of two Catholic Wilsons, but was of the opinion that she accepted books from both naming "but one, whom she supposeth freest from danger." Udall referred to John Wilson, Director of the St. Omer English College Press, and Laurence Warren, the Staffordshire printer, who occasionally adopted the pseudonym, John Wilson. The informer found any discussion with Mrs. Dabscot almost impossible since "the woman doth aequivocate."[42]

John Dabscot confessed that he had imported into England four bales of the offensive *Prvrit-Anvs*. His transgression resulted in his arrest, along with that of his wife and maid servant. Writing of their imprisonment the Venetian Ambassador to England, Marc-Antonio Correr, believed that it would fare "ill with them." When copies of the nefarious work were burned in August 1609, Dabscot, upon further interrogation, stated that he had brought them merely as merchandise. The prison term of 1609 failed to diminish the religious ardor of the Dabscots. They were committed to Newgate in March and May 1611/1612 and the following February for their refusal to take the Oath of Allegiance. There is the possibility that the Dabscots were acquainted with a book agent William Spencer who occasionally adopted the pseudonym Thomas Nichols. Spencer was indicted for recusancy in 1610 and 1611, also spending several months in Newgate.[43]

A memorandum submitted by Udall to Sir Julius Caesar in 1609 refers not only to Spencer but to eight other agents who acted as recipients and dispersers of controversial books. In addition to the better known names of William Wrench, the Dabscots, the "Widow Douce" and Roger Heigham, Udall refers to a certain Thomas Glepes [Sleeps?], Teak, Cabell and a member of the aristocracy, Lady Gray. The latter, the wife of Sir Thomas Gray of Chillingham, Northumberland, was a friend of Catholic refugees and made available her three London mansions for their security.[44]

The owner of Montague House on Aldersgate Street, Sir Henry Montague, was more prominent in matters of state than the husband of Lady Gray. Montague, the First Earl of Manchester, King's counsel and philosopher, was a convert to Roman Catholicism. Despite his Lordship's prominence, Udall could not refrain from mentioning several unpleasant disturbances at Montague's residence and in 1609 advised Sir Julius Caesar that his home had been searched. He stated, moreover, that his pursuivants had been "used in the most vile manner by the porter of the house and his wife; besides lewd words, they had theyre clokes mangled and spoyled."[45]

William Parker, Fourth Baron Monteagle, a colleague of Lord Montague, had been the first statesman to be advised of the impending Gunpowder Plot. Although Monteagle was never involved in the Conspiracy, he had strong Catholic leanings. His London home was frequently suspect. Books ferried across the Channel found their way to Monteagle's mansion and in 1609 Salisbury was advised that a shipper, Henry Parish, had stacked bales of *Prvrit-Anvs* and other Catholic texts in the residence.[46]

The homes of Lady Gray, Sir Henry Montague and Lord Monteagle were obviously known to some priests and Jesuits indicted as purveyors of orthodox texts. The author of *The Foote out of the snare* alludes to a "certain notorious Jesuitte lodging in a sanctuary not farre from the Sauoy . . . a great merchant for the commodity of these Popish pamphlets." He sarcastically states that this gentleman "hath thriven well thereby while hee fished in troubled waters." Gee comments upon his extensive stock, stating that he had "seene a greater store of bookes in quires at his chamber than [he] ever held in any stationers warehouse about Pauls having two or three roomes fitted out with heapes in this kinde to the very top." Gee may have alluded to John Fisher, known as Percy, a Jesuit of amazing didactic skill whose *Answer to a pamphlet, intituled: the Fisher catch'd in his owne net* had been recently printed at the secret press of Peter Smith in Bunhill. Fisher was at large in 1623 holding a series of disputations, several of which were attended even by James and his favorites.[47]

Among the books which proved attractive to the Catholic reading clientele in England was the recent English version of the *Flos sanctorum* of the Spaniard Alfonso de Villegas, translated by the brothers Edward and William Kinsman. The book is reported to have been printed in 1609 at Douai "by Peter Orroy an ordinary printer there." It is evident that the Kinsmans, priests, travelled between Flanders and England, since in 1609 William was questioned about his recent translation and association with the English import program. Udall branded him as a factor for Thomas Abington, the plotter for the cause of Mary Stuart, stating Kinsman was "known as the man which receaveth and disposeth of books from beyond the seas." He informed Sir Julius Caesar that Kinsman had recently delivered packets of books to the home of Sir Henry Montague. Kinsman was arrested in September 1609 and taken to Fleet Street Jail. He admitted that his brother had given him thirty-six copies of the Villegas translation "to make money for his relief." He denied that he had personally transported the books to England, avowing that they had been brought to him "by an unknown person in his residence in St. Owley Street."[48]

The participation of priests and Jesuits in the Catholic book program mentioned by Udall was to be specifically discussed by Gee more than a decade later. He declared that the distinguished Dr. Worthington marketed copies of his treatise, *The Anker of Christian Doctrine*, which had been printed by Lawrence Kellam at Douai in 1622. On a visit to London the former President of the Douai Seminary sold copies of the book at his lodging in Turnbull Street for fourteen shillings – although, according to his detractor, it was worth only five. Other author-priests, acting as agents, included Dr. Norris, "one that hath written diuers bookes of late;" Dr. Smith, "author of diuers pestilent bookes ... F[rater] Simons a Carmelite author of diuers late foolish pamphlets ... lodging on the lower end of Holbourn and F[rater] Heigham author of many loud-lying pamphlets." James complained to the Spanish Ambassador that Matthew Kellison's *The right and iurisdiction of the prelate and the prince*, imported from Douai, was being sold clandestinely by some of the diplomat's servants and the porter at the Spanish Embassy who had been arrested. Gee identifies with the Catholic book program several physicians and barber-surgeons: "D. Inquisoto an Italian, D. Lucatelli a mountebank lodging without Temple Bar, M. Covert an empiricall man in Holbourn, Monsieur a French doctor lurking about the Strand who occasionally heard mass near the Savoy."[49]

Gee reveals the prices of those "loud-lying pamphlets," and upon occasion is not reticent to give his appraisal of them. The Douai *Bible* – scarcely a pamphlet – sold for forty shillings, whereas a copy of the Rheims *New Testament* could be purchased for sixteen or twenty shillings. *An antidote against the pestiferous writings of all English sectaries* by Sylvester Norris realized eight shillings in spite of Gee's declaration that it "might be afforded for foure shillings." The same author's *Guide of faith* "sold at an vnreasonable rate," while his *Pseudo-Scripturist* brought five shillings. Gee waxed indignant over the price of George Musket's *The Bishop of London his legacy* printed at St. Omer in 1623. "They squeezed from Romish buyers six or seuen shillings apiece. A deare price for a dirtye lye. Yet I wish that they that haue any beliefe in it, might pay deare for it." The reader could buy copies of Brereley's *Protestants apologie* for seventeen shillings; Richard Smith's *Of the author and substance of the Protestant church and religion* for six shillings.[50]

The English Catholic paid dearly for his books and no less dearly for his very existence. From Gee's evidence, Udall's reports, the *Records* of the Stationers' Company, letters and diaries, a pattern of the clandestine Catholic press emerges. Despite Gee's allusion to "the swarme of [Catholic] bookes," the orthodox publishing and import program was small. The demand was limited – the danger omnipresent. The official policy of persecution, arrest and threatened imprisonment became an almost insurmountable barrier for the successful publication and circulation of Catholic books in England. The courageous survived – Wrench, Owen, the Dabscots, the Widow Douce; the more timid, the irresolute sank into obscurity – upon occasion suffering the stench and torture of Newgate!

Of the one hundred fifty-four titles mentioned by Gee one hundred twelve in English have been here identified. They were issued during the reigns of Elizabeth and James I by fifteen Continental firms and English secret presses. The total number of known English titles published by these houses is approximately four hundred thirty. Hence Gee's enumeration of one hundred fifty-four titles reflects his familiarity with domestic and Continental publications. Since apparently two-thirds of the books listed by Gee were printed abroad, it is essential to investigate these foreign suppliers of the English domestic Catholic market.

Gee cites fifty of one hundred thirty-four known books issued by 1626 at the English College Press at St. Omer. This Seminary, established in 1592 for the English Catholic exile, is of the utmost significance not only as an intellectual haven for the refugee but as a printing center whose press supplied to the English Catholic those texts denied him at home.

IX

CHESTS OF BOOKS AT ST. OMERS

The Seminary Presses

The majority of the "English bookes printed or reprinted or dispersed by the Priestes and their agents" in England were issued at the press of the English Jesuit College at St. Omer in the Spanish Netherlands. Allison and Rogers reveal that an approximate one hundred thirty-four books were printed from 1603 through 1625 at the St. Omer Seminary Press. The remaining Anglo-Catholic books issued during the period were printed at other Catholic colleges and by various Continental presses.

The Jesuit College of St. Omer had been founded by Father Persons in 1592. It was ideally located near the sea, being but "eight leagues [twenty-four miles] from Calais." Established within the dominion of Philip II of Spain, it received an annual pension from His Catholic Majesty. St. Omer superseded the small college of Eu in Normandy which had also been founded by Father Persons. Within three years after its establishment St. Omer counted one hundred scholars and by 1630 attendance had doubled.

The St. Omer College consisted of one large and several smaller buildings, a chapel having been added in 1610. Here the novitiates studied and aspired to the priesthood. The Catholic turncoat and government agent, Lewis Owen, in his biting, informative *Rvnning Register. Recording a Trve Relation of the State of the English Colledges, Seminaries and Cloysters in all forraine parts* stated that the student body embraced "Lords, Knights, Gentlemen and rich men's sonnes" who paid either forty or thirty pounds annually for their "dyet."[1]

According to Owen, the students had been practically hijacked by Jesuit agents stationed throughout the homeland for study at the English Catholic seminaries abroad. They "insinuate themselues into the Company of Masters and Bachelors of Arts . . . and . . . perswade them to become Roman Catholikes." Having convinced a young man to return to the church and ultimately to serve the true God, the Jesuit procured for him the necessary papers and passport. Owen's narrative, although probably prejudiced, presents a colorful portrait of prevailing corruption and intrigue. "This [Jesuit] agent doth procure a Passe vnder the hands of some of the Lords of His Majesties pr[i]vie Councell, for some Countrie Gentleman, that is either a Protestant or else some church-papist and two or three Seruinge men to travaile either into France or to learne the Language or else to Spaw, to drinke of those sower waters, for the recouery of his health, as he faineth, albeit there is no such matter: for this roaring Boy that liues about London and is maintained by them [Jesuits], will present himselfe before the Lords of the priuie Councell in his satten suite and his

Clok lined with velvet, to entreat their Honours to grant him their license for his more quiet passage into these forrayne parts; yea, this Gallant will take the Oath of Allegiance, but having obtained his passport, he deliuers it vnto some Iesuite, Monke, Frier or Seminarie Priests who, together with as many youths as are mentioned in this Passe, repaire to Douer or any other Seaport and thence saile all ouer into some of those forraine parts without any examination at all, Passe goode for 3 yeeres, they poast to and fro, from thence into England, and from England thither without any suspition, let or hindrance."[2]

Although young men were induced by Jesuits and missionaries stationed in England to attend the Continental seminaries, many boys went abroad of their own volition with ardor and enthusiasm. The Catholic Father John Gerard, whose *Memoirs* certainly suffer from his particular bias, declared that he had sent over "numbers of boys and young men to the Catholic seminaries abroad. On one occasion I had sent two boys on their way to St. Omers, and had given them letters of recommendation written with lemon-juice, so that the writing was not visible on the paper. They had to pass by Ostend which is not the usual way."[3]

Catholic students, laymen and priests did travel from the Netherlands to England without arousing any suspicion. Several arrived in the country in special vessels chartered by ambassadors. "I have known others," declared Owen, "that hired a Barke or Shallop at Dunkerke and were set ashore in the nightime neere Margate, in the Isle of Tenet in Kent, the place is called Starregate." Others, bound for the Continent, took sail at Portsmouth or Arundel, "departing at night and . . . away before morning." The shortest passage to the Continent was via Dover-Calais with another eight leagues by foot or horseback to St. Omer. More tedious journeys were undertaken via Waterford in Ireland "and from thence in the Trinitie or Jonas Shipps" escorted by an agent. South Shields in the mouth of the Tyne was known as a port of departure for "the conveying of youths and others beyond the seas to the seminaries." Here it was rumored that prior to their passage the Catholic boys were befriended by a certain Ursula Taylor who housed and fed them. Young women who aspired to life within the security of a Continental convent were, according to Gee, assisted by a London agent known as "Spanish John commonly called the Devils Factor a transporter of gentlewomen beyond the seas to become nunnes."[4]

Whatever the passage, the student and the "gentlewoman" arrived at St. Omer and the Continent to undertake a novitiate for the priesthood and the responsibilities of the cloistered life. Serious, sincere young Catholics had fled England not merely from fear of persecution but also "from contempt they felt for the scanty learning and bad teaching of the heretics." Eventually the seminarian was to bring Catholicism to England in the form of propaganda and the books issued by the Catholic presses at St. Omer and elsewhere.[5]

Even before the establishment of the English Jesuit College, St. Omer had been known as a book center. The Jesuit Henry Walpole declared in April 1594 that there were "diuers chests of books at St. Omers which were printed when the Armada was to have come over, sett out by Cardinal Allen as I have heard against her Matie." Walpole's remarks cannot refer to the actual printing at St. Omer, since the first known active local printer did not set up until 1604. He may have had in mind the importance of the town as an intellectual center, the hotbed of Jesuit activity, a community of extreme advantage for its proximity to the Channel.[6]

François Bellet emerges as the first licensed printer of St. Omer. He had served his apprenticeship to Plantin and Moretus at Antwerp. On October 8, 1601 he petitioned the Privy Council at Brussels for the right to establish a press at St. Omer stating: "There is a college of English students of considerable size which your Majesty established in this city as well as other colleges." He believed his services would benefit these institutions. There appears to have been no formal connection with the St. Omer College Press.[7]

Bellet was to publish principally the writings of Father Persons, several of which, despite the blockade of the Flemish ports, found their way into England. The salutary effect of Persons' treatises upon the English Catholic community is aptly expressed in a "Letter of the English Mission" of 1607. "Our Catholics are enabled to stand firm by means of the sacraments and other resources, among which is the reading of spiritual books and of treatises concerning religion, written as opportunity offers, in defence of the faith, and for the advancement of religion, by learned and pious men, one of whom according to opinion ... is Father Persons, for though his books do not bear his name, yet he is recognized in them by all. The elegance, propriety, gravity and simplicity of his style have won for him ... a foremost place among English writers." The "Letter" doubtless refers to Bellet's editions of Father Persons' *A treatise of three conversions of England from paganisme to Christian religion.* 1603–1604; *A relation of the triall beetweene the bishop of Eureux and L. Plessis Mornay.* 1604; *A review of the publike disputations.* 1604; *An answere to the fifth part of Reportes lately set forth by Syr Edward Cooke.* 1606; *The Christian directory.* 1607; *A treatise tending to mitigation towardes Catholicke-subiectes in England.* 1607. "News from England" circulated by the English Mission in February 1610 refers to "two contemporary books written in English and printed in quarto. It is supposed that they come from the pen of Father Persons. They do not treat of the oath but of other conversions. The first is against Dr. Morton ... the other book is the history of a conversion of a gentleman ... who gradually became and remains a good Catholic. All are of opinion that the fruit of good books is now immense in England."[8]

Bellet left St. Omer for Ypres in 1609, his activity having been superseded by the College Press established the previous year. As Lewis Owen wrote: "In the English Colledge at St. Omer the Iesuites haue a Printinge Press, to print such Popish Bookes and Seditious (yea Blasphemous) Pamphlets as are written by an English Iesuite." In Owen's opinion, the St. Omer Press realized a minimum of four hundred pounds annually. "They themselues are the Authours,

Correctors, Composers and Pressmen, in so much that it doth cost them nothing but Paper and Inke, and these bookes they doe sell at an unreasonable rate; for they are not ashamed to sell a booke, that contains not a quire of paper for fiue or six shillings, and to that purpose they have their Factors and Brokers in London, and all parts of England, to disperse and sell these Bookes and Pamphlets, and to transport the money vnto them at Saint Omer."[9]

Soon after his appointment as Prefect of the English Mission, Father Persons, determined to supply his co-religionists with pertinent texts, provided the St. Omer College Press with all necessary appurtenances for the printing and exportation of Catholic writings. The director of the Press, John Wilson, Persons' former secretary, was known as Persons' man. At Rome, Father Persons had employed several amanuenses, among them Father Walpole, Stephen Smith and the faithful Wilson. "They are in readiness and at noon Thursdays receive the great man's orders. The secretaries are kept hard at work, for Persons is untiring. John Wilson his man carries them [the letters] to the post to be conveyed according to their several directions."[10]

Wilson, a Catholic layman, was the author of *The English Martyrologe* and a *Treasury of devotion*, both published at the St. Omer English College Press. He was also the translator of four Anglo-Catholic texts. As Press director, he assumed editorial duties and wrote dedications for at least fourteen books. Udall refers to him in another capacity, implying that he may have been the "Wilson" who coöperated with the Dabscots in their program of smuggling books into England from the Continent.[11]

Wilson was doubtless involved in the export program, but his principal preoccupation from 1608 to 1640 was the supervision of the publication of an approximate one hundred ninety-one books of which one hundred thirty-four were issued by 1626. His presswork was regarded as greatly superior to that of other Continental printing houses producing English books. The expenses of the Press were considered high but nevertheless justifiable, since the new publications were designed to refute "the pernicious inventions and books which the heretics issue every day and do so much harm to the souls if not confuted. The Catholic books penetrate where the priests and religious cannot and serve as precursors to vndecieve many."[12]

Wilson's *Martyrologe* was in all likelihood the first book to have been printed at the St. Omer English College Press. It is of interest to observe that all works published by the Press appear without imprint. Wilson obviously chose anonymity to safeguard his publications from investigation by the searcher once they reached England. By 1612 the Press had attained its peak productivity issuing seven books annually for several years. The St. Omer publications reflect the principal desiderata of the English Catholic: writings of the Church Fathers, St. Albertus Magnus, St. Augustine, St. Jerome and St. Thomas a Kempis; devotional books including the treatises of Francesco Arias, Miguel de Comalada, Gaspare Loarte and Luis de Granada; Manuals of Prayer and Missals as well as the controversial writings which widened the breach between the Catholic and Protestant camps: the texts of Edward Coffin, Thomas Fitzherbert, John Floyd, Humfrey Leech, Sylvester Norris, Father Persons, John Percy, John Sweet and others.[13]

Owen refers to the importation of "Popish bookes and other Papist merchandise" which were transported into England "either secretly with some forrayne merchants goods or else with some Ambassador's goods." Gee alludes to St. Omer imprints which were circulating in London. Of the titles cited by him fifty have been identified as books printed at the College Press. Gee's listing usually includes only the title – often scarcely comprehensible – as well as a sarcastic, personal comment. According to the author of *The Foote out of the snare*, all of the texts which have been identified as St. Omer College Press imprints, were greatly overpriced.[14]

Gee's criticism also extended to the books published at Douai whose University on the River Scarpe, south of Lille, had been established more than thirty years before its sister seminary of St. Omer. The College at Douai had been founded by Cardinal Allen in May 1559 to supersede the English foundation of Liége. Allen seriously hoped to gather together at Douai English students and priests scattered over the Continent. The principal positions at the newly founded institution were held by English exiles, among them Richard Smith, former Regius Professor of Divinity at Oxford, who was to become the College's first chancellor. Dr. Allen obtained his licentiate at Douai in 1570 and was to become its Regius Professor in Divinity. The College was disbanded in 1578 because of extreme anti-English feeling. The students and faculty sought refuge in Rheims which was to produce its most enduring monument in 1582, the English translation of the *New Testament*. Allen refers to the vast undertaking in his diary of March 1582: "Hoc ipso mense externa manus Novo Testamento anglice edita imposita est." With order restored to Douai, the English exiles returned in 1593, re-establishing the College under the chancellorship of Dr. Richard Barrett. The College was to pursue Allen's original design, to train a body of clergy for the conversion of England.[15]

A 1620 report to the House of Commons declared that "many persons of great quality in the Court and other places have their sons in Dowa." Students were brought to Douai much in the same manner as to St. Omer. Udall reported to Lord Salisbury in December 1605 that Henry Kiene or Keene was known to be "a common transporter of young children to Douai." Henry Barker, the conveyor of priests and books – according to Udall – "who now dwelt at the further end of Tower Street leading to the River this weeke hath his jorney entended for the Low Countreyes."[16]

Although no printing press was maintained officially at the College, the town was of significance for the productivity of its presses which were to rival the St. Omer College Press in the exportation of Anglo-Catholic texts to the motherland. Udall refers to "Peter Orroy an ordinary printer" of the town and is familiar with five of his publications. Auroi, like Bellet, was an independent publisher, issuing an approximate twenty books at his premises on the Rue des Ecoles from 1596 to about 1628. His name is associated with the standard devotional treatises of Fulvio Androzzi, Ignacio Balsamo, Luis de la Puente and the first edition of the popular hagiography, *Flos sanctorum*, which had been translated by the Kinsmans. In addition he issued the controversial treatises of Matthew Kellison, Richard Broughton, Thomas Fitzherbert and others.[17]

Naturally Auroi and Bellet were well acquainted with the house of Boscard. Jacques Boscard had printed for the College of Douai during its brief exile at Louvain, his son Charles taking over the firm in 1596 although his mother apparently retained some control. A 1601 edition of Thomas Worthington's *Relation of sixtene martyrs* bears the imprint "Doway, widow of James Boscard." The younger Boscard continued his parents' press "At the Sign of the Golden Missal" until 1610, issuing only twelve books. In that year Boscard departed Douai for St. Omer probably lured by the brighter prospects of a fast developing college press. Bellet had either retired or died and as a printer Boscard could compete only with John Heigham in fulfilling commissions for the Seminary Press. Boscard remained at St. Omer until his death about 1630, after which his business was continued by his widow.[18]

Boscard had been offered some inducement to move to St. Omer. On condition that he remained in the town as a printer for three years, he was granted release from guard duty and from taxes on his dwelling, wine and beer. In addition, the magistracy offered him an annual stipend of one hundred florins. Boscard fulfilled his pledge, remaining at St. Omer where, "At the Signe of the Name of Jesus," he issued a variety of devotional and controversial books several of which were known to John Gee.[19]

One work only can be attributed to Henry Taylor, the English exile at Douai. He issued in 1624 an *Appendix of saints lately canonized and beatified by Paule the fift and Gregorie the fifteenth*. Taylor's publishing career is certainly of questionable significance. He emerges as a figure of ambiguity in the shadowy world of spies and counter-spies. As early as 1605, Sir Clement Fisher had informed the English Privy Council that he had received letters from one "Henry Tailor" who stated that he would inform their Lordships of "the many seminary priests that are harboured near us." The Council instructed Taylor to use "his old haunts and when he had renewed his familiar acquaintance" he was to forward to their Lordships "secret intelligence" for the arrest of priests and Jesuits. For his service Taylor was to be given a grant of ten pounds and to have his "press and prints" restored to him.[20]

The Council's employment of Taylor suggests that he had been formerly apprehended as an underground printer; his familiarity with Catholics was now to be made available to the Crown. Later Taylor abandoned the precarious role of informer or was dismissed as an agent by a dissatisfied regime. As a Catholic, he had sought exile abroad. He apparently spent some time in Louvain for he confessed in 1616 he had acted as typesetter, assisting with the composition of "that base lying pamphlet intitled Corona Regia." By 1622 the turncoat Taylor appears to have settled at Douai, where he informed the Rector of the College that the spy Richard Floyd had supplied the English agent, Turnbull, with a Catalogue of Catholic books printed at St. Omer "these past six years." He added that Turnbull had been informed of the publication of the notorious *Corona Regia* of Caspar Schoppe which had been issued with a French title "un fleau pour un Escossais."[21]

Taylor represents to some extent the flotsam of the English exile abroad, some teaching and working – others studying at the English seminaries in Flanders, France, Germany, Spain and Italy. With the overcrowding of the Douai College in 1579, Dr. Allen had sent students to Rome, where the Venerabile Collegium Anglorum de Urbe was established. The missionary movement was in full stream. Seminaries were founded at Tournai and Louvain, at Braunsberg in East Prussia. The printer, Adrian Quinqué of Tournai, issued one work, while the Press of the Irish Franciscans at Louvain published several titles in Gaelic, including the writings of Comalada, St. Bonaventure and the Rule of the Friars Minor. The Seminary at Braunsberg was attacked for having published controversial tracts assailing the English regime. In Spain, Jesuit Colleges were set up for English exiles at Valladolid and Seville. Giles Arkenstall, a wheat shipper to Spain, declared in 1605 that he had gained access to certain Spanish religious houses which harbored English priests. He referred to the printing in Seville of George Doulye's *Briefe instruction . . . concerninge the principall poyntes of Christian religion*. He was apparently unaware of the Salamanca broadsheet printed a year earlier by Artus Tavernier, entitled *An extracte of the determinacion and censure of the doctours of the vniversities of Salamanca and Valledolid touching the warres of Ireland.*[22]

The Seminaries of Rome, Rheims and Valladolid were vehemently denounced in Elizabeth's Proclamation of 1591 which described them as institutions where "certain principal seditious heads . . . gather together with great labor . . . a multitude of dissolute young men . . . to be instructed in sedition, and from thence to be secretly and by stealth conveyed into our kingdom with ample authority from Rome, to move, stir up and persuade as many as our subjects as they dare deal withal."[23]

Official condemnation scarcely quenched Catholic zeal. Creswell suggested to Philip II that traffic off the coasts of England, Scotland and Ireland would be profitable not only for Spanish merchantmen but also for the Catholic cause, since at the same time they "could carry away six or seven students to the continent."[24]

By 1616 the Jesuits were engaged in the erection of a new college at Liége, a haven for English Catholics. Carleton commented upon the rapid rise of the buildings, which offered work to forty craftsmen, "sometimes a hundred which are well paid in English gold." The "Relation of the English Mission in the State of Flanders" alluded in January 1616 to the training of its novitiates who "after completing their studies and the usual probation are straightaway called to the trials and persecution in England."[25]

The penetration of Catholic books into England by exporters and importers exposed the latter to the same hazards confronted by colleagues during the reign of Elizabeth. The Edict of 1586 still applied against the importation into England of foreign publications "contayning matter derogatorie to the soveraigne estate ... impugning the orders and rites established by lawe for the Christian religion and deuine seruice within the Realme." In June 1604 Parliament voted upon a bill for the "reformation of abuses in bringing into this Land, Printing, Buying and Selling of Seditious Popish vain and lascivious books."[26]

The expertise of the English and foreign agent prevailed. The Venetian Ambassador to England, Marc-Antonio Correr, referred to the English College in Flanders directed by the Jesuits who were engaged in sending books into England. In 1605 Christophe de Harlay, the French Ambassador to England, deplored the recent importation of Pierre Dampmartin's *De la connoissance et merueilles de l'homme* which exposed the projects of the Duke of Alençon in Flanders. A word of warning was received by Salisbury from Udall in November 1607 that "never more seditious bokes were readye to come abroade then nowe are in hand as well in Englande as beyond the seas." The informer declared that copies of Father Persons' *Treatise tending to mitigation towardes Catholicke-subiectes in England* were "comming over in greater plentye than as yet they haue done." The following month the same gentleman presented Salisbury with news of the arrival of "the long expected Bibles from Dowaye." He stated that "one partye who went ouer for the bokes" had been arrested and imprisoned. A second agent was awaited momentarily.[27]

A shipment of forty-one Catholic books smuggled into England from the Continent was brought to the attention of Sir Julius Caesar in August 1609. The cargo included the writings of Richard Bristow, Father Persons, John Wilson, Cardinal Bellarmine, the *Manual of Prayers*, and copies of the *New Testament*. The books had been issued by ten different Flemish firms, among them Auroi, Boscard and Bellet, two having been published at the St. Omer College Press. They obviously had been sent to a coastal agent who shipped them to England. A larger consignment dispatched to England from Dunkirk was seized by the customs officer, John Westenholme, on September 13, 1609. The agent's prize included "10 books entituled Loue of the soule [by Gregory Martin], 26 bookes entituled Christian Doctrine [by Cardinal Bellarmine], 7 bookes entituled the A.B.C. teaching how to help the preest to say Masse [also possibly by Cardinal Bellarmine], 5 bookes entituled a Mirror to Confesse well [Part I of *Six spirituall bookes*], 3 books entituled A short rule of good life [by Father Southwell], 1 booke of The unlawfull Resurrections of the Protestants [by Frarinus], 1 booke of the Life of Christe [by St. Bonaventure], 2 bookes of Prayer, 3 bookes of the Confutation of John Ryder [by Fitzsimon], 2 bookes entituled The suruey of the new religion [by Kellison], 3 bookes entituled A treatise of Pollicey and Religion [by Fitzherbert] and 1 booke of the Lives of the Saints [by Villegas]." The majority of these twelve titles can be identified as Douai and St. Omer imprints issued by the presses of Boscard, Auroi and Lawrence Kellam. St. Bonaventure's *Miroure of the blessed life of our Lorde and Sauioure Iesus Christe* and *A manual of prayers* had just been printed in 1609 by Boscard, while Auroi had circulated the English version of the *Flos sanctorum. The liues of saints* by Francesco de Villegas translated by the Kinsman brothers. The inclusion of such new titles indicates the continuing interest of the English recusant community in the most recent Catholic texts which were promptly supplied by the Continental agent.[28]

During the early months of 1610 Udall boasted to Sir Julius Caesar of his extreme vigilance and competence, asserting that not only every book imported into England had been intercepted by him, but also "theyre bringers and receauers." He referred to the expected arrival of various texts by Father Persons, Francis Walsingham, Thomas Fitzherbert and Cardinal Bellarmine.[29]

An advice of November 1610 states that about fifteen hundred copies of "a book printed in Latin and English attacking the King's book and the Kinge's person" had been unloaded at "the house of a very important person." It is quite possible that the writer alluded to the reply either of Cardinal Bellarmine or of Father Persons to James' *Apologie for the oath of allegiance*. The recipient, fearful of pending inquiry and possible arrest, had burned the entire consignment, with the possible exception of one copy which, along with another offensive text, reached Salisbury's desk. According to Marc-Antonio Correr, this work also castigated the person and philosophy of James I "directed with infinite scurrility against the King." He believed that the book had been printed at Cologne but had been shipped from France. Correr's allusion was in all likelihood to the notorious *Prvrit-Anvs*.[30]

Books continued to be smuggled into England from France and Flanders throughout James' reign. The Archbishop of Canterbury, the mouthpiece of official indignation, referred in 1616 to the infiltration of Jesuits, secular priests, seminarians – with their agents and factors – who brought in "diuers popish seditious and prohibited bookes." Priests bound upon their mission often escaped arrest – others were apprehended and their contraband seized. The Jesuit, John Sweet, using the pseudonym of John Douse, was arrested in November 1621, when the searcher found upon his person "popish bookes [and] vestmentes." At the same time an agent Hill was accused of distributing Catholic books, crucifixes and beads. Letters of the Port Commissioners of Dover and Sandwich allude to the seizure of "certain dangerous books, crucifixes and pictures of the saints, Jesuiticall books and manuscripts."[31]

Underground stationers in 1621 surreptitiously sold copies of books printed in France which were considered to be highly contemptuous of the state. "One states that the king has granted free exercise to the Catholics ... the other that Parliament deposed [the king] beheading his favorites. This has incensed the King and everybody, although the vendors have been punished despite their outcry. They are considered to be the work of the Jesuits."[32]

A message conveyed to Secretary Conway from the Commissioners of

Passage at Dover in 1623 refers to the seizure of a large shipment of Catholic books. A total of fifty-two copies had been impounded, including 23 copies of *A manual of prayers*, 11 *Primers, or office of the blessed Virgin Marie;* 5 copies of *The firme foundation of Catholike religion, against the bottomles pitt of heresies* by Jean de Caumont; 24 copies of Achilles Galliardi's *An abridgement of christian perfection;* 5 copies of Thomas Fitzherbert's *The first part of a treatise concerning policy, and religion;* 6 copies of *The rule of our holy mother S. Clare;* 4 copies of Sylvester Norris' *The pseudo-scripturist;* 6 *Introductions (to a deuoute life)* by St. Francis of Sales; 11 copies of the *Following of Christ* of St. Thomas a Kempis; 10 copies of John Wilson's *Key of paradise;* 18 copies of the ever popular *Catechism* of Laurence Vaux; 18 copies of the *Catechism* of Cardinal Bellarmine and 5 copies of *Babel or Monarchomalia protestantium*. This sizable lot had been taken from two passengers who had embarked at Calais for England. It is evident that they were agents for the St. Omer English College Press, Boscard and probably other Flemish firms. Bellarmine's *Short catechisme* was printed by Mangius at Augsburg and the English *Primer* by Henry Jaey of Mechlin.[33]

The role of the English Seminary Press at St. Omer, the Flemish, Parisian and other Continental Catholic presses dedicated to the dissemination of English orthodoxy is of obvious significance. Their publications, brought to England at great risk, reflect the interdependence of the Continental printer and the English domestic community. The domestic importer encountered considerable danger and was subject to interrogation, arrest and imprisonment as well as financial loss. His foreign supplier, the printer and publisher, gambled economically but confronted far less personal hazard. It is true that shipments might be lost at sea or sequestered by an infuriated English government, but for the most part his person remained free. The patience of the home government was to be further taxed by the enterprise of two English Catholic printers and publishers in exile, John Heigham and Lawrence Kellam.

X

HARTIE WEL WISHERS

John Heigham & Lawrence Kellam

John Heigham illuminates the role of the English Catholic publisher abroad. He was a man of many parts: author, translator, editor, publisher, book agent and even possibly ordained priest. Heigham has been the subject of an excellent essay by the recusant scholar, A. F. Allison. Since his career epitomizes that of the devout Catholic, who aspired to support and strengthen his persecuted fellow-religious through the publication and circulation of orthodox texts, it is essential to reëvoke his life as scholar, publisher, exporter and "smuggler."[1]

John Heigham – who, until about 1610 called himself inexplicably Roger Heigham – was born about 1568. There is some possibility that he was related to William Heigham of Essex who turned Catholic and sought refuge in Spain. A marginal reference in James Wadsworth's *The English Spanish pilgrime* alludes to Heigham as the "boy assistant to W.W. bokebinder in London." This remark is somewhat anachronistic. Either William Wrench, the bookbinder and Catholic underground printer, plied his trade earlier than has been presumed, since Heigham, a man in his early thirties at the turn of the century, can scarcely be called a boy or Wadsworth may have referred to William Williamson of St. Peter's in Cornhill or William Wood of St. Paul's, neither of whom however specialized as binders. The earliest accurate evidence concerning Heigham is a certificate from the Keeper of the Gatehouse which reveals his arrest as a Catholic in 1597. Two years later Heigham embarked for the Continent, since he is included in a list of Catholics apprehended in 1599: "Heigham a lay man has been arrested at Dover crossing the channel. He was committed to Bridewell."[2]

According to a petitition submitted to the Privy Council at Brussels in July 1622, Heigham, after leaving England, settled in Douai. In his petition he stated he had always maintained "the free exercise of the holy faith and the Catholic Apostolic religion." He informed the Council that he had dwelt in the Netherlands for a period of nineteen years, there having married Marie Boniface, the daughter of Pierre Bourgeois of Arras, and during the years acquired a family. He referred to his participation "en diuers arts, es mestiers et signament l'art de l'imprimerie."[3]

Heigham's reasons for setting up as a publisher in the Spanish Netherlands are clear. As a Catholic in England, he could no longer abide official intolerance or pursue his profession safely. If Wadsworth's hypothesis is to be accepted, he had gained some experience in the stationer's milieu of London – and a Catholic one – if associated with Wrench. His religious belief obviously motivated his choice of a profession which enabled him to promote the orthodox cause and bring essential books to the persecuted in England. Quite naturally he sought to settle in the Spanish Netherlands which were in easy access to England and which boasted splendid colleges maintaining influential faculties in constant need of books.

Heigham's Catholicism is as patent as his antipathy toward the Anglican Church. He repeatedly refers to "the deep, mortall and canckred mallice of the wicked heretikes, their most execrable blascheumyes, together with manie most fearfull, vilde and damnable facts done and committed by them, in hatred and contempt of this diuine sacrifice [of the Mass]." He declared that "the heretiks of our age do bear so rabide a rage, so mischeuous a mynde and so spitefull a spleane ioned with such audacious attempts, barbarous abuses and insolent outrages as neuer the like were heard of befour our dayes." Referring perhaps to personal experience in England, he recalled the outrages against the orthodox: "For some rushing violentlie into the church where the Priest was celebrating [the Mass they] stamp[ed] under their filthie feete the sacred host and spill[ed] vpon the ground the blessed bloud." With emotion he expressed his dedication to his faith: "Soe long as I liue, [I shall] cast myself under the feet of the meanest Priest in the world to serue him as his foot stole."[4]

Heigham was to fulfill his vow, for his press was to serve not only the needs of the "meanest Priest" but also the requirements of the layman. As a publisher in Douai, he addressed himself to his fellow Englishmen as their "hartie wel wisher and most affectionate countryman." Heigham was ever conscious of his responsibility to the English domestic community. In the thirteenth chapter of Ignacio Balsamo's *Instruction how to pray and meditate well*, which he and Thomas Everard had translated from French into English, Heigham suggested twenty-eight titles to the reader stating that "all of them are to be found in our English tongue." These included general Catholic texts published not only by Heigham but also by other Continental presses.[5]

There is some slight probability that Heigham was ordained as a priest or monk. He is listed by Gee – whose accuracy may be questioned – among the group of "Romish priests and Iesuites now resident about the city of London." He is alluded to as "F. [rater] Heigham author of many loud-lying Pamphletts."[6]

Actually Heigham was the author of only two "loud-lying" books, translator, editor and publisher of many. The first edition of his *Exposition of the holie masse, with ample declaration of all the rites and ceremonies* appeared at Douai in 1614; a second edition "reuiewed and augmented" by the author was issued in 1622. The book is ample testimony to Heigham's religious fervor. He cites his reasons for its composition and clearly defines the service of the Mass. The author states that "fower causes first moued [him] to explicate . . . the mysterres and Ceremonies of the holy Masse." He refers to its "incomparable dignitie and most excellent sublimitie of this diuine and dreadfull sacrifice." He had been inspired "by the most singular honor respect and revere[n]ce which the deuout and Catholike people of all places, of all ages, and of all callings haue ever borne and carried to this sacrifice." Lastly he had undertaken the work because of "great and long want of a full and perfect exposition of this diuine mysterie in our English toung, by reason that none of our nation have purposlie written of the same (or ought that I euer sawe) these fortie yeares." Hence Heigham's *Exposition* was animated by his own spirituality and the obligation he felt toward the English-speaking Catholic world wanting a missal in the vernacular. Now the simple man could follow the "sublimitie of this diuine and dreadfull sacrifice" in his own tongue. At the end of his career Heigham wrote and published his treatise, *Via vere tuta, Or the truly safe way*, in which he slashed at the opposing religious doctrine of the divines John Preston and Sir Humphrey Linde.[7]

His desire to support his faith is further attested by his editions of Peter Canisius' *Summe of Christian doctrine* and Nicholas Sanders' *A treatise of the images of Christ, and his saints*. He states in the former that he has included "A Catalogue of the Fathers and Doctours [who] are in this Booke alledged that thou maiest see how much auncient defendours we haue of the Catholike truth. In my iudgment 2 principall thinges thou shalt finde in this Book, of themselues sufficient to confirme thy own Faithe and to confound the negative Religion of all adversaries. The first is the very naked and sincere truth very plainly and expressly set down. The second is the multitude of witnesses of her sinceritie." He had believed it a most opportune time to issue Sanders' work: "First, that the labour of so learned a man should not utterly perish, nor lye any longer in obscuritie, as many other learned works, written by our Catholique Doctours now have done for many yeares, which by Gods assistance I haue resolued likewise to set forth a new. Secondly, for that this question of Images, seemeth still a great stambling [sic] block, to our adversaries, especially to the simple sort: and hath by none of our side been more clearly and more excellently handled in our English tongue, then by this Author." In order that the reader "myght better defende himselfe and be the more confirmed in [his] holy faith, and withall wonder at the blindnes and hardnes of Protestants harts," Heigham would not "fayle to ioyne with [them]."[8]

Heigham's linguistic skill was put to good use in his numerous translations. His knowledge of Latin may have been derived from his possible training in the priesthood. As a resident of the Spanish Netherlands, he naturally understood Spanish and French. It was from the latter language that he translated "A briefe and profitable exercise of the seauen principall effusions of the pretious bloud of our lorde and Sauioure Iesus" [1604], forming the sixth part of *Six spirituall bookes*, in all likelihood his first publication. The second edition of 1611 includes *A tratise [sic] of the loue of God* by the Spanish mystic Luis de Granada translated by Heigham. In 1618 Balsamo's *Instructions how to pray and meditate well* "Composed, att the request of certeine louers of pietie" appeared in Douai, having been translated "out of French into English by Iohn Heigham." The following year the Heigham Press issued *Meditations vppon the mysteries of our holy faith* by Luis de la Puente which was advertised as

"Translated out of Spanish into English, by Iohn Heigham." In 1622 he translated and edited St. Bonaventure's *The life of our blessed Lord and Sauiour Iesus* which was based upon the *Meditationes vitae Christi*. The same year Heigham published his French version of *The true Christion catholique* of Philippe d'Outreman.[9]

The Six spirituall bookes "ful of maruelous pietie and deuotion," probably Heigham's first publication, had been compiled and edited by him. His initials are appended to the second and third parts. "Certaine deuout and godlie considerations to be exercised whilst ... Masse is celebrated" reads "Newly set foorth by R. H." and "Diuers deuout considerations for the most woorthie receiuing of the Blessed Sacrament" bears the initials R.[oger] H.[eigham].[10]

A manual of prayers had been originally compiled by George Flinton, director of the Persons-Rouen Press which issued the work in 1583. By 1613 it reached its thirteenth edition when reprinted by "Iohn Heigham at Doway." Seven years later he issued a revised and enlarged edition announced as *A manuall of godly prayers and litanies taken out of many famous authors and distributed both for the morning and evening exercises for all the dayes of the weeke. With the hymnes and prayers for the principall holy-dayes. Whereunto is added all the psalmes of King David vsed in the Primer with the offices of the holy Crosse and the holy Ghost*. Like the *Manual of prayers*, the popular *Catechisme* of the English divine, Lawrence Vaux, had been printed eight times, having appeared in 1568 and 1574 with the Louvain and Antwerp imprints of John Fowler. A new edition was published in 1620: "Reuewed and amplified ... by Iohn Heigham." The Jesuit, William Kinsman, who had been detained and interrogated as the agent for Viscount Montague, had translated with his brother Edward *The liues of saints* of Alfonso de Villegas. Auroi had issued the first English edition at Douai in 1610. The work was revised and published in 1621 by Heigham, who announced the "second edition ... more correct, and more exact then the former." As a man of letters, Heigham wrote dedications of Jan van Paeschen's *Spiritual pilgrimage of Hierusalem* and *The life of the blessed virgin sainct Catharine of Siena* by Raymundus de Vineis.[11]

With the publication of *Six spirituall bookes* Heigham began his formal career as a publisher, a role which was to bring to the Catholic world at home and in exile an approximate sixty-six books largely of a devotional and controversial context. It must be emphasized that Heigham was a publisher, not a printer, who maintained two centers of activity, Douai and St. Omer. His earliest premises were at Douai, where he engaged the printer Pierre Auroi of the Pelican d'Or on the Rue des Ecoles in close proximity to the College. Auroi was to print for Heigham intermittently until the end of the publisher's career about 1631. At Douai, Heigham also engaged Charles Boscard at l'Escu de Bourgogne not distant from Auroi's premises. Boscard moved in 1610 to St. Omer where Heigham set up a second office and commissioned Boscard to print the majority of his books. Boscard died about 1630, his wife continuing to work for Heigham. There is some evidence that Heigham enjoyed a fairly close relationship with the St. Omer University authorities. According to Wadsworth, a student Anthony Browne who had become "wearied of their [the faculties'] tyrannical discipline and desirous to get his necke from their yoake" counterfeited a letter from his father to the University rector. He apparently used as his intermediary "one Higha[m] a booke seller, who liued in the Towne and vsed often to the Colledge, who deliuered it to the Poste which comes weekely fro[m] London to St. Omers, to that end he should give it to the Rector."[12]

It is none the less doubtful that Heigham had great sympathy with a fractious student. His interests were confined principally to his publications which embraced books of religious instruction, devotional and controversial treatises, church history and hagiography. The most popular of the Heigham imprints appear to have been his editions of the different *Primers*, the "Latin and English" issued in 1616 and 1621; the "Latin, with English rubrics" published in 1614 and 1623; and the "English" printed twice in 1631. *The Primer. The office of the blessed Virg. Marie, with the rubriques in English* – published in 1614 – was advertised "for the commoditie of those that doe not vnderstand the Latin tongve." Editions of his compilation of *Six spirituall bookes* appeared in 1604, 1611, 1618 and 1624, the last edition entitled *The psalter of Iesus*. The work contained at the end a privilege granted to Heigham for publishing "six liures spirituelles en Anglois."[13]

The ever popular *Introduction to a deuoute life* of St. Francis of Sales "translated into Englisg" [sic] appeared for the first time with Heigham's imprint in 1613, to be reprinted twice, in 1617 and 1622. The writings of the Spanish mystic, Luis de Granada were represented in the Heigham trade-list under the titles *A memoriall of a Christian life* and *Of prayer, and meditations* issued in 1612 and 1625. Other popular treatises sponsored by Heigham were the devotional writings of Fulvio Androzzi, Cardinal Bellarmine, Diego de Estella, Father Robert Southwell, Thomas a Kempis and others. Controversial polemics included those of Richard Broughton and Thomas Fitzherbert. Church history and hagiography were represented by the *History of England* of the Venerable Bede and by two editions of Villegas' *Liues of saints . . . Whereunto are added the liues of sundrie other saints of the vniversall chuerch*.[14]

Heigham's Douai and St. Omer texts were set by foreign craftsmen whose faulty English is occasionally evident. An *Introduction to a deuoute life* of St. Francis of Sales reads "translated into Englisg," while the imprint of the fourth edition of the *Psalter of Iesus* bears an inverted "n" and is "imprimted" at Douai. Heigham attributed the errors in Anthony Champny's *Treatise of the vocation of bishops* to the "authors absence from the presse" which fact had caused "diuers escapes in the print." He suggested that the reader consult the two-page errata inserted "for the correction of the most and chiefest of them." Press errors and delays were ascribed by Heigham in 1622 to the "continuall warres in this countrey and the manifolde difficulties which all those that liue here about doe feele." For these reasons he had been unable to complete to his full satisfaction the printing of the second part of the 1622 edition of *A summe of christian doctrine* of Peter Canisius. He regretted that he had been "constrained to finish the worke without ful accomplishment of [his] promise and purpose."[15]

Despite the prevailing difficulties, Heigham was to attain his zenith by 1624 when he issued nine books. Twelve Catholic texts, bearing his imprint, had been published between 1622 and 1623. Apparently confident of his position, Heigham in July 1622 petitioned the Privy Council at Brussels for the privilege to publish, sell and distribute nine books to the exclusion of his Flemish competitors. He stated that the late Archduke had granted him the right to print books of devotion and piety in English. With his appeal he sent an endorsement of Paul Boudot, Bishop of St. Omer, who referred to Heigham as a man of substance. The Bishop admitted his inability to render judgment upon Heigham's projected list of publications since he was unfamiliar with English, but was confident that the texts contained nothing contrary to faith or religious tradition – having consulted qualified scholars. Heigham's request appears to have been granted, since the works were published during the subsequent years.[16]

Heigham's Petition to the Brussels Privy Council to publish, sell and distribute his publications came to their attention in 1622. His personal activity as a shipper of Continental Catholic texts to the homeland was known far earlier to the foreign service of the English government. There is evidence that prior to his formal establishment as a Douai publisher, Heigham had been active as an exporter of Catholic books. A letter from Richard Fulwood, Father Garnet's assistant in England, informed Heigham that only half of the catechisms ordered from Dr. Worthington had arrived in England. Dr. Worthington at the time was Rector of the English University at St. Omer and well may have engaged Heigham as his shipper.[17]

Five years after Heigham's arrival at Douai there is mention of his participation in the traffic of Continental Catholic books. Udall expressed his amazement that when Heigham visited England in 1608 he had not been arrested by Bishop Bancroft, since the informer had "offr'd his grace the apprehension of Roger Higham who printeth and sendeth into England all the seditious bokes which come from Dowa and other partes." According to Udall, Heigham had slipped into England as an agent for the Jesuits attempting to "send them ouer yonge youths with good positions." He apparently had persuaded seven or eight to join the College of St. Omer.[18]

A report to Sir Julius Caesar of November 1609 refers to two books which were being dispatched to England from Calais under Heigham's supervision. Both publications, Thomas Fitzherbert's *The second part of a treatise concerning policy, and religion* and Villegas' *Lives of saints* had been recently printed by Kellam and Auroi at Douai. Udall added that Heigham had also been responsible for the distribution of Cardinal Bellarmine's reply to James' *Triplici nodo, triplex cuneus*. There is evidence that Heigham and the younger

John Fowler coöperated in the exportation of Catholic texts from the Continent. Sir Julius Caesar was informed in August 1609 that Sir William Waad had observed Heigham in the company of Fowler at "Callys" where they had "receaued fowr cases of bookes from Paris which they convayd to Saint Omers with great secresy." He believed that the material to be sent to England included among the suspect titles, "those leud bokes sent forthe in French against his Majesty" which "might with some care be intercepted." Sir Julius Caesar was to docket the information with the comment: "Touching 4 packs of vilde bookes sent from Paris to Saint Omers and from thence to England."[19]

Udall erroneously attributes to Heigham the publication of Father Persons' *The iudgement of a Catholicke English-man, living in banishment for his religion;* the work actually having been printed at the St. Omer College Press. Heigham however did act as agent for the College – as previously suggested – and attended to the exportation of the "whole impression" which, according to Udall, had "either latelie come [or] was to come immediately." As receiving agent in England, Heigham had sent over his Flemish-born wife, Marie Boniface, wearing the "habite of a Dutche woman." Referring to Mrs. Heigham and Joan Dabscot, Udall declared "two more dangerous women for these causes [are] hardly to be found." He averred that both ladies were familiar with the printing and distribution of *Prvrit-Anvs*. At the same time he excoriated the spouse of Marie Boniface, stating: "There hath not bin any boke of state, otherwise brought into England or printed beyond the sea but it hath ben performed by Roger Higham or his wife." Mrs. Heigham was arrested in England in 1609 and confined to the pursuivant's tender care for at least two weeks upon the charge of importing six copies of a treatise by the Irish Jesuit, Henry Fitzsimon.[20]

There is every reason to believe that Heigham persisted in the exportation of Catholic texts through 1624 when Gee refers to his presence in London. Either Marie Boniface had died or was no longer active since she does not appear among the group of ladies branded by Gee. Heigham published only ten books from 1621 through 1631. The disorders prevailing in the Netherlands and the renewed persecution of Catholics in England may have combined to discourage the veteran publisher. War had broken out between England and Spain and peace would not be restored until 1630. Heigham either died or retired in 1631 at the age of approximately sixty-three. He had completed a career which emboldened the Catholic cause in England. He had shirked no responsibility and had run the risk of arrest and possible death. He was a courageous, faithful Catholic who ever remained to the orthodox English community a "hartie wel wisher and affectionate countryman."

The activity and influence of Lawrence Kellam, the Elder, cannot be compared with that of Heigham. Kellam spent some time in England as a missionary, departing for the Continent where he established a press specializing in Anglo-Catholic texts. McKerrow's statement that Kellam was a German first heard of in

1598 must be corrected. Kellam lived in London where, as early as October 6, 1587, he was indicted as a recusant and referred to as "Lawrence Kellam yeoman."[21]

In a report two years later submitted by Tobias Matthew, Bishop of Durham, to Cecil, there is allusion to the importance of South Shields as a Catholic center. It is described as "a port town in the north of the Tyne," on the coast of the North Sea, a suburb of the Catholic stronghold Newcastle, "the chief landing place for Jesuits" who not only brought in books but also used the harbor for sending "boys and others beyond the seas to seminaries." Matthew remarked that the Jesuits had been granted the use of a house at South Shields "belonging to one Ursula Taylor a recusant to receive and lodge the boys and Lawrence Kellam a treasurer recusant there to furnish them with money and other needful provisions." Kellam's role appears to have been that of chief of the commissary and disperser of missionary funds. In all likelihood the Taylor home was raided after the reception of the good Bishop's letter in London and Kellam was compelled to seek a haven on the Continent. His whereabouts are not known until 1598, when he emerges as a printer at Louvain. Here he remained until 1600, having issued only three books: *A Christian directorie* of Father Persons; *A spiritual doctrine, conteining a rule to liue wel* by Luis de Grenada and *A facile traictise, contenand [sic] . . . ane infallible reul to discerne trew from fals religion* by the Scottish Catholic divine, John Hamilton.[22]

Kellam had moved by 1605 to Douai, certainly attracted to the city by the growing reputation of the English College. At his premises, "The signe of the Holy Lambe," he was to print until his death sometime between 1611 and 1613 twenty-four English Catholic texts. Like those of Heigham, they represent devotional and controversial writings by well-known English and Continental writers. The larger proportion of Kellam's imprints concerns controversial issues. Unlike Heigham, Kellam was not a publisher, but a printer who supervised press production. He occasionally associated himself with other craftsmen: Foigny of Rheims and the local printer, Pierre Auroi. Several of Kellam's publications were printed anonymously or appeared with a fictitious imprint. The controversial work, *The doleful knell of Thomas Bell* bears the colophon "Roane 1607." Like many of his contemporaries, Kellam was guilty of some carelessness in printing. His edition of the *Manual of prayers* advertised as "Now newly corrected" appeared with an inverted "n" and errors in the text.[23]

One of the first books printed by Kellam at Douai in 1603 was Matthew Kellison's *A suruey of the new religion* which Gee declared sold "at a high rate" in England. The Kellam list included the writings of such controversial authors as Thomas Fitzherbert, John Fraser, Richard Smith and Humphrey Leech. Devotional works comprised the ever popular *Contempte of the world* by Diego de Estella, the anonymous *Breefe collection concerning the loue of God towards mankinde*, and the much desired *Manual of prayers* not only "Now newly corrected," but also "more augmented and enlarged." Three hagiographical compilations grace the Kellam list: Pinelli's *The virgin Maries life;* Thomas Worthington's *Catalogue of martyrs in England* and St. Bonaventure's *Life of the holie father S. Francis.* Miscellaneous publications related to church doctrine and ritual. By 1604 the firm of Lawrence Kellam was sufficiently well known on the Continent to have ascribed to it George Doulye's *Briefe instruction . . . concerninge the principall poyntes of Christian religio[n]* which in all likelihood had been published by Francisco Perez at Seville.[24]

The crowning achievement of Kellam's career was his publication of *The holie Bible* "faithfully translated into English out of the authentical Latin. Diligently conferred with the Hebrew, Greeke and other Editions in diuers Languages." The translation had been done principally by Gregory Martin with the revisions of Cardinal Allen, Bristow, Rainolds and Worthington. The *Bible* bears the imprint "printed at Doway by Lawrence Kellam at the Signe of the holie Lambe. M.DC.IX." The dedication refers to the delays which retarded the translation: "they al proceeded (as manie do know) of one general cause, our poore estate in banishment." The translation had been finally completed in "these hardest of times, of aboue fourtie yeares since this college was most happely begune." Having reached England, copies of the Douai *Bible*, according to Gee, sold in London for "forty shillings . . . at an ordinary price might be afforded for tenne."[25]

The iustification and exposition of the diuine sacrifice of the masse of Henry Fitzsimon was probably the last publication bearing the imprint of the Elder Kellam. He died between 1611 and 1613. Edward Maihew's *Paradise of praiers* carries the colophon of the "widdow of Laurence Kellam, 1613." Mrs. Kellam was to print only five books through 1616, following her late husband's selection of texts. Either the "widdow Kellam" died in 1621 or relinquished the supervision of the press to her son Lawrence Kellam, the Younger, who was to continue the firm at least until 1639. His publications conform to the pattern established by his parents. The name, although suffering some slight alteration, had continued to bear influence, since in 1622 Dr. Worthington's *Anker of christian doctrine*, printed secretly in England, was attributed to the Douai press of "Thomas Kellam."[26]

Heigham and Kellam, the Elder, rank during the reign of James I as the principal English exiles publishing and printing Catholic books abroad for local and domestic consumption. Other Continental firms, stimulated partly by economic necessity and partly by conviction, made some contribution. The endeavors of the Flemish houses of Conincx, Seldenslach, Vervliet and Keerberg of Antwerp; Quinqué of Tournai; Jaey of Mechlin and the Irish Franciscans of Louvain; the French firms of Foigny of Rheims, Hamillon of Rouen and Prevosteau of Paris and others, cannot be overlooked. Their books, along with those of Heigham and the Kellams, found their way to the English agents to be shipped to the motherland; to fall occasionally into the hands of the pursuivants; to be destroyed by the fires piled high at St. Paul's Cross. Undeterred by harassment and danger, Heigham, Kellam and their colleagues epitomize the dedication of the Catholic stationer abroad to abet Catholicism at home.

XI

AN HONEST MAN SENT TO LIE ABROAD FOR THE GOOD OF HIS COUNTRY

The English Ambassador

The imprints of Heigham, Kellam and their predecessors, Fowler, Diest and Laet, made their way not merely to the modest homes of the English devout but also to the loftier residences of dignitaries and foreign plenipotentiaries.

The standard manual for the conduct of foreign ministers at the time of Elizabeth was *A Short Treatise about Ambassadors* by Bernard du Rosier which had been published in 1555. Rosier outlines the privileges of the diplomat whose status, he declares, had been clearly defined by civil and canon law. His own person was regarded sacred since "he acts for the general welfare" and the immunity granted him was to extend to members of his suite. His choice of religion was not to be questioned and his chaplain was to remain free of all molestation; both were permitted to import whatsoever they required for the observance of their faith.[1]

Obviously the ambassador – his "person sacred" – was beyond reproach or question. His was practically an unassailable position which sanctioned no criticism or censure from the resident government. As the minister of France, Spain and the Empire, the appointee was naturally a Catholic, employing a diplomatic corps of similar persuasion. Setting a pattern to the co-religionists of a foreign nation as well as to his own personnel, the ambassador punctiliously performed his religious duties. As a Catholic in England, where a foreign minister was at odds with the accepted faith, he not only exercised his religious duties scrupulously but encouraged orthodoxy.[2]

Both the foreign minister in England and his English counterpart abroad enjoyed, theoretically at least, an exalted position. None the less both were compelled to perform for their governments tasks – viewed from a modern point of view – somewhat trivial, among them the tracking down of offensive books. The correspondence of Lord Burleigh and Sir Francis Walsingham frequently alludes to the interception of books odious to Her Majesty's government. The action of the English minister reflects not only the sensitivity of Elizabeth to criticism but also English influence abroad.

A letter of Lord Burleigh to Walsingham of January 1572 refers to two noxious books, "the one of Carpenter the Apostate, the other by an unknown malicious French writer taught by a rebellious crafty priest of England, wherein ... he vomiteth his choler." Burleigh had advised Walsingham to arrest the authors, although he was fully aware of the difficulties involved. He was of the opinion that they could be tracked down through the printers of both works and suggested to Walsingham that he would gladly give a reward upon their apprehension. He urged the immediate destruction of the books, railing against "the licentiousness of those [who] inveighed against men by name in printed books." Burleigh had been infuriated by the publication of the anonymous *Lettre* of Pierre Charpentier, a Huguenot, who none the less, had approved the St. Bartholomew Day Massacre and attributed much of the civil and religious disorder in France to the reformed extremist. Burleigh inveighed violently against the *L'innocence de Marie royne d'Escosse* by François de Belleforest, the very book which had proved itself incriminating evidence against William Carter. A note of December 1588 refers to the titles of several seditious texts recently circulated, among them *Maria Stuarta regina*. A memorandum of two weeks later states that Walsingham intended to forward to Burleigh "a book of lies translated from the Spanish." Burleigh had importuned the assistance of the French ambassador in the detection and seizure of Belleforest's text, threatening that his government was prepared to take steps for noncompliance.[3]

A particular literary canker regarded by the English authorities as corrosive and corruptive was the publication of Cardinal Allen's *Admonition to the nobility and people of England and Ireland concerninge the present warres* which had been written in Rome and sent in manuscript by the Spanish Ambassador to Antwerp where it was anonymously printed at the order of the Duke of Parma. His Excellency planned to distribute it throughout England after the successful invasion of the Armada. Allen's vituperation of his Queen exceeded in virulence any of his earlier writings. The public and private life of Elizabeth was denounced and the role of Philip of Spain as the redeemer of England extolled. He was commended as the saviour who would drive this infamous woman from her throne and salvage the country for the greater glory of Catholicism. The vilification of a Queen of England and the castigation of her rightfully inherited Crown – by a born Englishman – infuriated her government. Allen's excoriation demanded immediate action. The involved mechanism of diplomacy, springing into play, with its detailed reports between the English foreign office and its Continental agents, foreshadows the official warnings of modern nations, threatening and counter-charging in the permanent cold war of the present.[4]

Sir Henry Killigrew, English Ambassador to the United Provinces, was instructed to receive all copies of Allen's work. By June 6, 1588, Killigrew had enlisted the services of the eminent Dutch diplomat Philip van Marnix, Sieur d'Aldegonde, the former burgomaster of Amsterdam. Killigrew assured Lord Burleigh that Aldegonde was pursuing every clue to discover copies of this "traiterous libel" and had even employed his wife who "hath good acquaintance in Antwerp." Through his own network of spies Killigrew had already learned the name of the printer and the place of printing. He had also heard from Aldegonde that the *Admonition* had been printed in Antwerp "by order from the Duke but secretly and it is to be spread among the fugitive English and Irish." The Ambassador continued that steps had been taken to trap the dispersers of the book. He had already written to his Antwerp agent for a description of "the stature, countenance of those who receive these books and give them abroad to England." A week later Cardinal Allen arrived in Bruges, where he gave "encouragement and counsel to his familiars to hearten them upon their voiage to England." Writing to Lord Burleigh, Sir John Conway, Governor of Ostend, stated that the *Admonition* was "to be sent and spread in England to sow sedition before hand at the first landing."[5]

Obviously infuriated by the prospective circulation of the *Admonition* in England, Elizabeth herself sent instructions to her Commissioners in the United Provinces, informing them if the work were not suppressed, diplomatic relations between the two countries would be suspended. She declared: "We are assured of certain vile books printed in Antwerp by his [Parma's] command and a Bull of Pope Sixtus V. If he shall say he is not acquainted with this book and bull nor assented to be executioner of the bull you shall require him in our name that the printers of the book and bull may be taken and punished according to the quality of their offence and the books burned." If Parma refused, the Commissioners were to depart the Netherlands.[6]

Alessandro Farnese, Duke of Parma, appears to have been somewhat shaken by the wrath of Elizabeth, Queen of England. A report of Killigrew, dated June 30, 1588, states that Don Ambrosio Madragon, Parma's Commander of the Horse, had arrested and jailed a disperser of Cardinal Allen's book. He informed Lord Burleigh that Madragon was retaining the remaining copies and hence "the books by this means will not be so common." Don Ambrosio's detention of one disperser proved to be scarcely sufficient appeasement. Killigrew continued to remain in close contact with Aldegonde and the Pensionary Roels both of whom had acquired as many copies as possible. By July 11, 1588 Dr. Valentine Dale had been summoned by the home government to deal personally with the Duke of Parma. His message to the Lord Secretary must have left Burleigh somewhat confused since he stated that Parma had not "precisely insisted upon the punishment to be inflicted upon the printer of those seditious pamphlets which commonly are said to be printed in one place when indeed they are printed in another. And it is commonly reported that these libels were printed at Arras."[7]

Four days later, July 15, 1588, Dr. Edward Burnham informed Walsingham that Aldegonde's wife had, upon a recent visit to Antwerp, hoped to obtain a copy of Allen's *Admonition*, but, he added, "there is not one to be got and the printer is in prison." Parma, apparently alarmed by Elizabeth's threats to suspend diplomatic relations, had ordered the imprisonment of the printer who appears to have been the Antwerp stationer and publisher of Anglo-Catholic texts, Arnout Conincx. Despite this official step Killigrew anticipated exportation of available copies of the *Admonition* to England by clever Catholic agents. On July 18, 1588 he sent to Lord Burleigh "pictures of Cardinal Allen's factor and the Jesuit by whose means the books are to come abroad." Notwithstanding Killigrew's measures and the efforts of Aldegonde, Roels and their agents, copies of the *Admonition* circulated in England before and after the Armada. Had not the infuriated Burleigh demanded the impeachment of dispersers of this infamous work "on the grounds of treason"? The printing and importation of the Cardinal's libel into England were no mere tempest in a teapot. The *Admonition* was designed and recognized by the English government as a literary salute to the Armada – a herald of the glorious triumph of the Spanish fleet and the Catholic conquest of England.[8]

Killigrew had worked diligently as a trusted and faithful servant of the Crown. Other diplomats had striven earlier to call in foreign printed books and tracts odious to Her Majesty's government. In July 1583 Sir Henry Cobham, English Ambassador to France, reported to Walsingham that the Jesuits had shipped to Rouen "two dryfatts" full of books to be circulated in England, Scotland and Flanders. He named as their agent one Pierre l'Huillier, "librairier of the city." Their plan was to conceal the books in a boat transporting Cobham's personal effects to England. The material is described as "their newly translated testaments, catechisms and some pamphlets concerning the Jesuits miracles done in sundry countries."[9]

Lord Burleigh's treatise, *The execution of justice in England for maintenance of publique and christian peace*, was published in England in 1583. In it the author strove to prove the equality and mercy of English justice. It provided the official justification of Elizabeth's treatment of the Catholics and it is the best statement of Burleigh's position in this matter, emphasizing above all the English struggle against the ancient and long-standing enemy, the papacy. Reaction to the work was far-flung and diversified. The clemency of the government described by Lord Burleigh had been scarcely granted to members of the Catholic faith.[10]

The Execution of Justice in England, addressed to the English public and foreign governments, was promptly translated into French, Italian and Latin. After the appearance of the 1584 Latin edition, issued in London, an agent, William Herle, reported to the Queen that he had taken to the Netherlands two dozen copies of the recent Latin translation as well as the French and Italian versions. With enthusiasm, he declared that he had distributed copies which were "marvelously liked, insomuch that the Archbishop of Cologne caused them to be translated into High Dutch to be dispersed all Germany over." The Dutch edition, *D'executie van iustitie in Engelandt*, was published by Richard Schilders at Middleburg.[11]

The reaction of William, Cardinal Allen to the treatise of William, Lord Burleigh differed totally from that of his eminence, the Archbishop of Cologne. The English churchman made an immediate protest and issued his *True sincere and modest defence of English catholiques that suffer for their faith . . . against a false . . . libel intituled the Execution of Justice in England*. Sir Edward Stafford, Cobham's successor as English Ambassador to France, reported Allen's reply to Lord Burleigh in August 1588, announcing that he was sending him a copy. "It is printed, as I hear at Rheims though they say in Germany, marvellously closely kept here from selling, not to be had for money. I got those I have from one of their faction who tells me that 'two companies' [lots] of them are gone into England, two hundred in a company. There is I think no speaking of having them called in first because they are secretly sold, secondly because they would make men believe it is because we are touched to the quick; thirdly for speaking against the publishing of them maketh them more desired and better believed by a great many."[12]

Two months later Stafford informed Walsingham that an Englishman using a false name "Stinter" had visited Rouen, having brought with him three or four copies of Allen's *Defence*. Stafford advised the Secretary of State that he knew where another two copies were concealed, adding that they were "very closely kept. There is a bruit that three or four hundred of them were taken to one port of England." The scrupulous Stafford, alert to the circulation of books unsympathetic to the Crown, had unfortunately not familiarized himself with foreign type-faces, since he reported to Walsingham that he had been unable to find out where the *Defence* had been printed: "They themselves say in England or Flanders, which I think true for it could hardly be done either at Rouen or here [Paris] without my knowing of it." Alas, poor Stafford! *A true sincere and modest defence of English catholiques* by William, Cardinal Allen had been recently printed at the Rouen press of the Jesuit, Father Robert Persons![13]

A year earlier Stafford had sent Walsingham "the coppie of a leafe of a booke" which was in the process of printing. The Ambassador had dispatched a plate of a forthcoming illustrated book, *Briefve description des diuers cruautez que les Catholiques endurent en Angleterre pour la foi* originally published in English at Antwerp. The plates had been engraved by Richard Verstegan, the former printer of Smithfield. Stafford assured Walsingham that the "discoverer" of this enterprise would bring him "to the light of all the rest when ytt is donne." He inquired whether he was to request the French authorities to suppress those plates already printed.[14]

Shortly after this communiqué Stafford sought the help of the French Queen-Mother, Catherine de' Medici whose assistance appears to have been prompt. Verstegan's press was searched; "the son of the printer ... the corrector and an Englishman arrested." Stafford urged the French Secretary of State, Claude de Pinart, Sieur de Cramailles, to continue his pursuit of "the authours and accomplices" because the work "touched upon the honour of the Queen." Consequently Verstegan's plates were confiscated and the author imprisoned with the printer. Despite the suppression of the plates, the book was published at the end of December. The papal nuncio, Girolamo Ragazzoni, chided Henry III of France who, as a Catholic, could have hindered the appearance of a book which delineated the persecution of the Catholics in England. Actually, however, since Verstegan's work assailed the English Queen, the diplomatic entente between France and England had been violated and the anti-defamation law challenged. The author and engraver, the news-agent and spy, the former "Smythfield Prynter," Verstegan, remained in prison until July 1584.[15]

Stafford still at the embassy in the summer of 1586 continued to supply Walsingham with dubious foreign publications: "a new knavishe book yesterday only published abroad." He took umbrage at the French edition of *Vallenger's Martyrdome of M. Campion Jesuite* originally issued by the recently incarcerated Master Verstegan. Through royal intervention Stafford had its dispersers jailed, having secured the assurance of Henry Valois that he "would not suffer anything that might touch her Majesty to be published here." Had not Henry III of France, the former Duke of Anjou, been a suitor to the artful and astute Elizabeth?[16]

Despite the French King's desire to appease the English Queen, anti-English books continued to circulate in Paris. They were particularly attractive to the Leaguists, avowed enemies of Elizabeth. Their leader, Henry Duke of Guise, was nephew of Mary Stuart whose head was to fall at Elizabeth's command in February 1587. Stafford expressed his indignation in June 1587 at the appearance in Paris of the vicious *Advertissement des Advertissements* by Jean de Caumont who had castigated Elizabeth for her treatment of Mary Stuart. The Ambassador attempted to have all copies of the work suppressed. He advised Walsingham that he had searched for the printers and sellers of the book, but they had fled; "some were put in the guard and the books which were very few in respect of the great number printed were torn and burnt." Orders had been given that existent copies "in towne be kept secret."[17]

A letter of January 1588 forwarded by Stafford to Walsingham reflects the growing general awareness of the forthcoming naval encounter between Spain and England. "They carried a book yesterday here of the defeat of a great many of our ships ... by the Prince of Parma's forces. Every body here knoweth it to be false and laughed at it; but yet it maketh a noise in the street." The following April he advised Lord Burleigh of the publication of the "villainest book that ever was set out ... there is not possibly another yet to be got; they be sold secretly."[18]

Four books of Anglo-Catholic interest were published by Continental presses in 1589, three of them in the Netherlands, one in Paris. In June 1589 an English agent, stationed at Middleburg, sent Walsingham "one of the many gibing books which are now printed in these countries [Flanders]." There is every reason to believe that he referred to Father Creswell's *Copy of a letter, lately written by a Spanishe gentleman, to his freind [sic] in England; in refutation of sundry calumnies, there falsly bruited*, which had been anonymously issued by Trognaesius at Antwerp. The printer had informed the English agent John Gylles that he had published this and other books upon order of the States. Their circulation was eventually prohibited but only after they had been "sold openly on the Bourse for six days."[19]

By the time James had succeeded to the throne, the overt practice of Catholicism by members of the diplomatic corps had begun to irk the regime with its fast developing Puritan segment. The tendency of James on the other hand to shower affection and lavish praise upon a new favorite was to continue and eventually to envelop the person of the Spanish ambassador to England. In his concept of kingship, James was disposed habitually toward exalted beings, notably foreign diplomats who were men of noble birth, traveling with large, wealthy, lavishly accoutred retinues. Demanding the nation be ever mindful of the "great Reuerence and Respect" owing to "Ambassadors, Agents and publique Ministers of forraigne Princes and States," the monarch insisted that they were to suffer no "insolencie, misbehauiour, inciuilitie, disgrace or affront" and that all Englishmen were to show to them and their attendants "courtesie both in speech, gesture and otherwise as is most fitting to proceede from persons of ciuill behauiour vnto men of that eminence . . . vpon paine of his Maiesties highest indignation and displeasure."[20]

The embassies in London which housed these "publique ministers" were invested with richly appointed chapels, frequented by many English Catholics denied the public observance of their faith. Writing to the Doge and Senate, Marc-Antonio Correr, Venetian Ambassador to England, referred to the services which had formerly been conducted by the "second chaplain" of the late French Ambassador to England. "He ministered not only to foreigners but to the many English Catholics who openly attend my chapel especially since the departure of the Spanish ambassador who had four chaplains in his suite." It was reported further that Mass was celebrated attended by "diuerse Catholickes" at the residence of the Spanish Ambassador in Seething Lane, where an Indulgence sent from Rome had been read to the worshipers. In August 1606 many faithful were arrested by pursuivants upon leaving the Spanish Embassy. Udall, in all likelihood striving to impress Salisbury, boasted that Fowler had brought to the Spanish Embassy a shipment of two thousand five hundred books![21]

The French Ambassador to England, Christophe de Harlay, Comte de Beaumont, became an intimate of James I and was dubbed "an earnest suitor to the King in behalf of the Catholic." He attempted to promote the cause of the Catholic Appellant group, presenting James with copies of their "books, petitions and memorials including Colleton's *Supplication*. When the King began to read it he fell into great passion and with many oaths trod it under his feet, and yet after took it up and perused it."[22]

The Venetian Ambassador to England, Torzi Giustiniani, considered the publication in London of a broadside, *News from Venice*, a work of "insolencie and incivilitie." This ephemeron had been presumably issued by the bookseller Francis Burton of the White Lion and written by "an English gentleman a resident of many years in Italy who had freely discussed Italian princes and their government." The author had averred that "the preachers in Venice preach loudly against Free Will, teaching the people that we have free will only to evil." Giustiniani took immediate exception to its appearance, demanding that all copies be seized and burned. He declared the work anti-Catholic propaganda replete with "falsehoods prejudicial to the undiminished fame of the Republic for piety." Salisbury, disturbed by this affront to a foreign court and a resident dignitary, ordered its immediate suppression and demanded that "all [copies] found at the printers and booksellers [be] forbidden them on the pain of death." The author was to be confined to his residence "until the Grand Duke's pleasure be known."[23]

Giustiniani's successor as Venetian Ambassador to England, Marc-Antonio Correr, was to find his diplomatic residence in London in May 1609 a source of considerable embarrassment and the provocation of English indignation. According to Correr's testimony, he had very kindly maintained on his staff "a wretched priest" who had been second chaplain to the late French ambassador. Wotton affirmed that the cleric was English-born at Bruges and educated at the College of Douai. Correr informed his home government that the priest had been the cause of "anxiety and great trouble" to him, averring that he ministered "not only to foreigners" but also to the many English who "openly attend my chapel especially since the departure of the Spanish ambassador."[24]

Despite his protestations Correr had inquired not too deeply into the activity of his priest who had deposited at the Embassy, among other books, copies of the odious *Prvrit-Anvs*. Correr stated that the books had been taken out "one by one" by the agent of a certain person "as they were required for sale and circulation among Catholics." He maintained his complete ignorance of the entire affair, assuring the home government of his zealous prosecution of this distasteful matter. Contrary to his statement that copies were taken out "one by one," he added that for all his diligence he could not detect that "any copies of the book *[Prvrit-Anvs]* had been brought to the house except four in the hands of the priest who says he gave one to the French Embassy, one . . . to me and others to private individuals."[25]

Correr could not have been too surprised by the visit of the Secretary of the Council, Sir Christopher Parkins, to the Venetian Embassy, where six hundred copies of *Prvrit-Anvs* were discovered in the porter's lodge. Correr's aplomb – if not his position – was at stake. Thereupon he himself "forced the doors of the priests room but found nothing." The Embassy cellar was now thoroughly searched and "3 cases and some bales of books in English" were seized.[26]

An inventory of the "cases and bales" found in the Embassy is docketed "A Catalogue of Books received from the Ambassador at Venice taken from the Dutch priest at his house." The List which cites copies as "many" or "some" includes twenty-five titles of which two have been struck out. One, however, is still discernible – *Prvrit-Anvs*. Quite possibly, aware that the List had been compiled by Parkins or some agent for the State Department, Correr had importuned the official to delete the offensive name to spare him further embarrassment. Correr's "wretched priest" was apparently a Continental book agent having brought with him not only copies of *Prvrit-Anvs* but also of other titles issued by the St. Omer College Press, Boscard, Bellet and Antwerp and Rouen firms. The shipment included among others several treatises by Father Persons, Southwell's *Short rule of good life*, *The dialogues* of St. Gregory, *The spiritual conflict* of Lorenzo Scupoli and *The firme foundation of Catholike religion* by Jean de Caumont, Worthington's *A catalogue of martyrs in England, The history of our B. Lady of Loreto* of Orazio Torsellino, writings by Bristow, Woodward and others. The dossier cites a copy of the Rheims *New Testament* and Doulye's *Briefe instruction . . . concerninge the principall poyntes of Christian religion* ascribed to the printer Perez of Seville.[27]

The "Correr Affair" brought not only discomfort to the Ambassador of the Venetian Republic but disrepute to the domestic Catholics. James advised all foreign dignitaries in 1610 not to admit English subjects to Mass in their chapels and not to permit English priests to conduct services. Apparently his warning was not heeded too seriously since the following year Sir Thomas Lake informed Salisbury that if English subjects did not desist from attending Mass at the Spanish Embassy, it would prove imperative for the government to station a guard at the residence for their arrest.[28]

English officialdom desired no open rupture with Spain and in 1612 when the Spanish Ambassador complained that a consignment of books addressed to him for the use of his chaplain had been seized by a customs man, the Earl of Northampton promised the immediate release of the shipment. He explained that this action had been an error on the part of the inspecting officer who believed the package had been intended for an ordinary person. The matter was immediately referred to the Privy Council and the Catholic books delivered to Zuñiga.[29]

On the other hand the home government failed to yield to the protest of the Venetian Ambassador, Antonio Foscarini, who in 1615 had taken umbrage at the sale of a book in England of "the worst nature." The diplomat referred to the recently published *Squitinio della liberta Veneta*, a satirical denunciation of Venice, attributed to the Marquis de Cuevas, copies of which had been brought to London by English stationers attending the Frankfurt Book Fair. Bemoaning its scurrilous attack upon the Republic, Foscarini denied that the book had been printed at "Mirandola," stating that the publisher had lied as "to time and place." He informed his home government that he had entertained some idea of prohibiting it, "as it seems prejudicial to your service that such a thing should be publicly sold but . . . being better advised I have covertly bought all copies I have found and have thus provided a remedy."[30]

With the shifting mood of the nation moulded by the King's desire for the Spanish marriage of Charles, the requests of the Catholic diplomats in England were carefully heeded. Writing to the homeland in June 1618, Contarini remarked that the Spanish Ambassador had requested James to release all the Catholic priests "now in prison here, the number being very considerable. I understand that with few exceptions they have all been granted on condition of quitting the country." Not long thereafter James had "beene pleased at the earnest instance of M. le Mareschall Cadinet, late ambassador extraordinaire with his Majesty from the French King, to release from prison seminary priests and other religious and ecclesiastical persons." They were to be banished from England with their "bookes, vestments and other thinges." The influence of the Spanish Ambassador was such that Jesuits were released from prison at his request and later sought asylum at the Embassy, where they "were visited by many men of the Spanish faction, including some Catholics, of whom there are many in the Kingdom and in London."[31]

An anti-Spanish writer was later to denounce the brashness and arrogance of the Spanish Ambassador to England, Diego da Sarmiento de Acuña, Count of Gondomar, who asserted that he had "dasht the authority of the High Commission; upon which there are diverse Pursevants (men of the worst kind of condition) resembling our Flies and Familiars attending upon the Inquisition whose office and Imployment is to disturb the Catholicks, searching thier [sic] Houses for priests, Holy Vestments, Books, Beades . . . and the like religious Purtenances. I haue caused the execution of their office to be slackened."[32]

Although many demands of the Spanish Ambassador had been met, he had scarcely won the respect of the anti-Spanish publicist Thomas Scott who lampooned his presumption and arrogance in the *Vox Populi*. A Venetian informant declared the work was circulating in certain London quarters, adding: "The Spanish Ambassador foams with wrath in every direction and it is said he has sent it *[Vox Populi]* to the King to make complaint." The news specialist, Nathaniel Butter, was confined to jail for a month in May 1622 for his publication of *More news from the Palatinate*, a work "displeasing to the Hapsburg ruler."[33]

Ferdinand of Hapsburg was to become England's enemy in the Thirty Years War and despite the temporary Anglo-Spanish entente much anti-Catholic sentiment prevailed. The House of Commons had complained in 1621 that the principal cause of the increase of popery was the indulgence granted Catholics to attend Mass at the chapels of the foreign ambassadors. The indifference of the embassy heads to the proscription of Catholic books is reflected in the shipments addressed to the Spanish and French ambassadors.[34]

The Mayor of Dover advised Lord Zouch that a Frenchman, Abraham Siroise, had just brought over a load of one hundred eight dangerous books. He admitted that he had been unable to detain the gentleman because he had with him "a packet addressed to the French Ambassador." Upon returning to England after the absence of twenty-three years, Mary Bachelor, a Catholic, the companion of Lady Ratcliffe, declared that the beads found on her person were for the purpose of making bracelets, while the books she had brought over were intended as presents for the servants of the French ambassador. In August of the same year a shipment of one hundred seventy-one Popish books was landed at Dover "with notes of 152 which were demanded by the Spanish Ambassador." It appears that a printing press had actually been set up in the Spanish Embassy in London where it was rumored "a scandalous book is said to have been printed." Wary of official English reaction, the Spanish Ambassador was reported to have had his porter imprisoned for circulating copies. Earlier a publication, *The King and the Prelate*, had been found at the Spanish Embassy designed to counterbalance James' text, *God and the King*.[35]

Despite the growing hostility of the nation, the outspoken opposition of the House of Commons and the infractions of the Spanish and French ambassadors, James, in his admiration for "superior beings" brooked no "insolencie, misbehaviour, inciuilitie, disgrace or affront" to the resident diplomatic corps. Aware of the abuse directed against his favorite Acuña, Count of Gondomar, James issued his Proclamation of 1621 designed to restrain "prentices and other people from abusing or offering wrong to ambassadors, their followers ... in gesture, word or action."[36]

The ambassador to the English Court endeavored to protect the best interests of his country and – if possible – to abet the Catholic cause. The English ambassador, "an honest man sent to lie abroad for the good of his country," also strove to serve and protect the needs of his nation and – if possible – to stem the Catholic cause. His mission was not merely to preserve English relations abroad but also to acquaint the Continent with the particular virtuosity of his monarch, poet, statesman and theologian!

XII

THE FOREIGN CIRCULATION OF ROYAL TEXTS

James I, Author

As King of England, James was omniscient not only in matters of statecraft but also in the fields of belles-lettres and theology. The young prince at the age of ten, a pupil of the distinguished Scottish savants, George Buchanan and Peter Young, was "able extempore to read a chapter out of the Bible out of Latin into French and out of French into English." James, a devotee of poetry, in 1584 made his debut in literary criticism, with his *Essayes of a prentise in the diuine art of poesie* "containing some reulis and cautelis to be observit and eschewit in Scottis poesie." His poetic licence was further aired in the publication of *His Majesties poeticall exercises [The Furie, The Lepanto, la Lepanthe]* issued by the controversial printer Robert Waldegrave. For the most part the monarch's literary talent was applied however less to poetry than to prose and political and theological pedantry.[1]

James had published in 1598 *The true law of free monarchies* which reflected his concept of the kingship, an hereditary office, bestowed upon him by divine right: "The king is overlord of the whole land, so he is the master over the life and death of every one of them. For although a just prince will not take the life of any of his subjects without a clear law, yet the same law, whereby he taketh them are made by himself or his predecessors and so the power flows always from himself." Referring to James' assertions, Father Persons informed Cardinal Borghese that the work "treat[ed] of a free and absolute monarchy, maintaining that an absolute king is subject not to law, but is absolute lord of all things. If His Holiness wishes we will have it translated, for it is a small book but pestilential." There is no indication that His Holiness Pope Clement VIII ordered a translation.[2]

A David, exhorting his Absalom, James reiterated his political maxims in his *Basilicon Doron*, designed for the enlightenment of his son Prince Henry, aged four, stressing the patriarchal nature of kingship. The edition was printed privately in 1599 since James, vain and somewhat apprehensive regarding its reception, did not wish to offend his Presbyterian elders. Referring to this limited edition of seven copies, the author was to write: "I only permitted seven of them to be printed and these seven I dispersed among some of my trusted servants to be kept closely by them." The *Basilicon Doron* was to enjoy great popularity, being reprinted twelve times. The second edition appeared on the public market a few days after Elizabeth's death arousing general interest since Englishmen were eager to ascertain the talent and personality of their new monarch. Copies were avidly purchased for home consumption, while others were sent abroad by diplomats to acquaint their governments with the virtuosity of the English king. The work was translated into Gaelic in 1604 and appeared under various titles: *A princes looking glasse* and *The fathers blessing: or second councell to his sonne*. No matter how entitled it carried always the same message:

"God gives not kings and the style of gods in vain,
For on his throne his scepter do they sway;
And as their subjects ought them to obey,
So kings should fear and serve their God again. –
And so ye shall in princely virtues shine,
Resembling right your mighty king divine."[3]

The young monarch who had frequently been the victim of intrigue and cabal viewed the Gunpowder Plot with dismay. New anti-Catholic legislation was quickly introduced at the Parliamentary sessions of 1605/1606; the anti-recusant laws being accompanied with a new oath of allegiance. Those who took the oath declared not against the Pope's right of excommunication but against his claim to depose kings and to authorize their subjects to take up arms against them. Pope Paul V promptly denounced the Oath of Allegiance and Cardinal Bellarmine, in a letter to the Archpriest Blackwell, assailed James' position. By pronouncing the Oath of Allegiance inadmissible, the Pope placed English Catholics, who desired to remain loyal subjects of James and Rome, in an awkward if not impossible position.[4]

Piqued by the Papal breves and Bellarmine's letter, James composed his celebrated *Triplici nodo, triplex cuneus: or an apologie for the oath of allegiance ag.[ainst] the two breves of Pope Paulus Quintus a.[nd] the late letter of Cardinal Bellarmine to G. Blackwel the arch-priest*. Although the work appeared anonymously in 1607, having been printed by the King's printer Robert Barker, its royal authorship was an open secret. James had become so involved in its writing that Bishop Montagu stated: "I know not how it came to pass but the king's pen ran so fast that in the compass of six days his Majesty had accomplished that which he now calleth his Apology." James tauntingly challenged Cardinal Bellarmine to prove that "the pope may give leave to his subjects to violate his person." He enunciated the temporal rights of kings and recorded the infringements of their power by the Papacy. The staunch defenders of Rome, Cardinal Bellarmine and Father Persons, subsequently took up their cudgels and promptly replied to James' accusation. Udall was to report to Sir Julius Caesar in September 1609 that "From three seuerall places there are bokes unlawfull shortly to be conveyed into England. From Cologne (where Matheus Tortus was printed) commeth an answer to the kings boke. From Doway and St. Omers come an English answer to the kings boke." James had now initiated a flyting warfare which, according to the French ambassador, La Boderie, "put the author in his element for this is the science of which he knows the most and in which he most delights."[5]

Detecting some errors in the 1607 and 1608 editions of the *Apologie*, James set about to revise the text with the help of John Barclay. The new edition was reported to be on the press as late as March 1609. "His Majesty has little spared the Pope or his party which others do frankly imitate both in books and preachings without straining courtesy or mincing the matter any longer."[6]

The revised version, *An apologie for the oath of allegiance. Together with a Premonition to all most mightie Monarches*, appeared on April 8, 1609 following the royal proclamation the previous day which had called in all copies of the earlier editions. These, it declared, reflected the rashness of the printers and the delinquency of the examiners who had permitted the work to appear "incorrect of some faults varying from the original copies which do not a little pervert the sense." Booksellers were informed that copies of the earlier editions could be exchanged "without further cost" for copies of the new edition. On May 22, 1609 the new edition, *An apologie for the oath of allegiance: first set forth without a name, now acknowledged. Together with a Premonition to all most mightie Monarches* advised the Continental rulers of the Papal pretensions and ambition to curtail their royal sovereignty.[7]

James' political ideology is reiterated in the treatise, *Deus & Rex: sive dialogus quo demonstratur Jacobum regem immediate sub Deo constitutum justissime sibi vendicare quicquid in juramento fidelitatis requiritur* which appeared in 1615 and was reprinted six times. *God and the King*, although occasionally attributed to Richard Mocket, censor of the press from 1610 to 1614 and Warden of All Souls, Oxford, was in all likelihood written by James, since a royal command demanded that it be taught in all schools and universities and by all ministers of the church. It was to be purchased by all householders in England and Ireland, where the work was to be "universally receaved, dispersed and taught ... all parents and masters of families and every teacher or teachers, as well as men as women, private or public, teaching either in the English or Latin tongues, within the realm of Ireland [were] to take special care that all their youths and scholars generally and respectively may forthwith receive and be taught the said book either in English or Latin." The patentees of the Stationers' Company in Dublin were instructed to have a sufficient number of copies on hand "to furnish the realm from time to time" and were advised not to charge more than the official rate of six pence per copy. Thus, the king's interpretation of his divinely given stewardship over the entire realm was to be acknowledged in every city and hamlet.[8]

In 1616 James issued his *Declaration pour le droit des rois*, a reply to the criticism of his *Apologie* by Cardinal du Perron. There is every indication that he had been assisted in its composition by the Huguenot divine Pierre du Moulin who shortly after its publication was awarded a Doctor of Divinity degree at Cambridge, a prebendary worth two hundred pounds annually, a house and a gold chain.[9]

James – who had advised his young son in matters of state – also prepared commentaries on books of the Bible and kindred subjects. His interest in theological problems was deep and probing. The scholar Isaac Casaubon observed that "hardly a day passed in which some new pamphlet is not brought to him [James] mostly written by the Jesuits on the martyrdom of English Catholics or matters of that description. Neither his private affairs nor public business interest his Majesty so deeply as do affairs of religion."[10]

With a collected edition of his writings in mind, James expressed his dissatisfaction at the carelessness of his previous printers in a fairly lengthy letter of July 1, 1616 to the Master and Wardens of the Stationers' Company. The King declared that because of the "grose errors . . . o[u]r royall meaninge may be misinterpreted and thereby we may Consequentlye be abused." He thought it advisable not only "to p[er]use all such o[u]r writeings and works whiche haue ben formerly published to the ende that all former errors may be corrected and amended. But also wee haue Caused them, together wth such o[u]r works as haue not heretofore ben published, to be redvced into one volume, and haue authorished, licensed and Com[m]anded o[u]r trustie and welbeloued Seruant John Bill and his assignees onely, from henceforth as his and their proper Copie to imprint all such o[u]r works as heretofore wee haue written or hereafter shall be pleased to write." The *Workes* of James, King of Britain, France and Ireland appeared in three editions from 1616 to 1620.[11]

As an author James desired due acclamation for his writings. His *Apologie for the oath of allegiance* was sent abroad to be distributed by his ambassadors among the crowned heads of Europe. Copies were "bound in velvet with the coats of arms and corner pieces of gold, stamped with the rose and thistle, the lion and the lilies." Although James was certainly piqued at the cool reception of his princely dicta by his foreign colleagues, he remained totally indifferent to the reactions of other authors whose writings he had proscribed in England, often condemned and had tracked down by his ambassadors abroad. James' ministers became his literary agents, his censors. They distributed his *Apologie;* they helped destroy books offensive to their master.[12]

In the execution of their duties the royal plenipotentiaries were occasionally compelled to submit to their princely author uncomplimentary reports. Early in his reign James would have taken exceeding pleasure in the reaction of one of his most stubborn opponents, Father Persons, to the *Basilicon Doron*, a copy of which he had received from his Majesty. Writing to Father Garnet, Persons described the book as "a princely gift and a princely work. The reading of this book hath so exceedingly comforted me, as I have imparted also the same comfort to other principal men of this place and namely yesterday to His Holiness, who I assure you could scarce hold [his] teares for comfort to hear passages in favour of virtue and hatred to vice."[13]

The tears of Pope Paul V were to flow later with indignation and rancor at the publication of James' *Apologie for the oath of allegiance* – copies of which were circulated abroad by the English diplomats. The correspondence of Sir Henry Wotton reflects the reaction of Catholic Europe to the distribution of copies of the *Apologie* "bound in velvet, stamped with the rose and thistle, the lion and lilies." Writing to Sir Thomas Edmondes from Venice in July

1609, Wotton declared: "The principal subject of discourse at present through Italy is our good master's excellent work which the Deuil would fain hurt. France is said to have much openly approued it; Spain to have refused it." The *Apologie* which now had become a conversation piece in Italian political circles was to meet a fate akin to other literary effusions condemned by the royal author. Wotton hesitantly informed James in August 1609 that he had secured "a copy of that censure (for so they call it) which the Pope with his own hands delivered to the Venetian ambassador's secretary ... to forbear this state from receiving your Majesty's blessed labours – [The sumptuously bound copy presented to the Venetian Republic was to remain unopened in the state archives!] And the Pope seemeth to have dispatched the like to all Princes of his own colour with so incredible celerity."[14]

Despite the papal proscription of the *Apologie* Wotton attempted to assuage his master's wounded feelings and requested James to send him additional copies of the book by "His Majesty's best ships" since he had been "secretly solicited by divers persons to procure them copy." This note of comfort was rather hollow. Wotton was shortly compelled to inform James that Cosimo II, Grand Duke of Tuscany, had received "one of his Majesty's books and [had] consigned the same to his confessor who by order of the Inquisition there hath burned it. The Pope hath forbidden it in Rome by public edict and for the greater defamation coupled it with Beza's Confessions." Two weeks later Wotton informed Salisbury that the Venetian booksellers had been instructed to surrender their copies of the *Apologie* to the General Inquisitor. Aware of the curiosity aroused by a forbidden text, Wotton suspected duplicity on part of the Venetian book trade and therefore dispatched the author, Giovanni-Battista Biondi, to investigate the premises of the bookdealer, Giovanni-Battista Ciotto who, in his opinion, was the most Jesuitical of all. Biondi was advised to return to the dealer's shop within a few days since Ciotto expected a new shipment of the *Apologie* from Basle. Wotton added judiciously: "This prohibition will do nothing in this place but increase the desire and price of the thing prohibited."[15]

A Catholic convert, the highly popular Henry IV of France, presented with a copy of the *Apologie* threw it down, exclaiming "the writing of books was no fit business for a king." Philip III of Spain, Albert Archduke of Austria, Governor of the Netherlands, and the Holy Roman Emperor Matthias displayed less tolerance toward their Protestant cousin, refusing the copies presented them. Henry Howard referred to the reaction of the Spanish Ambassador who had spurned a copy of the work, an action which "gave some distaste."[16]

James had naturally been hurt by the harsh and indifferent reception of his political opus abroad. In October 1610 he waxed indignant about the circulation of a "slanderous French book against him." James probably alluded to *La Religion Catholique soustenue en tous les poincts de sa doctrine, contre le livre addresse aux Rois ... par ... Jacques I* by the Jesuit Pierre Pelletier who, the irate monarch suggested, was to be seized by the French government before he "sought refuge in the pope's dominions." Two months later James expressed his indignation at the delaying tactics of the French Parlement which had stayed the promulgation of an edict condemning Cardinal Bellarmine's *De potestate papae*, a reply to the *Apologie*. Infuriated, James had requested his ambassador to intercede with Marshal Villeroy and the Queen Mother, Marie de' Medici.[17]

James' vanity had been wounded by the reaction of Catholic Europe to his political manifesto. He was to vent his anger later against the German publicist Caspar Schoppe, author of the *Corona regia*, a taunting and offensive reply to the *Apologie*. Schoppe, a well-known German philologist, had abjured Protestantism and been awarded a pension by the Pope. Thereafter he spent much of his time heaping abuse upon reformers and scholars, slinging some of his most acrimonious darts against James Stuart. In 1614 he visited Madrid where, according to the Venetian Ambassador, he had received "handsome acknowledgments for his writings." Sir John Digby, English Ambassador to Madrid, complained to the Duke of Lerma and other Spanish dignitaries about Schoppe's vilification of his master. Realizing the complete indifference of the Spanish official corps, Digby resolved upon a course of action and "set ten of his servants upon the man [Schoppe] in the public street with orders to slay him." Schoppe escaped his assailants with a slight wound and sought refuge in a monastery where he declared his intention to draft other works against that "schismatic tyrant."[18]

James, never positive that Schoppe had written *Corona regia*, ascribed it tentatively to the Flemish philologist, Henri de Putte and commissioned his ambassador to the United Provinces, Sir Dudley Carleton, to pursue the putative author and his printer and "to stay all copies of the book." Carleton's delicate mission is revealed in a letter written to him by Chamberlain in November 1616 which states that the English plenipotentiary is to "demaund justice against him that made the scandalous libel called Corona regia which they finde by goode proofe to be Puteanus, the reader at Louvain." The search for the author and the printer was to become a minor *cause célèbre* and was to drag on for years.[19]

The case required the diplomatic skill of Sir John Bennet, Ambassador Extraordinary to the Archduke Albert and the harassed Carleton. According to the dispatch of the Venetian Ambassador to England, Giovanni-Battista Lionello, Bennet's mission concerned "a book which Dr. Puteanus of Louvain had written against his Majesty, not only in blame of his religion but full of slanders and especially with respect of his character." Lionello informed his home government that James desired the book to be suppressed since he felt this attack "more than any other thing that might befal him."[20]

The Schoppe affair lasted until 1623 involving the expertise of the English diplomatic corps which at times behaved almost ludicrously. Wotton advised Sir George Calvert in November 1623 that he had arranged a meeting at Cologne with one Bilderbeck, an agent for the States General, "a well affected and well intelligenced man" who enjoyed the confidence of the Count Palatine and "seemeth to be an instrument of good abilities." Bilderbeck had recognized the *Corona regia* as the work of Schoppe and assured Wotton that it had been printed by a former craftsman of Louvain, Christopher Flavius who was seeking now refuge near Cologne. He continued that Flavius had denied any knowledge of the work having stated that the type was French. He himself had bemoaned the circulation of so scurrilous a tract "by its first dispersers in Louane and Bruxelles" who he declared "were certaine Frenchmen that sold wafers and carried some of the copies up and down in boxes on their backs." Henry Taylor, the Catholic book agent and possible informer, also stated that Flavius had printed the work, admitting he had assisted with the composition.[21]

Wotton ascertained that Flavius was not at Cologne but at "Confluentia" [Coblentz] where he was engaged in the printing of certain pamphlets "which the Jesuits do feed him, but is extremely poor and kept in fear." To appease his outraged monarch, Wotton suggested to Bilderbeck the possibility of kidnapping the unfortunate Flavius who occasionally visited his former master, the printer Heyrat of Cologne. "I should think it no hard matter to snatch up Flavius and to convey him against his will in a covered boat down the Rhene to the confines of the States and so to England." There is no evidence that the victim of Wotton's madcap scheme ever reached England to stammer his apologies before the cold, supercilious Court of High Commission.[22]

A champion of the established faith, James had earlier directed his high office against the Arminian heresy. Holland had been stirred at the beginning of the century by the anti-Calvinist ideology of Jacob Arminius whose followers, including the German free thinker, Conrad Vorst, opposed the tenets of predestination and election. Concerned about the infiltration of Arminian doctrine into England, James in August 1609 importuned his ambassador to the United Provinces, Sir Ralph Winwood, to oppose the appointment of Vorst as Professor of Theology at the University of Leyden. Little attention was paid to the King's request. Copies of Vorst's heretical treatise, *Tractatus Theologicus de deo*, entered England illegally, motivating James' decision to have copies burned at St. Paul's and at Oxford and Cambridge. The monarch in 1612 busied himself with his personal condemnation of the Arminian doctrine of Conrad Vorst in five proclamations in French, Latin and English, *Concerning his proceedings in the cause of D. C. Vorstius*. One hundred copies were dispatched "with all speed" to Winwood who obviously was to acquaint the Dutch authorities with the sentiment of the English monarch and was to expedite their circulation. Winwood, supporting his king, referred to the reasons "which did move him to declare himself against Vorstius. We have under the press many answers to Vorstius his Apologies which come forth so much the more slowly, because in Holland inhibitions are made to write against him, but for him free Liberty and Permission is granted."[23]

The Dutch indulgence toward Vorst rankled James and to rescue England from the Arminian infection, Carleton, Winwood's successor as Ambassador to the

United Provinces, was informed in May 1617 that certain Arminian texts had been translated into English and had been printed at Hasselt a town not far from Utrecht. Carleton was advised to ascertain the facts – and if true – to "prevent the transport of them to England." The detailed correspondence between Carleton and Winwood reflects the irksome minutiae assigned to members of His Majesty's foreign service. Carleton promptly reported that he had sent agents to Hasselt and Campen ("a town well affected towards Arminians") and had been informed by them that "no books of Arminius translated into English had been printed in either town." Apparently unconvinced, Carleton sought to engage the coöperation of the municipal authorities of Hasselt and Campen to assist in the detection of Arminian texts, a search which proved fruitless.[24]

Provoked by his failure, the frustrated Ambassador delivered before the Dutch Estates in Autumn 1617 a caustic speech which initiated a series of indignant replies, among them the *Weegh Schael, Om in alle billickheydt recht te over weghen de Oratie van ... Dvdley Carleton Ambassaduer van den ... Coningh van Groot Britannien* attributed to Jacob Taurinus, leader of the Remonstrant faction. Carleton considered the reply "seditious against the state, scandalous to the reformed religion and personally injurious." By its very nature it reflected "dishonour upon the King his master." Carleton demanded that the Dutch government issue immediately an edict calling in and burning all copies. He personally promised a reward for the detection of the author and pardon to the printer if he gave himself up within two weeks. The case hung in balance. Carleton appealed to Barneveldt, claiming that wrong had been done to the English king "by those in Holland."[25]

The "wrong" done by Taurinus' tract was not amended since the work appeared in a French translation in 1618 enlarged with a sarcastic preface and a lampoon of the motto of the Order of the Garter. Carleton, having voiced his indignation with some vehemence, ultimately won the attention of the Dutch States General which agreed the matter had gone too far and that the international law of libel had been offended. They ordered that within the following three days the Dutch stationers deliver copies of the book which were to be burnt in "the chamber of their assembly." Secretary Lake believed that had it been done in the market place there would have "beene some satisfaction."[26]

Carleton was removed from his diplomatic post when the texts of a German publicist, David Pareus [Waengler], a disciple of Arminius, were surreptitiously exported to England. Tarred with the odious taint of Arminianism, Pareus was accused of entertaining positive opinions about the efficacy of tyrannicide. Knowledge of the circulation of Pareus' texts evoked in 1622 a decision of the Privy Council to condemn his doctrine as "dangerous and false." Since his books had been distributed among "the stationers of the cittie of London," the Bishop of London was to expedite "a speedie and diligent search in the houses, shopps and stoarehouses of all and every the said stationers" for these books. Upon their apprehension the texts of Pareus were "to be publickley burned in Paules church by the comon executioner of that citie" who was to be very careful that "not any one of the said bookes be saved or escapt the fyer upon any pretence whatsoever." Similar instructions were delivered by his Lordship to the Chancellors of the Universities of Oxford and Cambridge.[27]

The books of Pareus and Vorst had been banned and burned; the writings of Arminius searched out; copies of the *Apologie* of King James "bound in velvet and stamped in gold" had been presented to the Continental monarchs by those faithful emissaries of the King of England, his ambassadors. As his representatives, Wotton and Carleton, Bennet, Digby and Winwood had hoped to bolster and magnify the position of their monarch among his European colleagues. They had aspired to perform faithfully their every chore; immersed themselves in the minutiae of their office; withstood the rebuffs of indignant heads of state appalled at the effrontery of a Protestant prince – their agents had stalked the authors and printers of offensive tracts and books. They remained the officers of good will, ministers abroad personifying the dignity of England and the tenets of its established faith before the cool, calculating Catholicism of the Continent. Despite the panoply of office, theirs was scarcely an enviable role – enduring the whims and caprices of the aging monarch whom they conscientiously served.

XIII

AN ADMONITION TO THE PARLIAMENT
Puritan Reform

Elizabeth and James in the pyramidal structure of the nation represented the apex, the personification of authority invested in them as supreme heads of church and state. Political hostility to them and their realm implied lèse majesté, religious enmity, heresy. The Elizabethan and Stuart governments had applied to the Catholic opposition various modes of reprisal: arrest, imprisonment, torture and even death. The Catholic represented not merely a religious menace but a hostile, foreign danger, a political body emboldened by Continental power and strength. To the Crown his ambition suggested no striving for life celestial but a daily exercise in intrigue and plot, connivance with Jesuit cohorts, the circulation of insidious, treacherous propaganda. His was the determination to crush the state, to destroy the Crown bestowed upon Elizabeth and bequeathed by her to James I.

The Puritan lacked the vitality and unholy design of his dissident countryman, the Catholic. He accepted his monarch; he threatened no political revolution. His was a cause of high moral purpose; a purification of the Established Church, a diminution of panoply and pomp. He attracted a host of simple people who desired the regeneration of the country, a nation more chaste, undefiled. He criticized, but he did not rebel. He neither sought nor received foreign help. He suffered and endured persecution; he was upon occasion to flee his country and to observe his belief in a foreign land. Like the Catholic, the Puritan was sustained by his own conviction, his direct association with God, his communion of spirit, his temple of one or more, a tabernacle of worship. His affirmation of faith enabled him to plant congregations on the Continent and to build houses of prayer in the wilderness of a new and distant world.

The seeds of Puritanism were sown during the reign of Mary, burgeoning rapidly under Elizabeth into expressions of distaste against the Established Church which, according to the leaders of reform, had abandoned Christ for antichrist. Puritanism developed upon the bedrock of Calvinism; adopted the Pauline doctrine of faith, insisting upon the over-ruling power of God and His immanence in the individual soul. The Puritan identified himself with his own exclusive church, a congregation of saints, admitting to its number only those who could offer satisfactory proof of their divine election. Predestination was its canon and sainthood of the elect its aspiration.[1]

Divergence from the Established Church by the Catholic and Puritan groups concerned the state; to some extent moulding its domestic policy during the first year of Elizabeth's reign. A Proclamation of December 1588 forbade subjects to preach or to listen to preaching other than that of the Gospel and the Epistle of the day and "the ten Commandments in the vulgar tongue without exposition." They were to heed no public prayer except that established by law. Such legislation was issued for "the true advancement of religion." Apparent indifference to royal statute had provoked an official decree of 1571 which insisted upon no other service than that established by the Book of Common Prayer.[2]

The first public manifesto of the Puritan Party was issued in 1572, *An Admonition to the Parliament* by John Field and Thomas Wilcox, Puritan divines. The work marks the initial hostility of the reform group toward the national church. It was basically an appeal to the civil authorities that Parliament correct the abuses within the church and change it in accordance with Scriptural strictures. Its requests included a simplified service, bereft of pomp and extravagance, and the equality of ministers. The authors deplored the moral degeneration of their country which "so far from having a church rightly reformed according to the prescript of God's word that as yet we are not come to the outward face of the same." In their demand for a simplified service they attacked the Prayer Book as "an imperfect booke culled and picked out of that popishe dunghill, the masse book, full of abominations."[3]

Field and Wilcox were preachers in the Minories, the original home of Puritanism, imparting their message of reform to the "godly," their disciples gradually becoming known as the "new Catharites, the church-goers of purity." Their influence and the impact of the *Admonition* were observed by the authorities, among them Sandys, Bishop of London, who informed Lord Burleigh that the city would never be tranquil until these authors of sedition, who "are now esteemed as gods, Field and Wilcox, Cartwright and others be far removed. The people resort unto them as in popery they were wont to run on pilgrimages." Whitgift, the arch-foe of nonconformity, heaped ridicule and scorn upon the authors and their Manifesto, stating that it had been issued not only out of time but also out of order – "in the manner of a libel, with false allegations and applications of scriptures, opprobrious speeches and slanders. For if you ask of the time, the Admonition was published after the Parliament to the which it was dedicated was ended. If you speak of the place it was not exhibited in Parliament (as it ought to have been) but spread abroad in corners and sent into the country." The request of Bishop Sandys was to be met. Wilcox and Field spent a term in Newgate eventually to be released and to continue their reform crusade.[4]

The demands presented in the *Admonition* were swiftly heeded and the cause of the authors supported by one of the greatest of the Puritan reformers, Thomas Cartwright, whose *Second Admonition to the Parliament* followed promptly in 1572. His views were subsequently refuted by Whitgift whose charges were answered by Cartwright and others – a flyting warfare having been initiated by both sides.[5]

AN ADMONITION TO THE PARLIAMENT

Thomas Cartwright, "the head and most learned of that sect of dissenters called Puritans," was one of the most popular preachers in the reform group. It was declared that his sermons attracted such vast audiences of enthusiastic listeners that "the sextone was fayne to take down the windows of St. Mary's so great was the crowd that came to hear." His reputation had prompted Walsingham as early as 1582 to request him to compose a reply to the Rheims *New Testament* "and other books of the Jesuits" for which he was promised an annual stipend of one hundred pounds. According to Cartwright, God had revealed his will in the Scriptures alone which in turn laid down a rule of church government. The church was to act independently of all civil authority and was to render its first allegiance to God, its second to Caesar. Cartwright's ecclesiastical ideology and church organization were crystallized in a platform drawn up by the Puritan Walter Travers. His work, *A full a. plaine declaration of ecclesiasticall discipline*, was written in Latin and translated into English in 1574 by Cartwright. The survey treats the calling, conduct, knowledge and apparel of a minister, the office of bishop and pastor, the functions of a consistory. The *Declaration* attempted to bring to the simple and pure the tenets and fabric of the ideal church described in the Scriptures, "the discipline of Christ's church that is necessary for all times."[6]

The reform platform had been drawn up; the disciples of the ecclesiastical utopia fanned throughout the country, challenging the state, bearing pressure upon Burleigh already rankled by Catholic plot and scheme. "I do what I can," he wrote on August 5, 1573, "to procure fitte men to preache at the Crosse, but I cannot know their hartes, and these tymes have altered opinions. Such as preached discretlie last yeare now labour by raylinge to feede the fansies of the people." Bitterly he referred to a recent sermon delivered at Oxford the content of which "ray[ls] against this present state and affirm[s] to be good whatsoever Mr. Cartwright in writing hath sett downe. Such men must be restrained if the state shall stand saffe."[7]

As a student of Cartwright at Cambridge, Robert Browne had found his master's ideas too narrow, his concept of presbyterianism too inflexible. Browne left Cambridge to organize the church according to his own concept. His distinguished treatise, "Reformation without tarrying for anie," published in Holland in 1582, is the first work written by an Englishman which demands a full measure of religious liberty. The magistrate was to exercise no ecclesiastical authority whatsoever. A church, consisting of one or more, represented a group of "true Christians united in a company, a number of believers who placed themselves under the government of God and Christ." Browne's concept of a true religious existence was to be found in the voluntary association of individuals in a body independent of every other man. The influence of Browne and his disciple Robert Harrison upon the extremist Puritan circle is reflected in the Proclamation of June 1582/1583 which forbade the circulation of their writings in the homeland. Their printed books, it was declared, had been sent from Zeeland "to deprave [the] ecclesiastical government and to breed schism among the unlearned." The books were to be turned in to an Ordinary and their distribution forbidden. The first Independent Church established in Southwark was to be later dismissed by Bacon as "a very small number of silly and base people here and there in corners dispersed and now by good remedies suppressed and worn out so there is scarce any news of them."[8]

While the Brownist Church struggled for its existence, adherents of other reform sects, among them members of the Family of Love, also sought a haven in London. Henry Niclaes of Leyden had received early in the sixteenth century a divine summons to become a prophet and establish a Familia Caritatis. He wrote extensively on his mystic crusade eventually arousing the suspicion of local and more prominent authorities, among them, the high tribunal at the Council of Trent whose officers placed his writings on the Index. Between 1552 and 1553 members of the sect drifted into England where they taught the love of humanity and Anabaptist doctrine. According to an Address of the gentry of Suffolk to the Council, adherents could not sin, although their writers "cri[ed] out in the bitterness of their sould [sic] and groan[ed] before God under the burden of their sins yet labour[ing] to keep themselves and their profession undamnable before the world." The tenets of the Family of Love appealed as little to the government of Elizabeth as to the See of Rome. In October 1580 the sect was banned by royal proclamation condemning its "damnable heresies . . . as absurde and fanatical, as by fayning to themselues a monstrous new kind of speach neuer found in the Scriptures . . . by which they do moue ignorant and simple people." All persons suspected "to be either teachers or professors of the foresaid damnable sect" were to be seized and prevented "from further infecting [the] Realme."[9]

The country during the national crisis of 1588 had not suffered from the defection of the Puritans. Their loyalty was well attested in the Diary of the preacher Richard Rogers who had been deeply moved "with thinckinge on our late deliuerance from the rage of Spain as memorable a woorcke of God as ever was in my remembrance more than that of Monsieur" [the Duke of Anjou whose proposed marriage with Elizabeth was extremely unpopular]. Nonetheless the nation clamped down upon the Puritan sectaries as well as upon the menacing Catholics. In 1589 non-licensed preachers were denied the right to deliver sermons in London and the following year it was suggested that members of the Family of Love, Anabaptists and Brownists "overthrowers of the Church and common weal" all be punished.[10]

Although the Puritans had never sought foreign help for their spiritual crusade, Elizabeth considered them as dangerous as the Catholics. With some incredulity Sir Francis Knollys viewed her distrust of them since "she cannot be ignorant that the Puritans are not able to change the government of the clergy." Yet the Queen and her realm frowned upon the reformed sect who on the other hand viewed with dismay the position of many of their leaders confined to jail. Cartwright had been imprisoned in the Fleet; "Fenne of Coventry with many more in the Clink; [John] Udall sentenced to death. All these things seem but a way to bring in popery for atheism is here already, and soon will overflow the land."[11]

The prison abodes of the Catholic recusants, Newgate, the Clink, Marshalsea and the other stinking, loathsome jails were by 1593 to house members who refused the rites of the Anglican Church – sentenced to terms of three months. The Puritans' resentment against the Crown was further inflamed by the illegal arrest of the distinguished sectaries, Henry Barrow and John Greenwood, who were tried and sentenced to death for their religious principles. Writing to a correspondent in April 1593, Thomas Phelippes stated that a bill had been brought against the Barrowists and Brownists making it a felony to maintain any opinions against the ecclesiastical government. He declared that Barrow and Greenwood with others had been condemned "upon the statute" for writing and publishing seditious books. "They were hanged early this morning." The official intolerance of the government toward its politically non-hostile Puritan element was to drive from the nation some of its most high-minded citizens. Eventually, having sought liberty of conscience in the Netherlands, a small group was to establish in the new world a community of faith for its own, albeit bigoted religious opinions.[12]

The echoes of official reprisal against the Puritans in England were heard by the enemy abroad. Ever the man of news, the former English citizen, Richard Rowlande, now the Catholic correspondent, Richard Verstegan of Antwerp, apprised Father Persons in April 1593 that eighty Puritans had lately been arrested "at a sermon in Finisbury Field and with them Mr Martin Marprelate [John Penry] is thought to be taken. There was a Brownist hanged for his seditious tongue."[13]

The repressive measures of Elizabeth had silenced neither the Catholic nor the Puritan. Under James, Puritanism was to splinter among sectary groups and to achieve invincibility, to become almost a theocracy during the reign of his son, to divide a great nation, to cause strife and havoc unknown to Elizabeth and James.

Presbyterianism, which regarded itself as an independent spiritual power with authority to hold kings to account before God, could scarcely have been acceptable to James Stuart, God's appointee to rule his island kingdom. James could little accept the Puritan equation that if all men be equal before God, the sovereign must share the same position and submission. All mankind partook equally of the grace of the spiritual overlord Christ who reigned supreme above the temporal monarch, James Stuart.[14]

James had expressed his dislike of the Puritan sectaries in his kingly admonition to Prince Henry, his *Basilicon Doron*, referring to them as "uerie pestes in the church and common-weale." His first Speech to Parliament alludes to "a sect rather than a Religion . . . the Puritanes and Nouelists."[15]

A Catholic memorandum of April 1603 which pledged the loyalty of this minority to the new monarch referred to the prevailing sects in the Kingdom: "Protestants who domineered all the late religion; Puritans who have crept up amongst us [and] atheists who live on brawls." Fully aware of a growing divisiveness among the Protestant sectarian groups, James was soon to advise his subjects "to leave the care of the church to [his] princely care." He urged them not to use "contemptuous behauiour to ecclesiasts or indiscreet speeches in the pulpit or otherwise." His admonition was prompted by his desire to reign unruffled by theological debate and to preserve "the state Ecclesiastical and Politic."[16]

James, however, did not remain indifferent to the Puritan request for reform, and heeding the group's desire, summoned a conference at Hampton Court in 1605/1606. Soon wearied of the ministers' wrangling and disputation, James dissolved the meeting and relegated to his bishops power to expel nonconformists. In July 1604 he had assailed intractable individuals who, having failed to abide by orders, were to be handed over to the authorities.[17]

Although Chamberlain reported in February 1604 that the Puritans had been silenced and suspended, the sectaries continued to meet in London and other parts of the country. In 1616 a revitalized Independent Church was established at Southwark by Henry Jacob "on a day of solemn fasting and prayer." This followed the founding of several Anabaptist congregations at Gainsborough, in London at Pinners Hall and at Newgate under the leadership of John Murton. By 1621 the ultra-reform group had gained ascendancy, their influence felt strongly in the Commons where it was suggested that debate begin with a sermon. The Puritan sway is reflected in a letter of Joseph Mead who peevishly declared that "much was spoken at every hand against the Papists and cannon shot provided against them but never a word spoken against the Puritans, or so much as a mouse trap proposed for them."[18]

The ascendancy of the Puritan party had been gained through the vigorous determination of its divines and disciples. Their sermons, delivered from pulpits and street corners, were fast transmuted into the printed word. The Puritan press, like its Catholic counterpart, became the ancillary of the movement. Although the early Puritan printers were to issue manifestoes and dogma anonymously in England or from a haven on the Continent they never experienced the opprobrium and aversion displayed toward their Catholic colleagues. In their espousal of the reform movement they circulated countless sermons and tracts, homilies and moral lessons, triumphing eventually with the collapse of the kingship, when Puritan stationers were appointed printers to the Commonwealth.

XIV

PRINTING IN CORNERS

The Domestic Puritan Press

Robert Crowley has been regarded as the first English printer of Puritan doctrine. To his office he brought a strong conviction of faith and purpose. A 1582 Fellow of Magdalene College, Oxford, Crowley was to author a variety of treatises and was to serve with abounding confidence the Puritan cause under Edward VI and Elizabeth. His press and his pulpit have been described as "two prolific sources of faction [which] happily coöperated in propagating his principles of predestination – his shop and his sermons were alike frequented."[1]

Crowley wrote eighteen treatises of which more than one half reflect his Puritan allegiance. His *Briefe discourse against the outwarde apparell of the popish churche* indicates his participation in the "Vestments Controversy" which expressed itself in its criticism of the show and pomp of the Established Church. Crowley's high moral purpose is revealed in five works written between 1549 and 1551 which manifest some attempt to inquire into the baneful influence of a rigid social hierarchy. *An informacion and peticion agaynst the oppressours of the pore Commons of this realm* discloses to some extent the lot of the poor, their degradation and the indifference of the upper classes to their misery. *The voyce of the last trumpet blowen bi the seue[n]th angel* fulminates against sin advising each individual of his high moral responsibility. The first and second estates were to set an example to the third which was always to heed the lessons of virtue and obedience. In 1550 Crowley wrote two works of social significance, *One and thirty epigrams* and *The way to wealth*. The former, a series of short verse essays, exposes glaring social and moral abuses, while the latter presents the mutual distrust and hatred between the wealthy and the poor. The author condemns the upper class as "gredie comerauntes," but none the less advises the downtrodden artisan and peasant against rebellion and avarice. He reiterates the sin of greed in his *Pleasure and payne, heaven and hell* in which he deplores the "rakeyng togyther of the treasures of this vayne world." In 1587 Crowley "having had more spare time than in long time before" wrote his *Deliberat answer*, a refutation of opinions aired by the eminent Catholic divine, Edward Rishton.[2]

Crowley's literary career spanned some thirty years; his publishing role embraced two shorter periods. Setting up as a printer at Ely Rents, Holborn, in 1549, he was to issue through 1551 fourteen books, the majority of which reflect his Puritan association. These – in addition to his translation of the *Psalms* – include writings by the Welsh lexicographer, William Salesbury:

Baterie of the pope's Botereulx, commonly called the high altare; his translation of the *Bible* from Welsh into English and two works in Welsh. As a nonconformist, Crowley issued in 1550 *The true copy of a prolog written in an olde English Bible* by Wiclif, the most notable of early English religious dissenters. Crowley's three editions of Langland's *Vision of Piers Plowman* rank as his most notable literary publications.[3]

No known work appears to have been issued by the Master of Ely Rents during the last two years of Edward's reign. In 1551 he formally solemnized his religious profession by receiving orders as a deacon from Nicholas Ridley Bishop of London. With the accession of Mary in 1553, Crowley departed England for Frankfurt where he joined other Puritan malcontents, returning to London at the beginning of Elizabeth's reign. The past career of Robert Crowley as a Puritan and publisher had not been forgotten by his religious associates and professional colleagues.[4]

Shortly after his return Crowley was admitted to the archdeaconry of Hereford where he occupied himself largely with ecclesiastical discipline, holding simultaneously a living at St. Peter the Poor in London. He was to become vicar of St. Giles without Cripplegate in 1566, composing this time his *Briefe discourse against the outwarde apparell of the popishe churche*, *The opening of the wordes of the prophet Joell* and a treatise directed against the priest Thomas Watson. Crowley was active as a preacher at Paul's Cross where he declared "Christ only and not godly magistrates must appoint what is necessary for His ministry."[5]

Although Deacon Crowley was extensively preoccupied with matters theological, he retained his association with the Company of Stationers which in 1578 created him a freeman by redemption. Crowley was active in bookselling since in 1580 and 1584 he engaged apprentices, Thomas Merye of St. Saviour, Southwark, and Allen Riche of Eastrodeham, Norfolk. In 1586 he was requested by the Master of the Stationers' Company to deliver "the electyon day" sermon for which he was paid vis., 8d. and two years later was designated with eight others as licenser of books. Crowley died a few weeks after his appointment in June 1588 – his role as publisher and bookseller to be remembered by his guild. In September 1592 his widow "in respect for her pou[er]tye" was granted a pension of "ffoure nobles by the yere towards her relief," one noble to be given each quarter.[6]

Crowley's career reflects the Puritan credo of work, godliness and reform. Through preaching he aspired to cleanse the soul of man and through the printed text he strove to impress indelibly upon the minds of the unreformed the message of faith and spiritual regeneration.

While Crowley proclaimed the doctrine of predestination to a rapt audience, the hostility of left-wing Puritanism was expressed in the first printed manifesto, *An Admonition to the Parliament*, written by John Field and Thomas Wilcox. The work which appeared with a pseudonymous imprint "Wandsworth" had been printed by a gentleman whose career to some extent bears comparison with that of Robert Crowley. John Strowd, a Somerset clergyman, had been deprived of his living in 1568. He was to become a free-lance preacher and printer for a short period, confessing that he had "wante of long training vp in this mysterie." The location of Strowd's press which issued the *Admonition* and other Puritan works was, according to its master, located an approximate "one hundred miles off" from London, its whereabouts somewhat confusing – designated as either Hemel in Hampstead or Hampstead in Essex. The "Wandsworth" books found their way to London where they were distributed by the wife of the London goldsmith and Warden of the Mint, Richard Martin.[7] Twelve years later Lady Martin's scrupulous husband, now an alderman of the Capital, was to send his deputy to search the home of one of the country's foremost historians, Speed, for suspect literature!

Strowd not only admitted his inexperience as a printer but also confessed to the paucity of equipment, stating that he had "no wealth to furnish the Print with sufficient varietie of letters," since he was "a poor man" and used "one letter for three or foure tongues." He declared that he was both typesetter and corrector, acknowledging that upon occasion he had omitted "divers quotations in the margent," these lacunae having been caused by the "want of healpe." Since he was not in close proximity "eyther unto the author or to some that is made privie unto hys books," he found himself at an additional disadvantage. He had been motivated to print his books not "of any gaine but only for the desire . . . to aduaunce the glory of God."[8]

The first edition of the Field-Wilcox *An Admonition to the Parliament* was printed at "Wandsworth" in 1572 to be followed almost immediately by a second edition. To bolster its influence, Cartwright wrote his *Second Admonition to the Parliament* which was also printed by Strowd in an edition of one thousand copies. The manifestoes were followed by the "Wandsworth" edition of *Certain articles collected by the Byshops out of an Admonition to the Parliament* by Field and Wilcox. The impact of both manifestoes upon the government faction is expressed in a letter written by Archbishop Parker in June 1572 in which he declared that despite the best efforts of church and state "some good fellows still labour to print out the vain Admonition to the Parliament. Since the first printing it hath twice been printed and now with new additions. We wrote letters to the Mayor and some aldermen of London to lay in wait for the charects, printer and corrector but I fear they deceive vs. They are not willing to disclose this matter."[9]

Infuriated by the audacity of the Puritan writers and their elusive printer, both "Admonitions" were banned by a royal proclamation of June 11, 1573 which referred to the "vnqviet" nature of some persons "redy to fynde fault with al wel established orders" who used "other rites and ceremonies then are by the lawes of the Realme vsed." The Edict alluded to those who had "rashly set foorth, and by stealth printed certaine bookes vnder the title of An admonition to Parliament, and one other also in defence of the sayde admonition . . . whiche bookes do tende to no other ende, but to make diuision and dissention in the opinions of man." It was declared that every printer and stationer who had in his keeping one or both titles was to surrender them to the Bishop of his diocese or a member of the Privy Council.[10]

A month later Lord Burleigh was informed by Parker of the failure of the Proclamation. "The whole Citie of London, where no doubt is great plentie, hath not brought one to my handes and I can hardley think yat your Lordships of her Majestys privy Counsell haue receyved many, whereby it may easely appeare, what boldenes and disobedience the new writers have already wrought in the myndes of the people and that agaynst the Ciuill Magistrates." He declared the *Articles* by Field and Wilcox were as common in London "in ye Innes of Court and ellswheare, as in ergo in the scholes and as I heare they were abroade before yat came in to your Lordships handes."[11]

The government and Stationers' Company, rankled by the failure of the Proclamation, were now fully determined to locate the offending press. Their efforts proved successful. Strowd was "to come into the hands of his persecutors" in August 1573 when John Harrison the Elder of the Stationers' Company had been advised by the Archbishop of Canterbury "to serche out" the press. Entries in the *Records* of the Stationers' Company specify the expenditure incurred in the quest for the "Wandsworth" press: "Item laid owte the xxvith of August 1573 for Harrisons Jorney in Hempsteade with the purseuaunt xixs; item to the carter yat brought the presse xs.; item to ye constable of Hempsteade for bringinge vp ye men viiis.vid., to the pursevaunt for his paines."[12]

With his two assistants, John Lacy and Thomas Asplyn, Strowd was arrested and brought before the Court of Ecclesiastical Commission. Questioned regarding the whereabouts of Cartwright's *Second Admonition*, the printer declared that he had given thirty-four copies of it to the Bishop of London "in one bundell," adding that his wife had burned the others. "And for the rest they were dispersed abroade, he knew not where for they never came into his hands for he was an 100 miles off." At the same time a message of Lord Burleigh dolefully reports that "Hir Majesties Proclamation toke none effecte ... not one boke brought in. Mr. Cartwright is said to lye hid in London with great respect unto him."[13]

A letter of November 22, 1573 reiterates Parker's complaints about the government's inability to chasten the left-wing press and the license of Puritan authors who "throughout all the realm ... slander us with infamous books and libels, lying they care not how deep. We have sought as diligently as we can for the press of the puritans but we cannot possibly find it. The more they write the more they shame our religion."[14]

After his confrontation with the Court of Ecclesiastical Commission Strowd had sought a haven in Kent and despite the government's efforts continued his dual role as a preacher and printer. In 1574 – indifferent to the official ban against Cartwright's *Admonition* – he issued two editions of his *Replye to an answer made to Doctor Whitegift*. Strowd's preface to the second edition reflects his courage and aspiration: "Some perhaps will marvel at the new impression of thys booke ... notwithstanding our most gracious princes late published proclamation. But cease to muse, good christian reader, whosoever thou art: and learne to know that no lawes, were they never so hard and severe can put out the force of Gods spirit in his children." He stated that the work had been issued for "the profite ... of the godly and their instruction," although he anticipated personal "daungers and trobles" if he came "into the hands of the persecutors." His immediate fate is not known. A directive of the Privy Council of March 31, 1573/1574 instructed two Northamptonshire knights, Sir John Spencer and Sir Robert Lane, "to make enquerye for a booke likely to be printed in the countie of Northampton an answer against Whitegiftes booke ... to committ the principall doers to prison [and] to send up the bookes and to advertise what they finde." Strowd was to remain in apparent obscurity until 1586 when he printed *A proclamation and edict of the Archbishop of Culleyn* and acted as colporteur for the distribution of the important Presbyterian manual, *Declaration of ecclesiasticall discipline* of Walter Travers.[15]

Archbishop Parker had alluded to the press of the Puritans. Strowd had been briefly silenced only to reëmerge. Other Puritan establishments issued the writings of Brownist and Anabaptist whose sermons had been rapidly transmuted into the printed word. The press became a powerful adjunct of the Puritan pulpit. The dissenter, seeking a reform of the church and a higher level of personal conduct, found ready identification with the 1584 publication of *A briefe and plain declaration concerning the desires of all those faithful ministers that have and do seeke for the discipline and reformation of the churche of Englande* which has been attributed to William Fulke, the "accerimus Papastamix," defender of the Established Faith and author of the "Catalogue of ... Papist Books." The work, known as "A Learned Discourse of Ecclesiastical Government" is a statement of the responsibilities of the church to the people emphasizing the importance of preaching. The "Declaration" evoked the reply of John Bridges, Bishop of Sarum, whose 1,400-page volume entitled *A Defence of the gouernment established in the Church of Englande for ecclesiastical matters* protested innovation and extremist religious reform. The respectable Dean had initiated a flyting warfare which was to reach its climax in the anonymous publication by the radical Puritan camp of the clever, pungent satires known as the Marprelate tracts.[16]

The Marprelate series which derided episcopacy: its rigidity, luxury, arbitrary authority, its "bishops of the devil" indicates the identification of a sympathetic press with the extremist movement. As a Puritan, Robert Waldegrave associated himself with the radical group becoming the printer of four of the Marprelate pamphlets. Since the Marprelate Controversy has been thoroughly analyzed in books and articles, it is of present interest principally to review Waldegrave's connection with the Puritan extremists and his role as a printer of several of their writings and the Martinist tracts.

Robert Waldegrave arrived in London from Worcester in 1568 to be apprenticed to William Gryffith. He set up his own press without Temple Bar in the Strand "near unto Somerset House," where in 1578 he issued his first work, *A castle for the soule*. Through the following ten years Waldegrave was to print approximately seventy books of which eighty percent are Puritan in content. They include among others two editions of *The confession of the true and christian faith* (adopted by the reformed church of Scotland); two works by Master John Knox, *A godly letter sent to the fayethfull in London* and *An exposition upon the fourth of Matthew*. In 1581 he printed *A caueat for Parsons Howlet* by John Field, a reply to the hostile criticism of the Puritans by Father Persons, issuing also Field's *Godly exhortation by occasion of the late judgement of God at Parris garden*. Other Waldegrave imprints appear in *A discourse of the true and visible markes of the Catholique church* by the prominent Huguenot divine, Theodore de Bèze, translated into English by Field's former associate Thomas Wilcox, the Genevan *Booke of the forme of common prayers*, sermons and tracts by the eminent Puritan divines, Laurence Chaderton and Dudley Fenner.[17]

In a lighter vein Waldegrave printed during this decade several works which stirred the people's souls to matters more zestful than the hell and damnation preached by the Puritan zealots. He issued in 1581 *The ioyfull entrie of the dukedome of Brabant* and *A brief declaration of the shews performed before the Queens Maiestie and the French ambassadours*. More romantic and useful texts included the *Aduentures of lady Elgerie, Daphnis and Chloe, Vpon the life and death of Sir Philip Sidney* and *The English Secretorie*, a manual on the "inditing of all manner of Epistles" – these last three compositions by the prolific author, Angell Day. The more immediate needs of the public were supplied by publications in the fields of medicine and domestic economy. Waldegrave printed two editions of Walter Bailey's *Briefe treatise touching the preservation of eyesight* and Thomas Hill's *Profitable arte of gardening*. The requisites of the schoolboy were gratified by his publication of a treatise on mnemonics and a translation of Pierre de la Ramée's *Latin grammar*.[18]

During this period Waldegrave engaged two apprentices, Henry Kirkham and Edward Ungle, who assisted in his setting type for John Harrison, the Younger, Thomas Man of the Talbot, Paternoster Row, Henry Carre and Thomas Woodcock of the Black Bear, who had been confined to Newgate in 1578 for selling copies of Cartwright's *Admonition to the Parliament*, and was later to assist in a raid upon Waldegrave's premises.[19]

The growing attachment of Waldegrave to the more radical wing of Puritanism prompted him in 1584 to print not only Fulke's "Learned Discourse of Ecclesiastical Government," but also *A dialogue concerning the strife of our Church*. The Court of High Commission was quick to pounce upon the disseminator of works critical of established church policy. It advised the Wardens of the Stationers' Company to seize Waldegrave, his workmen and his press along with his unlicensed books. The Court's order was promptly heeded and the printer was confined for six weeks to the White Lion Prison in Southwark where he was returned shortly for a longer stay of five months.[20]

Waldegrave's two terms of imprisonment failed to chasten his enthusiasm for a more radical Puritanism and the literature it inspired. In 1588 he printed four treatises by the outspoken Puritan divine, John Udall, *The true remedie against famine and warres, The combate betwixt Christ and the Deuill, The Amendment of life* and his highly controversial reflections, *The State of the Churche of Englande laid open in a conference between Diotrephes, a bishop, Tertullus a papist.* Known popularly as "Diotrephes," Udall's text was a trenchant denunciation of episcopacy which he considered to be the root of all social and religious evils. The book had been issued anonymously by Waldegrave whose association with it became public knowledge. His new premises at the Sign of the Crane, St. Paul's Churchyard, were raided on May 13, 1588 by the Warden of the Stationers' Company assisted by the reformed Thomas Woodcock who had earlier suffered imprisonment for his sale of Cartwright's *Admonition.* "Upon serche," the gentlemen "did seise and bringe to the stacon[er]s hall a presse with twoo paire of cases with certen pica Romane and pica Italian letters with diu[er]s books entituled The state of the church of England laid open in a conference between Diotrephes a byshop Tertullus a papist." Since the Master of the Crane had issued this treatise without authority and "contrary to ye said decrees, it was determined that ye said books shall be burnte and the said presse letters and printinge stuffe defaced and made vnserviceable."[21]

In his first Marprelate tract, *The Epistle,* its Puritan author, either Udall or John Penry, was to decry the seizure of Waldegrave's press, declaring that the state and Stationers' Company had shown greater indulgence to a Catholic printer. The writer declared that several printers had offered to purchase Waldegrave's press and type wishing to donate the proceeds "towards the relief of the man's wife and children." Their request had been denied by the Company officials. The author continued that the "popishe Thackwell though he printed papist and traiterous bookes [had] the favour to make money of his presse and letters." The writer claimed that Thackwell was at liberty "to walk where he will, and permitted to make the most he could of his presse and letters; whereas Robert Waldegrave dares not shew his face for the bloodthirstie desire for his life, onely for the printing of bookes which toucheth the bishops myters." The press, he avowed, had been "sawed and hewed in pieces, the yron worke battered and made vnserviceable his letters melted." All this had been done by the express order of "John Wolfe, alias Machivaell, Beadle of the Stacioners, and most tormenting executor of Waldegrave's goods and he himself vtterly deprived of ever printing again having a wife and sixe small children."[22]

Waldegrave, his wife and children escaped the fury of Machiavelli's heir, John Wolfe, finding refuge at the home of Mrs. Crane in East Mosely near Kingston-on-Thames, the abode of a widow of a leftist Puritan deprived of his pulpit and a friend of John Udall. Here Waldegrave was welcomed by Udall's friend, John Penry, the dedicated Welsh Puritan, who persuaded him to issue in 1588 *An exhortation vnto the governours and people of Wales.* Waldegrave had now associated himself with one of the future authors of the

Marprelate tracts. He had committed himself to the vanguard of extreme Puritanism, issuing from East Mosely *The demonstration of discipline* and Penry's *Defence of that which hath bin written.* The Puritan authors, Udall and Penry, associated with the printer Waldegrave, were poised to challenge the Established Church through a powerful literary weapon, a series of satires designed to discredit English episcopacy. Determined upon their mission, Penry and Udall wrote the Martinist series, four of which were printed by Robert Waldegrave.[23]

The Marprelate tracts never enjoyed the approval of the serious Puritan divine who deplored their jocular, derisive strain. The series jeered at a solemn matter with its broad scurrility and failed to bolster the reform cause. A Puritan source berates "those hateful libelles of Martin Marreprelate . . . all printed with a kinde of wandering presse . . . shameless libell[s] . . . fraught only with odious and scurrilous calumniacions against the established government." The Martinist lampoons were held in ridicule by the Catholic camp, its propagandist, Creswell, stating that "the Martinists or Puritans [were] much more dangerous for domestical broyles than the Spaniardes for open warres . . . for that they muste needes hate her Maiestie and the Protestante Councell most deadly, as both by reason and by their bookes."[24]

The earliest "booke" of the Martinists was printed at the Crane home in East Mosely in black letter type of several sizes which had been shipped to Waldegrave from the Continent. The first of the series, *The Epistle*, appeared in October 1588. Written in a scornful, mordant vein, the work attacked those prelates who had been particularly obnoxious to the Puritans, Whitgift, John Aylmer, Bishop of London and Thomas Cooper, Bishop of Winchester. The sesquipedalian title of *The Epistle* lampoons the high-churchmen: "Oh read ouer D. John Bridges for it is a worthy worke . . . Compiled for the behoofe and overtherrow of the Parsons Fyckers and Curats that have lernt their Catechismes, and are past grace. By the reverend and worthie Martin Marprelate, gentleman, and dedicated to the Confocation house." Waldegrave's participation is concealed in the colophon: "Printed overseas in Europe, within two furlongs of a Bounsing Priest, at the cost and charge of M. Marprelate, gentleman."[25]

Aware of Waldegrave's association with *The Epistle* but uncertain of his whereabouts, the episcopal pursuivants sought him at his London premises where in their holy zeal they broke through the main wall of the house. The designates of the Court of Ecclesiastical Commission proceeded "to serch out the authors and the[i]r complices, and ye printers and ye secret dispersers of ye same, and to cause them to be apprehended and committed."[26]

The printer and authors, cognizant of their hazardous situation, departed East Mosely for a more secure haven at the manor house of the well-known Puritan patron Sir Richard Knightley at Fawsley in Northamptonshire, former sheriff and M. P. for the shire. One Jeffs, a tenant farmer of Upton, had been persuaded to haul "a load of stuff" from East Mosely to Fawsley. Completely ignorant of the nature of his shipment which had been covered with hay, Jeffs had transported the press and type to the Knightley residence. The "load" was deposited in a small upper room where Waldegrave, known as "Sheme" or "Shamme", printed in November 1588 the second Marprelate tract, *The Epitome*. Although this satire assails Dr. Bridges, its principal target was Aylmer, Bishop of London, who was regarded by the Puritans with even greater contempt than Whitgift. The imprint reads "Printed on the other hand of some of the priests."[27]

While the more radical Puritan element enjoyed the ribaldry of the lampoon, the pursuivants continued their search for "a suspected press." The cause of episcopacy was further supported by Bishop Cooper of Winchester whose *Admonition to the people* castigated the left-wing Puritan camp which was also officially chastised by a royal Proclamation of February 13, 1588/1589 directed against "certain seditious and euill disposed persons towards her Maiestie and the Government established for causes Ecclesiasticall." The state declared that subversive elements had "deuised, written, printed or caused to be seditiously and secretly published and dispersed sundry schismaticall and seditious bookes, diffamatorie Libels and other fantasticall writings against her Maiesties Subjectes, containing in them doctrine very erroneous ... and slanderous to the state, and against the godly reformation of Religion and Gouernment Ecclesiastical ... and also against the persons of the Bishops ... in rayling sorte and beyonde the boundes of all good humanities." It was declared that such books introduced "a monstrous and apparaunt daungerous Innouation within her Majesties dominions and countries." For this reason all such literature was to be turned in and information given regarding its "Authors, Writers, Printers or dispersers thereof."[28]

Neither the *Admonition* of the Bishop of Winchester nor the Proclamation of the Queen of England had proved deterrents sufficiently severe to intimidate the authors and printer of the Marprelate series. The group had found a third refuge in late January 1588/1589 at the home of John Hales of Coventry where a week after the publication of the royal Edict they issued a satirical broadside, *The Minerall Conclusions*, a reply to Cooper's criticism. The lampoon contained thirty-seven "Minerall and Metaphysicall School Points to be defended by the reverende Bishops and the rest of my cleargie masters of the Convocation house." The bishops were accused of supporting ludicrous religious tenets postulated by medieval schoolmen. The work was printed by Waldegrave who a month later issued a more substantial attack, *Hay any worke for Cooper or a briefe Pistle [sic] directed by waye of an Pistle to the reverend bishopps*, bearing the colophon "Printed in Europe not farre from some of the bouncing priestes." The tract, the fourth in the Martinist series, is a lengthy satire indulging in inventive word play upon the good Bishop's name. It is none the less the most serious of the tracts attempting to confute Cooper's defense of the civil authority of the bishops.[29]

By the Spring of 1589 Waldegrave had become deeply concerned about his identification with the radical Puritan element. He had consulted with several Puritan divines who had expressed indignation with the extremist tone of the Martinist campaign. It is even possible that Waldegrave had conferred with Cartwright who lived in close proximity in Warwick. The distinguished reform leader had assured Lord Burleigh that he had not "anie hand or so much a finger in the bookes under Martin's name" and emphasized his "mislike and sorrow for such kind of disordered proceeding." Waldegrave, now troubled by his radical association, apprehensive for his future, concerned for his family, withdrew his support as printer of the tracts, stating that "all the preachers I have conferred withall do mislike yt." According to the bookbinder Henry Sharpe, he "wolde no longer meddle or be a dealer in this course." Waldegrave departed Coventry around Easter 1589 ultimately finding refuge in the Huguenot city of La Rochelle where in all likelihood he printed only two books: Penry's *M. Some laid open his colours* and *A dialogue wherin is plainly laid open the tyrannical dealing of the L. Bishopps against Gods children*.[30]

Shortly thereafter Waldegrave found his way to Edinburgh where he received a license from the Scottish Privy Council to print the *Confession of faith* and ironically on October 9, 1590 he was designated royal printer by King James VI of Scotland, the future James I of England. Lord Burleigh wryly commented upon the new role of the former Martinist printer: "They [the Puritans] have founde such fauour, as to procure their cheife instrument, and old seruant Waldegraue, to be the King of Scots printer." Waldegrave was to continue in office until his death shortly after his master's accession to the English throne.[31]

Despite Waldegrave's defection the Martinist series continued – printed by another craftsman with the help of two assistants. *Martin Junior or Theses Martinianae, Martin Senior or the iust censure and reproofe* and *The Protestation* were printed in the Spring of 1589 by John Hodgkins known as "a salpetreman" and two aides, Arthur Tomlyn and Valentine Symmes. Of the three, Symmes is the best known. He is first heard of in connection with the Marprelate Controversy and was to continue as a fractious member of the Stationers' Company. Tomlyn and Symmes had been engaged to do job printing in the North and had been compelled to take "a corporal oath" not to divulge the nature of their venture. The three had proceeded not to Coventry but to Walston Priory where the Martinist Press had now found its fourth haven. Here at the home of Roger Wigston they installed the press in "a low parlour." The printers completed their work on *Martin Junior* and *Martin Senior* in July 1589. Like his predecessor, Waldegrave, Hodgkins became apprehensive of detection and decided to move his assistants and equipment to a more remote, secluded area. They packed up "three payres of cases with lettres of three sortes," ink and about "twelve ream of pape[r]" which were placed on a cart also disguised with hay. As they proceeded through the small town of Warrington pieces of type rolled to the ground catching the attention of bystanders. Although Hodgkins assured the group that they were merely "shott," he and his assistants were arrested two weeks later at Newton Lane, "a mile from Manchester."[32]

The printer, accomplices and patrons of the Martinist series now confronted an irate government. The three men were sent with escort to London, examined by the Council and committed to Bridewell. The state proclaimed its indignation against those "who print[ed] in corners and spread thyngs imprinted," declaring that all "Brownist books and such other seditious books should be suppressed and burnt." During several examinations Hodgkins, Tomlyn and Symmes were put to torture to force confessions. Hodgkins was transferred to the Tower and there is some evidence that "having been condemned of felonie" he was executed. Confessions were wrested from Tomlyn and Symmes for their participation in the printing program. Later, Sir Richard Knightley stood trial for his involvement being fined two thousand pounds, while Mrs. Crane suffered imprisonment in the Fleet in 1590 and was penalized a thousand marks. After a short prison term, Symmes was to emerge in 1590, becoming a large-scale printer and publisher, issuing the first edition of Shakespeare's *Much ado about nothing, The tragedie of King Richard the second, The tragedie of King Richard the third* and the first and second parts of *The history of Henrie the fourth.*[33]

The Marprelate Campaign reflects not only the attitude of the Puritan extremists critical of the uncompromising attitude of the established church, but also the role of the sympathetic underground press which had become a ready adjunct to a program of invective and criticism. Waldegrave and his successor placed their skills at the service of the dissenting group to print their tracts which – with other Puritan writings – were disseminated in London by agents of like persuasion. The distribution of this literature and the government's reaction to it bear some small comparison with the circulation of underground Catholic texts and the attitude of the Crown toward its recusant minority.

The method of distribution of Puritan nonconformist literature is scarcely comparable with that of the highly organized Catholic machine which employed its missionaries and priests to convey books into England and to bring them from the provinces to the metropolis. The Puritans adopted no such plan since many stationers were Puritan sympathizers, selling nonconformist literature openly in their shops. The writings of their fellow-faithful presented for the most part no real danger to the country – the books they wrote contained no pattern of revolt, no suggestion of foreign usurpation – theirs were manifestoes of purification and reform.

Richard Boyle is designated by the author of *Martin Junior* as a purveyor of Puritan books at his shop at the Rose in London. Boyle was active from 1584 to 1615, having been apprenticed to Thomas Woodcock who had sought the Company's intervention for his participation in the sale of the Field-Wilcox *Admonition*. Hence Boyle as a malleable young man had been well indoctrinated in leftist Puritan propaganda. The Master of the Rose was to play no conspicuous role as a stationer, publishing merely an approximate twenty-three books of which two-thirds are Puritan in content. They include various treatises of the Puritan divine, James Balmford, translations of Huguenot writings, an edition of the Psalms, and miscellaneous works parading virtuous conduct and reform. Boyle's publishing list was small; his role as a bookseller was more extensive. His publication program cannot compare with that of the larger firms of Robert Dexter of the Brazen Serpent, St. Paul's Churchyard; John Beale of Fetter Lane; Thomas Man at the Talbot, Paternoster Row; Edward Brewster of the Bible, St. Paul's; and John Legate of Cambridge – houses which published the writings of Richard Greenham, the Puritan apostle to the "poore and peevish;" William Gouge; John Dod, celebrated for his commentaries on the Proverbs and Ten Commandments; Richard Rogers, the diarist; William Perkins, author of *A golden chaine, or the description of theologie* which was reprinted by Legate five times, having also been issued by Waldegrave.[34]

Boyle and Man, Dexter and Beale, Brewster and Legate sold the Puritan sermons, polemics and commentaries at their shops at the Rose, the Brazen Serpent and their stalls at St. Paul's. The Martinist tracts and other extremist nonconformist writings could not be sold in the open. Their publishers and printers relied on sympathetic agents and London factors. Humphrey Newman, known as Brownbread, was the principal disperser of the Marprelate tracts. He is described as a cobbler who for a short time was attached to the household of Sir Richard Knightley wearing his livery or "a greene cloake and a greene hat." Newman covered the Midlands and London, traveling to the Capital via Northampton in order to avoid any identification with the secret press. He received from Waldegrave and his successor Hodgkins the printed sheets of Penry's writings and the Martinist series which he brought to the bookbinder Henry Sharpe of Northampton. Sharpe stitched the sheets of these works, Newman taking with him nine hundred copies of Penry's *Supplication* and seven hundred of *Hay any worke for Cooper* to London. Sharpe also sewed the sheets of *Martin Senior* and *Martin Junior*, and seven or eight hundred copies of the former were packed by Newman as a bundle of leather to be forwarded by the Warwick carrier via Banbury to London. This shipment and others were eventually deposited at the Sarazin's Head on Friday Street, a narrow thoroughfare running south from Cheapside across Cannon Street. Nicholas Tomkins, a servant of Mrs. Crane, identified Newman as "the principall vtterer of them [distributor of the Marprelate tracts] and hath had six or seven hundred at once of them."[35]

Newman with other participants in the Marprelate Series was arrested and pressured by the authorities to admit his guilt in the "spreadinge" of books of "a seditious infamous and slanderous character" and to confess "the lewdness and greevousness of [his] said former practises which [he] with all [his] hart and sole [did] detest." Although Newman's fate is not known, he had persistently and conscientiously worked for the extremist Puritan cause.[36]

To its support came other agents canvassing the country and the Capital. Copies of *The Epistle* were distributed and sold in close proximity to the Crane home itself. At the residence of Mark Collyns "one of the Baylies of the Town of Kyngston and at the house of Robert Doddeson ... the bookes or libelles called by the name of Martin Marprelate" could be obtained. Copies of *The Epistle* were priced at 11d. apiece and the author of the tract declared that his readers would gladly purchase his books if "they could tell where to find them." In London, Giles Wiggington, a deprived Yorkshire minister, received copies of *The Epistle* and *The Epitome*. According to Mrs. Crane's servant, Tomkins, Wiggington had dispersed copies of the books and shortly thereafter had been arrested by one of Whitgift's pursuivants. During his interrogation at Lambeth Wiggington was urged "to speak more boldly of church government and of two bookes extant of M[artin]." Not dissimilar in calling and purpose from the Widows Douce, Fowler, Bulloch and Udall, Mrs. Margaret Lawson, known as "the shrew of Newgate," conducted a brisk trade in the distribution of the Martinist tracts.[37]

It is dubious that Melanchthon Jewel, a Devonshire Puritan divine, was acquainted with the "Baylie of Kyngston" or Mrs. Lawson. Jewel was arraigned before the Court of Star Chamber in 1590 for having "penned and delivered forth illicit books" for which delinquency he suffered confinement in the White Lion. After his release Jewel returned to Devonshire where he resumed his career as a hedge-priest and book peddler. He was arrested within a year or two for selling seditious Puritan books. Jewel was apparently not easily discouraged. In December 1604 the home of the "schismatic Puritan" Melanchthon Jewel was searched where incriminating evidence in the form of books, paper and lists was found.[38]

The Barrowist John Greenwood overshadows in importance the person of Melanchthon Jewel. Greenwood had been confined illegally to the Clink, his arrest based upon the statute against writing and publishing seditious books. According to the omniscient Verstegan, Greenwood had been jailed for approving a book entitled *A conference betwixt him and certayne ministers* "wherein first he disaloweth the Booke of Common Prayer ... and proved the Congregation of England profane and Babell like." During a visit to Greenwood, Henry Barrow and John Penry were immediately arrested and "detained upon reason of the same statute." Barrow, the leader of a group of faithful disciples, had condemned the Church of England as a false church which his conscience had compelled him to desert. His influence was analyzed by Bishop Bancroft who declared that "diverse ministers well reckoned of heretofore for their learning are lately fallen from Cartwright, and his secte into another new frenzy of Barrowisme. I know the nature of the schismatickes to bee of such giddiness, as that no one thinge will content them longe."[39]

The prison stay of Greenwood, Barrow and Penry was to terminate with their execution in 1593. Prior to their death they wrote a full account of their confinement and treatment by the civil authorities entitled *The examinations of H. Barrowe J. Grenewood and J. Penrie*. The prisoners strove to acquaint their Puritan audience with the intolerance of English authority and through the deft help of several sympathizers were able to have the work smuggled out of jail for publication abroad. The Barrowists, Robert Bull and Robert Stokes, visited the prisoners and took with them the manuscript written on slips which they forwarded to a Dutch agent, Bowles or Bouler, who arranged with Hanse, the printer of Dort, to issue the book in an edition of two or three hundred copies. This work and *The plain refutation of Mr. Giffardes booke* were printed in Dort under the supervision of a Barrowist exile, Arthur Byllet, originally from Llanteglos in Cornwall, who is described as "a scholler and a soldiour." Byllet acted as proofreader; Stokes bore the financial responsibility. Both publications destined for exportation to England were examined at Flushing and Brill where they were impounded. The interception of *The plaine refutation of Mr. Giffardes booke* is to be attributed largely to the efforts of a later Barrowist sympathizer, Francis Johnson, who at the time was preacher to the English merchants at the Gasthuis Church at Middleburg. Johnson had strongly disavowed Barrowist teaching and, according to William Bradford, had been "so zealous against this way of separation that [when] Mr. Barrow's and Mr. Greenwood's Refutation of Gifford was privately imprinting in this city, he not only was a means to discover it, but made the ambassador's instrument to intercept them at the press and see them burnt; the which charge he did well perform, as he let them go until they were wholly finished, and then surprised the whole impression, not suffering any to escape, and then by the magistrate's authority caused them all to be openly burnt, himself standing by until they were all consumed to ashes." Master Bradford's report is not absolutely correct. Not all copies had been destroyed. Johnson himself had reserved two copies and upon ultimately reading the text was to become so deeply impressed with Barrowist doctrine that he visited London to confer with the authors in the Clink. He returned, a convert to Barrowism, to Amsterdam, where he caused "the same books, which he had been an instrument to burn, to be new printed and set out at his own charge."[40]

The sponsors of the Barrowist publications at Dort were arrested and brought for examination before Gabriel Goodman, Dean of Westminster in April 1593. It was declared that Byllet had been "the man that putt Barrowes and Greenwood their bookes to the printer at dorte." Byllet admitted his part in the publications, confessing that he had supervised the printing and informed his interrogators that, despite their attempt to stifle the circulation of Barrowist doctrine, copies of such books would be found in the homes of English sympathizers. Verstegan alluded to Barrow's treatise, *A briefe discoverie of a false church*, which had been written during the author's prison confinement, the manuscript having been surreptitiously taken from the prison by the author's admirer Daniel Studley who brought it to Dort to be issued by Hanse.[41]

Aroused by the circulation of the Barrowist writings, the state and the Stationers' Company continued their search for subversive Puritan authors, printers and agents. In July 1593 the Company agents spent three days at Billingsgate Market in pursuit of "11 barrelles and 11 fyrkins" of books which had been dispatched to London from Scotland. The raid proved successful since within the "barrelles and fyrkins" were found copies of *A parte of a register, contayninge sundrie memorable matters, written by diuers godly and learned in our time, which stande for, and desire the reformation of our churche, in Discipline and Ceremonies, according to the pure worde of God and the Lawe of our Lande.* This ponderous title graced an anonymously printed corpus of forty-two tracts written by extremist Puritan authors, Edmund Dering, Anthony Gilby, Richard Greenham, Dudley Fenner and John Udall. Bancroft, who believed the book had been printed by Waldegrave, referred with rancor to the literary persuasion of the extremist group: "Their rayling pamphlets ... their tribolar chartals. They have taken upon them to make a register, all ready to come from thence and finished." There is reason to doubt Bancroft's attribution of the *Register* to Waldegrave. The fonts appear to be those of Richard Schilders of Middleburg who apparently had sent the sheets to Scotland for binding.[42]

The execution of the Barrowist leaders, the denunciation of the Brownists, the search for their books and authors had scarcely "extinguished the sect." Puritan agitators swept the country and it has been asserted that from "the close of the 16th-century to the outbreak of the Revolution ... the Puritan writers probably did more than any others of the time to keep the printers and booksellers busy and the common public supplied with reading matter." A 1590 memorandum to Lord Burleigh had referred to the unsettled state of the country disrupted by papists and "the turbulent sect of Puritans." By 1592 it was observed that the nation was divided among three mighty factions of Catholics, Protestants and Puritans.[43]

Preachers with their message of reform and godliness found ready audiences. During his lifetime the sermons of the popular Puritan divine, Richard Greenham, had circulated in manuscript only. After his death in 1594 his writings were published "to the delight of many loving friends which have long desired and expected the impression of all his workes." Between 1598 and 1612 seven editions of Greenham's *Works* were issued. During their publication Verstegan advised Father Persons that the wholesale London publisher John Norton had become involved in the Puritan cause, "having been sent by them to Scotland to print their bookes." Norton had opened a branch office in Edinburgh about 1587 and in 1589, in arrangement with the Scottish publisher Andro Hart, had obtained the privilege of importing books from the Continent free of duty. According to their petition to the Estates of Scotland, Hart and Norton had "two years earlier enterprisit the hamebringing of volumes and buikis furth of Almane and Germanie." Three known Puritan titles can be identified with Norton's Scottish venture: the *Tractatus de vera excommunicatione* of Theodore de Bèze, *A discouerie of the conspiracie of the Scottish papists* and *A plaine discovery of the whole revelation of Saint John* by John Napier printed for him by Waldegrave. Upon his return to London Norton was arrested and briefly imprisoned.[44]

Strowd, Waldegrave and Hodgkins had been the victims of the pursuivants' unannounced visits, their premises raided, their presses battered and destroyed. The authors of extremist Puritan literature suffered indignities similar to those endured by their Catholic colleagues. As early as June 1557/1558 a royal proclamation referred to "divers books filled with heresy and treason . . . imported from abroad or secretly published" in England. It was stated that "any one who is found to have any of these books shall be taken for a rebel and executed against martial law." The government had taken violent exception to the Genevan edition of *How superior powers ought to be obeyd of their subjects and wherein they may be lawfully and by Gods word restrained*. The treatise, smacking of rebellion, had been written by Christopher Goodman, Puritan divine and former Lady Margaret Professor at Cambridge. He had joined the Puritan exiles abroad during Mary's reign and in his treatise he had bitterly attacked the Queen and the government of women in general. He referred to the ungodly evils which had swept the land and believed it was the duty of counselors to restrain government license. If they failed to thwart the Crown's wayward behavior, the people were to resist. Goodman did not return to England until another queen had ascended the throne. He was brought up on charges before the Court of Ecclesiastical Commission and compelled to recant his published opinions.[45]

With the death of Edmund Grindal, Elizabeth in August 1583 appointed John Whitgift as Archbishop of Canterbury. A man of great energy, he strove to enforce discipline throughout the church, finding Puritan doctrine most uncongenial. Determined to stifle Puritanism, Whitgift promptly increased the power of the Court of High Commission, prohibiting all preaching, reading or catechising in private homes. All preachers were compelled to subscribe to the royal supremacy and to accept the Book of Common Prayer. Whitgift's rigorous, uncompromising attitude alienated the substantial Puritan element, which – loyal to the government – none the less resented an imposition upon its spiritual freedom. In 1586 Whitgift aspired to eliminate adverse criticism through his Star Chamber decree which insisted upon the licensing of all books by the Archbishop of Canterbury and the Bishop of London. He was granted the privilege "to inquire into all heretical opinions, seditious books, conspiracies, false rumors" without any legal writ or warrant.

The liberties taken by Whitgift's pursuivants are bemoaned by the Puritan divine, Dudley Fenner, who referred to the indignity visited upon Puritans. "Their righteous soules must bee vexed with seeing and hearinge the prophane speeches and the evill example of those thrust upon their charges: reproached, scoffed at, and called seditious and rebellious. It is grievous to be a freeman borne, and to be a free minister to be brought into a slavishe subjection to a Commissaire as at his pleasure upon every trifling complaint to be summoned."[46]

Referring to the "furye" of the searchers when his home was raided in January 1590, Penry commented upon the violence of the chief pursuivant Richard Walton who with his assistants made entry "into all the houses, shops to apprehend all those he should in any waies suspect, and to commit them at his discretion to the next Gaol or prison." According to his statement, Walton had invaded his home in Northampton, "ransacked the study, and took away with him all such printed books and written papers as he himself thought good. He offered violence unto diuers persons and threatened not only to breake open doores (having no such commission) but also to vntile houses." In his *Appellation* Penry stated that the Warden of the Stationers' Company had seized five hundred copies of his *Humble Supplication*.[47]

At the height of the Marprelate Controversy the Puritan divine, Edmund Snape, feared the arrival of pursuivants and the consequent search for books not authorized. To elude detection he promptly concealed copies of his *Defensive of the ecclesiastical discipline* and other illegal publications in a "backhouse" belonging to a tanner.[48]

The royal Proclamation of February 1589 against the Martinist tracts, Waldegrave's defection, the arrest of Hodgkins, Symmes and Tomlyn, Sir Richard Knightley and Mrs. Crane helped terminate the extremist movement. By 1590 it was declared that London was no longer a city of Puritan agitators. None the less agents provocateurs haunted the book stalls in St. Paul's Churchyard; insidiously mingled with Puritan clergymen pretending sympathy for the cause. Occasional criticism of the government's repressive policy was to be expressed. As late as March 1605 the study of the Puritan Bywater was searched and a libel of the late Archbishop and my Lord Bishop of London entitled *The lamentation of Dickie for the death of his brother Jockey* was found. Upon examination Bywater declared that the text was not his but had been dictated to him by one Lewis Pickering.[49]

When James I ascended the throne many of the extremist Puritans had fled the country to pursue their religious beliefs abroad. Like the Catholics in exile, they sought a refuge in Calvinist Holland. There, through the medium of the press, they issued sermons and texts which were to be forwarded to England for the gratification of the faithful and the indoctrination of the unregenerate.

XV

A LIBERTY OF PRINTING

The Puritan Press in the Netherlands

The Lowlands, split into Catholic Flanders and Protestant Holland, afforded shelter to the religious deviates of the age. In 1573 the Reformed religion, as taught at Geneva, was adopted by the United Provinces. As the South had given comfort and strength to the Catholic axis, supplying its cause with presses and aid for the support of orthodoxy, the North offered its cities to the Puritan extremists whose printers, abetted by native craftsmen, aspired through the printed word to purge and reform the England they had abandoned. In their resolute and courageous quest for religious freedom they had forfeited family and country, profession and security. "Seeing themselues molested [in England]," wrote their great leader, William Bradford, convinced that "there was no hope of their continuance there, by a joint consente they resolued to go into the Low-Countries, where they heard was freedom of religion for all men. Their desires were set on the ways of God, and to enjoy His ordinances ... they rested in His providence and knew Whom they had believed." The Puritans were to remain in Holland for a short time. Their victory was to be attained ultimately in England only after the deaths of their founding spiritual leaders and the departure of many zealots for an unexplored, distant world.[1]

The Puritan, like the persecuted Catholic, was supported in his quest for religious and political self-expression by the help of the press. At Middleburg and Dort, Amsterdam and Leyden the printer in exile brought to his community and the sectaries at home significant spiritual and controversial texts.

In their search at Billingsgate Market in July 1593 the pursuivants of the Stationers' Company had found among the "11 barrelles and 11 fyrkins" copies of *A Parte of a register*, the weighty anthology of Puritan writings which has been attributed to the press of Richard Schilders of Middleburg. Schilders, originally from Angers in Anjou, had emigrated to England about 1567 when he found employment with the printer Thomas East with whom he lived as "a seruaunt by pryntinge." Here Schilders and his wife Trokyn became members of the Huguenot Church of London. In May 1568 he was admitted as a member of the Stationers' Company with the proviso that he print books only in English, a stipulation which he disobeyed, since he issued in 1575 *Den Spiegel des Howelicks.*[2]

Apparently uncomfortable in his foreign milieu or chafing at the criticism of an indignant guild, Schilders departed England in 1577 for Middleburg, the capital of Zeeland, an important commercial and religious center. He became the first printer and publisher of the town and during his lengthy residence was to issue an approximate seventy books of which almost ninety percent consist of the writings of the Puritan extremists abroad and their co-religionists at home.

In 1582 the first group of English Separatists arrived at Middleburg headed by their leader Robert Browne who was granted a house of worship, the Vischmarkt-kerk. The first known book to bear Schilders' Middleburg imprint – anglicized Richard Painter – is Browne's *Book which sheweth the life and manners of all true Christians*, the second part of which contains his extremely important "Treatise of Reformation without tarrying for anie." The printing of this politico-religious work, which urged the convocation of all true believers to bind themselves together by mutual covenant, – issued in an edition of one thousand copies – was not completed. The text was broken off in the middle of a sentence, a copy in the British Museum stating, perhaps in Browne's hand, that "by reason of trouble the print was staid." It has been surmised that the author lacked funds for the completion of the composition.[3]

The unfinished publication, none the less, caused such an impact upon the public that the English government issued a proclamation against the circulation of Browne's writings which had been sent from "Zeelande to deprave the ecclesiastical government and breed schism among the unlearned." The censure asserted that copies had been secretly sold and "dispersed in sundry places within the Realme" and demanded that anyone having a copy of Browne's treatise was to yield it immediately to an Ordinary of the diocese "to the intent that [it] may bee burned, or vtterly defaced."[4]

Walsingham had been advised as early as August 1582 by the Deputy of the English Company of Merchant Adventurers stationed at Middleburg that the work had been written by "one Browne, an Englishman now at Middleburg" where "as it is said, he exercises a ministry in a corner." The writer continued that copies of the book had been offered for sale publicly on the English "burse" by one William Pagett, a former brewer's clerk of London. Walsingham was assured that the book had been disavowed by the pastor of the Company who had detected in its reading "sundry points of doctrine to be erroneous and the whole scope thereof . . . tending not to the peace nor edification of the church." The Company authorities had sought to have Pagett arrested and with his books deported to England for examination. While the Dutch had denied the Company the right to seize Pagett, they did permit the confiscation of Browne's book. Writing to Lord Burghley in September 1582, Awdley Danett stated that he had visited Middleburg where he found "Brownes book sold openly." He added that despite the efforts of the Prince of Orange to suppress its sale, many copies had already been shipped to England.[5]

Although Thomas Cartwright had earlier acted briefly as Chaplain to the Company of Merchant Adventurers at Middleburg only two of his writings were issued by Schilders: *A brief apologie ag. M. Sutcliffe* and *A Christian letter of certaine English protestants vnto Mr. R. Hoo[ker]*. However, numerous texts by his disciple Dudley Fenner were to be printed by Schilders from 1584 to 1602. Fenner had served as curate in the village of Cranbrooke where the Puritan printer and clergyman John Strowd had been suspended. One of the ablest exponents of Puritan views, Fenner had followed Cartwright to Middleburg where, as a leader of the reformed church, he preached and wrote. Many of his theological texts bear Schilders' imprint, among them: *A defence of the reasons of the counter poyson for maintenance of the Eldership; A defence of the godlie ministers against the slaunders of D. Bridges;* the *Groundes of religion.*[6]

With the defection of Waldegrave from the Marprelate Controversy in the Spring of 1589, Schilders became the last hope of the radical Puritan group. His reputation is attested in the Marprelate tract, *The Epitome,* whose author remarks: "Put every man to his othe and fynde meanes, that Schilders of Middleburg shall be sworne to, so that if any refuse to sweare then he may be thought to be the printer."[7]

Between 1590 and 1616 Schilders printed the works of several of the most influential Puritan divines: Barrow's *Petition,* Udall's *Demonstration,* Calvin's *Catechisme,* the *Psalms* "used in the Kirk of Scotland" and Fenner's translation of the *Song of Songs.*[8]

To avoid any contravention of English law which forbade the exportation of bound books to England, Schilders shipped to the Island some unbound sheets which were apparently bound by Thomas Gibson of Bury, printer, binder and bookseller. According to Strype, Gibson bound copies of Browne's books which had been dispatched by Schilders who also sent the sheets of the *Psalms* and the *Song of Songs.* The London bookseller Henry Hooke declared in September 1600 he had received from a merchant Eldredge "xii bookes of psalters and psalmes printed at Middleborough by Ric. Skilders," nine of which had been bound by Eldredge.[9]

Among the English arrivals in Middleburg was the semi-Separatist, Henry Jacob, who preached a complete purge of the existing Church of England. His several treatises bear Schilders' colophon: *A treatise of the sufferings and victory of Christ* in two editions; *A defence of the churches and ministery of Englande; Reasons taken out of Gods word proving a necessitie of reforming our churches in England.* Copies of this latter work found their way into England and proved an irritant to James. He immediately demanded the Bishop of Winchester to reply to Jacob whom the ecclesiast considered "only a man of bold face and his book a packet of words . . . having neither sap nor substance." The Bishop alas was unable to satisfy his monarch's request because of a physical discomfort caused by "sciatica and a continual singing in [his] head . . . many obstructions and extreme windiness."[10]

In 1609 Schilders printed Jacob's *Request to the right high and mightie Prince James an humble supplication for tolleration.* Although James read his exiled subject's appeal – the copy in Lambeth Palace Library bearing the monarch's marginal notes – Jacob's request was not granted. He did not return to England until 1616 when he established the Southwark Meeting House, the first organized Congregational Church in England which he was to abandon briefly for a proselytizing mission among the Virginia colonists.[11]

Unlike Jacob, the distinguished Hebrew scholar, Hugh Broughton, established no splinter sect. Like Jacob, he wrote an *Epistle* addressed not to the "high and mightie" Prince James, but to "the learned nobilitie of England touching the translating of the Bible" printed by Schilders in 1597. Broughton had also visited Middleburg where he preached for a short time to the English Congregation and composed numerous treatises printed by Schilders. Known to Jacob and Broughton was the Scottish Puritan, John Forbes of Alford, Aberdeenshire, who visited Middleburg, becoming in 1611 preacher to the Puritan church in exile. Schilders issued not only his writings but also several by his father Patrick, Bishop of Aberdeen.[12]

No known work was published by Schilders after 1616. The English Crown had been long aware of the activity of Richard Painter and the other presses in exile. A report of 1606 refers to "sundry factions and schismatical persons who have planted themselves in the Low Countries where they have liberty without impeachment or contradiction to publish in print many books and baptistical pamphlets slandering the ecclesiastical government in England." The temerity of the writers and printers aroused James sufficiently to instruct Sir Noel Caron to "suppress and restrain certain books now in hand to be printed in Amsterdam." In 1616 the English Ambassador to the United Provinces, Sir Dudley Carleton, was to express his master's indignation at the leniency of the Dutch government toward Schilders' press. He stated that James had been wronged by the States' permitting "a liberty of printing at Middleburg for any passionate or discontented spirit to publish what he pleases to the disquiet of both church and state in his Majesty's kingdoms."[13]

Scarcely the rivals of Schilders in the publication of English Puritan literature, the presses of Hanse and Isaac Canin issued a few important texts at Dort [Dordrecht], close to Rotterdam, one of the first towns in the Netherlands to embrace the Reformed Religion. The Barrowists, Robert Bull and Robert Stokes, had smuggled from the jail cell of Barrow, Greenwood and Penry the prisoners' account of their examination which they forwarded to an English agent at Dort. The manuscript and other Barrowist tracts were printed by Hanse of Dort from 1590 to 1593. A few years later a local craftsman Isaac Canin emerges as the agent of the Scottish printers Andro Hart and Charteris. In 1601 Canin issued for "the aires of H. Charteris and A. Hart in Edinburgh" the *Psalms of David in metre* followed by two editions of the *New Testament* translated into English from the version of Theodore de Bèze. The heirs of Henry Charteris, probably his son Robert, and Andro Hart, in collusion with the large-scale firm of Norton of London, had availed themselves of Canin's service to profit from cheaper foreign labor and to avoid any involvement with the English Crown in the shipment of bound books to England. Their association aroused the indignation of the royal printer Robert Barker who declared that Hart had persuaded English printers to reside at Dort for printing the Bible and

Psalms. The firm of Barker, which enjoyed the Bible patent, had published twenty-two editions of the English *New Testament* from 1575 to 1601, and viewed the Norton-Canin edition as a personal affront. With some vehemence Barker referred to the Dort publishers as "persons of the most disordered sort [who] also attemp[ted] to publish lewd and seditious books."[14]

English printing at Dort was continued to some extent by George Waters. In 1611 he was briefly associated with the English news-publisher, Nathaniel Butter, who had commissoned him to print "divers great quantityes and nvmbers of primers." By this action Butter had greatly offended the Company since the patent for the publication of "Prymers Psalters and Psalmes" had been granted to the holders of the English Stock of the Stationers' Company. Butter was summoned before the Wardens of his guild in October 1611 to reply to charges for this dereliction. He was accused of having sent Waters not only specific instructions for the printing of primers but also the copy of an English primer which was to serve as the specimen for the Dort reprint. Printed copies had been brought to England by Jacob Benhill a tailor who, along with a certain Green of London Bridge, had acted upon Butter's behest as agents for the circulation and sale of the Dort primers. Butter was severely reprimanded by the Company and was compelled to give up all available copies of the work and to surrender his yeoman share in the English Stock. The matter was further investigated abroad – Waters being examined at Dort by the "Burroughmasters, Aldermen and Councell there."[15]

Waters was apparently sufficiently chastened to desist from printing any book until 1614 when he issued *The unreasonablenesse of the separation* by William Bradshaw. He was to continue to publish until 1623, circulating a small list of books of political and literary content.[16]

From 1607 through 1619 Giles Thorp, a member of the Amsterdam Separatist community, issued a few books. Thorp had settled in Amsterdam, where he became a member of Henry Ainsworth's congregation. He had probably been instructed in the mystery of printing by Ainsworth who during his early years at Amsterdam had worked for a local bookseller. Thorp was presumably the author of an unpublished book, *The hunting of the foxe, part I* which was acrimoniously criticized by the nonconformist divine John Paget in his *Arrow against separation of the Brownists* in which he referred to "the disguised pamphlets that are come out [which] do in part shew disguised practises of your separation." Paget alluded to Thorp as deacon of Ainsworth's congregation which he faithfully served, becoming an elder in 1618.[17]

As a result of his close association with Ainsworth, Thorp printed four of his books: *The Communion of Saincts; A defence of the holy scriptures, worship and ministerie against M. Smith; An animadversion to Mr. Clyftons Advertisement* and his *Annotations upon the book of Psalms*. A Separatist treatise of interest, bearing Thorp's imprint, is Richard Clyfton's *Plea for the infants and elder people directed against the teachings of the she-baptist,* John Smythe. Works by Randal Bate and John Harrison may also be ascribed to Thorp's press.[18]

Thorp's publication of an occasional Brownist work is completely overshadowed by the brief but concentrated productivity of the secret "Pilgrim Press" of Leyden whose score of books rank as American incunabula.

The English Separatist Congregation had departed in early 1609 for Leyden, a city described by Bradford as "fair and beautiful . . . of a sweet situation . . . made more famous by the university." Here the exiles, denied the more varied employments offered by Amsterdam, nevertheless "fell to such trades and employments as best they could," attaining "at length a competent and comfortable living, but with hard and continual labor."[19]

The part-time employment chosen by one of their ablest leaders, William Brewster, assistant to pastor John Robinson, was the direction of the underground printing press. The history of the Pilgrim Press at Leyden has been traced with bibliographical precision and the keenest scholarship by Rendel Harris and Stephen K. Jones. Little can ever be added to their findings. None the less the role of this minority press, a threat to the authority of the English home government, must be considered in an analysis of contemporary subversive printing.[20]

William Brewster, having attended Cambridge for a brief period, entered service with Sir William Davison, Ambassador to the Low Countries, remaining with him until 1587 when he withdrew to the country. Here, according to his biographer Bradford, he passed time in promoting and furthering religion. At Scrooby Manor, where he was Master of the Post, Brewster encouraged a growing group of Separatists who joined in communion with him on the Lord's Day. Emigrating with the Separatists to Holland, he returned to his academic pursuits at Leyden, teaching English to Dutch students, many of whom "attained it with great facility for he drew rules to learne it by after the Latin manner." Bradford believed Brewster to be "qualified above many . . . wise and discreet . . . of an humble and modest mind." By 1617 with the financial assistance of a Kentish gentleman, Thomas Brewer, "a man of means" and "the help of some friends" – William Brewster set up a secret press on the Pieterskerkkoorsteeg.[21]

Brewster had been introduced to the mystery of printing by the Brownist exile, Edward Winslow, who is described as a "Printer of London." The authors selected for publication at the new press upheld extremist Separatist doctrine. The printer enjoyed a warm personal relationship with the divines, John Robinson, Francis Johnson and William Ames, David Calderwood, Robert Harrison, Walter Travers and Thomas Cartwright, the latter ejected from England, now having sought exile in Holland. Hence printer and writer were welded by a mutual spirituality, a desire for reform and the aspirations of the religious exile for his ecclesiastical utopia.[22]

The Pilgrim Press from 1617 through 1619 issued twenty books of the Separatists: notably those by William Ames, David Calderwood, John Dod and Robert Cleaver, William Euring, John Robinson, Francis Johnson, Thomas Dighton, Walter Travers and Thomas Cartwright. Of these only three bear

Brewster's name: "Prostant Lvgdvni Batavorvm, apvd Gviljelmvm Brewstervm in Vico Chorali" and "Tot Leyden Voor Guiliaem Brewster Boekdrucker." The remainder, branded by Sir Dudley Carleton as Brewster imprints, have been definitely identified by Harris and Jones.[23]

The work of his secret press kept Brewster fully occupied, as Bradford was to write: "[He] had employment enough; and by reason of many books which would not be allowed to be printed in England, they might have had more than they could do." It was not until after the publication of nine works, that Carleton, embodying the authority of the English state and in the manner of his predecessors, Cobham and Stafford, complained to the Prince of Orange of the publications of the Leyden underground press.[24]

With the appearance of Calderwood's *De Regimine Ecclesiae Scoticanae Brevis Relatio*, Carleton determined that the printer and the press be investigated as "an example to others." The books were to be suppressed and the identities of the printer and author revealed. In 1618 Brewster printed the treatise of the Scottish Puritan divine David Calderwood who was to visit Holland the following year when his larger work, the *Perth Assembly* was printed by Brewster. Carleton suspected Schilders to be responsible for Calderwood's treatise. He had him examined by the Dutch authorities in March 1618, hinting at the possibility of severe punishment were the truth to be withheld.[25]

While Schilders denied all responsibility, copies of the *Perth Assembly* which Carleton castigated as "writte with much scorn and reproach of the proceedings in Scotland concerning the affairs of the church" were on public sale by July 17, 1619. The ambassador advised Sir Robert Naunton, English Secretary of State, that the book had appeared "without name, either of author or printer. I am informed it is printed by a certain English Brownist of Leyden as are most of the Puritan books sent over of late days in England." He referred to the underground press's infringement of the English and Dutch laws against the exportation of controversial material to England and expressed his hope for the prompt identification of the printer and the location of the press.[26]

Carleton's hopes were soon rewarded. In a letter of July 22, 1619, he suggested to Naunton that the *Perth Assembly*, copies of which had been shipped to England, and the *De Regimine Ecclesiae Scoticanae Brevis Relatio* had been printed by one and the same person, "William Brewster a Brownist who hath been for some years an inhabitant and printer at Leyden but is now within these three weeks removed from thence and gone back to London where he may be found and examined not only of this book ... but likewise of the Perth Assembly of which if he was not the printer he assuredly knows both the printer and the author." Carleton continued that Brewster had his hand in "all such books as have been sent over to England and Scotland," referring specifically to the two Pilgrim Press imprints: Cartwright's *Confvtation of the Rhemists Translation, Glosses and Annotations on the Nevv Testament* and the anonymous tract, *De vera et genvina Iesv Christi Domini et Salvatoris nostri Religione*. As definite proof that Brewster was the printer of the latter work and of Calderwood's *Relatio*, the Ambassador indulged in some bibliographical research. He dispatched to Naunton a title-page of the *De vera . . . Religione* which he requested his correspondent to compare with the title-page of the *Brevis Relatio*. Upon close scrutiny he would agree they were "of the same character."[27]

Carleton's mention of Brewster's visit to England is in all likelihood correct. Enjoying several pseudonyms, Williams and Wincob, a friend of the Dutch and the holder of an English passport, Brewster could easily slip in and out of the country. Carleton of course had hoped to apprehend him. A Dutch pursuivant, "a dull drunken fellow," sent to arrest him, mistakenly seized Brewster's patron, Thomas Brewer, taking "one man for another." Brewer was clapped into the Leyden University jail, while his "printing letters were found in a garret where he had hid them." At the Ambassador's request his books and papers were immediately impounded to be examined by Carleton's agents who found among them copies of Brewster's first imprint, the *Reply* of William Ames to the Dutch Remonstrant divine, Nicholas Grevinchovius. "By that character," Carleton declared, "he is condemned of the rest; and certain experienced printers which have viewed the letters, affirm that all and every one of the books with which he is charged . . . were printed by him."[28]

While Brewer remained in the University jail, subject to English interrogation, Brewster, according to Naunton, had been "fryghted back in the Low Countries by the Bishopps pursuivants."[29]

The activity of the short-lived underground press on the Pieterskerkkoorsteeg was reviewed by the English Ambassador. Carleton stated that Brewster had neither maintained an open shop nor printed many books appropriate for public sale in the provinces. His "practice was to print prohibited books to be vented underhand in his Majesty's kingdoms."[30]

Brewster's financial patron Brewer, a graduate of the University of Leyden, enjoyed the protection of his alma mater's authorities. In due course he was returned to England having been promised that he would not "be touched either in body or goods by the English government." Having decided against the Pilgrim venture to America, Brewer remained in England where he purportedly wrote a "most pestilential book" prophesying the ruin of all religions by James I. The English Separatists departed from Delft aboard the "Speedwell" on July 22, 1620, possibly carrying with them from Holland one part of their underground press. Legend persists that "the great iron screw" brought by the passengers from Leyden – used to support the main beam of the Mayflower during a violent storm – had been the original screw of the Brewster press![31]

Even though Carleton established Brewster's association with the Leyden underground press, it is quite evident that its activity would shortly have been terminated. The ideology of the extremists had been expressed – their books printed and circulated in Holland and England – some to arrive in the New World. The Pilgrim leaders had accomplished their immediate goal; a greater ambition lay ahead. As early as 1617 the project of emigration had preoccupied members of the Leyden refugee community. By September 1619 when the grant was given to John Robinson and Robert Cushman by the Virginia Company to settle in America, the Leyden underground press had completed its work and its printer was prepared to accompany the colonists to a distant clime. Together they forsook "that goodly and pleasant city which had been their resting place near twelve years; but they knew they were pilgrims and looked not much on those things, but lift[ed] up their eyes to the heavens, their dearest country and quieted their spirits." At Plymouth Colony, the Elder Brewster, far beyond the reach of pursuivant and royal plenipotentiary, was to teach and preach. Upon his death in 1643 he left a library of three hundred books among which were to be found thirteen imprints of the Pilgrim Press of Leyden.[32]

With the dispersal of the more radical Separatists to the New World, the literature of the leftist Puritan wing diminished. The Crown continued to oppose nonconformity in the press and the royal Proclamation of 1623 referred to "the printing in the parts beyond the Sea, and elsewhere as well sundry, seditious, schismaticall, and scandalous Bookes and Pamphlets." James' renewal of the Proclamation in 1624 urged a stricter licensing of books by the Archbishops of London and Canterbury and the Vice-Chancellors of the Universities whose scrutiny would prevent Popish and Puritanical books and pamphlets. Conway advised Attorney-General Coventry that James had refused to sign the Proclamation unless the words be added "as also all seditious Puritanicall bookes and scandalous to our Person and State, such as have been lately vented by some Puritanicall spirits."[33]

James, prey to his own impatience and indecision, victim of his own tantrums and poor health – ridiculed and rejected – was not long to survive the "Puritanicall spirits." He was to die in March 1625, those "spirits" conquering the realm he had bequeathed his son. Charles was to find himself ultimately indefensible against the powerful Puritan hold upon the people. The crusade of Puritanism had been achieved by its agitators – supported by its press: the Martinists and Barrowists, Independents and Presbyterians – Waldegrave and Hodgkins, Schilders and Brewster! Its initial goal was to be intensified and relentlessly pursued by later reformers who set the final stage for revolution. The faith, which had sought a purification of the soul, the cleansing of a worldly church, became heady with success and in its violence ruptured the Kingdom and slew its monarch!

CONCLUSIONS

At their stalls in St. Paul's, Ludgate, Little Britain, Old Bailey and the Royal Exchange, the English printer-bookseller sold the popular texts of the age: literature and drama, classics and verse, ballads and news-books, legal manuals and medical compendia, Anglican sermons and homilies, herbals and almanacs, treatises on husbandry and astrology, jest books and chap books, volumes on geography, travel and exploration. As loyal subjects of their Majesties and law-abiding members of their guild, these stationers were involved in little political controversy or religious disputation. They served no faction but pursued their careers, preoccupied with the problems of daily existence.

Unlike them, the Catholic and Puritan printer-publishers maintained their underground presses as literary bastions for the minority faiths which they designed to support and extend. Neither printing minority was large. It would appear that the Catholic press, supported by a few wealthy English aristocrats and a powerful foreign missionary program – viewed favorably by the King of Spain – should have achieved greater success than the Puritan. Yet it was the poorer, unorganized Puritan press which was to spread its message effectively in England – to witness the complete triumph of its gospel of Godliness and spiritual regeneration.

The victory of Puritanism stems from its inherent loyalty to the Crown. Although it criticized the worldly Established Church and strove to strip it of pomp and panoply, at no time did it challenge the government or appeal to a foreign power for aid and invasion of the motherland. Puritanism was a faithful religion – whereas Catholicism yielded much of its allegiance to a foreign monarch, the Vicar of Rome! The militant Catholic strove to cleave England, to withhold his fidelity, to seat upon the English throne a Continental prince. Puritanism, non-subversive, wholly English, abetted by a helter-skelter, unorganized press, eventually won the country. Catholicism was to retreat, its influence to diminish, its press to become less forceful.

In 1624 approximately 124 stationers were active in England. Of these a little more than one-third were involved in some capacity with the minority presses. Forty-three were associated with the Catholic program, contradicting Gee's statement that Catholic books "hvmm[ed] vp and downe in euery corner both of city and country."* Gee's findings none the less are not to be lightly dismissed since they represent a microcosm of the underground and overseas Catholic

---

* According to Allison & Rogers an approximate 700 Anglo-Catholic books were printed between 1558 and 1625 in several editions either secretly in England or on the Continent by foreign firms and English presses in exile.

printing program. The identified members of the Puritan underground and Continental press, including such elusive participants as Humphrey Newman, Melanchthon Jewel and Mrs. Lawson, "the shrew of Newgate," total eleven. Crowley and Boyle obviously found no need to conceal their traffic in non-subversive Puritan texts.

Throughout the history of both movements certain similarities emerge. Each retained underground presses, brief and transient, quickly dismantled at the approach of the pursuivant or Messenger of the Press; both included Continental firms whose masters had sought exile from English reprisal, intent upon exporting their books to the homeland.

Although Catholic and Puritan confronted hazard and reprisal from the English Crown, the Catholic printer experienced less tolerance than his professional Puritan colleague. The former's political philosophy branded him a renegade – an avowed enemy of the state. The Puritan printer whose propaganda was critical – but never seditious – seldom evoked the authorities' real wrath. Five Catholic stationers were executed – their guilt based upon the possession and circulation of subversive texts. In contrast, only one Puritan, the printer Hodgkins, may have been hanged.

The differences between the Catholic and Puritan operational printing programs are vast. The Catholic plan, supported by Jesuit acumen, relied upon a chain of skilled aides; the Puritan depended upon an occasional patron and distributor. Abroad well-established presses supplied the orthodox movement with appropriate literature; on the Continent the Puritan faction found some small support from impecunious English exiles and for a brief period hailed the achievements of its small but influential Leyden Press. The Catholic book project affords a far more illuminating picture than that of the Puritan bereft of any real organization, any concentrated program.

London, with its maze of alleys, lanes and warrens, proved a suitable center for some secret presses and the hideout of scouts, brokers and Catholic missionary agents. Much of the underground printing, however, was pursued in the provinces: Lancashire, Staffordshire, Worcestershire and Northamptonshire, the latter, the home of Sir Richard Knightley, who provided a brief haven for the Martinist press under Waldegrave's direction.

The highly organized Catholic press with its factors traveling between London and the provinces, the Continent and the remote Channel ports, bringing books into England concealed in greatcoats or hidden within shipments of indigo and cochineal, covered with fish in barrels and "fardels" – occasionally transported within "some Ambassador's goods" – presents a vivid portrait of the contemporary traffic in illicit books.

The Catholic book program depended also upon missionaries and intelligencers abroad: Verstegan at Antwerp, Humphrey Shelton at Rouen, Edward Barlow at Bruges and other agents posing as scholars, travelers, pilgrims, jugglers or gentlemen in retirement. Texts were conveyed to England by "certain common carriers of papisticall bookes and letters from one papist to another," Godshall, Marsham and Moore, the latter a Master of Arts from Cambridge and a graduate of the Rheims Seminary. The Jesuit, Father Emerson, on one trip successfully dispatched four priests to England who smuggled over 800 books into the country. It was alleged that the St. Omer English College Press maintained a regular corps of "Factors and Brokers in London, and all parts of England, to disperse and sell [their] Bookes and Pamphlets, and to transport the money vnto them at Saint Omer."

Catholic agents often sought a dwelling in proximity to a foreign port in order to take "trips to the coast to arrange for boats to convey people across ... whilst others [take] charge of the preparation and introduction into the country of books written in English and both on spiritual and devotional subjects and in matters of controversy and in answer to the calumnies with which the heretic assails us." Hilles, a spy in the Spanish service, settled near Petworth where he worked as an under-cover man and prevailed upon Catholic carriers to bring books into England.

The Jesuit William Kinsman confessed that he had transported to the homeland copies of his translation of Alfonso de Villegas' *Flos sanctorum. The liues of saints*, while the Dabscots suffered interrogation and arrest for their role in the importation of the obnoxious *Prvrit-Anvs*,* having smuggled other books "out of France or the Low Countries especially from Roane."

The expertise of the publisher Heigham had not escaped official notice. According to Udall, there had not been any book of stature "otherwise brought into England or printed beyonde the sea but it hath ben performed by Roger Higham or his wife." As a shipper, Heigham sent over copies of books by Worthington, Fitzherbert, Fitzsimon, Bellarmine, Villegas and other Catholic worthies. The exasperated Udall affirmed that Heigham had shipped to England "all the seditious bokes which come from Dowa and other partes." At South Shields the Jesuits landed newly printed Continental Catholic volumes, also exporting two "dryfatts" of books, "containing newly translated testaments, catechisms" to be circulated in England and Scotland. Feigning innocence of any complicity in the underground press, the resident diplomats in London protested English investigation of their residences. Had not a Flemish priest deposited bales of the vile *Prvrit-Anvs* in the cellar and porter's lodge of the Venetian embassy?

A group of dedicated ladies received and sold Catholic literature at their London stalls and domiciles. The widows Douce and Fowler, Bulloch and Udall acted as agents for Catholic texts, while Joan Dabscot and Marie Boniface, the wife of John Heigham, were considered to be "two ... dangerous women for these causes," arriving in England from the Continent concealing Catholic books.

Like the Catholic distribution program, the Puritan scheme retained agents who circulated texts and carried Martinist lampoons from the country to the Capital. The Puritan factor Humphrey Newman, alias Brownbread, traveled to London for that purpose. At the Capital, Martinist tracts were sold by Mrs.

---

* The Dabscots were not the only agents for the circulation of *Prvrit-Anvs*. Reference is made in 1609 to its distribution in England "in spite of the danger of those who sell it."

CONCLUSIONS

Lawson and Lady Richard Martin, wife of the Master of the Mint. Banned copies of Robert Browne's notable work, *A booke which sheweth the life and manners of all true christians*, were "dispersed in sundry places within the Realme," while copies of *The examinations of H. Barrow J. Grenewood and J. Penrie* – spirited out of jail in manuscript to be printed in Holland – were found in the homes of English sympathizers. Unbound sheets of Schilders' publications were shipped to England to be bound and sold, while the distinguished Brewster had his hands "in all such books as have been sent over to England and Scotland." Finding a limited welcome in England, he slipped in and out of the country assailed by the government as the printer of "prohibited books to be vented underhand in his Majesty's Kingdoms." Enjoying a variety of pseudonyms, like Heigham, he traveled between Holland and England bringing with him the publications of his Leyden Press. Melanchthon Jewel, the hedge-priest, suffered imprisonment for the sale of Puritan texts.

The texts circulated by the agents of both factions were issued for the most part in smaller editions than the popular fare carried by the masters of the Gilded Cup, the Three Crowns, Popes Head Palace and the Mermaid. A book designed for general consumption such as Wither's *Motto* appeared in several editions two of which consisted each of 6,000 copies. The circulation of the poem with its barbed allusion to current corruption and the venality of Stuart officials attests to its enormous appeal.

The size of Catholic editions varied. It is not at all surprising that the Rheims *New Testament*, a landmark in orthodox scholarship, was printed in an edition of 5,000 copies. Father Persons' *News from Spayne and Holland*, issued in an edition of 4,000 copies, indicates the great Jesuit's influence. On the other hand, Gregory Martin's *Treatise of Schisme*, printed by Carter, consisted of 1,250 copies.

Puritan books appeared in somewhat smaller editions. Cartwright's *Second Admonition to Parliament* and Browne's *Book which sheweth the life and manners of all true Christians* were printed each in editions of 1,000 copies. Humphrey Newman alludes to the distribution of 900 copies of Penry's *Supplication*, 700 and 800 copies of the Martinist tracts, *Hay any worke for cooper* and *Martin Senior*. Printed abroad at great difficulty and designed for a specific audience, the Barrowist treatise, *The examinations of H. Barrow J. Grenewood and J. Penrie*, was printed in an edition of either 200 or 300 copies.

The prices of Catholic texts – far exceeding the Puritan – were exorbitant according to Gee. Certainly they contravened the "Ordinance against the excessive prices of books" issued in 1598 by the Stationers' Company which berated those dealers "enhancing the prices of books and selling the same at too high and excessive rates and prices." It was decreed that all books printed in pica letter were to be sold "not above a penny for two sheets," while those printed in brevier were to cost a penny for one sheet and a half.* Disregarding

---
* Greg & Boswell, *Records*, p. 58.

the statute, Catholic factors in London demanded forty shillings for the Douai *Bible* and sixteen to twenty for the Rheims *New Testament*. Books by Worthington, Norris, Musket, Brereley and Smith ran the scale from seventeen to five shillings. On the other hand *Deus et Rex* of James I, issued certainly in large editions, since it was to be distributed throughout the realm, cost only six pence. Copies of the Marprelate tract, *The Epistle*, were sold at eleven pence. With the exception of Brereley's *Protestants apologie*, the writings of the Catholic authors indicated were printed at Douai and St. Omer and hence imported into England. The expense of importation obviously influenced the asking price. In contrast to the prices of sectarian books a copy of Shakespeare's *Sonnets* cost the actor Edward Alleyn five pence, while the first edition of *Venus & Adonis* issued by Field in 1593 fetched three times as much. An edition of the First Folio cost half the price realized by the Douai *Bible*.*

To stifle the circulation of high-priced Catholic texts and the cheaper literary pabulum of the Puritan the government exercised its power of reprisal: a constant but often ineffectual harbor patrol, raid, search, arrest and imprisonment. Its "many eyes, [its] many tongues ... scouts and crafts" had been bewailed by Father Campion. By the reign of James I the Crown still found it imperative to stem the tide of defamatory literature, heeding Udall's advice that "never more seditious bokes were readye to come abroade then nowe are in hand as well in Englande as beyonde the seas."

Both Catholic and Puritan printer suffered from the raids of the Crown's ruffian gang of pursuivants, "thieves rude and barbarous" and the Messengers of the Press, the official investigators of the Stationers' Company, who strove to abort the infiltration of nonconformist books within England. The informer "hatefull to the better sort" is personified by the unctuous braggart Udall, the prototype of the opportunist, the betrayer, the hoodlum, eager to sacrifice and to destroy for personal advancement. Factors and agents, allured by the government with financial rewards, were encouraged to advance information. The Catholic printer Henry Taylor was promised ten pounds and the return of his "press and prints" if he forwarded "secret intelligence."

With an unholy zeal the searcher pounced down upon the minority press which was "sawed and hewed in pieces ... battered and made vnserviceable, the letters melted." With a similar enthusiasm he "beset their homes on every side, corners ransacked even womens beds and bosomes." The walls were sounded to locate hiding places and the "highways laid." The coöperative policy of the Stationers' Company is reflected in its readiness "to seek out unauthorized printers, to seize any printed or bound stock which had been produced contrary to the form of any statute, act or proclamation." Success in detection was often celebrated in a "serch dinner," an award banquet.

The Catholic and Puritan offender on the flimsiest pretext was arrested and thrown into jail, Newgate, Bridewell, the Clink or the Poultry, "slaughter

---

* Rostenberg, *Publishing in England*, II, p. 425.

houses" where the victims "succumbed like dogs in their corner... many laden with chains and braces." The possibility of a fair trial for a recusant was remote. Was not the sympathetic jury at the trial of the bookseller Duckett informed by Popham, Lord Chief Justice of England, to consult once again and to return with the sensible verdict "guilty"?

While the transgressor languished in jail, his books were banned and frequently burned.* Had not Elizabeth herself perused Bacon's *Declaration of the practices and treasons committed by Robert late Earle of Essex* to excise any passages which might possibly render honor to her late favorite or diminish homage to be tendered her royal person? Raleigh's *History of the World* had been banned since it proved "too saucy in censuring princes." Books printed abroad which impugned the authority of the Crown were to be tracked down and destroyed by the royal emissary, the diplomat. The assignments of the English ministers, Cobham, Stafford, Digby and Carleton, wearisome in their minutiae, included the detection of offensive texts, the possible murder of an author, the kidnapping of a printer. Working with a staff of minor officials, the diplomat did not always achieve success. Carleton expressed his indignation to James that the States of Holland permitted "a liberty of printing... for any passionate or discontented spirit to publish what he pleases to the disquiet of both church and state in his Majesty's kingdoms." Yet Cobham, Stafford and Carleton achieved some success – authors were arrested and their texts confiscated. The Catholic and Puritan printers and the works they issued at home and abroad rank among the earliest victims of the vicious practice of censorship in its long and noxious history.

The efforts of the state to stifle and harass the printing and distribution program of the minority factions achieved no great success. As early as 1565 the Spanish ambassador to England, Guzman de Silva, declared that the books shipped from Louvain had done an incalculable service in spreading the faith. Less than a decade later, Bishop Parker bemoaned the influence of the Puritan authors upon a sympathetic public, reporting the "boldness and disobedience... which the new writers have already wrought in the myndes of the people and that against the Ciuill magistrates."

Creswell assayed the influence of the "Martinists or Puritans [as] much more dangerous for domestical broyles than the Spaniardes for open warres... for that they muste needes hate her Maiestie and the Protestante Councell most deadly, as both by reason and by their bookes." The government, alarmed by the insidious spread of nonconformist texts, issued a series of proclamations against those books "secretly published and dispersed... containing in them doctrine very erroneous... and slanderous to the state."

The Catholic community had been able "to stand firme not only by means of the sacraments and other resources, among which is the reading of spiritual books and of treatises concerning religion... by learned and pious men." The

---

* The report that entire editions were burned is of course exaggerated – consider the many copies of such books which exist today in public and private collections.

influence of Father Persons upon the English orthodox group was considerable – "for though his books do not bear his name, yet he is recognized in them by all. The elegance, propriety, gravity and simplicity of his style have won for him ... a foremost place among English writers." He regarded his own books and others "printed in Flanders and elsewhere as a most efficacious means for helping the Catholic cause abroad and at home whither many copies were exported." By 1610 the "fruit of [Catholic] good books" was extensive in England. The texts which "penetrat[ed] where the priests and religious cannot" were recommended as "weapons against the heretics [whose books] issue[d] every day do so much harm to the souls if not confuted."

The dedication of the Catholic Heigham to his faith is revealed in his multiple role as author, translator and publisher. His *Deuout Exposition of the holie masse* was inspired by the "great long want of the full and perfect Exposition of this diuine mysterie of the English toung." From his press came Catholic texts which were not "to lye any longer in obscuritie."

The Puritan printer Strowd affirmed his high moral credo in his circulation of books not based on the motive "of any gaine but only for the desire ... to aduaunce the glory of God." To him no law could extinguish "God's spirit in his children."

The eventual complete victory of Puritanism in England may be partially attributed to the printers and booksellers who from "the close of the sixteenth century to the outbreak of the Revolution ... supplied the common public with reading matter."

The cause of the religious minorities in England was inestimably served by the underground press – domestic and in exile – and by the sympathetic Continental printer-publisher. Both orthodox and Puritan craftsmen circulated in the country their texts brought from the provinces and warrens of London, imported from the Flemish towns and the cities of France and the Empire.

Strength and optimism omnipresent, the minority printer ever remained "a hartie wel wisher and affectionate countryman" to his co-religionists. Imbued with religious intensity, he found a greater reward in his service than in economic remuneration. The factional printer was sustained by his faith, by his labor.

Yet the Catholic stationer confronted greater hazard than the Puritan. The state was his implacable enemy, determined to evict and destroy him. He represented a foreign authority, a book program developed by Jesuitical shrewdness. The tool of an overseas power, he became a national threat.

Thus, despite the recusant printer's devoted support of Catholicism, it was Puritanism that attained an ultimate national victory, thanks in part to the Puritan stationer whose loyalty had seldom been questioned. Allied as he was with "phanaticall spirits," he was never associated with a Continental monarch or a foreign church. The books he circulated bore no message of treason, no disloyalty to the Crown. Although he irritated his Majesty and Parliament, he was never (with one possible exception) made to endure the extreme penalty suffered by several Catholic stationers. Indeed the future government, the Commonwealth, ever mindful of his service, was in time to bestow upon him the laurel, "Printer to the State"!

ILLUSTRATIONS

Queen Elizabeth I. Full-page engraving from Henry Holland, *Herwologia Anglica*. [Arnhem 1620]. Attributed to Crispin van de Passe. Courtesy, Rare Book Division, The New York Public Library.

William, Cardinal Allen, described by Elizabeth's admirers as "ill deserving to be accounted English." Full-page engraving from Isaac Bullart, *Academie des Sciences et des Arts*. Amsterdam 1682. Engraving attributed to Esme de Boullogne. Courtesy, Rare Book Division, The New York Public Library.

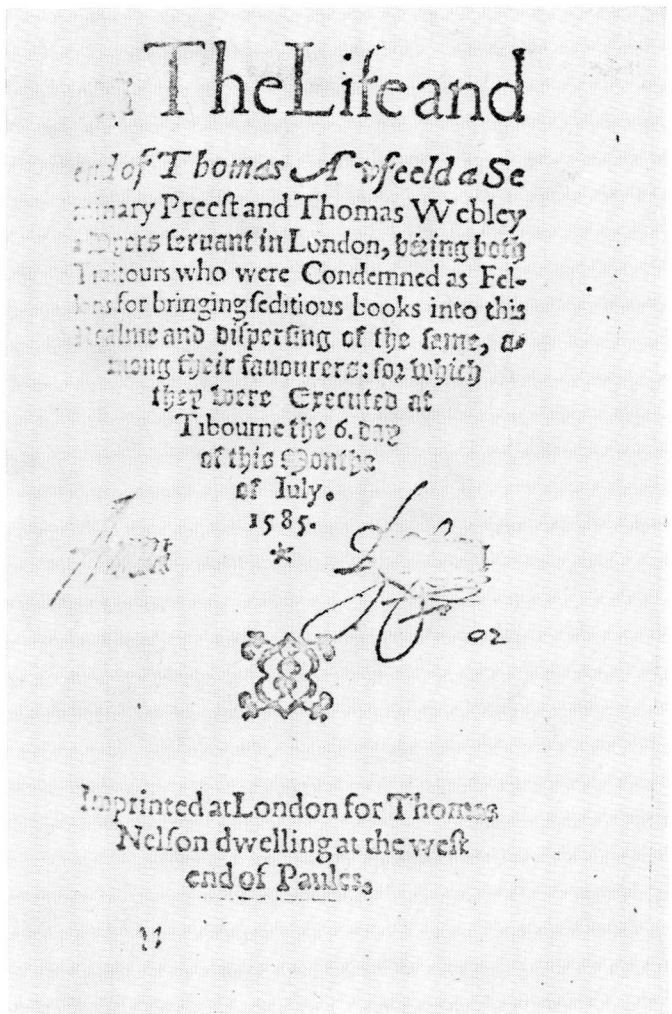

Father Persons' "Man," Thomas Awfield, priest and book scout. Title-page of *The Life and end of Thomas Awfeeld a Seminary Preest and Thomas Webley a Dyers seruant*. London 1585. Courtesy, The British Museum Library.

William Cecil, Lord Burleigh. With Walsingham, "Grand Master of Espionage." Full-page engraving from Henry Holland, *Herwologia Anglica*. [Arnhem 1620]. Attributed to Crispin van de Passe. Courtesy, Rare Book Division, The New York Public Library.

A DIALOGVE BETWIXT A SE-CVLAR PRIEST, AND A LAY GEN-TLEMAN.

Concerning some points obje-
cted by the Iesuiticall faction against such
Secular Priests, as haue shewed their dislike
of M. *Blackwell* and the Iesuits
proceedings.

Printed at Rhemes. M D C I.

The Archpriest Controversy. Title-page of [John Mush], *A Dialogve Betwixt A Secv ar Priest, and a Lay Gentleman.* "Rhemes 1601." The fictitious imprint indicates the publisher's wish not to be publicly identified with the Controversy. The book was actually printed by Adam Islip, London 1601. Courtesy, The Henry E. Huntington Library.

Full-page engraving of James I in robes of state with regalia from Thomas Milles, *The treasurie of aunciant and moderne times*. London 1613–1619. Artist unidentified. Courtesy, Rare Book Division, The New York Public Library.

1. An Answere to Sr. Edw. Cooke [?]
2. Motives of Bristow   2
3. Hæggens   2
4. Leader   2
5. wystons 3 conversions   2
6. A Christian directory   2
7. Firm foundation of Cath: religion 2
8. English martyrologie   2
9. Equivocation   2
10. Dialogues of st Gregory   2
11. Historie of ye L of Loretto   2
12. Popish prayers   2
13. C. Bedanus his English workes   2
14. An answere to Sr E. Cooke   2
15. Rules of good life   [?]
16. The spirituall conflict   2
17. Golden Knotts or
    Loan Bell
18. Bells triall examined   2
19. Rosary of our Lady   2
    A popish booklet   1

These bookes above named of ye Right Honorable
Sr Jul: Cæsar Aug: 1. 1609
   I remitt.   Richard Etkins.

Manuscript List of 20 intercepted Catholic books submitted to Sir Julius Caesar, August 1, 1609. Signed by Richard Etkins. Courtesy, Department of Western Manuscripts, The British Museum.

PRVRIT-ANVS,
VEL
NEC OMNE, NEC EX OMNI.

SIVE

Apologia pro PVRITANIS, *& Nouato-*
ribus Vniuerfis.

IN QVA

Et mores, & opiniones Nouorum Hominum no-
ftri temporis, auctoritate Scripturæ affir-
mantur & infirmantur

AD

Reformatos huius fæculi Fratres, Germanos,
Gallos, & Britannos.

Si malè, nil peius; si bene, nil melius.

LVTETIAE BRITANNORVM,
Apud ISAACVM IACOBI, M. DC. IX.

Title-page of the "vile book" known as *Prvrit-Anvs* attributed to Horatio Dolabella, a work "stuffed with ... horrible blasphemies," a slashing polemic against James I. Probably printed abroad, 1609. Courtesy, Rare Book Division, The New York Public Library.

IX

❧ By the King.

❧ A Proclamation for the search and
apprehension of Iohn Cotton
Esquire.

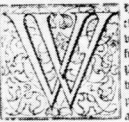hereas Iohn Cotton of Warblington, otherwise of Subberton, in
the Countie of Southhampton, Esquire, is vehement strong and
vehement presumptions, discouered to haue committed matter
full of very strange and execrable high Treasons, against Our
Personand State. And the same hath seemed, as it should appeare
by all circumstances, hath, vpon a guiltie conscience, and some
priuie intelligence of search intended for him, fled from his house
and dwelling, and lurketh or wandreth in vnknowne places. Al-
though it standeth not with the course of Iustice to condemne any man vnheard, yet for that
the presumptions and proofes appeare to bee so forcible against him, as if after this publike
notice, he shall not forthwith come in, and render himselfe, wee shall haue iust cause to con-
clude him guiltie, we haue thought fit, besides Our more secret directions, to haue recourse
to the ministrie and loue of Our people, which neuer failed Us, in any case that concerned
Our safetie or honour, for his bringing forth or apprehension.

Wherefore we do charge and command all our Iustices, Maiors, Sheriffes, Bailiffes,
Headboroughs, and Constables, and also all officers of Our Portes, to doe their best and
vtmost endeuours, to search for, and apprehend the said Iohn Cotton. Of whom, for the better enforming of those that know not his person, wee haue caused a description to be hereunto
annexed. And doe neuerthelesse require all Our louing Subiects, not onely to bee ay-
ding and assisting to Our said Officers therein; But likewise to vse their owne particular
diligence, care and industrie, aswell for the finding out and apprehending of the said Iohn
Cotton, as for the giuing intelligence and aduertisement vnto any of our Iustices or Officers, where he hath beene at any time lately seene or met, or otherwise where there is any
likelyhood that he should harbor, repaire or be receiued.

And for the better encouragement of our louing Subiects to doe their duetie in this
case (which wee take so much to heart) wee doe hereby declare, signifie, and promise,
that whosoeuer shall apprehend and bring into the handes of any Our Officers of Iustice,
the person of the said Iohn Cotton liuing, that haue for his reward the summe of one thousand
Crownes.

And on the other side, if any of Our Subiects shall voluntarily receiue, harbour,
conuey, fauour or conceale the said Iohn Cotton, wee do signifie vnto them all, that we shall
account them as partakers, and abettors of the said Treasons: And if any of Our Officers,
or others shall neglect or let passe any opportunitie, occasion, or meanes for the performance,
or executing of their duetie in this behalfe, wee shall proceede against such persons to their
condigne punishment with all seueritie according to our Lawes.

Giuen at Our Pallace of Westminster the eleuenth day of Iune, in the eleuenth
yeere of Our Reigne of Great Britaine, France, and Ireland.

God saue the King.

Iohn Cotton is of the age of fourtie eight yeeres, or thereabouts, of a reasonable tall
stature, slender of bodie, the haire of his head and beard flaxen, but now inclining to
white, well complexioned, with somewhat a long and leane visage.

¶ Imprinted at London by Robert Barker,
Printer to the Kings most Excellent Maiestie.
ANNO DOM. 1613.

James I, *A Proclamation for the search and apprehension of Iohn Cotton* "a west county gentleman" and author of a "very scandalous and railing book" against the government. London 1613. Courtesy, The Henry E. Huntington Library.

x

A Catalogue of Popish Books.

ging in *Turnbull street*, for fourteene shillings, which might bee afforded for fiue shillings.

The Protestants Apologie, written by *Brerely*, reprinted and sold for seuenteene shillings, and might bee afforded for six shillings, or lesse.

Saint Augustines Confessions, translated by *Tob. Mathew*, and sold for sixteene shillings, beeing but a little booke in *octauo*, and might bee afforded for two shillings six-pence.

Two other bookes in *octauo*, lately written by *Tob. Mathew*, and sold very deare.

The Author and substance of Protestant Religion, written by *Smith* a Priest now in *London*, and sold for six-shillings, and might bee afforded for twelue-pence.

Luthers his life and doctrine, a railing booke, written by *Lewella* Priest, who is at this present in *London*, sold for eight shillings, worth two shillings.

An Antidote against the pestiferous writings of English Sect aries, in two parts, written by *D. No-rice* a Priest, now resident in *London*, sold for eight shillings, might bee afforded for foure shillings.

The Guide of Faith, written by the said Author, and sold at an vnreasonable rate.

The Pseudo-Scripturist, by the same Author, a booke of some twelue sheetes of paper, and sold for fiue shillings.

The Christian Fore, by the same Author, a book of ten sheetes of paper, and sold for two shillings six-pence.

The

A Catalogue of Popish Books.

The lewd lying Pamphlet, tearmed, *The Bi-shop of Londons Legacie*, written by *Muskei* a Iesuite, and reprinted with a preface of a new disguise : the booke containing about sixteene sheetes : they squeezed from some Romish buyers, six or seuen shillings a peece. A deare price for a dirty lye. Yet I wish, they that haue any beliefe in it, might pay dearer for it.

The summary of Controuersies, written by *D. Smith*, sold as deare as the rest.

The new Religion, no Religion, written by one *Floud*, a Priest now in *London*, sold at a high rate, and so are all the rest following.

The sum of Christian Doctrine, written in Latine by *Petrus Canisius*, and translated into English by *I. Heigham* a Priest in *London*.

The true Christian Catholick, by the same Author.

The life of Saint Katharine of Sienna, by the same Author.

The Protestants Consultation, a dangerous book, lately written by an vnknowne Author.

Iesus, Maria Ioseph, lately come out of the Press, printed in *London*, by Simons *a Carmelite* now in *London*.

Two other Bookes, written by the same Author, called, *The way to finde ease, rest, and repose vnto the soule*.

Bellarmines steps in English.

His art of dying well, in octauo.

The exercise of a Christian life, by *S.B.*

The vocation of Bishops, by *D. Champney* now in *London*.

The

Titles of "Popishe trashe" listed by John Gee in *The Foote out of the snare*. London 1624. Despite the author's prejudice the book remains a "microcosm of the underground English publishing world." Courtesy, Rare Book Division, The New York Public Library.

THE ENGLISH MARTYROLOGE

CONTEYNING

A SVMMARY OF THE LIVES
of the glorious and renowned Saintes
of the three Kingdomes,

ENGLAND, SCOTLAND, AND
IRELAND.

COLLECTED AND DISTRIBVTED
into Moneths, after the forme of a Calendar,
according to euery Saintes festiuity.

WHERVNTO
Is *annexed in the end a Catalogue of those, who haue suffered
death in England for defence of the Catholicke Cause, since King
Henry the 8. his breach with the Sea Apostolicke, vnto this day.*

By a Catholicke Priest.

Eccles. 44.
Nomen eorum viuet in generationem & generationem.
Their memory shall liue from generation to generation.

Permissu Superiorum. Anno 1608.

Title-page of [John Wilson], *The English Martyrologe*. St. Omer 1608. The first book published at the St. Omer English College Press written by its first director. Courtesy, The Henry E. Huntington Library.

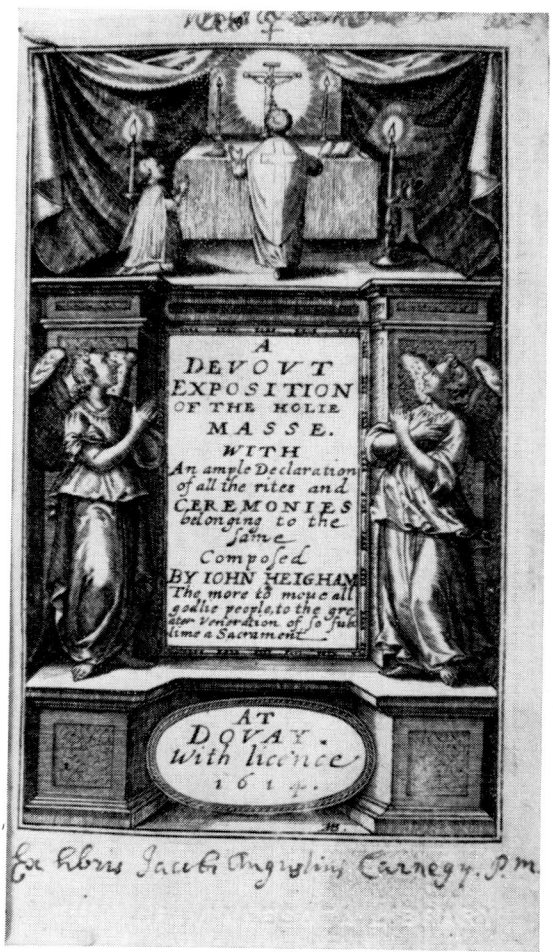

Title-page of John Heigham, *A Devovt Exposition of the Holie Masse.* Douai: Heigham, 1614. Written and published by the Catholic bookman and author, John Heigham, "a hartie wel wisher and affectionate countryman." Courtesy, The University of Minnesota Library.

Manuscript list of recusant books deposited at the Venetian Embassy in London in 1609 causing the ambassador Marc-Antonio Correr much embarrassment. Reflection of diplomatic involvement in the importation of Catholic literature into England. Courtesy, Department of Western Manuscripts, The British Museum.

By the King.

A Proclamation for Ambaſſadours and forreigne Miniſters.

HE Kings moſt Excellent Maieſtie, conſidering the great Priuiledges, which by the Lawes of GOD and Nations are attributed vnto the perſons of Ambaſſadors, Agents, and publique Miniſters of forreigne Princes and States, and the great Reuerence and Reſpect, which of right appertaineth vnto them, and weighing the manifold and important Reaſons thereof, and how neerely euery ſmall neglect and diſreſpect of them, toucheth not onely thoſe Princes and States by whom they are imployed, but all others in example and conſequence, and as a neceſſarie dependant thereupon, the vniuerſall weale and tranquillitie of all Kingdomes and States, hauing entercourſe, commerce, or correſpondence together; And willing that as great obſeruance be vſed towards them within this His Maieſties Realme, as in other the beſt gouerned Kingdomes and Nations, Hath thought fit hereby to forewarne all perſons whatſoeuer, That they not onely forbeare to vſe any inſolencie, miſbehauiour, inciuilitie, diſgrace, or affront, vnto any Ambaſſadors, Agents, or publique Miniſters of any forreigne Princes or States, and their followers, ſeruants, and attendants, but also doe vpon all occaſions performe vnto them, all ſuch reuerence, reſpect and courteſie, both in ſpeech, geſture and otherwiſe, as is moſt fitting to proceede from perſons of ciuill behauiour, vnto men of that eminencie for place and employment, vpon paine of His Maieſties higheſt indignation and diſpleaſure, and ſuch ſeuere puniſhment as the offenders of this His Royall Command may deſerue. And His Maieſtie doeth hereby charge and command, not onely the Lords of His Maieſties Priuie Councell, but alſo all Maiors, Sheriffes, Iuſtices of Peace, and all other His Maieſties Officers, Miniſters and Subiects, That they, and euery of them in their ſeuerall places, doe not onely vſe their beſt endeauour to preuent and reſtraine all inſolencies, miſbehauiours, and offences afore-mentioned, but alſo take order that all offenders therein may receiue ſpeedie and condigne puniſhment according to their demerits, to the terror and example of others.

Giuen at Our Court at Whitehall, the eight day of March, in the one and twentieth yeere of Our Reigne of Great Britaine, France and Ireland.

God ſaue the King.

Imprinted at London by Bonham Norton and Iohn Bill, Printers to the Kings moſt Excellent Maieſtie. M.DC.XXIII.

James I, *A Proclamation for Ambassadours and forreigne Ministers*. London 1623. Courtesy, The Henry E. Huntington Library.

By the Queene.

The Queenes Maiestie consydering that notwithstanding that by great and mature deliberation of the wysest of this Realme, a godly & good order of publique prayer and administration of the Sacramentes hath ben set foorth and allowed by Parliament, and commonly through the whole Realme, in al the tyme of her Maiesties raigne receiued and vsed: yet some persons of theyr natures vnquietly disposed, desyrous to change, and therefore redy to fynde fault with al wel established orders, do not only refrayne from comming to the Church, where the diuine seruice and common prayer is orderly vsed, but also do vse of theyr owne deuises, other rites and ceremonies then are by the lawes of the Realme receiued and vsed: and besydes that, some of them haue rashly set foorth, and by stealth imprinted certayne bookes vnder the title of an admonition to the Parliament, and one other also in defence of the sayde admonition, the whiche bookes do tende to no other ende, but to make diuision and dissention in the opinions of men, and to breede talkes and disputes agaynst common order. Her highnesse therefore, both to represse suche insolent and inordinate contemptes of suche as refuse to come to common prayer and diuine seruice, accordyng to the order established by Parliament, to the euill and pernitious example of others, and to kepe her subiectes in one vniforme, godly, and quiet order within her Realme, to auoyde al controuersies, scismes, and dissentions that may aryse: doth strayghtly charge & commaunde al her Maiesties faythful and true subiectes, them selues to kepe, and to cause others suche as be vnder them, to kepe the order of common prayer, diuine seruices, and administration of the Sacramentes, accordyng as in the sayde booke of diuine seruice they be set foorth, and none other contrary or repugnant, vpon payne of her hyghnesse indignation, and of other paynes in the sayd acte comprysed.

And as concerning the said bookes, called, The admonition to the Parliament, and al other bookes made for the defence of the sayde admonition, or agreeable therewith, the whiche bookes do cheefely tende to the deprauyng and fyndyng fault with the sayde booke of common prayer, and administration of the Sacramentes, and of the orders receiued here in this Churche and common wealth of Englande: Her highnesse strayghtly chargeth and commaundeth al and euery Prynter, Stationer, Booke bynder, Marchaunt, and al other men of what qualitie or condition he or they be, who hath in theyr custodie any of the sayd bookes, to bryng in the same to the Byshop of the diocesse, or to one of her hyghnesse priuie Counsel, within t'wentie dayes after that he shal haue notice of this Proclamation, and not to kepe any of them without licence or allowance of the sayde Byshop, vpon payne of imprysonment, and her highnesse further displeasure.

Geuen at our Manour of Grenewiche, the .xi. day of June. 1573. the fyfteenth yere of our raigne.

God saue the Queene.

Imprinted at London in Powles church-
yarde, by Richarde Jugge, Printer to the Queenes
Maiestie.

Cum priuilegio Regiæ Maiestatis.

Elizabeth I, *A Proclamation* [confiscating Cartwright's *Second Admonition to the Parliament.*] London 1573 – a work by "the head and most learned of that sect of dissenters called Puritans." Courtesy, The Harvard College Library.

By the Queene.

A Proclamation against certaine seditious and scismatical Bookes and Libelles, &c.

He Queenes most excellent Maiestie being giuen to vnderstande that there are sent frō the partes beyond the seas, sundry seditious, scismaticall, and erronious printed Bookes and libelles, tending to the deprauing of the Ecclesiastical gouernment established within this Realme, set foorth by Robert Browne and Richard Harrison, fled out of the Realme as seditious persons, fearing due punishment for their sundry offences, and remaining presently in Zealande: which seuerall bookes, doe manifestly conteine in them very false, seditious, and scismatical doctrine and matter, and haue notwithstanding bene secretly solde, published, and dispersed in sundry places within this Realme, to the end to breede some scisme among her Maiesties subiectes, being persons vnlearned, and vnable to discerne the errors therein conteined: Her highnesse therefore perceiuing the wickednesse of these euil spirits, and the malicious disposition of lewde and euill disposed persons to be readie to violate and breake the peace of the Church, the Realme, and the quietnesse of her people, and knowing it also to be most requisite and conuenient for her highnesse to vse those meanes which God hath appointed for preuenting thereof, doeth will, and also straightly charge and commaunde that all maner of persons what so euer, who haue any of the sayde Bookes or any of like nature in his or their Custodie, that they and euery of them doe foorthwith vpon the publishing hereof, bring in and deliuer vp the same vnto the Ordinarie of the Diocesse, or of the place where they inhabite, to the intent they may bee burned, or vtterly defaced by the sayde Ordinary. And that from henceforth no person or persons whatsoeuer, be so hardy as to put in print or writing, sell, set foorth, receiue, giue out or distribute any more of the same or such like seditious bookes or libels, as they tender her Maiesties good fauour, and wil answere for the contrary at their vttermost perils, and vpon such further paynes as the Lawe shall inflict vpon the offendours in that behalfe, as persons maintayning such seditious actions, which her Maiestie myndeth to haue seuerely executed. Giuen at her Maiesties Mannor of Greenewich the last day of June, in the fiue and twentieth yeere of her highnesse Reigne.

God saue the Queene.

Imprinted at London by Christopher
Barker, Printer to the Queenes most excellent Maiestie.

Elizabeth I, *A Proclamation* [forbidding the importation of the writings of the Separatists Robert Browne and Robert Harrison into England]. London 1573. Both men were regarded by the state as "seditious persons [whose] bookes . . . conteine . . . very false seditious and scismatical doctrine." Courtesy, The Harvard College Library.

❧ By the King.

¶ A Proclamation against Seditious, Popish, and Puritanicall Bookes and Pamphlets.

FOR that the printing, importing, and dispersing of Popish and seditious Bookes and Pamphlets, and seditious Puritanicall Bookes and Pamphlets, scandalous to Our person, or State, such as haue beene lately vented by some Puritanicall spirits, is growen so common, and practised so licentiously, both to the traducing of Religion, and the State, as that great inconueniencies may grow thereby, if they be not preuented and punished: Therefore, We doe straitly charge and command, That from hencefoorth no person or persons whatsoeuer, presume to print any Booke or Pamphlet, touching, or concerning matters of Religion, Church gouernement, or State, within any Our owne Dominions, which shall not first be perused, corrected, and allowed, vnder the hand of the Lord Archbishop of Canterburie, the Lord Archbishop of Yorke, the Bishop of London, the Vicechancelour of one of the Vniuersities, of Oxford, or Cambridge, for the time being, or one of them, or of some other learned person or persons, to that purpose appointed by them, or one of them; And that no Merchant, or other person whatsoeuer, from hencefoorth presume to impost, or bring into this Kingdome any such Booke or Pamphlet, and set, or offer the same to sale, or otherwise dispose thereof, before the same be first perused and allowed by the Lord Arch-Bishop of Canterburie, Lord Arch-Bishop of Yorke, or Bishop of London, for the time being, or by some other learned person or persons, to that purpose appointed by them, or one of them, who shall testifie their allowance thereof, vnder his or their hands: And that no Booke-binder, or Booke-seller, or other person whatsoeuer, shall from hencefoorth presume to sell, or offer to sell, or otherwise disperse or dispose any such Booke or Pamphlet, not so perused and allowed, vpon paine of Our high displeasure, and such other seuere punishment, as by Our Lawes, or by Our Prerogatiue Royall, can, or may be inflicted vpon them for such their contempt. And We doe straitly charge and command all Maiors, Iustices of the Peace, Shiriffes, and all other Our officers and ministers whatsoeuer, and all other Our louing Subiects, whom it shall, or may appertaine, and especially the Master and Wardens of the Company of Stationers of London, that from time to time they doe their vtmost endeauors, for the due obseruance of the Premisses, and for the discouery and searching out of all Offences and Offenders against this Our Royall command.

Giuen at Our Court at Nottingham the fifteenth day of August, in the two and twentieth yeere of Our Reigne of Great Brittaine, France and Ireland.

God saue the King.

¶ Imprinted at London by Bonham Norton, and Iohn Bill,
Printers to the Kings most Excellent Maiestie.
ANNO DOM. M.DC.XXIIII.

James I, *A Proclamation against Seditious, Popish, and Puritanicall Bookes and Pamphlets.* London 1624. Courtesy, The Henry E. Huntington Library.

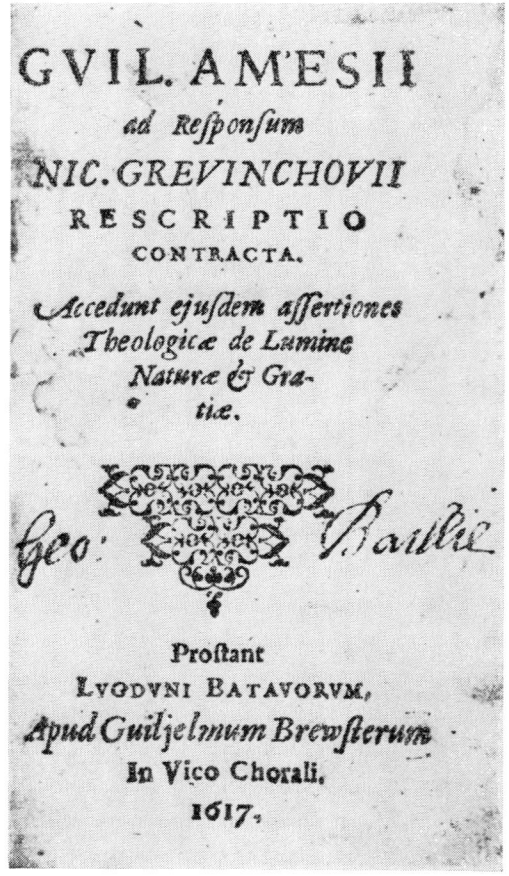

Title-page of William Ames, *Ad Responsum Nic. Grevinchovii Rescriptio Contracta*. Leyden: Brewster, 1617. The first book printed by the "Pilgrim Press" at Leyden and one of the three to bear William Brewster's name in the imprint. Courtesy, The Yale University Library.

NOTES

CHAPTER I

1. G. P. Gooch, *English Democratic Ideas in the Seventeenth Century* (New York, 1959), p. 34.
2. The propaganda program of Spain and the Papacy is discussed in Elizabeth Jenkins, *Elizabeth The Great* (New York, 1967), pp. 101, 156, 240; A. L. Rowse, *The England of Elizabeth* (New York, 1966), pp. 438 ff., G. B. Harrison, ed., *The Elizabethan Journals . . . 1591-1597* (New York, 1967), Vol. I. pp. 213, 241.
3. Robert Steele, *Bibliotheca Lindesiana. A Bibliography of Royal Proclamations of the Tudor and Stuart Sovereigns* (Oxford, 1910), Vol. I, pp. 51, 68.
4. Arnold A. Meyer, *England and the Catholic Church under Elizabeth* (New York, 1967), p. 76.
5. *Ibid*, p. 84; Edward Arber, *A Transcript of the Register of the Company of Stationers 1554-1640 A.D.* (London, 1875), II, pp. 182 ff.
6. A. W. Pollard & G. R. Redgrave, *A Short-Title Catalogue Of Books printed in England, Scotland & Ireland . . . 1475-1640* (London, 1946), 8032. (henceforth designated as *STC*).
7. Jenkins, *op. cit.*, p. 158; *STC* 8064; Steele, *op. cit.*, p. 74
8. Meyer, *op. cit.*, p. 271; Conyers Read, *Lord Burghley & Queen Elizabeth* (New York, 1960), p. 247.
9. Harrison, *op. cit.*, p. 241; *Calendar of State Papers, Domestic Series of the Reign of Elizabeth 1591-1594* (London, 1867), p. 161. (henceforth designated as *C.S.P.D.S. Elizabeth*).
10. St. George K. Hyland, *A Century of Persecution under Tudor and Stuart Sovereigns* (London, 1920), pp. 162 ff., *C.S.P.D.S. Elizabeth, 1595-1597* (London, 1869), p. 39; *C.S.P.D.S. Elizabeth, 1581-1590* (London, 1865), p. 66.
11. Albert J. Loomie, *The Spanish Elizabethans* (New York, 1963), p. 584; Steele, *op. cit.*, pp. 81, 82; *C.S.P.D.S. Elizabeth, 1581-1590*, p. 161.
12. Meyer, *op. cit.*, p. 286.
13. *STC* 8146.
14. Loomie, *op. cit.*, p. 198; Steele, *op. cit.*, p. 83.
15. P. R. Harris, "The Reports of William Udall, Informer 1605-1612" in *Recusant History* (London, 1966), Vol. 8, Pt. II, no. XI; Hugh R. Williamson, *The Gunpowder Plot* (London, 1951), p. 314; J. H. Pollen, ed., *Unpublished Documents Relating to the English Martyrs, 1584-1603* (London, 1914), I, p. 307.
16. Steele, *op. cit.*, p. 89; *STC* 22590; *Calendar of State Papers Foreign Series of the Reign of Elizabeth, July-December 1588* (London, 1936), XXII, p. 74. (henceforth designated as *C.S.P. F.S. Elizabeth*).
17. *STC* 368; A. F. Allison & D. M. Rogers, *A Catalogue of Catholic Books in English Printed Abroad or Secretly in England 1558-1640* (London, 1964), no. 5. (henceforth designated as A & R); Meyer, *op. cit.*, pp. 325 ff., Clancy Thomas, "English Catholics and the Papal Deposing Power 1570-1640" in *Recusant History* (Bognor Regis, 1961), Vo. VI, No. 3, Part I, p. 122; William Cecil, Lord Burghley, *The Copie Of A Letter Sent Owt of England to Don Bernardin Mendoza* (London, 1588), Aig., A3 & A3v.
18. A. C. Southern, *English Recusant Prose, 1559-1582* (London, 1950), p. 15; Arber, *op. cit.*, I, p. 533; II, pp. 231, 234, 236, 237.
19. *STC* 15412 – attributed to Richard Leigh.
20. *Ibid*.
21. *C.S.P. D.S. Elizabeth, 1591-1594*, p. 42; John Morris, ed., *The Condition of Catholics under James I. Father Gerard's Narrative of the Gunpowder Plot* (London, 1872), p. xvii., Harrison, *op. cit.*, I, pp. 60 f.; Anthony G. Petti, "The Letters and Dispatches of Richard Verstegan" (London, 1956), LII, p. 40.
22. Harrison, *op. cit.* I, pp. 93, 125.
23. *The Chamberlain Letters*. Ed. by Elizabeth M. Thomson (New York, 1965), p. 13.

NOTES

24. *C.S.P. D.S. Elizabeth, 1598–1601* (London, 1869), p. 499; Meyer, *op. cit.*, p. 354.
25. *STC* 19398; A & R 271.
26. Ethelred L. Taunton, *The History of the Jesuits in England 1580–1773* (London, 1901), p. 276.
27. *Ibid*, p. 275.
28. *Diary of John Manningham of the Middle Temple 1602–1603* (Westminster, 1868), p. 146.

CHAPTER II

1. For press control under the Tudors and Stuarts, see Frederick S. Siebert, *Freedom of the Press in England 1476–1776* (Urbana, 1952), pp. 32 ff., 55 ff.
2. H. S. Bennett, *English Books & Readers 1558 to 1603* (Cambridge, 1965), p. 75; Siebert, *op. cit.*, pp. 57 ff.
3. Siebert, *op. cit.*, p. 82.
4. Steele, *op. cit.*, pp. 70, 75.
5. For Caly, see E. G. Duff, *A Century of the English Book Trade Short Notices of all Printers, Stationers ... from ... 1457 ... to the Introduction of the Company of Stationers in 1557* (London, 1905), p. 21., (Gardiner) *STC* 11592; (Brooks) *STC* 3839; (Feckenham) *STC* 10744; (Watson) *STC* 25113; (St. John Fisher) *STC* 10896; (St. Vincent of Lerins) *STC* 24754; *(Manuale ad usum Sarum) STC* 16151; *(Breviary portiforium) STC* 15840; In 1557 Caly was fined by the Stationers' Company for printing a book without license and on July 22, 1565 he was compelled to pay four pence for another infraction – see Arber, *Transcript*, I, p. 70, p. 316.
6. For Carter, see *Dictionary of National Biography*. Ed. by Leslie Stephen & Sidney Lee (New York, 1908), III, p. 1116; R. B. McKerrow, *A Dictionary of Printers and Booksellers In England, Scotland and Ireland ... 1557–1640* (London, 1910), p. 62; Arber, *Transcript*, I, p. 196; (Loarte) A & R 466; *STC* 16646, A & R 469; (Suso) A & R 801; (St. Peter Canisius) A & R 198; *(Jesus Psalter)* A & R 415, Arber, *Transcript*, II, pp. 749–750.
7. *Short-Title Catalogue of Books printed in France and of French Books printed in other countries from 1470 to 1600 now in the British Museum* (London, 1924), p. 306; "Official Lists of Catholic Prisoners during the Reign of Queen Elizabeth" in *Miscellanea, Catholic Record Society* (London, 1906), p. 228; Arber, *Transcript* II, p. 149.
8. (Martin) *STC* 17508, A & R 535; Pollen, *op. cit.*, p. 30; *Middlesex County Records*. Ed. by John C. Jeaffreson (London, n.d.), I, 124: "True Bill for not going to any church, chapel or any usual place of common prayer. William Carter yeoman, 26 May, 23 Eliz."; "Tower Bills, Accounts sent by Lieutenant of the Tower for expenses of prisoners maintenance at expense of the state" in *Miscellanea*, p. 15.
9. *C.S.P. D.S. Elizabeth, 1581–1590*, p. 63; Pollen, *op. cit.*, p. 30; John Bridgewater, *Concertatio ecclesiae Catholicae in Anglia* (Treves, 1584), p. 127.
10. McKerrow, *op. cit.*, p. 275; (Alfield) *STC* 4537, A & R 4; for Vallenger, see Henry R. Plomer, "Stephen Vallenger" in *The Library* (London, 1901), N.S. II; Anthony Petti, "Stephen Vallenger 1541–1591, Norfolk Catholic" in *Recusant History* (Bognor Regis, 1962), Vol. VI, no. 6.
11. Southern, *op. cit.*, p. 508; P. R. Harris "William Fleetwood, Recorder of the City and Catholicism in Elizabethan England" in *Recusant History* (London, 1963), VII, no. 3, p. 114; (Martin) *STC* 17507, A & R 534; *STC* 20632, A & R 702.
12. A. F. Allison, "Biographical Studies 1534–1829" in *Recusant History* (Bognor Regis, 1954), II, no. 3., p. 38; (Robert, works by) A & R 726–729, *STC* 21077. The Martinist authors, John Udall or John Penry, well knew the history and trials of their stationer associate, Robert Waldegrave. Penry, a Welshman, may have had some information about the illusive Thackwell.
13. Allison, "Biographical Studies" I, no. 1, p. 37.
14. Bennett, *op. cit.*, p. 80; (Persons) *STC* 19394, A & R 616; (Bristow) *STC* 3802, A & R 151; (Hide) *STC* 1337, A & R 395; (Persons) *STC* 19392–19394, 19402, A & R 615–616, 627; *(A Manual or Meditation)* A & R 520–521.
15. For Awfield, see The *Life and end of Thomas Awfeeld a Seminary Preest and Thomas Webley a Dyers seruant in London* (London, 1585).

NOTES

16. "The Memoirs of Father Robert Persons," Ed. by J. H. Pollen in *Catholic Record Society's Miscellany* (London, 1905), II, p. 290.
17. *Ibid.*, pp. 17, 21., (Persons) *STC* 19402, A & R 627; (Campion) A & R 192.
18. Southern, *op. cit.*, p. 357f.
19. McKerrow, *op. cit.*, p. 107.
20. *Ibid*, p. 342., (Frarinus) *STC* 11333, A & R 344; (St. Thomas More) *STC* 18083, A & R 549; *(A brief fourme of confession) STC* 11181, A & R 143; *Short Title Catalogue of Books Printed in the Netherlands and Belgium . . . 1470 to 1600 Now in the British Museum* (London, 1965), p. 129 (henceforth designated as *STC Netherlands*).
21. (Sander) *STC Netherlands* 182; A & R 752; Fowler books printed at Louvain: (Reginald Pole, *A treatie (sic) of iustification*) *STC* 20088, A & R 657; (William Allen, *A treatise made in defense of the lawful power of priesthood to remitte sinnes*) *STC* 372, A & R 11; (Thomas Harding, *A reiondre to M. Jewels replie, against the sacrifice of the masse*) *STC* 12761; A & R 378; (Thomas Harding, *Detection of errours*) *STC* 12763; A & R 376; (Robert Pointz, *Testimonies for the Real Presence of Christes body and blood in the blessed Sacrame[n]t of the aultar*) *STC* 20982, A & R 656; Books published by Fowler at Antwerp in 1566: (Frarinus, *An oration*) *STC* 11333, A & R 344; (Thomas Harding, *A reiondre*) *STC* 12760, A & R 377; (John Rastell, *A third booke*) A & R 708.
22. Southern, *op. cit.*, p. 502; (William, Cardinal Allen, *A treatise*) *STC* 372, A & R 11; (Thomas Harding, *A detection of . . . foule errours*) *STC* 12763, A & R 376; (Thomas Stapleton, *A counterblast*) *STC* 23231, A & R 796; (Reginald Pole, *A treatie (sic) of iustification*) *STC* 20088, A & R 657; (John Leslie, *Copie of a letter*) *STC* 17566, A & R 451; (Leslie, *A treatise of treasons*) *STC* 7601, A & R 454; *(Hortulus anime) STC Netherlands* 99; (Richard Bristow, *Demaundes*) A & R 148.
23. McKerrow, *op. cit.*, p. 108.
24. *Middlesex Sessions Roll*, I, p. 123; James Wadsworth, *The English Spanish Pilgrime* (London, 1630), p. 24; Henry Foley, S.J., *Records of the English Province of the Society of Jesus* (London, 1877), I, p. 675.
25. "The Memoirs of Father Robert Persons," p. 31; McKerrow, *op. cit.*, p. 106; *(Manual of prayers) STC* 17263, A & R 495.
26. McKerrow, *op. cit.*, p. 49; (Persons, *A defence of the censure gyuen vpon two bookes of William Clarke and Meredith Hanmer*) *STC* 19401, A & R 626; (Persons, *An epistle of the persecution of Catholickes in Englande*) *STC* 19406, A & R 629; (Persons, *The first booke of the Christian exercise*) *STC* 19353–19362, A & R 619, 621; (Gaspare Loarte, *The exercise of a Christian life*) *STC* 16643, A & R 643; Diego de Estella, *The contempte of the world*) *STC* 10541, A & R 294.
27. McKerrow, *op. cit.*, pp. 92, 167, 40; Diest's publications include: (Ninian Winzet, *The buke of fourscoir-thre questions*) *STC* 25859, A & R 902; (St. Vincent of Lerins, *For the antiquitie and veritie of the Catholick fayth*) *STC* 24752, A & R 863; (John Rastell, *A confutation of a sermon pronou[n]ced by M. Iuell*) *STC* 20726, A & R 705; (Lewis Evans, *A brieue admonition vnto the nowe made ministers of England*) *STC* 10589, A & R 297; (Stanislaus Hosius, *A most excellent treatise of the beginning of heresyes in oure tyme*) *STC* 13888, A & R 403; (Osorio da Fonseca, *An epistle to Elizabeth Quene of England*) *STC* 18888, A & R 586; (John Rastell, *A replie against an answer intitled in defence of truth*) *STC* 20728, A & R 707; (John Rastell, *A copie of a challenge taken owt of the confutation of M. Iuells Sermon*) *STC* 20727, A & R 706; (Guilielmus Landinus, *Certaine tables wherein is detected . . . the doting dangerous doctrine*) *STC* 15653, A & R 461; (Thomas Harding, *A breefe answere touching certain vntruthes*) A & R 374; Laet's publications include; (John Martiall, *A treatise of the cross*) *STC* 17496, A & R 524; (Thomas Dorman, *A proufe of certain articles in religion denied by M. Iuell*) *STC* 7062, A & R 725; (Thomas Dorman, *A disproufe of M. Nowelles reproufe*) *STC* 7061, A & R 274; (William, Cardinal Allen, *A defense . . . of the Catholicke Churche*) *STC* 371, A & R 10; (Venerable Bede, *The history of the Church of England*)|*STC* 1773, A & R 82; (Thomas Harding, *A confutation of a booke intituled an Apologie of the Church of England*) *STC* 12762, A & R 375; (Osorio da Fonseca, *An Epistle to Elizabeth Quene of England*) *STC* 18888, A & R 585; (Fridericus Staphylus, *The Apologie*) *STC* 23230, A & R 794; (Thomas Stapleton, *A fortresse of the faith*) *STC* 23232, A & R 797; (Thomas Stapleton, *A returne of vntrvthes vpon M. Iewelles replie*) *STC* 23230, A & R 799.
28. (Adam Blackwood, *Martyre de la royne d'Escosse*) *STC* 3107, A & R 119; (John Leslie, *A defence of . . . Marie quene of Scotland*) *STC* 13505, A & R 452; (William, Cardinal

Allen, *An apologie and true declaration of the institution... of the two English colleges*) *STC* 369, A & R 6.
29. Father Person's work bears a fictitious authorship: R. Doleman, *STC* 19398, A & R 271.
30. (St. Peter Canisius, *Certayne necessarie principles of religion*) A & R 198; (St. Peter Canisius, *A summe of Christian doctrine*) *STC* 4573, A & R 200; (Gaspare Loarte, *The exercise of a Christian life*) A & R 462–463, *STC* 16643; (Luis de Granada, *A memoriall of Christian life*) *STC* 16903–16904, A & R 472–473; (Luis de Granada, *Of prayer and meditation*) *STC* 16907–16908, A & R 476–477; (Laurence Vaux, *A catechisme or a Christian doctrine*) *STC* 4801, *STC* 24626, *STC* 5645, *STC* 24627, A & R 834–837; *(Jesus psalter)* *STC* 14565, A & R 414; *(A manual of prayers)* *STC* 17263–17264, A & R 495–496.
31. Fulke's *Catalogue* is reproduced in Southern, *op. cit.*, pp. 537–541. The *Catalogue* first appeared in Fulke's *D. Heskins, D. Sanders, and M. Rastel, accounted (among their faction) three pillers of the Popish Synagogue... overthrown* (London, 1579) and revised, enlarged editions in *Thomas Stapleton and John Martiall Confuted* (London, 1580); also Fulke's *Retentive to stay good Christians* (London, 1580).

CHAPTER III

1. For Scottish printing, see H. G. Aldis, *Books Printed in Scotland before 1700* (Edinburgh, 1904), p. 118; Taunton, *op. cit.*, p. 89; Joseph Creswell, *An Advertisement written to a Secretarie of my L. treasurers of Ingland, by an Inglishe intelligencer as he passed througthe Germanie towardes Italie. Concerninge an other booke newely written in Latine... against her Maiesties late proclamation, in searche and apprehension of seminary priestes and their receauers.* (N.p., 1592), p. 5 (listed under John Philopatris); Bennett, *op. cit.*, p. 77; (Robert Persons, *Newes from Spayne and Holland conteyning. An information of English affayres in Spayne.* (N.p., 1593).
2. Bennett, *op. cit.*, p. 77; Southern, *op. cit.*, p. 36.
3. A. G. Petti, "Richard Verstegan and the Catholic Martyrolgies of the Later Elizabethan Period" in *Recusant History* (Bognor Regis, 1959), Vol. 4, no. 2; Verstegan's anti-English works include: *A declaration of the true causes of the great troubles presupposed to be intruded against the realm of England*. 1592; *L'Origine et present Estat de la secte Calvinienne*. 1611 (broadside); see Petti, "Bibliography" nos. 6, 13a, 13b, 13c; the latter listed in A. G. Petti, "A Bibliography of the Writings of Richard Verstegan c. 1550–1641" in *Recusant History* (London, 1963), Vol. VII no, 2 gives editions of the *Theatrum Crudelitatum haereticorum nostri temporis*. (1587–1588), see 4a–4i; an edition of 1883 is listed!
4. Loomie, *op. cit.*, p. 262; Pollen, *op. cit.*, p. 259; *C.S.P.D.S. Elizabeth, 1595–1597*, p. 478.
5. Petti, "The Letters and Dispatches of Richard Verstegan," pp. 86, 219; *(Trial of Trueth)* *STC* 24274; (Lewkenor, *Discourse*) *STC* 15562–15565; this work was published four times.
6. Loomie, *op. cit.*, p. 57; *C.S.P. D.S. Elizabeth, 1595–1597*, p. 588; Petti, "The Letters of Richard Verstegan," pp. 187, 256; (Sutcliffe, *A treatise*) *STC* 23471–23472; (Rainolds, *A treatise*) *STC* 20633, A & R 703; *(Statuta anno xxxv Reginae Elizabethae.* 1593) *STC* 9489–9492; (Holinshed, *Chronicles*) *STC* 13568–13569; (Thomas a Kempis, *The following of Christ*) *STC* 23968, A & R 814; Petti, "Bibliography," no. 5; Edward Arber, *An Introductory Sketch to the Martin Marprelate Controversy* (London, 1879), p. 140; William Pierce, *An historical introduction to the Marprelate tracts* (London, 1909), p. 330.
7. Loomie, *op. cit.*, p. 58.
8. *Ibid; C.S.P.D.S. Elizabeth, 1601–1603*, (London, 1870), p. 146; Southern, *op. cit.*, p. 37; *Letters and State Papers Relating to English Affairs Preserved in the Archives of Simancas* (London, 1899), IV, p. 555; for Hosius' writings, see A & R 403–404.
9. Williamson, *op. cit.*, p. 30; *Calendar of the Manuscripts of the Marquis of Salisbury preserved at Hatfield House* (London, 1899), Pt. VII, p. 186; Pt. XVIII (London, 1940), p. 230.
10. Williamson, *op. cit.*, p. 30.
11. Southern, *op. cit.*, p. 34; "Memoirs of Father Robert Persons," p. 157; Pollen, *op. cit.*, p. 105; "Official Lists of Catholic Prisoners during the Reign of Queen Elizabeth," p. 249. Southern, *op. cit.*, p. 35; Harrison, *The Elizabethan Journals... 1591–1597*, I, p. 225;

NOTES

Christopher Devlin, *The Life of Robert Southwell Poet and Martyr* (London, 1956), p. 101; *Calendar of the Manuscripts of the Marquis of Salisbury*, Pt. VII, p. 195.

12. Steele, *op. cit.*, p. 92; Harrison, *op. cit.*, p. 60.
13. *C.S.P. D.S. Elizabeth 1581–1590*, pp. 78, 91; Pollen, *op. cit.*, p. 38; Southern, *op. cit.*, p. 37; *Calendar of the Manuscripts of the Marquis of Salisbury* (London, 1904), Pt. IX, p. 203; According to "Official Lists of Catholic Prisoners During the Reign of Queen Elizabeth 23 March 1583, p. 233, Peter Lanson was committed to the Marshalsea on February 1, 1582.
14. *C.S.P.D.S. Elizabeth, 1598–1601*, p. 344.
15. Harrison, *op. cit.*, I, p. 205; Foley, *op. cit.*, VI, p. 726.
16. *(The primer, or office of the blessed virgin Marie in Latin and English)* STC 16094, A & R 680; *Calendar of the Manuscripts of the Marquis of Salisbury* (London, 1910), Pt. X, p. 62; Ernest James Worman, *Alien Members of the Book Trade During the Tudor Period* (London, 1896), p. 70.
17. Bennett, *op. cit.*, p. 117.
18. Analysis of Fulke's "Catalogue": Caly imprints: (Feckenham, *Scruples*) STC 10745, (Feckenham, *Apologie*) STC 10744; Fowler imprints: (Harding, *Reiondre*) STC 12760, A & R 377; (Sander, *The supper of our Lord*) STC 21695, A & R 753; (Stapleton, *A counterblast*) STC 23231, A & R 796; (Certain *deuout & godly petitions commonly called Iesus psalter*) STC 14565–14506, A & R 413; (Sander, *Rocke of the church*) STC 21692, A & R 570; (Sander, *Defence of images*) STC 21696, A & R 754; (Bristow, *Demaundes*) A & R 148; (Allen, *Defence of priestes authoritie to remitte sinnes*) STC 372, A & R 11; (Vaux, *A Catechisme*) STC 4801, A & R 834; (Pointz, *Poyntes of the sacrament*) STC 20082, A & R 656; (Frarinus, *Oration*) STC 11333; A & R 344; Laet Imprints: (Harding, *Against the apology of the English church*) STC 12762, A & R 375; (Dorman, *Against M. Iewel*) STC 7062, A & R 274; (Dorman, *Disproufe of M. Nowels reproofe*) STC 7061, A & R 274; (Allen, *Defence of purgatory*) STC 3731, A & R 10; (Harding, *A confutation of a book by Bishop Iewel intituled an Apologie of the Church of England*) STC 12762, A & R 375; (Stapleton, *A fortresse of the faith*) STC 23232, A & R 797; (Stapleton, *A returne of vntrvthes*) STC 23234, A & R 799; Diest Imprints: (Harding, *Against M. Iewels Challenge*) A & R 734; (Rastell, *A replie against an answer ... in defence of truth*) STC 20728, A & R 307; (Rastell, *Against M. Iewels Chalenge*) STC 20727, A & R 706; (Hosius, *A most excellent treatise of the beginning of heresyes in oure tyme*) STC 13888, A & R 403; *(Maister Evans answered by himselfe)* A & R 297; *(Rastells Replye)* STC 20728, A & R 707; Beller Imprint: (Rishton, *Discourse*) STC 21058; Silvius Imprint: (Heskyns, *The Parliament of Chryste*) STC 13284, A & R 393; Bogard Imprints: (Martial, *A replie to Calfhills blasphemous answer*) STC 17497, A & R 523; (Hosius, *Of the expresse word of God*) STC 13889, A & R 404; Carter imprints; (Albyn de Valsergues, *A notable discourse*) STC 274, A & R 3; (Martin, *A treatise of treasons*) STC 17508, A & R 535; (St. Peter Canisius, *Certayne necessarie principles of religion*) A & R 198.
19. *Letters and Memorials of Father Robert Persons, S.J.* (London, 1942), I p. 85.
20. *C.S.P.D.S. Elizabeth, 1581–1590*, p. 63.
21. *Ibid*, p. 493; Southern, *op. cit.*, pp. 38, 183; T. G. Law, *Documents Relating to the Dissension of the Roman Clergy, 1597–1602* (London, 1896), I, 109; (Persons, pseud. R. Doleman, *A conference about the next succession to the crowne of Ingland*) STC 19398, A & R 271; (Bristow, *A brief treatise of diverse ... wayes*) STC 3801, A & R 147–148; (Allen, *An admonition to the nobility and people of England*) STC 368, A & R 5; (Stapleton, *A fortresse of the faithe*) STC 23232, A & R 797.
22. *C.S.P.D.S. Elizabeth, 1591–1594*, p. 354; Persons, *An epistle of the persecution of Catholickes in Englande*. 1582, STC 19406; A & R 629; Campion, *Rationes decem*. 1581. STC 4534, A & R 192.
23. For Alfield's life, see *The Life and end of Thomas Awfeeld*.
24. Foley, *op. cit.*, VI, p. 721.
25. *The Life and end of Thomas Awfeeld;* "Official Lists of Catholic Prisoners During the Reign of Queen Elizabeth 24 March 1583," p. 239.
26. P. R. Harris, "William Fleetwood, Recorder of the City and Catholicism in Elizabethan England," p. 115; Allen, *A true sincere and modest defence* of *English Catholiques that suffer for their faith*. 1584. STC 373, A & R 13.
26. *The life and end of Thomas Awfeeld*.
27. *Ibid*.

NOTES

CHAPTER IV

1. Williamson, *op. cit.*, p. 30; Bennett, *op. cit.*, p. 76.
2. *Acts of the Privy Council of England, 1601–1604.* Ed. by John R. Dasent (London, 1907), N.S. Vol. XXXIII, p. 412.
3. J. R. Tanner, *Tudor Constitutional Documents* (New York, 1930), p. 246; Southern, *op. cit.*, p. 573.
4. Loomie, *op. cit.*, p. 70.
5. Southern, *op. cit.*, p. 33.
6. Petti, "The Letters and Dispatches of Richard Verstegan," p. 1; Pollen, *op. cit.*, p. 521; *Calendar of State Papers Relating to Scotland* (London, 1858), II, p. 612.
7. *C.S.P.D.S. Elizabeth, 1601–1603*, p. 166; *Ibid, 1591–1594*, p. 497; Mirkell is referring in all likelihood to Father Persons, *Newes from Spayne and Holland conteyning. An information of Inglish Affayres in Spayne.* STC 22994, A & R 634; Bede the Venerable, *The History of the churche of England.* 1565. STC 1778, A & R 82.
8. *C.S.P.D.S. Elizabeth, 1598–1601*, p. 340; Pollen, *op. cit.*, p. 30.
9. Loomie, *op. cit.*, p. 55; Steele *op. cit.*, p. 93.
10. *Ibid*, p. 68; STC 372, A & R 11.
11. Steele, *op. cit.*, p. 83.
12. Arber, *Transcript*, I, p. 61.
13. Bennett, *op. cit.*, p. 13; Meyer, *op. cit.*, p. 172.
14. Bennett, *op. cit.*, pp. 76 ff.
15. B. I., *The Copy of a Letter Lately Written By a Spanishe Gentleman, To his Friend in England, in refutation of sundry calumnies.* N.p., 1589, p. 5.
16. Morris, *op. cit.*, p. 36; *C.S.P.D.S. Elizabeth, 1598–1601*, p. 226.
17. Morris, *op. cit.*, p. 211; Pierce, *op. cit.*, p. 14, 131 f.; Patrick Collinson, *The Elizabethan Puritan Movement* (London, 1967), p. 152.
18. Morris, *op. cit.*, p. xv.
19. Arber, *Transcript*, I, pp. 244, 242, 505, 515, 526.
20. *Ibid*, p. 393.
21. Partial analysis of Stowe's "Cataloguy": (Thomas Heskyns, *The parliament of Chryste*) STC 13250, A & R 393; (Stanislaus Hosius, *A most excellent treatise of the beginning of heresyes in oure tyme*) STC 13888, A & R 403; (Robert Pointz, *Testimonies for the Real Presence of Christes Body . . . in the Sacrame[n]t of the aultar*) STC 20082, A & R 656; (John Rastell, *A briefe shew of the false wares; A confutation of a sermon; A copie of a challenge; A replie against an answer; The third book . . . to beware of M. Iewel; A treatise . . . beware of M. Iewel*) STC 20725–20729, A & R 704–709; (Thomas Dorman, *A disproufe of M. Nowells reproufe; A proufe of certeyne articles in religion; A request to M. Iewell*) STC 7061–7063, A & R 274–276; Caly Imprints include: no. 10. Roger Edgeworth, *Sermons very fruitfull, godly and learned.* 1557. STC 7482; no. 20. Richard Smith, *The second parte of a Boucklier of the Catholyke fayeth.* 1555. STC 22817; no. 22. John Standish, *A discourse wherein is debated whether the scripture should be in English.* 1554. STC 23207–23208; no. 23. St. Vincent of Lerins, *The waie home to Christ.* 1554. STC 24754; no. 25. John Feckenham, *Two homilies upon the Credo.* 1555. STC 10745; no. 27. James Brooks, *A sermon very notable . . . made at Paules crosse.* 1553. STC 3838; no. 28. Miles Hogarde, *The displaying of the Protestantes.* 1556. STC 13557; Diest Imprints include: no. 4. Stanislaus Hosius, *A most excellent treatise of the beginning of heresyes in oure tyme.* 1565. STC 13888, A & R 403; no. 34. John Rastell, *A copie of a challenge.* 1565. STC 20727, A & R 706; Laet Imprints include: no. 8. Venerable Bede, *The history of the church of Englande.* 1565. STC 1778, A & R 82; no. 14. Thomas Dorman, *A proufe of certeyne articles in religion, denied by M. Iewell.* 1564. STC 7062, A & R 275; Fowler Imprints are: no. 32. Robert Pointz, *Testimonies for the Real Presence of Christes body and blood in the blessed Sacarame[n]t of the aultar.* 1566. STC 20082, A & R 656; no. 30. John Rastell, *A briefe shew of the false wares.* 1567. STC 20725, A & R 704.
22. *Inventory of 30 "books and reliques" found in studies of George Brome and his two sisters, Elizabeth and Briget, August 27, 1586.* MS: British Museum, Lansdowne 50, item 76, folios 163v–164r; Partial identification of the Brome Collection: *(Catechisme)* Jacques-Charles Brunet, *Manuel du Libraire Et de L'Amateur de Livres* (Berlin, 1921), I, p. 1657; (Loarte) STC 16643, A & R 463; Dante Alighieri, *Lo'nferno, e 'l purgatorio e 'l paradiso*

NOTES

(Venice, 1550), *Short-Title Catalogue of Books Printed in Italy . . . From 1465 to 1600 Now in the British Museum* (London, 1958), p. 209; Luis de Grenada, *A memoriall of a Christian life* (Rouen, 1586); *Of prayer and meditation* (Paris, 1582; Rouen, 1584) *STC* 16903, A & R 472; *STC* 16907–16908, A & R 476–477; *A Manuall of Prayers* N.p. 1583, *STC* 17263, A & R 485; *Certaine deuout and godly petitions, commonly called Iesus psalter.* (Antwerp 1575; London, 1579; Rouen, 1579–1580) *STC* 14565–14564, A & R 413–416.
23. *C.S.P.D.S. Reign of Elizabeth, 1581–1590*, pp. 198–199.
24. Arber, *Transcript*, I, p. 492; 1. (Bristow) A & R 148; 2. (Leslie) *STC* 7601, A & R 454; 3. (More) *STC* 18083, A & R 549; 4. (Possevino) A & R 659; 5. *(Primer) STC* 20373–20381; 6. (Bede) *STC* 1778, A & R 82.
25. Arber, *Transcript* II, 99.
26. *Ibid*, II, p. 40; *STC Netherlands*, p. 180, 194.
27. McKerrow, *op. cit.*, p. xi.

CHAPTER V

1. Meyer *op. cit.*, p. 394.
2. *Ibid*, p. 402; Thomas G. Law, *A Historical Sketch of the Conflicts between Jesuits and Seculars in the Reign of Queen Elizabeth* (London, 1889), no. 80; (Bagshaw) *STC* 1188, A & R 65.
3. Law, *Documents*, I, p. xiii; Meyer, *op. cit.*, p. 413; Law, *Historical Sketch*, p. lxxxvi.
4. Law, *Documents*, II, pp. 178, 173.
5. Steele, *op. cit.*, p. 106.
6. Lewis Owen, *Relation of the state of the English Colledges, Seminaries and Cloysters in all forraine parts* (London, 1626), pp. 111–112.
7. McKerrow, *op. cit.*, p. 102; For Field, See E. M. Kirkwood, "Richard Field Printer, 1589–1624" in *Transactions of the Bibliographical Society* (London, 1931), XII, no. 1.
8. *Ibid;* Worman, *op. cit.*, p. 16; Desserans and Vautrollier took up an agency in London at Plantin's request; the latter promising Desserans $16^2/_3\%$ on sales. The arrangement did not work out-the agency lasted about a year.
9. Law, *Historical Sketch*, no. 9; no. 16; (Bluet) *STC* 25125, A & R 122; (Colleton) *STC* 5557, A & R 246.
10. Law, *Historical Sketch*, nos. 13, 12; (Watson) *STC* 25123, A & R 883; (Copley) *STC* 5735, A & R 257.
11. (Preston, *Apologia*) *STC* 25596, A & R 661; (Preston, *Responsio*) *STC* 25597, A & R 674.
12. W. W. Greg & E. Boswell, eds., *Records of the Court of the Stationers' Company* (London, 1930), p. 36; for Ward, see McKerrow, *op. cit.*, p. 282.
13. McKerrow, *op. cit.*, p. 148; Law, *Historical Sketch*, no. 2; (Mush, *A dialogue*) *STC* 25124, A & R 553; (Mush, *Declaratio*) *STC* 3102; A & R 552.
14. Law, *Historical Sketch*, no. 15; (Preston, *A theologicall disputation*) *STC* 25603, A & R 676.
15. McKerrow, *op. cit.*, p. 80; (Shakespeare editions), see *STC* 22315–22318; 22322; 22289; 22299; Law, *Historical Sketch*, nos. 5, 4; *(The copies of certaine discourses)*, *STC* 5724, A & R 254.
16. McKerrow, *op. cit.*, p. 229; (Shakespeare editions) *STC* 22276; 22296; 22303.
17. McKerrow, *op. cit.*, p. 66; Devlin, *op. cit.*, p. 234; Charlewood published several treatises by the Puritan-preacher-publisher, Robert Crowley, whose contributions will be discussed in Chapter XIV; see *STC* 6075, 6088, 6089, 6091, 6095.
18. Greg, *op. cit.*, pp. xix & 55.
19. Law, *Historical Sketch*, no. 10.
20. *Ibid*, nos. 20 & 18.
21. McKerrow, *op. cit.*, p. 274; Greg, *op. cit.*, pp. xx, 56; William A. Jackson, ed., *Records of the Court of the Stationers' Company 1602 to 1640* (London, 1957), p. 21.
22. Law, *Historical Sketch*, nos. 8, 12; for Barker, see McKerrow, *op. cit.*, p. 18; Law, *op. cit.*, no. 19; no. 6; (Persons), *STC* 19392, A & R 614.
23. Law, *Historical Sketch*, no. 21; for Bankworth, see McKerrow, *op. cit.*, p. 17.
24. Meyer, *op. cit.*, p. 456.

219

NOTES

25. McKerrow, *op. cit.*, p. 5; Greg, *op. cit.*, p. 57; Arber, *Transcript*, II, p. 988. Allde's father, John, a printer, had tangled with the government in 1568 when he printed for the Flemish dealers, Hans Stell and Arnould Vaukyll, a tract against the Duke of Alva, *Copie des pointz ou articles arrêtes par le duc d'Albe . . . en est euidemment à cognoistre les horribles Tirainnes cruautez et larrecins du Duc d'Alba*, see Arber, *Transcript* II, 745.
26. Jackson, *op. cit.*, p. 5; (James I, *Basilicon Doron*) STC 14354.
27. (Preston, *Disputatio*) STC 25602, A & R 667.
28. Jackson, *op. cit.*, pp. 138, 158.
29. *Ibid*, p. 137; 159; *(A briefe description)* STC 11353.
30. McKerrow, *op. cit.*, p. 83; Arber, *Transcript*, II, pp. 144, 706; Greg, *op. cit.*, p. 21.
31. (Shakespeare editions), see STC 22328, 22322, *(Strange sightes)* STC 21321, Arber, *Transcript*, II, pp. 658, 667; *(A most horrible murther)* STC 17748.
32. Greg, *op. cit.*, p. 56; Arber, *Transcript*, II, p. 580; *(Jesus psalter)* A & R 417.
33. Greg, *op. cit.*, p. 33.
34. McKerrow, *op. cit.*, p. 65; (Lyly) STC 17075–17076.
35. Duff, *op. cit.*, p. 23; (Southwell writings) STC 22950–22951, 22956, 22958–22959.
36. Morris, *op. cit.*, p. xlvii; *Short Title Catalogue of Books Printed in the German Speaking Countries . . . From 1455 to 1600 now in the British Museum* (London, 1962), p. 703.
37. (Bristow, *Demaundes*) STC 3801, A & R 149; for Bulloch, see McKerrow, *op. cit.*, p. 55; Joseph Gillow, *A Literary and Biographical History, or Bibliographical Dictionary of the English Catholics* (New York, n.d.), II, p. 133; (Caumont) STC 4868, A & R 212; Richard Challoner, *Memoirs of Missionary Priests* (New York, 1924), p. 236; *Middlesex County Records* I, p. 222.
38. Quoted in J. H. McDonald, *The Poems and Prose Writings of Robert Southwell, S.J. A Bibliographical Study* (Oxford, 1937), p. 117.
39. *Ibid*, p. 118.

CHAPTER VI

1. *The Chamberlain Letters*. Ed. Thomson, p. 25; Taunton, *op. cit.*, p. 280.
2. For James' life and personality, see David Harris Willson, *King James VI and I* (London, 1966); William McElwee, *The Wisest Fool in Christendom. The Reign of King James I and VI* (New York, 1958).
3. Rowse, *op. cit.*, pp. 261 ff; 264 ff; 268 ff.
4. Gooch, *op. cit.*, p. 56; J. N. Figgis, *The Divine Right of Kings* (Cambridge, 1934), p. 137.
5. J. R. Tanner, *Constitutional Documents of the Reign of James I 1603–1605* (Cambridge, 1961), p. 15; McElwee, *op. cit.*, p. 129.
6. Taunton, *op. cit.*, p. 279; Williamson, *op. cit.*, p. 108; Hyland, *op. cit.*, p. 236.
7. *The Gunpowder Treason: with a Discourse of the Manner of its Discovery* (London, 1679), Pt. II, p. 21.
8. *Ibid*, p. 135; Taunton, *op. cit.*, p. 289.
9. Williamson, *op. cit.*, p. 143.
10. G. B. Harrison, *A Jacobean Journal* (New York, 1941), p. 250.
11. Taunton, *op. cit.*, p. 35f; Samuel R. Gardiner, *History of England from the Accession of James I. to the Outbreak of the Civil War* (New York, 1965), II, p. 17.
12. Arber, *Transcript*, III, 131b; 132b; 133b; 134, 138b.
13. G. B. Harrison, *A Second Jacobean Journal* (London, 1958), p. 33.
14. Logan Pearsall Smith, *The Life and Letters of Sir Henry Wotton* (Oxford, 1907), p. 380.
15. Taunton, *op. cit.*, p. 360; Foley, *op. cit.*, pp. 1016, 1034.
16. *The Chamberlain Letters*. Ed. by Thomson, pp. 124, 126.
17. Hyland, *op. cit.*, p. 236; *The Chamberlain Letters*. Ed. by Thomson, p. 237; 127; Steele, *op. cit.*, p. 139; Meyer, *op. cit.*, p. 63.
18. (James I, *God and the King*) STC 14419; Steele, *op. cit.*, p. 139.
19. *Calendar of State Papers and Manuscripts. English Affairs. Venetian, 1617–1619* (London, 1909), nos. 658, 679. (henceforth designated *C.S.P. Venetian*).
20. Smith, *op. cit.*, p. 124; *C.S.P. Venetian*, no. 679.
21. *Ibid*, no. 416, no. 641.

NOTES

22. *Ibid*, no. 613; *Journals of the House of Commons from November the 8th 1547 to March the 2nd 1628* (London, 1803), I, pp. 684, 694, 709.
23. *The Chamberlain Letters*. Ed. by Thomson, p. 333.
24. *Acts of the Privy Council June-December 1626* (London, 1938), p. 222.

CHAPTER VII

1. *Journals of the Hose of Commons* I, pp. 229, 981.
2. *Journals of the House of Lords* (London, 1846), II, p. 421; *Journals of the House of Commons* I, p. 496.
3. Steele, *op. cit.*, p. 137; *The Chamberlain Letters*. Ed. by Thomson, p. 187; Harris, "The Reports of . . . Udall," No. XI.
4. Smith, *op. cit.*, I, p. 368.
5. Harrison, *A Jacobean Journal*, p. 44; Morris, *op. cit.*, p. cixii.
6. "The Reports of William Udall," Edited by P. R. Harris, presents an excellent survey of the activities of this odious individual; see no. 8.
7. *Ibid*, nos. 15, 33.
8. *Ibid*, nos. 15, 33; *Calendar of the Manuscripts of the Marquis of Salisbury* (London, 1938), XVIII, p. 139.
9. *Acts of the Privy Council, 1616–1617* (London, 1927), p. 40.
10. *C.S.P.D.S. James I, 1603–1610* (London, 1857), I, p. 502, 533; *The Chamberlain Letters*. Ed. by Thomson, p. 202; Harrison, *A Second Jacobean Journal* p. 91; William Parker, Fourth Baron Monteagle, 1575–1622, enjoyed a close relationship with the principal Roman Catholic families in England and for years displayed great enthusiasm for Roman Catholicism. Upon the accession of James I, he withdrew his support. It was to Monteagle that the letter was brought on October 26, 1605 warning him about the pending Gunpowder Plot: "Shift your attendance at this Parliament." He took the letter to Lord Salisbury – the conspirators were shortly thereafter apprehended.
11. *C.S.P.D.S. James I, 1611–1618* (London, 1858), pp. 402, 484; Harris, "Reports of Udall," no. 25.
12. Siebert, *op. cit.*, pp. 142ff; *STC* 8714, 8736.
13. Theodore F. T. Plucknett, *A Concise History of the Common Law* (Boston, 1956), p. 485; Siebert, *op. cit.*, p. 117; *STC* 8714, 8723. 8736.
14. (Stubbs) *STC* 23400; Pierce, *op. cit.*, p. 30; Jenkins, *op. cit.*, p. 225.
15. For Singleton, see Duff, *op. cit.*, p. 148; also H. J. Byrom "Edmund Spenser's First Printer Hugh Singleton" in *Transactions of the Bibliographical Society* (London, 1933), N.S. XIV, no. 2; *STC* 8114.
16. Harrison, *The Elizabethan Journals* II, p. 182; Leona Rostenberg, *English Publishers in the Graphic Arts 1599–1600* (New York, 1963), p. 9, plate 1.
17. For John Wolfe, see McKerrow, *op. cit.*, p. 296f; *STC* 12995; Harrison, *The Elizabethan Journals* II, pp. 169, 209.
18. *C.S.P.D.S. Elizabeth, 1598–1601*, p. 450.
19. *Ibid*; Harrison, *The Elizabethan Journals* II, p. 170.
20. (Essex, *Apologie*) *STC* 6788 cites the work as entered to Burby; Harrison, *The Elizabethan Journals* II, pp. 154f; for details of the controversy about the printing of the *Apologie*, see Jackson *op. cit.*, p. 9 – there was much involved litigation.
21. (Bacon, *Declaration*) *STC* 1133; Harrison, *The Elizabethan Journals* II, p. 241.
22. (Woodhouse, *Almanac*) *STC* 532; Harrison, *The Elizabethan Journals* II, p. 10.
23. Arber, *Transcript* III, p. 316; (Marston, *Metamorphosis*) *STC* 17482; (Marston, *The Scourge of villanie*) *STC* 17485; (Guilpin, *Skialetheia*) *STC* 12504; (Davies, *Epigrammes*) *STC* 6350; (M. T., *Micro-cynicon*) *STC* 17154; (La Sale, *The fyftene joyes of maryage*) *STC* 15258.
24. (Rowlands, *The letting of humours blood*) *STC* 21393; William H. Hart, *Index expurgatorius anglicanus: or, A descriptive catalogue of the principal books printed or published in England which have been suppressed* (London, 1872–1878), no. 31; (Darrell, *A true narration*) *STC* 6288; Harrison, *The Elizabethan Journals* II, p. 257; *Journals of the House of Lords, 1578–1614*, II, p. 557.

NOTES

25. For Sandys, see *STC* 21715–21717, *The Chamberlain Letters*. Ed. by Norman E. McClure (Philadelphia, 1939), I, p. 214; (Cowell, *The interpreter*) *STC* 5900.
26. Hart, *op. cit.*, p. 50; Steele, *op. cit.*, p. 128; Harrison, *A Second Jacobean Journal*, p. 183.
27. Owen, *op. cit.*, p. 14; *C.S.P.Venetian, 1607–1610* (London, 1904), XI, no. 536.
28. *Prvrit-Anvus*, Foreword.
29. Harris, "Reports of Udall," nos. 24, 18.
30. Owen, *op. cit.*, p. 14; Harrison, *A Second Jacobean Journal*, p. 143; *C.S.P. Venetian, 1607–1610*, no. 564; Harris, "Reports of Udall," p. 204.
31. *Ibid*, no. 30; for Ely, see McKerrow, *op. cit.*, no. 99.
32. *Calendar of the Manuscripts of the Marquis of Salisbury* (London, 1965), XIX, p. 419; For apprehension of J. Cotton, *STC* 8487.
33. *Ibid*.
34. Hart, *op. cit.*, p. 53; *Acts of the Privy Council, 1617–1619*, p. 455.
35. (Raleigh, *The History of the world*) *STC* 20637–20641; *The Chamberlain Letters*. Ed. by Thomson, p. 196; Jackson, *op. cit.*, p. 357.
36. Thomas Birch, *The Court and Times of James The First* (London, 1848), II, p. 266.
37. (Wither's *Motto*) *STC* 25924–25929; Jackson, *op. cit.*, p. 135; *C.S.P. James I, 1619–1623* (London, 1958), p. 275; Allen Pritchard, "George Withers Quarrel with the Stationers: An Anonymous Reply to the Schollers Purgatorie" in *Studies in Bibliography. Papers of the Bibliographical Society of Virginia* (Charlottesville, 1963), p. 34.
38. Greg, *op. cit.*, p. 89; *C.S.P. James I, 1619–1623*, pp. 268, 274, 275.
39. For Wood, see McKerrow, *op. cit.*, p. 298; Jackson, *op. cit.*, p. 170.
40. Pritchard, *op. cit.*, pp. 37 ff.
41. *Journals of the House of Commons*, p. 27.

CHAPTER VIII

1. John Gee, *The Foote out the snare. With a Detection of Sundry Late Practices and Impostures of the Priests and Iesuites in England* (London, 1624).
2. For dossier of Catholic printers and agents, see Foley, *op. cit.* I, p. 675.
3. Gee, *op. cit.*, E3v.
4. *C.S.P.Venetian, 1617–1619*, no. 439.
5. *Calendar of the Manuscripts of the Marquis of Salisbury* (Dublin, 1906), Part XI, p. 88; *C.S.P.F.S., Elizabeth*, XVIII, p. 363; Harris, "The Reports of Udall," no. 4.
6. Greg, *op. cit.*, p. 58; See Henry R. Plomer, "Bishop Bancroft and a Catholic Press" in *The Library* (London, 1907), pp. 167, 174; for Jeffes and Wrench, see McKerrow, *op. cit.*, pp. 156, 392; (Bristow, *Demaundes*) *STC* 3801, A & R 149; Wrench is mentioned by Gee; see Foley, *op. cit.*, I, p. 675.
7. Arber, *Transcript*, II, p. 734; Greg, *op. cit.*, p. 81; for Boulter and Danter, see McKerrow, *op. cit.*, pp. 43, 83f.
8. Publications attributed to Wrench and the unidentified printer of John Brerely's *Apologie* include: Thomas Wright, *Certaine articles Discouering the palpable absurdities and ... errors of the Protestants religion* (N.p., 1604–1605) A & R 922; William Bishop, *A reformation of a Catholike deformed* (N.p., 1604) *STC* 3096, A & R 115; Miguel de Comalada, *A most godly ... dialogue, teaching the true ... way by which we may attaine to the perfect loue of God* (N.p., 1604) *STC* 6777, A & R 250; Robert Southwell, *An epistle of comfort* (N.p., 1605) *STC* 22947, A & R 782; John Colleton, *The apologie of the Romane church* (N.p., 1604) *STC* 3604, A & R 131; Ralph Buckland, *Seauen Sparkes of the enkindled soule* (N.p., 1604–1605) *STC* 4008, A & R 181; *A manual of prayers* (N.p., 1604 – in 2 editions) *STC* 17267, 17269, A & R 501, 504; *A Petition apologeticall, presented to the Kinges most excellent maiesty* (Douai, 1604) *STC* 4835, A & R 646; John Radford, *A directorie teaching the way to truth ... against the heresies of the time* (N.p., 1605) *STC* 20602, A & R 701; Philip Woodward, *The fore-runner of Bels downefall* (N.p., 1605) *STC* 19407, A & R 909; Victor, Bishop of Vita, *The memorable and tragical history*, of the persecution in Africke. (N.p., 1605) *STC* 24714, A & R 847; John Colleton, *Supplication* (N.p., 1604) *STC* 14432, A & R 247; John Percy, *A treatise of faith* (N.p., 1605) A & R 608.
9. Plomer, "Bishop Bancroft and a Catholic Press," p. 166; "London Sessions Records 1605–1685" in *Catholic Record Society* (London, 1934), pp. 5, 49, 60.

NOTES

10. Harris, "Reports of Udall," no. 24.
11. *Ibid*, no. 40.
12. Cyril Davenport, *Royal English Book Bindings* (London, 1896), p. 59 ff., William Y. Fletcher, *English Book Collectors* (London, 1902), p. 55 f.
13. Falconer Madan, *Oxford Books. The Early Oxford Press 1468–1640* (Oxford, 1895), p. 276, 297; Among the publications issued at Oxford by Lichfield and Wrench are the Greek texts of Christopher Angelos. *STC* 638–639; John Hales, *A Sermon. STC* 12628; Thomas Jackson, *Nazareth and Bethlehem, and Mankinds comfort. STC* 14314; M.T., *Digesta. STC* 17152; Oxford University. *Jacobi ara ceu in Jacobis regis reditum e Scotia in Angliam gratulatoria. STC* 19023; John Terry, *The reasonablenesse of wise & holy truth. STC* 23912.
14. Harris, "Reports of Udall," no. 4.
15. "London Sessions Records 1605–1685," p. 5; Foley, *op. cit.*, I, p. 675; Morris, *op. cit.*, p. lvii; For Owen, see McKerrow, *op. cit.*, p. 209; "Bishop Bancroft and a Catholic Press," pp. 166, 175.
16. Publications attributed to Owen and Duckett: Luca Pinelli, *Briefe meditations of the most holy sacrifice* (N.p., 1595–1600) *STC* 19937, A & R 648; Lorenzo Scupoli, *The spiritual conflict* ["Antwerp" (Secretly in England), 1598] A & R 759; Luis de Granada, *A memoriall of Christian life* ["Rouen" (Secretly in England), 1599] *STC* 16905, A & R 473; Laurence Vaux, *A Catechisme* (N.p., 1599) A & R 840; Thomas Wright, *Certaine articles* (N.p., 1600) A & R 920–922; *STC* 23618; Robert Persons, *A brief discours* ["Doway" (Secretly in England), 1601] *STC* 19395–19396, A & R 617–618; Thomas Hill, *A quatron of reasons of Catholike religion* ["Antwerpe" (Secretly in England), 1600] *STC* 13470, A & R 400–401; Robert Southwell, *An humble supplication* (N.p., 1601) *STC* 7586, A & R 784; Richard Broughton, *An apologeticall epistle* ["Antwerpe" (Secretly in England), 1601] A & R 152; D.T.H., *Nine rockes to be auoided* ["Doway" (secretly in England), 1600] A & R 267; *Jesus psalter* (N.p., 1595–1600?) A & R 417; *A manual of prayers* (N.p., ca. 1593) *STC* 17266 cites ["Calice" (secretly in England), 1599] A & R cite 1593, as well as 1599, no. 500; see Harris, "Reports of Udall," nos. 13. 4.
17. *Acts of the Privy Council of England, 1601–1604* XXXIII, p. 85; Harris, "Reports of Udall," no. 4; Foley, *op. cit.*, I, p. 675; "John Bird freed by redemption 202.10"; A John Bird had been bound to Humphrey Lowndes, 1-9-1600; see D. F. McKenzie, *Stationers' Company Apprentices 1605–1640* (Charlottesville, 1961), no. 759.
18. For Pauley, see McKerrow, *op. cit.*, p. 211; Leona Rostenberg, *Literary, Political, Scientific, Religious & Legal Publishing, Printing & Bookselling in England, 1551–1700: Twelve Studies* (New York, 1965), I, p. 162.
19. Jackson, *op. cit.*, p. 436.
20. For a detailed study of James Anderton, see C. A. Newdigate, Jr., "Birchley or St. Omers?" in *Transactions of the Bibliographical Society* (London, 1926), N.S. VII, no. 3; Arthur J. Hawkes, "The Birchley Hall Secret Press" in *Transactions of the Bibliographical Society* (London, 1926), N.S. VII, no. 2.
21. For London of the early Stuart period, see Norman G. Brett-James, *The Growth of Stuart London* (London, 1935), pp. 31, 74, 87, 194, 230; According to Sir Walter Besant, *London in the Times of the Stuarts* (London, 1903), p. 6; there were 408 convictions for recusancy in Middlesex during the last 24 years of Elizabeth's reign. The majority came from Westminster, Clerkenwell, Tottenham, Stepney in Holborn, This area continued to attract clandestine Catholic activity during James' reign; Harris, "The Reports of Udall," no. 3.
22. Foley, *op. cit.* I, p. 675; *Calendar to the Sessions Records, 1614–1615* (London, 1935), II, p. 216; *Ibid*, 1615–1616 (London, 1937), III, p. 50; *Middlesex Sessions Roll* (London, n.d.), II, pp. 114, 216, 237, 240; McKerrow, *op. cit.*, p. 248.
23. Jackson, *op. cit.*, p. 169; for Stansby, see McKerrow, *op. cit.*, p. 256; (Percy, *Answer to a Pamphlet*) *STC* 4957, A & R 603; Foley, *op. cit.*, I, p. 195.
24. Foley, *op. cit.*, I, p. 195; for Gubbins, Newman and Orwin, see McKerrow, *op. cit.*, pp. 119, 200, 208; Arber, *Transcript* II, p. 698; 237; (Boccaccio, *Fiametta*) *STC* 3179; (Udall, *Amendment of life*) *STC* 24490; (Udall, *The combate betwixt Christ and the deuill*) *STC* 24493; (Udall, *The true remedie against famine and warres*) *STC* 24507; Arber, *Transcript* II, 237.
25. Arber, *op. cit.*, II, p. 205.
26. Harris, "Reports of Udall," no. 23.
27. (Brathwaite, *The Prodigals teares*) *STC* 3579; (Greene, *Disputation*) *STC* 12234–12235.

28. Foley, *op. cit.*, I, p. 675; *Middlesex County Records*, II, p. 77; McKenzie, *op. cit.*, 1334–1339.
29. Foley, *op. cit.*, I, p. 675; *Middlesex County Records* II, pp. 84, 210, 237.
30. For Ely, see McKerrow, *op. cit.*, p. 99; Harris, "Reports of Udall," no. 31; Foley, *op. cit.*, I, p. 675; *C.S.P.D.S. Charles I 1627–1628* (London, 1858), p. 56; (Cotton, *Short History of Henry III*) STC 5864.
31. For the Brownes, see Foley, *op. cit.*, I, p. 675; McKerrow, *op. cit.*, p. 51 f., Foley, *op. cit.*, I, p. 675; the Browne musical publications include: William Corkine, *Ayres, to sing and play to the lute and basse violl*. 1610; *The second booke of ayres*. 1612. STC 5768–5769; Henry Lichfield, *The first set of madrigals*. STC 15588; Francis Pilkington, *The first set of Madrigals and Pastorals*. 1613; *The second set of Madrigals and Pastorals*. 1624. STC 19923–19924; Thomas Bateson, *The second set of Madrigales*. 1618. STC 1587; Michael East, *The fourth set of bookes. Anthemes*. 1618; *The fift set of books*.1618; *The sixt set of bookes*, 1624. STC 7463–7466; John Dowland, *A pilgrimes solace. Wherein is contained musical harmonies*. 1612. STC 7098; Thomas Ravenscroft, *Pammelia. Musickes Miscellanie*. 1618. STC 20760; (Drayton, *Poly-Olbion*) STC 7226–7227; (Peacham, *Graphice*) STC 19507–19508; (Granada, *Treatise of Consideration and prayer*) STC 16913–16914; (Jenison, *The Christians apparelling Christ*) STC 14488; *C.S.P.D.S. Charles I, 1627–1628*, p. 56.
32. Foley, *op. cit.*, I, p. 675; *Middlesex County Records*, II, p. 81; McKenzie, *op. cit.*, no. 71.
33. Foley, *op. cit.*, I, p. 675; McKenzie, *op. cit.* no. 830, 833.
34. Foley, *op. cit.*, I, p. 675.
35. Harris, *op. cit.*, nos. 10, 4; 23; *Manual of Prayers* (Douai: Boscard, 1605) STC 17270, A & R 505; Fulvio Androzzi, *Certaine deuout considerations* (Douai: Auroi, 1606) STC 632; A & R 26; St. Thomas More, *Dialogue* (Antwerp: Fowler, 1537) STC 18083, A & R 549; Leslie, *Defence of ... Marie ... of Scotland* (Louvain: Fowler, 1572) STC 13505, A & R 451; John Percy, *Treatise of faith* (Secretly in England, 1605) A & R 608; Robert Persons, *Christian Directory* (Rouen: Persons Press, 1582–1585) STC 19353–19362, A & R 619–621; Foley, *op. cit.*, I, p. 680 – he quotes Gee's reference to "Two priests lodging in Mistress Fowler's house in Fetter Lane; names I cant learn."
36. Foley, *op. cit.*, I, p. 675.
37. *Ibid*; *Middlesex Sessions Roll*, II, pp. 114, 127, 144; *Calendar to the Sessions Records 1612–1614* (London, 1935), I, pp. 246, 251, 451; II, pp. 240, 296; III, p. 50; Harris, "Reports of Udall," nos. 32, 13.
38. Foley, *op. cit.*, I, p. 675; Harris, "Reports of Udall," p. 237.
39. *C.S.P.D.S. James I, 1603–1610* I, p. 309; *Middlesex Sessions Roll* I, pp. 50, 143; III, p. 50.
40. *Ibid*, II, pp. 79, 107, 126, 134, 146, 237; *Calendar to the Sessions Roll*, II, pp. 240, 296.
41. Harris, "Reports of Udall," no. 31; *London Sessions Record 1605–1685*, p. 3.
42. Harris, "Reports of Udall," Memorandum no. 22, no. 19; *London Sessions Record, 1605–1685*, p. 87.
43. Harris, "Reports of Udall," nos. 18, 19, 29, 32; *C.S.P.Venetian, 1607–1610*, nos. 588, 564.
44. Harris, "Reports of Udall," no. 32; *London Sessions Record, 1605–1685*, p. 62.
45. Harris, "Reports of Udall," Addenda no. 25.
46. *Ibid*, p. 204.
47. Gee, *op. cit.*, Rv; Percy, *Answer to a pamphlet*. STC 4957, A & R 603.
48. (Villegas, *Flos sanctorum*) STC 24730, A & R 851; Harris, "Reports of Udall," nos. 25, 26; Foley, *op. cit.*, I, p. 680; Gillow, *op. cit.*, IV, p. 367.
49. Gee, *op. cit.*, Q3r–Q3v; (Worthington, *An anker of Christian doctrine*) STC 2600, A & R 910; (Norris, *An antidote*) STC 18657–18658, A & R 572a–573; Gee, *op. cit.*, Q4v, (Smith, *Answer*) STC 22809, A & R 771; (Smith, *Of the author and substance of the Protestant church*) STC 22812, A & R 776; (Smith, *The prudentiall ballance of religion*) STC 777, A & R 22813; Gee, *op. cit.*, Folio S; Gillow, *op. cit.*, III, p. 682; Foley, *op. cit.*, I, p. 680.
50. Gee, *op. cit.*, Q3v; (Musket, *The bishop of London his legacy*) STC 18305, A & R 555; (Brerely, *The protestants apologie*) STC 3605, A & R 132–133; Gee, *op. cit.*, Q3v; (Smith, *Of the author and substance of the Protestant church*) STC 22812, A & R 776; *(The holie bible)* STC 2207, A & R 107; *(The New Testament of Jesus Christ)* STC 2884, (2898, 2923, A & R 567–569; (Norris, *An antidote*) STC 18657, A & R 572a, 572b, 573; (Norris, *The guide of faith*) STC 18659, A & R 574; (Norris, *The pseudo-scripturist*) STC 18660, A & R 576.

NOTES

CHAPTER IX

1. For St. Omer, see Owen, *op. cit.*, p. 4; C. A. Newdigate, "Notes on the Seventeenth Century Printing Press of the English College at Saint Omers" in *The Library* (London, 1919), 3rd Series, X, no. 38.
2. Owen, *op. cit.*, p. 110.
3. Morris, *op. cit.*, p. lxxix.
4. Owen, *op. cit.*, p. 111; Harrison, *The Elizabethan Journals* I, p. 214; Loomie, *op. cit.*, p. 203; *Calendar of the Manuscripts of the Marquis of Salisbury* (London, 1904), X, p. 203; Foley, *op. cit.*, I, p. 675.
5. "Notes on the English Mission" in Foley, *op. cit.*, I, p. 115.
6. Pollen, *op. cit.*, p. 259.
7. Newdigate, "Notes on the Seventeenth Century Press," p. 181.
8. Gardiner, *op. cit.*, I, p. 218; "News from England" cited in Foley, *op. cit.*, VII, p. 983; (Persons, *Treatise of three conversions*) *STC* 19416–19417, A & R 640–641; (Persons, *A relation of the triall made before the king of France*) *STC* 19413, A & R 637; (Persons, *A review of the publike disputations*) *STC* 19414, A & R 638; (Persons, *An answere to the ... Reportes ... by ... Cooke*) *STC* 19352, A & R 611; (Persons, *The Christian directory*) *STC* 19371, A & R 623.
9. Owen, *op. cit.*, p. 14.
10. Newdigate, "Notes on the Seventeenth Century Press," p. 182.
11. (Wilson, *The English martyrologe*) *STC* 25771, A & R 889; (Wilson, *The treasury of deuotion*) *STC* 25773, A & R 891.
12. *Calendar of State Papers and Manuscripts existing in the Archives and Collections of Milan* (London, 1912), I, p. 653.
13. (St. Albertus Magnus, *The paradise of the soule*) *STC* 269, A & R 2; (St. Augustine, *The confessions*) *STC* 910, A & R 44; (St. Jerome, *Certaine selected epistles*) *STC* 14502, A & R 412; (St. Thomas a Kempis, *The following of Christ*) *STC* 23987, A & R 816; (Francisco Arias, *The iudge*) *STC* 741, A & R 37; (Miguel de Comalada, *Desiderius*) A & R 251; (Gaspare Loarte, *The exercise of a christian life*) *STC* 16644, A & R 465; (Luis de Granada, *Prayer and meditation*) *STC* 16922a, A & R 480; (*A Manual of prayers*) A & R 515; (*Missale paruum*) *STC* 16226, A & R 543; (Edward Coffin, *A refutation*) *STC* 5475–5476, A & R 243–244; (Thomas Fitzherbert, *An adioynder, The obmutesce, The reply*) *STC* 11022, 11020, 11023, A & R 309, 314, 315; (John Floyd, *The church conquerant*) *STC* 11110, A & R 323; (John Floyd, *The ouerthrow of the Protestants pulpit-babels*) *STC* 11111, A & R 326; (John Floyd, *A suruey of the apostasy of Marcus Antonius de Dominis*) *STC* 11117, A & R 332; (John Floyd, *A word of comfort*) *STC* 11118, A & R 333; (Humfrey Leech, *Dutifull and respectiue considerations*) *STC* 15362, A & R 449; (Sylvester Norris, *An antidote*) *STC* 18657–18658, A & R 572a–573; (Sylvester Norris, *The guide of faith, An appendix to the antidote, The pseudo-scripturist, A true report*) *STC* 18659, 18660–18661, A & R 574–577; (Robert Persons, *A Christian directory, A discussion of the answere of M. William Barlow, The iudgment of a Catholicke Englishe-man, A quiet and sober reckoning*) *STC* 19376, 19378, 19409, 19408, 19412, A & R 624–625, 628, 630, 635; (John Percy, *An answer, A catalogue, A treatise of faith, True relations*) *STC* 4957, 10911–10912, 10916, 10915, A & R 603–606, 609–610; (John Sweet, *A defence; Monsignr. fate voi*) *STC* 25328–23529, A & R 802–803.
14. Owen, *op. cit.*, p. 111; Gee, *op. cit.*, Q3v refers to the works of Coffin, Norris, Floyd, Persons, Percy and others printed at St. Omer.
15. Meyer, *op. cit.*, p. 93f.; Peter Guilday, *The English Catholic Refugees on the Continent 1558–1795* (London, 1914), p. 10; Owen, *op. cit.*, p. 110.
16. *Journals of the House of Commons* p. 607; Harris, "Reports of Udall," no. 1.
17. *Ibid* no. 26; H. K. Duthilloeul, *Bibliographie Douaisienne* (Douai, 1842), II, p. 406; (Fulvio Androzzi, *Certain deuout considerations*) *STC* 632, A & R 26; (Ignacio Balsamo, *An instruction how to pray*) A & R 67; (Luis de la Puente, *Meditations*) A & R 697; (Alfonso de Villegas, *Flos sanctorum*) *STC* 24730, A & R 85; (Matthew Kellison, *The right and iurisdiction of the prelate*) *STC* 14910–14911, A & R 427–428; (Richard Broughton, *A booke intituled: The English Protestants recantation*) *STC* 10414, A & R 153; (Richard Broughton, *A demonstration*) *STC* 10403, A & R 155; (Thomas Fitzherbert, *The first part of a treatise concerning policy, and religion*) *STC* 11018–11019, A & R 313, 316.

18. Duthilloeul, *op. cit.*, Pt. II, p. 407; (Thomas Worthington, *A relation of sixteene martyrs*) A & R 917.
19. Duthilloeul, *op. cit.*, Pt. II, p. 407.
20. Newdigate "Notes on the Seventeenth Century Printing Press," p. 186; *(An appendix of the saints)* STC 24738, A & R 33; *Calendar of the Manuscripts of the Marquis of Salisbury* XVII, p. 328.
21. Smith, *op. cit.*, p. 92; Newdigate, "Notes on he Seventeenth Century Printing Press," p. 186.
22. Loomie, *op. cit.*, p. 185, 197; Meyer, *op. cit.*, p. 115 f., Owen, *op. cit.*, p. 69 ff.; *Calendar of State Papers . . . existing in the Archives . . . of Milan* I, p. 653; Among the works attributed to the press of the Irish Franciscans: (Leadbhar) STC 6778, A & R 252; (MacAingil) STC 17157, A & R 489; (Ó Heó Ghusa) STC 18791, A & R 581–582; (Suim) A & R 800a; *C.S.P.D.S. James, 1603–1610*, p. 261; [Warford (Doulye) *A briefe instruction*] STC 25068, A & R 877; *(An extracte of the determinacion . . . of the doctours of the vniversities of Salamanca and Valledolid touching the warres of Ireland)* STC 21595, A & R 298.
23. Loomie, *op. cit.*, p. 185.
24. *Ibid*, p. 197.
25. *Letters to and from Sir Dudley Carleton during his embassy to Holland.* Ed. by Philip Yorke, 2nd Earl of Hardwicke (London, 1780), p. 43; *Calendar of State Papers . . . existing in the Archives . . . of Milan* I, p. 653.
26. *Journals of the House of Commons . . . 1547–1628*, p. 986.
27. *C.S.P. Venetian* XIX, no. 588; Harrison, *A Jacobean Journal*, p. 239; Harris, "Reports of Udall," nos. 8, 9.
28. Receipt of 20 "popish" books delivered to Sir Julius Caesar by the Bishop of London through Sir Julius Caesar's secretary Richard Etkin, dated Aug. 1, 1699, MS. British Museum, Lansdowne 153, fol. 73r., see Sears Jayne, *Library Catalogues of the English Renaissance* (Los Angeles, 1956) – the List cites twenty titles – however these appear in several copies totalling forty one:
"1. Answer to Tho Bel 4" (possibly one of the treatises by Philip Woodward, *Bel's trial examined*; *The dolefull knell, of Thomas Bell; The foreunner of Bells downefall.*) STC 19403, 19407; A & R 905, 907, 908; "2. Motiues of Bristow 2" (Richard Bristow, *Demaundes*) STC 3801, A & R 148–149; "3. Higgons 2." (Theophilus Higgons, *The apology; The first motiue*) STC 13452, 13454, A & R 396–397; "4. Lecester 2." (Possibly, *The copie of a letter, wryten by a master of arte of Cambrige (sic) . . . about . . . some proceedings of the Erle of Leycester*) STC 19399, A & R 261; "5. ? 3 conversions 2." (Robert Persons, *A treatise of three conversions of England*) STC 19416, A & R 640; "6. A Christian directory 2." (Robert Persons, *The first booke of the Christian directory*) STC 19353–19354, 19362, 19368, 19371, A & R 619–623; "7. Firme foundation of Ca: religio[n] 2." (Jean de Caumont, *The firme foundation of Catholike religion*) STC 4968, A & R 212–214; "8. English martyrologe 2." (John Wilson, *The English martyrologe*) STC 25771, A & R 889; "9. Equivocation 2." (Robert Persons, *A treatise tending to mitigation*) STC 19417, A & R 641; "10. Dialogues of St. Gregory 2." (St. Gregory, *The dialogues*) STC 12349, A & R 367; "11. Historie of L. of Loretto 2." (*The History of our Bl. Lady of Loreto* translated out of Latyn into English by Thomas Price) see Gillow, *op. cit.*, V, p. 368; "12. Popish prayers 2." *(A manual of prayers)* STC 17270, A & R 505; "13. C. Bellarmine, his christia[n] doctrine 2." (St. Robert Bellarmine, *An ample declaration of the Christian doctrine*) STC 1834, A & R 87; "14. An answer to Sr E. Cooke 2." (Robert Persons, *An answere to the fifth part of Reportes lately set forth by Syr Edward Cooke*) STC 19352, A & R 611; "15. Rules of good life 4." (Robert Southwell, *A short rule of good life*) A & R 787–790; "16. The spirituall conflict 2." (Lorenzo Scupoli, The *spiritual conflict*) A & R 759; "17. Dolefull knell of Thomas Bell." (Philip Woodward, *The dolefull knell, of Thomas Bell*) STC 19403, A & R 907; "18. Bels triall examined 2." (Philip Woodward, *Bels trial examined*) A & R 905; "19. Rosary of our Lady 2." (Thomas Worthington, *The rosarie of our Ladie*) STC 17546, A & R 918; "A Rheims Testam[en]t 1." *(The New Testament of Iesus Christ)* STC 2884, 2898, A & R 567–568; Harris, "Reports of Udall," no. 27; (Gregory Martin, *The loue of the soule*) STC 17504–17505, A & R 526–528; (St. Robert Bellarmine, *An Ample declaration of the Christian doctrine*) STC 1834–1835, A & R 87–89; (St. Robert Bellarmine, *A short Christian doctrine*) STC 1844, A & R 101; this work was not published until 1633; the work may refer to *A catechisme, or christian doctrine neces-*

NOTES

sarie for chyldren. (Louvain, 1568) *STC* 4801; *(Six spirituall bookes* (1) *A mirroure to confesse well) STC* 3369, A & R 766; (Robert Southwell, *A short rule of good life*) *STC* 22969, A & R 787–790; (Petrus Frarinus, *An oration against the vnlawfull insurrections of the Protestants of our time*) *STC* 11333, A & R 344; (St. Bonaventure, *The life of our blessed Lord and Sauiour Iesus*) *STC* 13034, A & R 124; *(A manual of prayers) STC* 17263–17271, A & R 495–506; (Henry Fitzsimon, *A Catholike confutation of M. Iohn Riders clayme of antiquitie*) *STC* 11025, A & R 319; (Matthew Kellison, *A suruey of the new religion*) *STC* 14912–14913, A & R 429–430; (Thomas Fitzherbert, *The first part of a treatise concerning policy, and religion*) A & R 311; (Alfonso de Villegas, *Flos sanctorum*) *STC* 24730, A & R 851.

29. Harris, "Reports of Udall," no. 33.
30. *C.S.P. Venetian, 1610–1613* (London, 1905), XII, p. 92.
31. *Acts of the Privy Council, 1616–1617* (London, 1927), p. 40: *C.S.P. D.S. James I, 1619–1623* (London, 1858), p. 140.
32. *C.S.P. Venetian, 1621–1623*, no. 56.
33. *C.S.P. D.S. James I, 1623–1625* (London, 1859), pp. 61, 70, see also Newdigate, "Birchley or St. Omers," p. 316; *(Manual of prayer) STC* 17270, A & R 505; *(Primer) STC* 16096, A & R 688; (Jean de Caumont, *The firme foundation of Catholike religion*) *STC* 4868, A & R 212–214; (Achilles Galliardi, *An abridgement of Christian perfection*) A & R 349; (Thomas Fitzherbert, *The first part of a treatise concerning policy and religion*) A & R 311; *(The rule of our holy mother S. Clare)* A & R 237–238; (Sylvester Norris, *The pseudoscripturist*) *STC* 18660, A & R 576; (St. Francis of Sales, *An introduction to a deuoute life*) *STC* 11317, A & R 338; (St. Thomas a Kempis, *The following of Christ*) *STC* 23987, A & R 815; *(The key of paradise)* A & R 432; (Laurence Vaux, *A catechisme*) *STC* 4801, A & R 834; (St. Robert Bellarmine, *A shorte catechisme*) *STC* 1843, A & R 100.

CHAPTER X

1. A. F. Allison, "John Heigham of S. Omer (c. 1568–c. 1632)" in *Recusant History* IV, no. 6; see also Duthilloeul, *op. cit.*, p. 409.
2. Gillow, *op. cit.*, III, p. 256; James Wadsworth, *The English Spanish Pilgrime*, p. 26; McKerrow, *op. cit.*, pp. 292, 299; *C.S.P.D.S. Elizabeth, 1598–1601*, p. 226. In Morris, *op. cit.*, p. 789; Father Gerard states that he had transferred the custody of his London house and garden to "a very godly and discreet matron of good birth, whom the Lord honoured with martyrdom. Her maiden name was Heigham (Anne Line). Her brother Wm. Heigham is now in Spain, a lay brother of the Society."
3. Allison, *op. cit.*, Appendix B.
4. John Heigham, *A Devout Exposition of the Holie Masse. With an ample Declaration of all the rites and ceremonies, belonging to the same* (Douai, 1614). Preface.
5. Ignacio Balsamo, *An instruction how to pray and meditate well.* Tra[n]slated out of French into English by John Heigham. (Douai, 1618); A. F. Allison, "Biographical Studies" 1534–1829, I, no. 1, p. 209.
6. Gee, *op. cit.*, S4 "F. Heigham."
7. Heigham, *A deuout exposition of the holie masse*, Preface; Heigham, *Via vere tuta.* (St. Omer, 1631) *STC* 13037, A & R 392.
8. St. Peter Canisius, *A summe of Christian doctrine* (St. Omer, 1622), Printer to the Reader.
9. *Six spirituall bookes. A briefe and profitable exercise of the seaven principall effusions of the pretious blood of our Lorde and Sauioure Iesus.* (Douai, 1611); *A tratise of the loue of God* (signed by Heigham); Ignacio Balsamo, *An instruction how to pray and meditate well* (Douai, 1618); Luis de la Puente, *Meditations vppon the mysteries of our holy faith* (St. Omer, 1619); St. Bonaventure, *The life of our blessed Lord and Sauiour Iesus* (St. Omer, 1622); Philippe d'Outreman, *The true Christian catholique* (St. Omer, 1622) *STC* 3669, 20486, 13034, 18902, A & R 766–767, 698, 124, 588.
10. *Six spiritual bookes* (Douai, 1604): *STC* 3369, A & R 766.
11. *A manual of prayers* (Rouen, 1583); *A manual of prayers* (Douai, 1613), *A manuall of godly prayers and litanies* (St. Omer, 1620) *STC* 17262, 17273, 17276, A & R 495, 507, 512; Laurence Vaux, *A catechisme* (Louvain, Antwerp, 1568, 1574) *STC* 4801, 24626,

NOTES

A & R 834–835; Alfonso de Villegas, *The liues of the saints* (St. Omer, 1621) *STC* 24731b, A & R 854; Jan van Paeschen, *The spiritual pilgrimage of Hierusalem* (Douai, 1604–1605) *STC* 12574, A & R 594; Raymundus de Vineis, *The life of the blessed virgin* (Douai, 1609) *STC* 4830, A & R 864.

12. Wadsworth, *op. cit.*, p. 85.
13. *The primer, or office of the blessed Virgin Marie* (St. Omer, 1616, 1621) *STC* 16098, A & R 682–683; *The office of the blessed Virg. Marie, with the rubriques in English* (Douai, 1614, 1623) A & R 685–686; *The primer or office of the blessed Virgin Marie in English* (St. Omer, 1631) two issues *STC* 16099–16100, A & R 691–682; *The psalter of Iesus* (Douai, 1624) *STC* 14570, A & R 769.
14. St. Francis of Sales, *An introduction to a deuoute life* (Douai, 1613) *STC* 11317, 11320, 11320a, A & R 338, 340–341; Luis de Granada, *A memoriall of a Christian life* (Douai, 1612) *STC* 16905, A & R 474; Fulvio Androzzi, *Certain deuout considerations of frequenting the blessed sacrament* (St. Omer, 1618, 1624) A & R 27–28; St. Robert Bellarmine, *An ample declaration of the christian doctrine* (Douai-St. Omer, 1617–1624) *STC* 1837, A & R 91–92; Diego de Estella, *The contempte of the world* (St. Omer, 1622) *STC* 10544, A & R 296; Father Robert Southwell, *A short rule of good life* (St. Omer, 1622) *STC* 22970, A & R 791; St. Thomas a Kempis, *The following of Christ* (St. Omer, 1624) *STC* 23990, A & R 820; Richard Broughton, *A demonstration* (Douai, 1616) *STC* 10403, A & R 155; Thomas Fitzherbert, *The second part of a treatise concerning policy, and religion* (Douai, 1615) A & R 317; The Venerable Bede, *The history of the church of Englande* (St. Omer, 1622, 1626) *STC* 1778–1779, A & R 83–84; Alfonso de Villegas, *The liues of the saints* (St. Omer, 1621, 1630) *STC* 24371b, 24734, A & R 854, 857.
15. St. Francis of Sales, *An introduction to a deuoute life* (Douai, 1613) *STC* 11317, A & R 338; *The psalter of Iesus* (Douai, 1624) *STC* 14570, A & R 769; Anthony Champny, *A treatise of the vocation of bishops* (Douai, 1616) *STC* 4960, A & R 233; St. Peter Canisius, *A summe of Christian doctrine* (St. Omer, 1622) *STC* 4572, A & R 201.
16. Allison, *op. cit.*, Appendix B.
17. *Calendar of the Manuscripts of the Marquis of Salisbury* (London, 1933), XVI, p. 32.
18. Harris, "Reports of Udall," no. 12.
19. *Ibid*, no. 11.
20. *Ibid*, no. 29; Persons, *The iudgement of a Catholicke English-man liuing in banishment for his religion*. *STC* 19408, A & R 630; Fitzsimon, *A Catholike confutation of M. Iohn Riders clayme of antiquitie*. *STC* 11025, A & R 319.
21. McKerrow, *op. cit.*, p. 163; *Middlesex Session Roll*, p. 173.
22. *Calendar of the Manuscripts of the Marquis of Salisbury* X, p. 203; Persons, *Christian directorie*. *STC* 19368, A & R 622; Granada, *A spiritual doctrine*. *STC* 16922, A & R 479; Hamilton, *A facile treatise*. *STC* 12730, A & R 371.
23. Duthilloeul, *op. cit.*, p. 407; Philip Woodward, *The dolefull knell, of Thomas Bell*. *STC* 19403, A & R 907; *A manual of prayers*. *STC* 17268, A & R 503.
24. Kellison, *A survey of the new religion*. *STC* 14912, A & R 429; Fitzherbert, *The first part of a treatise concerning policy, and religion*. A & R 311–312, *STC* 11017; Fraser, *A learned epistle*. *Offer maid to a gentilman of qualitie*. *STC* 11335, 11337, A & R 346, 348; Smith, *An answer to Thomas Bels late challeng*. *STC* 22809, A & R 771; Leech, *A triumph of truth*. *STC* 15363, A & R 450; Estella, *The contempte of the world*. A & R 295; *A breefe collection concerning the loue of God towards mankinde*. *STC* 5534, A & R 142; *Manual of prayers*. *STC* 17268, A & R 503; Pinelli, *The virgin Maries life*. *STC* 19940, A & R 651; Worthington, *A catalogue of martyrs in England*. A & R 916; St. Bonaventure, *The life of the holie father S. Francis*. *STC* 3217, A & R 126; Doulye, *A brief instruction*. *STC* 25068, A & R 877.
25. *The holie bible*. *STC* 2207, A & R 107; Gee, *op. cit.*, Q3.
26. Fitzsimon, *The iustification and exposition of the diuine sacrifice of the masse*. *STC* 11025, A & R 119; Maihew, *A paradise of praiers*. *STC* 17197, A & R 492; Worthington, *An anker of Christian doctrine*. *STC* 26000, A & R 910.
27. *Acts of the Privy Council*, 1621–1623, p. 232.

NOTES

CHAPTER XI

1. Garrett Mattingly, *Renaissance Diplomacy* (London, 1954), p. 44; Rosier's treatise appeared in Nicolas Bertrand, *Les Gestes des Tolaisans*. 1555. See *STC of Books Printed in France*, p. 51.
2. E. R. Adair, *The Exterritoriality of Ambassadors in the Sixteenth and Seventeenth Centuries* (London, 1929), pp. 186, 232.
3. Read, *op. cit.*, p. 95; *C.S.P.D.S. Elizabeth 1581–1590*, pp. 365, 567; [Pierre Charpentier], *Lettre ... addresse à Fr. Portes Candiois, par lequelle il monstre que les persecutions des Eglises de France sont aduenues, non par la faulte de ceux qui faisoient la profession de la Religion, mais de ceux qui nourrissoint les factions et conspirations qu'on appelle la cause* (N.p., 1572); François de Belleforest, *L'innocence de Marie, royne d'Escosse* (N.p., 1572); [Robert Turner], *Maria Stuarta, regina Scotiae*. (Ingolstadt, 1588).
4. William, Cardinal Allen, *An admonition to the nobility and people of England*. STC 368, A & R 5.
5. *C.S.P.F.S. Elizabeth, January-June 1588* (London, 1931), XXI, Pt. IV, pp. 461, 489.
6. *Ibid*, p. 528.
7. *Ibid*, p. 533; *C.S.P.F.S. Elizabeth, July-December 1588*, XXII, pp. 2, 26.
8. *Ibid*, pp. 49, 60.
9. *C.S.P.F.S. Elizabeth, July 1583–July 1584* (London, 1914), XXIII, p. 28. L'Huillier certainly does not appear to have been active in Rouen as a Catholic agent; when he took up residence in Paris only one work appears to have been associated with him as partner of Jamet Mettayer in 1595: Alexander de Pont-Aymery, *Discours d'estat*. (Paris & The Hague, 1595).
10. William, Cecil, Baron Burghley, *The execution of justice in England for maintenance of publique and christian peace*. STC 4902.
11. STC 4905–4907.
12. William, Cardinal Allen, *A true sincere and modest defence of English catholiques that suffer for their faith*. STC 373, A & R 13; *C.S.P.F.S. Elizabeth, August 1584–August 1585* (London, 1916), XIX, p. 35.
13. *Ibid*, p. 126.
14. A. G. Petti, "Richard Verstegan and the Catholic Martyrologies of the Later Elizabethan Period," p. 70; A. G. Petti, "A Bibliography of the Writings of Richard Verstegan," no. 20.
15. Petti, "Richard Verstegan and the Catholic Martyrologies," p. 76.
16. *C.S.P.F.S. Elizabeth, June 1586–June 1587* (London, 1927), XXI, p. 48; *Ibid*, p. 48; *Martyrium Edmundi Campiani*. Tr. G. Estius. (Louvain, 1582) see *STC Netherlands*, p. 45.
17. *C.S.P.F.S. Elizabeth, June 1586–June 1587*, p. 315; for Caumont, see *STC of French Books*, p. 96.
18. *C.S.P.F.S. Elizabeth, June 1586–June 1587*, pp. 499, 585.
19. *C.S.P.F.S. Elizabeth, January–July 1589* (London, 1950), XXIII, p. 299; B.I., *The copy of a letter*; STC 1038, A & R 60.
20. James I, *For ambassadors*. 8 March 1624. STC 8723.
21. *C.S.P. Venetian, 1607–1610*, XI, p. 576; Harris, "Reports of Udall," nos. 1, 13.
22. Harrison, *A Jacobean Journal*, p. 127.
23. For Burton, see McKerrow, *op. cit.*, p. 57; *C.S.P. Venetian 1603–1607* (London, 1900), X, no. 730.
24. Harris, "Reports of Udall," p. 204; *C.S.P. Venetian 1607–1610*, p. 576.
25. *Ibid*.
26. *Ibid*.
27. "A Catalogue of books marked? for the ambassador of Venice taken from the Dutch priest at his house"; referred to in Jayne, *op. cit.*, p. 140 – original manuscript, British Museum: Lansdowne 153 fol. 681. The Venetian ambassador was Marc-Antonio Correr. The authors of the Catholic works are not cited since obviously the searcher was Protestant. "1. The Rosary of St Mary the Virgin. Many." Thomas Worthington, *The rosarie of our ladie* (Antwerp, 1600) A & R 918.
"2. St Maries Psalter or offices. Many." This work may be identified as either *A methode, to meditate on the psalter, or great rosarie of our blessed Ladie* (Antwerp, 1598) or *The primer, or office of the blessed Virgin Marie* (Antwerp, 1599, 1604) STC 17538, 16094–16095, A & R 541, 680–681.

"3. A treatise tending to mitigation of Equivocation." Robert Persons, *A treatise tending to mitigation towardes Catholicke-subiectes in England* (St. Omer, 1607) *STC* 19417, A & R 641.
(nos. 4 & 5 crossed out) 5. *Prvrit-Anvs* is discernible.)
"6. Th' Commen(?) of J. ffox his calendr Saints. Ma." John Foxe, *Acts and monuments* (London, 1583, 1596, 1597) *STC* 11225–11226A.
"7. Christian doctrine of C. Bellarmine translated. Ma." St. Robert Bellarmine, *An ample declaration of the Christian doctrine* ... Translated into English by Richard Hadock (N.p., 1602–1605; Douai, 1604–1605) *STC* 1834–1835, A & R 87–89.
"8. Christian directory. Many." Robert Persons, *A christian directory* (St. Omer, 1607) A & R 623.
"9. The Rule of good life. Many." Robert Southwell, *A short rule of good life* (N.p., 1596–1597, 1602–1605, Douai, 1603) *STC* 22964, 22969, A & R 787–790.
"10. Of three c[o]nv[er]sions of England. Many." Robert Persons, *A treatise of three conversions of England* (St. Omer, 1604) *STC* 19416, A & R 640.
"11. The English Martirologe, videl. the martirs of England Scotland & Ireland For 1608. Many." John Wilson, *The English martyrologe conteyning a summary of the liues of the glorious and renowned saintes of the three kingdomes England, Scotland, and Ireland* (St. Omer, 1608) *STC* 25771, A & R 889.
"12. The Rule of p[er]f[e]ction. Some." William Fitch, *The rule of perfection* (Rouen, 1609) A & R 306.
"13. An Answer to ye workes of Sr Edward Cook. Many." Robert Persons, *An answere to the fifth part of Reportes lately set foorth by Syr Edward Cooke* (St. Omer, 1606) *STC* 19352, A & R 611.
"14. Theophilus Higgons motives. Many." Theophilus Higgons, *The first motiue of T.H. maister of arts ... to suspect the integrity of his religion* (Douai, 1609) *STC* 13454, A & R 397.
"15. Demaunds unto all Heretiks. Many." Richard Bristow, *Demaundes to be proponed of Catholiques to the heretikes.* (Antwerp, 1576, N. p., 1596–1597) *STC* 3801, A & R 148–149.
"16. St. Gregories dialogues dedicated to o[u]r E. Stu[dents]. Many." St. Gregory, *The dialogues* (Douai, 1608). *STC* 12349, A & R 167.
"17. The Spirituall Conflict. Some." Lorenzo Scupoli, *The spiritual conflict* (Douai, 1603–1610) A & R 760.
"18. The firme foundation of Catholik religion. Some." Jean de Caumont, *The firme foundation of Catholike religion, against the bottomles pitt of heresies* (Douai, 1607–1608) A & R 214.
"19. Newes from Spaine. an. 1593. Some." Robert Persons, *Newes from Spayne and Holland* (Antwerp, 1593) A & R 634.
"20. A breefe Instruction ... the points of Relig. Some." William Warford (Doulye), *A briefe instruction, , , concerninge the principall poyntes of Christian religio[n]* (Seville, 1604) *STC* 25068, A & R 877.
"21. The following of Christ. Some." Thomas a Kempis, *The following of Christ* (Rouen, 1585) *STC* 23968, A & R 814.
"22. The Contempt of the Worlde. Some." Diego de Estella, *The contempte of the worlde and the vanitie thereof* (Douai, 1604) A & R 295.
"23. Bels triall examined. Some." Philip Woodward, *Bels trial examined.* (Douai, 1608) A & R 905.
"24. Rhemes testament. 4." *The New Testament of Iesus Christ* (Rheims, 1582) *STC* 2884, A & R 567.
"25. The history of our Lady of Loretto. Many." Orazio Torsellino, *The history of our B. Lady of Loreto* (St. Omer, 1608) A & R 825.
28. Adair, *op. cit.*, p. 190.
29. *Ibid*, p. 195.
30. *C.S.P. Venetian 1615–1617* (London, 1908), XIV, no. 48.
31. *C.S.P. Venetian 1617–1619*, no. 416; *Acts of the Privy Council of England, 1619–1621* (London, 1930), p. 351.
32. Richard Dugdale, *A Narrative of the Wicked Plots carried on by Seignor Gondamore for advancing the Popish Religion and Spanish Faction* (London, 1670), p. 15.

NOTES

33. *C.S.P. Venetian 1619–1621*, no. 644; *C.S.P. D.S. James I, 1619–1623*, p. 399; *More News from the Palatinate*. 1622. STC 19133.
34. Adair, *op. cit.*, p. 211.
35. *C.S.P.D.S. James I 1619–1623*, pp. 324, 479; *C.S.P. D.S. James I 1623–1625*, pp. 25, 70; Birch, *op. cit.*, II, p. 355.
36. Adair, *op. cit.*, p. 191; *STC* 8723 James I, *For ambassadors*. [8 Mar. 1624].

CHAPTER XII

1. For James' education and early writing, see Willson, *op. cit.*, p. 60f., *The Furies* STC 14379.
2. Tanner, *op. cit.*, p. 9; *STC* 14409; Clancy, *op. cit.*, p. 210.
3. *STC* 14348–14349; Robert Dickson & John P. Edmond, *Annals of Scottish Printing from the Introduction of the Art in 1507 to the Beginning of the Seventeenth Century* (Cambridge, 1890), II, p. 445; *STC* 14350–14360; J. William Hebel & Hoyt H. Hudson, *Poetry of the English Renaissance 1509–1600* (New York, 1930), p. 547.
4. Willson, *op. cit.*, p. 227 ff.
5. *STC* 14400; Charles H. McIlwain, *The Political Works of James I* (New York, 1965), p. lxff.; [St. Robert Bellarmine], *Responsio ad Librum inscriptum Triplici nodo, Triplex cuneus, sive apologie* (Cologne, 1608) (written under the name of Bellarmine's almoner, Matthaeus Tortus); Robert Persons, *The iudgement of a Catholicke Englishman liuing in banishment for his religion . . . concerninge a late booke set forth and entitled, Triplici nodo* (St. Omer, 1608); Harris, "Reports of Udall," no. 28; Willson, *op. cit.*, p. 232 ff.
6. *STC* 14401; Harrison, *A Second Jacobean Journal*, p. 131.
7. *STC* 14402; Willson, *op. cit.*, p. 237; McIlwain, *op. cit.*, p. lxi.
8. *STC* 14419–14420; *Calendar of State Papers Relating to Ireland, of the Reign of James I 1615–1625* (London, 1880), p. 144.
9. *STC* 14367; Willson, *op. cit.*, p. 241.
10. Willson, *op. cit.*, p. 230.
11. Jackson, *op. cit.*, p. 356f., *STC* 14344.
12. *STC* 14400; Harrison, *A Second Jacobean Journal*, pp. 133, 139.
13. Taunton, *op. cit.*, p. 283.
14. Smith, *op. cit.*, p. 462; Willson, *op. cit.*, p. 238.
15. Willson, *op. cit.*, pp. 465, 468.
16. *Ibid*, p. 238; Sir Ralph Winwood, *Memorials of Affairs of State in the Reigns of Q. Elizabeth and King James I* (London, 1725), IV, p. 55.
17. *C.S.P.D.S. Reign of James I, 1603–1610*, pp. 639, 651; McIlwain, *op. cit.*, p. liv.
18. *C.S.P. Venetian 1613–1615* (London, 1907), no. 224.
19. *Letters of Chamberlain*. Ed. by McLure II, p. 33.
20. *C.S.P.Venetian 1615–1617*, no. 718.
21. Smith, *op. cit.*, II, p. 92.
22. *Ibid*, II, p. 280.
23. Tracts by Arminius printed prior to and during 1609 include his *Disputatio publica* no. 4; *Theses Theologicae de natura Dei; Dignitatie van des menschen origen des will-keur ende hare crachten*, and others; *Chamberlain Letters*. Ed. by Thomson, p. 87; *STC* 9229–9233; Akrigg, *op. cit.*, p. 311; Winwood, *op. cit.*, III, p. 339.
24. *Letters to and from Sir Dudley Carelton*, p. 129.
25. Knuttel, *op. cit.*, no. 2506: *Balance pour peser en toute equite et droicture la Harangue Dv . . . Dudley Carleton*, (N.p., 1618); Carleton, *op. cit.*, p. 243; see also Knuttel, *op. cit.*, no. 2661 for *Placcaert van de Staten van Hollandt . . . tegens het seditieux spreechen*. (The Hague, 1618).
26. Walter Yonge, *Diary of Walter Yonge Esq. from 1604 to 1628*. Ed. by George Roberts (London, 1848), p. 67; *Acts of the Privy Council of England 1621–1623* (London, 1932), pp. 232, 237.

NOTES

CHAPTER XIII

1. William Haller, *The Rise of Puritanism* (New York, 1947), p. 174ff.
2. Steele, *op. cit.*, p. 71.
3. Collinson, *op. cit.*, pp. 86, 119; *STC* 10847.
4. Collinson, *op. cit.*, p. 86; Arthur J. Klein, *Intolerance in the Reign of Elizabeth* (Cambridge, 1917), p. 151.
5. Haller, *The Rise of Puritanism*, p. 10; *STC* 4713.
6. *STC* 24184; Collinson, *op. cit.*, p. 297; *C.S.P.D.S. Reign of Elizabeth 1581–1590*, p. 62.
7. W. H. Frere, C. E. Douglas, *Puritan Manifestoes A Study of the Origin of the Puritan Revolt* (London, 1954), p. xxii.
8. *STC* 3910; Haller, *The Rise of Puritanism*, pp. 176, 183; Donald J. McGinn, *John Penry and the Marprelate Controversy* (New Brunswick, 1966), p. 24; Steele, *op. cit.*, p. 82.
9. Haller, *The Rise of Puritanism*, p. 205; *STC* 8125; *C.S.P.D.S. Reign of Elizabeth 1581–1590*, p. 275.
10. *Two Elizabethan Puritan Diaries by Richard Rogers and Samuel Ward* (London, 1933), p. 81; *C.S.P.D.S. 1581–1590*, p. 275; Steele, *op. cit.*, p. 89.
11. Harrison, *The Elizabethan Journals* I, pp. 80, 12.
12. *C.S.P.D.S. Elizabeth 1591–1594*, p. 341.
13. Petti, "The Letters and Dispatches of Richard Verstegan," p. 114.
14. William Haller, *Liberty and Reformation in the Puritan Revolution* (New York, 1955), p. 6.
15. McIlwain, *op. cit.*, pp. xcff.
16. *C.S.P.D.S. James I 1603–1610*, p. 5; Steele, *op. cit.*, p. 112.
17. Steele, *op. cit.*, p. 115.
18. *Chamberlain Letters*. Ed. by Thomson, p. 35; for the Separatist sects, see Champlin Burrage, *The Early English Dissenters . . . (1550–1641)* (New York, 1967), passim; Birch, *op. cit.*, I, p. 229.

CHAPTER XIV

1. J. H. Couper, *The Select Works of Robert Crowley* (London 1872), p. xi.
2. *STC* 6078, 6080, 6086, 6094–6095, 6088, 6090, 6084; Bennett, *op. cit.*, p. 125; For an analysis of Crowley's wriings, see *The Cambridge History of English Literature*. Ed. by A. W. Ward & A. R. Waller (New York, 1909), III, pp. 112 ff.
3. Duff, *op. cit.*, p. 35; *STC* 2725; 21612–21617; 25588; 19906–19907a.
4. *Dictionary of National Biography* V, pp. 241ff; Duff, *op. cit.*, p. 35.
5. Collinson, *op. cit.*, p. 115.
6. Arber, *Transcript* II, p. 102; I, p. 514; Duff, *op. cit.*, p. 35; Greg, *op. cit.*, pp. 29, 43.
7. *STC* 10847; A. F. Scott Pearson, *Thomas Cartwright and Elizabethan Puritanism* (Cambridge, 1925), p. 86; Arber, *Transcript* I, p. 466; Collinson, *op. cit.*, p. 139.
8. Pearson, *op. cit.*, p. 86.
9. *STC* 10847–10849, 4713, 10850.
10. Frere & Douglas, *op. cit.*, p. xvii; *STC* 8063 (Confiscating Cartwright's *Admonition to Parliament*. London, 1573).
11. Arber, *Transcript* I, p. 466.
12. Collinson, *op. cit.*, I, p. 174; Arber, *Transcript* I, p. 467.
13. Arber, *Transcript* I, p. 466; Pearson, *op. cit.*, p. 111; Collinson, *op. cit.*, p. 174.
14. Frere, *op. cit.*, p. xxi.
15. *STC* 4711–4712; Pearson, *op. cit.*, pp. 86, 85; Collinson, *op. cit.*, p. 140; *STC* 24184–24185.
16. *STC* 10395; 3734; Pierce, *op. cit.*, p. 135.
17. McKerrow, *op. cit.*, p. 277; Pierce, *op. cit.*, p. 151; *STC* 24911, 22022, 15073, 15068, 10844, 10845, 2014, 16567, 4926–4927, 10770.
18. *STC* 3472, 11990, 4315, 6409, 6401, 1193–1194, 13495, 19065, 15252.
19. Arber, *Transcript* II, pp. 102, 106.
20. *STC* 6801; McKerrow, *op. cit.*, pp. 277ff.
21. *STC* 24507, 24492, 24490, 24505–24506; *Cambridge History of English Literature* III, p. 430; Greg, *op. cit.*, p. 27; Pierce, *op. cit.*, p. 152.

NOTES

22. Allison, "Biographical Studies 1534–1829," p. 38; Dickson, *op. cit.*, II, pp. 396ff.
23. *STC* 19605, 24499, 19604.
24. Collinson, *op. cit.*, pp. 391ff; Burrage, *op. cit.*, II, p. 25; Creswell, *op. cit.*, p. 19.
25. For a detailed study of the Marprelate Tracts, see Pierce, *op. cit.* and Arber, *Introductory Sketch to the ... Marprelate Controversy; Cambridge History of English Literature* III, 433; *STC* 17453.
26. Pierce, *op. cit.*, p. 315.
27. *STC* 17454; *Cambridge History of English Literature* III, p. 438; Pierce, *op. cit.*, p. 158.
28. *STC* 5682; *Cambridge History of English Literature* III, p. 438; Arber, *Introductory Sketch to the ... Marprelate Controversy* p. 109.
29. *STC* 17455–17456; *Cambridge History of English Literature* III, pp. 439, 610.
30. Pierce, *op. cit.*, p. 183; Collinson, *op. cit.*, p. 393; Pearson, *op. cit.*, p. 451; McGinn, *op. cit.*, pp. 145ff; *STC* 6805.
31. Dickson, *op. cit.*, II, p. 468.
32. Pierce, *op. cit.*, pp. 185ff.
33. *Ibid*, pp. 200, 205ff; for Symmes, see McKerrow, *op. cit.*, p. 245; *STC* 22304; 22307–22309, 22314, 22282, 22288–22288a.
34. McKerrow, *op. cit.*, p. 46; Pierce, *op. cit.*, p. 192; Balmford *STC* 1334–1339; Philippe du Plessis du Mornay *STC* 18135; Pierre Coton *STC* 5861; *Psalms STC* 2751; Edward Vaughan, *A diuine discouerie of death. STC* 24596; Linaker, *A comfortable treatise for such as are afflicted in conscience. STC* 15638; Perkins *STC* 19658–19659, 19662–19664.
35. Burrage, *op. cit.*, II, p. 85; Pierce, *op. cit.*, pp. 161, 181, 186; Arber, *Introductory Sketch to the ... Marprelate Controversy*, pp. 116, 131; Thomas Gibson, printer and bookbinder in Bury St. Edmunds, was summoned by Lord Burghley for examination as a distributor of Brownist books; see Mc Kerrow, *op. cit.*, p. 113; Henry M. Dexter, *The England and Holland of the Pilgrims* (Boston & New York, 1905), p. 795n.
36. Pierce, *op. cit.*, p. 201.
37. *Ibid*, pp. 155f.
38. Collinson, *op. cit.*, p. 409; *C.S.P.D.S. James I 1603–1610*, p. 181.
39. Petti, "The Letters and Dispatches of Richard Verstegan," p. 144; Verstegan may have referred to Barrows, *Collection of certaine sclaunderous articles, gyuen out by the bishops against such faithfull christians as they nowe deteyne in their prisons. STC* 1518; Burrage, *op. cit.*, I, pp. 130, 139.
40. *STC* 119; Burrage, *op. cit.*, I, pp. 26, 140–141, 143, II, p. 42, 59; Petti, "The Letters and Dispatches of Richard Verstegan," p. 144; *STC* 1523.
41. Petti, "The Letters and Dispatches of Richard Verstegan," p. 144; *STC* 1517.
42. *STC* 10400; Arber, *Transcript* II, p. 587; Dickson, *op. cit.*, II, p. 468; J. Dover Wilson, "Richard Schilders and the English Puritans" in *Transactions of the Bibliographical Society* (London, 1912), XI, p. 85.
43. *C.S.P.D.S. Elizabeth, 1581–1590*, p. 698.
44. *STC* 12312–12318; Petti, "The Letters and Dispatches of Richard Verstegan," p. 114; McKerrow, *op. cit.*, pp. 203, 127; *STC* 2048, 14938, 18355.
45. *STC* 7884, 1020; Gooch, *op. cit.*, p. 31.
46. Pierce, *op. cit.*, p. 82.
47. Arber, *Introductory Sketch to the ... Marprelate Controversy*, p. 173.
48. Collinson, *op. cit.*, p. 403.
49. Harrison, *A Jacobean Journal*, p. 192.

CHAPTER XV

1. William Bradford, *Of Plymouth Plantation*. Ed. by Samuel E. Morison (New York, 1952), p. 10f.
2. Wilson, *op. cit.*, pp. 70, 73; Worman, *op. cit.*, p. 59.
3. Wilson, *op. cit.*, pp. 76f, 80; *STC Netherlands*, p. 42.
4. Steele, *op. cit.*, p. 82; *STC* 8141.
5. *C.S.P.D.S. Elizabeth, May-December 1582* (London, 1909), pp. 265, 299.
6. *STC* 4706–4707, 10771–10773.

7. Wilson, *op. cit.*, p. 84.
8. *STC* 521, 24500, 4387a–4388, 2701, 2769–2770.
9. Greg, *op. cit.*, p. 79; McKerrow, *op. cit.*, p. 112.
10. *STC* 14340, 14335, 14338; *Calendar of the Manuscripts of the Marquis of Salisbury*, XVII, p. 5.
11. *STC* 14339.
12. *STC* 3862–3862a, 11131, 11134, 11136, 11146, 11150.
13. Harrison, *A Jacobean Journal*, pp. 278ff; *Letters to and from Sir Dudley Carleton*, p. 348.
14. See Chapter XIV, notes 39 & 40; Mc Kerrow, *op. cit.*, pp. 61, 127ff, 67f; *STC* 2702, 2901; *STC* 2903; Harrison, *The Elizabethan Journals* II, p. 252; Jackson, *op. cit.*, p. 20 n.l.
15. McKerrow, *op. cit.*, p. 284; Jackson, *op. cit.*, viii, 52, 344.
16. *STC* 3532.
17. McKerrow, *op. cit.*, p. 265; Burrage, *op. cit.*, I, p. 168f; A. F. Johnson, "The Exiled English Church at Amsterdam and its Press" in *The Library* (London, 1951), Series V, Vol. V, no. 4, p. 220.
18. *STC* 228, 235, 209, 224, 5450, 1580, 12858.
19. Bradford, *op. cit.*, p. 17.
20. Rendel Harris & Stephen K. Jones, *The Pilgrim Press A Bibliographical & Historical Memorial of the Books Printed at Leyden by the Pilgrim Fathers* (Cambridge, 1922).
21. Bradford, *op. cit.*, pp. 325–328.
22. Harris & Jones, *op. cit.*, pp. 7f.
23. *Ibid*, Appendix II.
24. Bradford, *op. cit.*, p. 327.
25. Harris & Jones, *op. cit.*, Appendix 10, 19; *Letters to and from Sir Dudley Carleton*, pp. 348, 353.
26. *Ibid*, p. 379.
27. *Ibid*, p. 380; Harris & Jones, *op. cit.*, Appendix nos. 16, 9.
28. *Ibid*, p. 389; Appendix no. 1.
29. Dexter, *op. cit.*, p. 580.
30. *Letters to and from Sir Dudley Carleton*, p. 389; Dexter, *op. cit.*, p. 580.
31. Dexter, *op. cit.*, pp. 405, 435; Bradford, *op. cit.*, p. 59.
32. Bradford, *op. cit.*, p. 47; Harris & Jones, *op. cit.*, pp. 38ff; H. M. Dexter, "Elder Brewster's Library" in *Proceedings of the Massachusetts Historical Society* (Boston, 1889).
33. *STC* 8714, 8736; *C.S.P.D.S. James I, 1623–1625*, p. 309.

WORKS CITED

PRIMARY SOURCES

Acts of the Privy Council of England 1601–1604, 1621–1623, 1626. Edited by John R. Dasent. (London, 1907, 1932, 1938), N.S.

[Awfield, Thomas]. *The Life and end of Thomas Awfeeld a Seminary Preest and Thomas Webly a Dyers seruant in London*. (London, 1585). Copy consulted, courtesy The British Museum Library.

B.I., *The Copy of a Letter Lately Written by a Spanish Gentleman, To his Friend in England, in refutation of sundry Calumnies*. (N.p., 1589). Copy consulted, courtesy Rare Book Division, The New York Public Library.

Balsamo, Ignacio, *An introduction how to pray and meditate well*. Tra[n]slated out of French into English by Iohn Heigham. (Douai, 1618). Copy consulted, courtesy The British Museum Library.

The holie Bible faithfully translated into English, out of authentical Latin. (Douai, 1609). Copy consulted, courtesy Rare Book Division, The New York Public Library.

Bradford, William, *Of Plymouth Plantation*. Edited by Samuel E. Morison. (New York, 1952).

Bridgewater, John, *Concertatio ecclesiae in Anglia*. (Treves, 1584).

[Brome, George, Elizabeth & Briget]. "Inventory of 30 books and reliques found in the studies of George Brome and his two sisters Elizabeth and Briget, August 27, 1586." MS., Lansdowne 50, folios 163v–164r. Courtesy Department of Western Manuscripts, The British Museum.

[Caesar, Sir Julius]. List of "20 popish books delivered to Sir Julius Caesar by the Bishop of London. Aug. 1, 1609. Signed Richard Etkins." MS., Lansdowne 153, fol. 73r. Courtesy Department of Western Manuscripts, The British Museum.

Calendar of the Manuscripts of the Marquis of Salisbury preserved at Hatfield House. (London, 1899, 1904, 1906, 1910, 1933, 1938, 1940, 1965), Parts VII, IX–XII, XVI–XIX.

Calendar of State Papers Domestic Series. Reign of Elizabeth, 1581–1590, 1591–1594, 1595–1597, 1598–1601, 1601–1603. (London, 1864–1865, 1869–1870, 1902).

Calendar of State Papers Domestic Series. James I, 1603–1610, 1611–1618, 1619–1623, 1623–1625. (London, 1857–1859).

Calendar of State Papers Domestic Series. Reign of Charles I, 1627–1628. (London, 1858).

Calendar of State Papers Foreign Series of the Reign of Elizabeth, July 1583–1584; August 1584–August 1585; January–June 1588; July–December 1588; January–July 1589. (London, 1914, 1916, 1931, 1936, 1950).

Calendar of State Papers Relating to Ireland, of the Reign of James I: 1615–1625. (London, 1880).

Calendar of State Papers Relating to Scotland. (London, 1858).

Calendar of State Papers and Manuscripts existing in the Archives and Collections of Milan. (London, 1912).

Calendar to the Sessions Records 1612–1614;1614–1615;1615–1616. (London, 1935, 1937).

Canisius, St. Peter, *A summe of Christian doctrine*. (St. Omer, 1622). Copy consulted, courtesy The British Museum Library.

[Carleton, Sir Dudley]. *Letters to and from Sir Dudley Carleton during his Embassy to Holland*. Ed. by Philip Yorke, 2nd Earl of Hardwick. (London, 1780).

Catalogue of State Papers & Manuscripts Relating to English Affairs Existing in the Archives & Collections of Venice, 1603–1607; 1607–1610; 1610–1613; 1613–1615; 1615–1617; 1617–1619; 1619–1621; 1621–1623. (London, 1900, 1904–1905, 1907–1911).

Cecil, William, Lord Burghley, *The Copie of a letter sent owt of England to Don Bernardino Mendoza*. (London, 1588). Recently copy of the author.

[Chamberlain, John]. *Chamberlain Letters*. Edited by Norman E. McClure. (Philadelphia, 1939).

[Chamberlain, John]. *The Chamberlain Letters*. Edited by Elizabeth M. Thomson. (New York, 1965).

WORKS CITED

Champny, Anthony, *A treatise of the vocation of bishops and other ecclesiastical ministers.* (Douai, 1616). Copy consulted, courtesy The British Museum Library.

[Correr, Marc-Antonio]. "A Catalogue of books received from the Ambassador of Venice taken from the Dutch priest in his house." 1609. MS., Lansdowne 143, fol. 68r. Courtesy Department of Western Manuscripts, The British Museum.

Couper, J. H., *The Selected Works of Robert Crowley.* (London, 1872).

Creswell, Joseph, *An advertisement written to a secretarie of my L. Treasurers of my L. Treasurers of Ingland by an Englishe intelligencer.* (N.p., 1592). Copy consulted, courtesy Rare Book Division, The New York Public Library.

Dugdale, Richard, *A Narrative of the wicked Plots carried on by Seignor Gondamore for advancing the Popish religion and Spanish Faction.* (London, 1670).

Elizabeth I, Queen of England, *A Proclamation made against seditious and trayterous Bookes, Bulles and Writinges.* (London, 1570). Copy consulted, courtesy The British Museum Library.

Elizabeth I, Queen of England, *By the Queene.* (Proclamation confiscating Cartwright's *Second Admonition to the Parliament.*) (London, 1573). Copy consulted, courtesy The Harvard College Library.

Elizabeth I, Queen of England. *By the Queene.* (Against slanderous books.) (London, 1573). Copy consulted, courtesy The British Museum Library.

Elizabeth I, Queen of England, *By the Queene* (Against Stubbs' *Gaping Gulf*). (London, 1579). Copy consulted, courtesy The British Museum Library.

Elizabeth I, Queen of England, *A Proclamation against the Sectaries of the Family of loue.* (London, 1580). Copy consulted, courtesy The British Museum Library.

Elizabeth I, *A Proclamation against certain seditions and scismatical Bookes and Libelles*, & c. (London, 1583). Copy consulted, courtesy The Harvard College Library.

Elizabeth I, Queen of England, *A Proclamation for the suppressing of seditious Bookes and Libelles.* (London, 1584). Copy consulted, courtesy The British Museum Library.

Foley, Henry, S. J., *Records of the English Province of the Society of Jesus.* (London, 1897).

Gee, John, *The foote out of the snare. With a detection of sundry late Practices and Impostures of the Priests and Iesuites in England.* (London, 1624). Copy consulted, courtesy Rare Book Division, The New York Public Library.

Greg, W. W. & Boswell, E., Editors, *Records of the Court of the Stationers, Company 1576–1602.* (London, 1930).

The Gunpowder Treason: With a Discourse of the Manner of its Discovery, (London, 1679).

Harris, P. R., "The Reports of William Udall, Informer 1605–1612," in *Recusant History.* (London, 1966), Vol. VIII.

Harrison, G. B., editor, *The Elizabethan Journals, 1591–1597.* (New York, 1967).

Harrison, G. B., *A Jacobean Journal.* (New York, 1941).

Harrison, G. B., *A Second Jacobean Journal.* (London, 1958).

Heigham, John, *A deuout exposition of the Holie Masse. With an ample Declaration of all the rites and ceremonies, belonging to the same.* (Douai, 1614). Copy consulted, courtesy The British Museum Library.

Jackson, William A., Editor, *Records of the Court of the Stationers' Company 1602 to 1640.* (London, 1957).

James I, King of England, *A Proclamation for the search and apprehension of Iohn Cotton Esquire.* (London, 1613). Copy consulted, courtesy The Henry E. Huntington Library.

James I, King of England, *A Proclamation for Ambassadors and forreigne Ministers.* (London, 1623). Copy consulted, courtesy The Henry E. Huntington Library.

James I, King of England, *A Proclamation against the disorderly Printing, Vttering, and dispersing of Bookes, Pamphlets* & c. (London, 1623). Copy consulted, courtesy The Henry E. Huntington Library.

James I, King of England, *A Proclamation against Seditious, Popish and Puritanicall Bookes and Pamphlets.* (London, 1624). Copy consulted, courtesy The Henry E. Huntington Library.

Journals of the House of Commons from November 1542 to March the 2nd 1628. (London, 1803).

Journals of the House of Lords. (London, 1846).

Law, T. G., *Documents Relating to the Dissensions of the Roman Clergy 1597–1602.* (London, 1896).

Letters and State Papers Relating to English Affairs Preserved in the Archives of Simancas. (London, 1899).

"London Sessions Records 1605–1685" in *Catholic Record Society* (London, 1834).

[Manningham, John]. *Diary of John Manningham of the Middle Temple 1602–1603.* (Westminster, 1868).

WORKS CITED

McKenzie, D. F., *Stationers' Company Apprentices 1605–1640.* (Charlottesville, 1961).
McKerrow, R. B., *A Dictionary of Printers and Booksellers in England, Scotland and Ireland . . . 1557–1640.* (London, 1910).
Middlesex County Records. Edited by John C. Jeaffreson. (London, n.d.).
Middlesex Sessions Roll. (London, n.d.).
Morris, John, Editor, *The Condition of Catholics under James I. Father Gerard's Narrative of the Gunpowder Plot.* (London, 1872).
"Official Lists of Catholic Prisoners during the Reign of Queen Elizabeth" in *Miscellanea, Catholic Record Society.* (London, 1906).
Owen, Lewis, *Relation of the State of the English Colledges, Seminaries and Cloysters in all forraine parts.* (London, 1626). Copy consulted, courtesy Rare Book Division, The New York Public Library.
A Parte of a register, contayninge sundrie memorable matters written by diuers godly and learned in our time, which standeth for, and desire the reformation of our churche. (Middleburg, 1593). Copy consulted, courtesy The British Museum Library.
[Persons, Robert]. "The Memoirs of Father Robert Persons." Edited by J. H. Pollen. in *Catholic Record Society.* (London, 1905).
[Persons, Robert]. *Memorials of Father Robert Persons S.J.* (London, 1942).
Pollen, J. H. Editor, "Unpublished Documents Relating to the English Martyrs, 1584–1603" in *Catholic Record Society.* (London, 1908, 1914).
Prvrit-Anvs vel nec omne, nec ex omni, sur apologia Pvritanis & Novatoribvs Vniversis. (St. Omer, 1609). Copy consulted, courtesy Rare Book Division, The New York Public Library.
[Rogers, Richard & Ward, Samuel]. *Two Elizabethan Puritan Diaries by Richard Rogers & Samuel Ward.* (London, 1933).
Sander, Nicholas, *A treatise of the images of Christ, and other saints.* (St. Omer, 1624). Copy consulted, courtesy The British Museum Library.
Six spirituall bookes, ful of maruelous pietie and deuotion. (Douai, 1604). Copy consulted, courtesy The British Museum Library.
Smith, Logan Pearsall, *The Life and Letters of Sir Henry Wotton.* (Oxford, 1907).
Tanner, J. R., *Constitutional Documents of the Reign of James I 1603–1605.* (Cambridge, 1961).
Tanner, J. R., *Tudor Constitutional Documents.* (New York, 1930).
[Verstegan, Richard]. Anthony G. Petti, "The Letters and Despatches of Richard Verstegan" in *Catholic Record Society.* (London, 1956), Vol. LII.
Wadsworth, James, *The English Spanishe Pilgrine.* (London, 1930). Copy consulted, courtesy Rare Book Division, The New York Public Library.
Winwood, Sir Ralph, *Memorials of Affairs of State in the Reigns of Queen Elizabeth and King James I.* (London, 1725).
[Yonge, Walter]. *Diary from 1604 to 1628.* Edited by George Roberts. (London, 1848).

SECONDARY SOURCES

Adair, E. R., *The Exterritoriality of Ambassadors in the Sixteenth and Seventeenth Centuries.* (London, 1929).
Akrigg, G. P. V., *Jacobean Pageant or The Court of King James I.* (Cambridge, 1962).
Allison, A. F., "Biographical Studies 1534–1829" in *Recusant History.* (Bognor Regis, 1951).
Allison, A. F., "John Heigham of S. Omer (c.1568–c.1632)" in *Recusant History.* (Bognor Regis, 1958).
Arber, Edward, *An Introductory Sketch to the Martin Marprelate Controversy.* (London, 1879).
Bennet, H. S., *English Books and Readers 1558 to 1603.* (Cambridge, 1965).
Besant, Sir Walter, *London in the Time of the Stuarts.* (London, 1903).
Birch, Thomas, *The Court and Times of James the First.* (London, 1848).
Brett, Norman G., *The Growth of Stuart London.* (London, 1935).
Burrage, Champlin, *The Early English Dissenters . . . 1550–1641.* (New York, 1967).
Byrom, H. J., "Edmond Spenser's First Printer Hugh Singleton" in *Transactions of the Bibliographical Society.* (London, 1933), N.S., Vol. XIV, no. 2.
The Cambridge History of English Literature. Edited by A. W. Ward & A .R. Waller. (New York, 1909), Vol. III.

WORKS CITED

Collinson, Patrick, *The Elizabethan Puritan Movement*. (London, 1967).
Davenport, Cyril, *Royal English Bookbindings*. (London, 1896).
Devlin, Christopher, *The Life of Robert Southwell Poet and Martyr*. (London, 1956).
Dexter, H. M., "Elder Brewster's Library" in *Proceedings of the Massachusetts Historical Society*. (Boston, 1889).
Dexter, H. M., *The England and Holland of the Pilgrims*. (Boston & New York, 1905).
Dictionary of National Biography. Edited by Leslie Stephen & Sidney Lee. (New York, 1908), Vol. III.
Duff, E. G., *A Century of the English Book Trade. Short Notices of all Printers, Stationers ... from ... 1457 to the Introduction of the Company of Stationers in 1557*. (London, 1905).
Figgis, J. N., *The Divine Right of Kings*. (Cambridge, 1934).
Fletcher, William Y., *English Book Collectors*. (London, 1902).
Frere, W. H. & Douglas, E. C., *Puritan Manifestoes A Study of the Origin of the Puritan Revolt*. (London, 1954).
Gardiner, Samuel R., *History of England from the Accession of James I. to the Outbreak of the Civil War*. (New York, 1965).
Gooch, G. P., *English Democratic Ideas of the 17th Century*. (New York, 1959).
Guilday, Peter, *The English Catholic Refugees on the Continent 1558–1795*. (London, 1914).
Haller, William, *Liberty and Reformation in the Puritan Revolution*. (New York, 1955).
Haller, William, *The Rise of Puritanism*. (New York, 1947).
Harris, P. R., "William Fleetwood, Recorder of the City and Catholicism in Elizabethan England" in *Recusant History*. (London, 1963), Vol. VII.
Hawkes, Arthur J., "The Birchley Hall Secret Press" in *Transactions of the Bibliographical Society*. (London, 1926), N.S., Vol. VII, no. 2.
Hebel, William J. & Hudson, Hoyt H., *Poetry of the English Renaissance 1509–1660*. (New York, 1930).
Hyland, St. George K., *A Century of Persecution under Tudor and Stuart Sovereigns*. (London, 1920).
Jenkins, Elizabeth, *Elizabeth the Great*. (New York, 1967).
Johnson, A. F., "The Exiled English Church at Amsterdam & its Press" in *The Library*. (London, 1951).
Kirkwood, E. M., "Richard Field, Printer, 1589-1624" in *Transactions of the Bibliographical Society*. (London, 1931), Vol. XII, no. 1.
Klein, Arthur J., *Intolerance in the Reign of Elizabeth*. (Cambridge, 1917).
Law, Thomas G., *A Historical Sketch of the Conflicts between Jesuits and Seculars in the Reign of Queen Elizabeth*. (London, 1889).
Loomie, Albert J., *The Spanish Elizabethans*. (New York, 1963).
McElwee, William, *The Wisest Fool in Christendom the Reign of King James I and VI*. (New York, 1958).
McGinn, Donald J., *John Penry and the Marprelate Controversy*. (New Brunswick, 1966).
McIlwain, Charles H., Editor, *The Political Works of James I*. (New York, 1965).
Mattingly, Garrett, *Renaissance Diplomacy*. (London, 1955).
Meyer, Arnold A., *England and the Catholic Church under Elizabeth*. (New York, 1967).
Newdigate, C. A., "Notes on the Seventeenth Century Printing Press of the English College at Saint Omers" in *The Library*. (London, 1919), 3rd Series, Vol. X, no. 38.
Newdigate, C. A., "Birchley or St. Omers" in *Transactions of the Bibliographical Society*. (London, 1926), N.S., Vol. VIII, no. 3.
Pearson, A. F. Scott, *Thomas Cartwright and Elizabethan Puritanism*. (Cambridge, 1925).
Petti, A. G., "Richard Verstegan & The Catholic Martyrologies of the Later Elizabethan Period" in *Recusant History*. (Bognor Regis, 1959).
Petti, Anthony, "Stephen Vallenger, 1541–1591," in *Recusant History*. (Bognor Regis, 1962), Vol. VI.
Pierce, William, *An historical introduction to the Marprelate tracts*. (London, 1909).
Plomer, Henry R., "Bishop Bancroft and a Catholic Press" in *The Library*. (London, 1907).
Plomer, H. R., "Stephen Vallenger" in *The Library*. (London, 1901), N.S., Vol. II.
Plucknett, Theodore F. T., *A Concise History of the Common Law*. (Boston, 1956).
Pritchard, Allen, "George Withers Quarrel with the Stationers. An Anonymous Reply to the Schollers Purgatory" in *Studies in Bibliography. Papers of the Bibliographical Society of Virginia*. (Charlottesville, 1963).
Read, Conyers, *Lord Burghley & Queen Elizabeth*. (New York, 1960).

WORKS CITED

Rostenberg, Leona, *English Publishers in the Graphic Arts 1599–1700*. (New York, 1963).
Rostenberg, Leona, *Literary, Political, Scientific, Religious & Legal Publishing, Printing & Bookselling in England, 1551–1700: Twelve Studies*. (New York, 1965).
Rowse, A. L., *The England of Elizabeth*. (New York, 1966).
Siebert, Frederick S., *Freedom of the Press in England 1476–1776*. (Urbana, 1952).
Southern, A. C., *English Recusant Prose, 1559–1582*. (London, 1950).
Taunton, Ethelred L., *The History of the Jesuits in England 1580–1773*. (London, 1901).
Thomas, Clancy, "English Catholics & the Papal Deposing Power 1570–1640" in *Recusant History*. (Bognor Regis, 1961), Vol. VI, no. 3.
Williamson, Hugh R., *The Gunpowder Plot*. (London, 1951).
Willson, David Harris, *King James VI and I*, (London. 1966).
Wilson, J. Dover, "Richard Schilders and the English Puritans" in *Transactions of the Bibliographical Society*. (London, 1912).
Worman, Ernest James, *Alien Members of the Book Trade During the Tudor Period*. (London, 1896).
Wright, Louis B., *Middle-Class Culture in Elizabethan England*. (Ithaca, N.Y., 1958).

BIBLIOGRAPHIES

Aldis, H. G., *A List of Books Printed in Scotland before 1700*. (Edinburgh, 1904).
Allison, A. F. & Rogers, D. M., *A Catalogue of Catholic Books In English Printed abroad or secretly in England 1558–1640*. (London, 1964).
Arber, Edward, *A Transcript of the Register of the Company of Stationers 1554–1640 A.D.* (London, 1875).
Brunet, Jacques-Charles, *Manuel Du Libraire Et De L'Amateur De Livres*. (Berlin, 1921).
Dickson, Robert & Edmond, John P., *Annals of Scottish Printing from the Introduction of the Art in 1507 to the Beginning of the Seventeenth Century*. (Cambridge, 1890).
Duthilloeul, H. R., *Bibliographie Douaisienne*. (Douai, 1842).
Gillow, Joseph, *A Literary and Bibliographical History, or Bibliographical Dictionary of the English Catholics*. (New York, n.d.).
Harris, Rendell & Jones, Stephen K., *The Pilgrim Press a Bibliographical & Historical Memorial of the Books Printed at Leyden by the Pilgrim Fathers*. (Cambridge, 1922).
Hart, William H., *Index expurgatorius anglicanus: or a descriptive catalogue of the principal books printed or published in England which have been suppressed*. (London, 1872–1878).
Jayne, Sears, *Library Catalogues of the English Renaissance*. (Los Angeles, 1956).
Knuttel, W. P. C., *Catalogus van de Pamfletten-Verzameling Berusten de in de Koninklijke Bibliotheek*. (The Hague, 1889).
Madan, Falconer, *Oxford Books. The Early Oxford Press 1468–1640*. (Oxford, 1895).
McDonald, J. H., *The Poems and Prose Writings of Robert Southwell, S.J. A Bibliographical Study*. (Oxford, 1937).
Petti, A. G., "A Bibliography of the Writings of Richard Verstegan c.1550–1641" in *Recusant History*. (London, 1963).
Pollard, A. W. & Redgrave, G. R., *A Short-Title Catalogue of Books Printed in England, Scotland & Ireland . . . 1475–1640*. (London, 1946).
Short-title Catalogue of Books printed in France and of French Books printed in other countries from 1470 to 1600 now in the British Museum. (London, 1924).
Short-Title Catalogue of Books Printed in The German speaking Countries . . . From 1455 to 1600 Now In The British Museum. (London, 1962).
Short-Title Catalogue of Books Printed in the Netherlands and Belgium . . . Now In The British Museum. (London, 1965).
Short-Title Catalogue of Books Printed In Italy . . . From 1465 to 1600 Now In The British Museum. (London, 1958).
Steele, Robert, *Bibliotheca Lindesiana. A Bibliography of Royal Proclamations of the Tudor and Stuart Sovereigns*. (Oxford, 1910).

INDEX

Abbot, Richard, 69
Abington, Thomas, 106
Acts of Supremacy and Uniformity, 7
Acuña, Diego Sarmiento de, Count Gondomar, 26, 73–74, 144–145
Aduentures of lady Elgerie, 175
Agazzari, Alphonso, 37, 46, 53
Ainsworth, Henry, 194
    Animadversion to Mr. Clyftons Advertisement, An, 194
    Annotations upon the book of Psalms, 194
    Communion of Saincts, The, 194
    Defence of the holy Scriptures, A, 194
Albert, Archduke of Austria, 153–154
Albertus Magnus, St., 114
Albin de Valsergues, Jean de, 37
Alfield, Thomas, 22–23, 38–39, 43
All shall be well the pope is now proued vicar of hell, 9
Allde, Edward, 59–60, 63
Allde, John, 59
Allen, Cardinal William, 10–12, 14, 25, 27–28, 31–33, 35, 38–39, 44, 54, 113, 115, 117, 131, 137–138
    Admonition to the nobility and people of England, An, 12, 38, 136–138
    Apologie and true declaration of the institution and endeavours of the two English Colleges, 28
    Treatise made in defence of the lawful power and authoritie of the priesthod (sic) to remitte sinnes, 45
    True sincere & modest defence of English Catholiques, 21, 38–39, 138–139
Alleyn, Edward, 206
Alsop, Bernard, 101

Alvarez de Toledo, Fernando, Duke of Alba,
    "Manifesto against Elizabeth," 48
Ambassador, role of, 4, 135–145, 152, 183, 204, 207
Ames, William, 195, 197
    Rescriptio, 197
Amsterdam, 10, 183, 190, 193–195
Anderton, James, see Brereley
Andrews, Thomas, 100
Androzzi, Fulvio, 116, 127
    Certaine deuout considerations, 102
Antwerp, 12, 15, 21, 25–27, 32–34, 36–37, 49, 55, 97, 126, 131, 136–137, 139–140, 142, 165, 203
Apianus, Petrus, 27
Appellant Clergy & Writings, 53–56, 58–59, 63, 141
Appendix of saints, An, 116
Aquaviva, Claude, 31
Archer, Thomas, 60
Archpriest Controversy, 53–59, 63, 69
Arias, Francesco, 114
Arkenstall, Giles, 117
Armada, Spanish, 4, 11, 13, 99, 113, 136, 138
Arminius, Jacob, & Arminianism, 155–157
Arnauld, Antoine, 58
Arras, 123, 137
Arundel, Thomas, First Baron Arundel, 57
Asplyn, Thomas, 173
Atee, Francis, 80
Atkinson, William, 80
Audin, Martin, 36
Augustine, St., 114
Auroi, Pierre, 106, 115–116, 118–119, 126, 128, 130

INDEX

Avery, Richard, 101
Aylmer, John, 20–21, 177–178

Babel or Monarchomalia protestantium, 120
Bachelor, Mary, 144
Bacon, Sir Francis, 7, 14, 83–84, 164
   Declaration of the practises and treasons committed by Robert late Earle of Essex, A, 84, 207
Bagshaw, Christopher, 57
   Relatio compendiosa turbarum quas Iesuitae Angli, vna cum D. Georgio Blackwello ... sacerdotibus seminariorum populoq., Catholico co(n)ciuere, 57
   Sparing discoverie of our English Iesuits, 58
   True relation of the faction begun at Wisbich, 53, 58
Bailey, Walter
   Briefe treatise touching the preservation of eyesight, 175
Baily, Richard, 101
Bakel, 44
Ballad of thankes gyveinge vnto God, for his mercy toward his Maiestie, A, 13
Ballad of the obteyning of the galeazzo wherein Don Pedro de Valdez was chief, A, 13
Ballet called Garnettes arraynement of the popes looking glasse, A, 71
Balmford, James, 181
Balsamo, Ignacio, 116
   Instruction how to pray and meditate well, 124–125
Bancroft, Richard, 56, 59, 94–95, 128, 182, 184
Banks, Thomas, 49
Bankworth, Richard, 59
Barber, Henry, 101
Barclay, John, 151
Barker, Henry, 115
Barker, Robert, 58–59, 84, 150, 193–194
Barlow, Edward, 33, 203
Barneveldt, John van Olden, 156
Barrett, Richard, 115

Barrow, Henry, & Barrowism, 165, 182–184, 193, 198, 205
   Brief discovery of a false church, A, 183
   Examinations of H. Barrowe J. Grenewood and J. Penrie, The, 182–183, 193, 205
   Petition directed to her most excellent maiestie, A, 192
   Plaine refutation of Mr. Giffardes booke, The, 183
Bass, 45
Bate, Randal, 194
Bateson, Thomas, 101
Beale, John, 181
Bede, The Venerable, 44
   History of the Church of Englande Translated ... into English by Thomas Stapleton, The, 44–45, 49, 127
Begynninge and endynge of all popery, The, 9
Bell, Thomas
   Anatomie of popish tyrannie, The, 59
Bellarmine, Robert, St., 118–119, 127, 150, 204
   A.B.C. teaching how to helpe the preest to say Masse, 118
   Ample declaration of the Christian doctrine, An, 118
   Catechism, 120
   De potestate papae, 154
   Responsio ad librum inscriptum Triplici nodo, 150
Belleforest, François de
   Innocence de Marie, royne d'Escosse, L', 21, 136
Beller, Balthazar, 37
Bellet, François, 86, 113, 115–116, 118, 142
Benhill, Jacob, 194
Bennet, Sir John, 154, 157
Bennet, John
   Hope of Peace, The, 57
Berden, Richard, 37, 44
Berden, William, 37
Bèze, Theodore de, 153
   Discourse of the true ... markes of the Catholique Church, A, 175

INDEX

Tractatus de vera excommunicatione, 184
Bible, The
  Douai Version, 106, 118, 131, 206
  English Version translated from Welsh, 171
  "Barker" Version, 194
Bilderbeck, 154–155
Bill, John, 152
Biondi, Giovanni-Battista, 153
Birchley Hall, 98
Birde, John, 97
Bishop, George, 49
Bishop, William, 55, 95
Blackwell, Robert, 15, 53, 56–57, 150
Blackwood, Adam, 28
  Martyre de la royne d'Escosse, 28
Blount, John, 44
Bluet, Thomas, 53, 55
  Important considerations, which ought to move all true and sound Catholickes ... to acknowledge ... that the proceedings of her Majesty ... have bene both mild and mercifull, 55
Boccaccio, Giovanni, 99
Bock Heinrich, 62
Bogard, Jean, 27, 37
Bolt, John, 62
Bonaventure, St., 117
  Life of the holie father S. Francis, 131
  Life of our blessed Lord ... Iesus, 118–119, 126
  Meditations, 35
Booke against woemen, The, 85
Booke of common prayers, 175
Boscard, Charles, 116, 126, 142
Boscard, Jacques, 116, 118–120
Bostock, 73
Boudot, Paul, 128
Boulogne, 34–35
Boulter, John, 94–95, 98
Bourgeois, Pierre, 123
Bourne, Anthony, 35
Bowin, Francis, 104
Bowles, or Bouler, 183
Boyle, Richard, 180–181, 203
Bradford, William, 183, 190, 195–196
Bradshaw, William

Unreasonablenesse of the separation, The, 194
Brathwaite, Richard
  Disputation between a hee conny-catcher and a shee conny-catcher, 100
  Prodigals teares, The, 100
Braunsberg Seminary, 117
Bray, William, 100
Braynless blessynge of the bull, Ye, 9
Breefe collection concerning the loue of God towards mankinde, 130
Breife description of the declaration of the Ban made against the King of Bohemia, A, 60
Brereley, John, 98, 206
  Apologie of the Romane church, The, 95
  Protestants Apologie, 107, 206
Brewer, Thomas, 195, 197
Brewster, Edward, 181
Brewster, William, 195–198, 205
Bridges, John, 178
  Defence of the gouernment established in the Church of Englande for ecclesiastical matters, A, 174
Bridgewater, John, 22
Brief declaration of the shews performed before the Queens Maiestie, The, 175
Brief fourme of confession, A, 59
Brinkley, Stephen, 23–24, 27
Bristow, Richard, 23, 118, 131, 143
  Demaundes to be proponed of Catholiques to the heretikes, 25, 38, 49, 62–63, 94
Brome, George, Elizabeth & Briget, 49
Brooks, James
  Sermons, 20
Broughton, Hugh, 193
  Epistle, 193
Broughton, Richard, 116, 127
Browne, Anthony, 127
Browne, Francis, 23
Browne, John, Sr., & Jr., 100–101
Browne, Robert, & Brownists, 163–165, 174, 180, 184, 191, 195, 198
  Book which sheweth the life and manners of all true Christians (containing)

247

'Reformation without tarrying for anie', 163, 191, 205
Bruges, 21, 33, 137, 142, 203
Brussels, 72, 113, 123, 128, 155
Buchanan, George, 149
Bull, Robert, 183, 194
Bulloch, Peter, 61–63, 94, 97, 103, 182
Bulloch Mrs., 101, 103, 204
Bulmer, Robert, 101
Burbie, Cuthbert, 71
Burnham, Dr. Edward, 137
Burning of Books, 19, 49–50, 83–85, 87, 105, 119, 131, 137, 140–141, 153–157, 173, 176, 180, 183, 191, 206
Burre, Walter, 88
Burton, Francis, 141
Busino, Horatio, 93
Butter, Nathaniel, 71, 144, 194
Byllet, Arthur, 183
Bywater, 186

Cabell, 105
Cabinet de l'âme fidele, Le, 49
Caesar, Sir Julius, 80, 86, 95–96, 102–106, 118–119, 128, 150
Calais, 34–36, 44, 50, 79, 81, 86, 97, 100, 111–112, 120, 128–129
Calderwood, David, 195
  De Regimine Ecclesiae Scoticanae Relatio, 196–197
  Perth Assembly, 196
Calvert, Sir George, 154
Calvin, John, & Calvinism, 69, 161, 186
  Catechisme, 192
Caly, Robert, 20, 25, 37, 49
Cambridge, 11, 19, 37–39, 81, 85, 155, 157, 163, 181, 185, 195, 204
Camden, William, 43, 54
Campion, Edmund, 10, 22, 45–46, 49, 62, 206
  Rationes decem, 24, 38
Canin, Isaac, 193–194
Canisius, St. Peter, 28, 37
  Catechisme, 21
  Summe of Christian doctrine, A, 125, 128
Carleton, Sir Dudley, 73, 78, 154–157, 193, 196–197, 207

Caron, Sir Noel, 193
Carr, William, 34
Carre, Henry, 175
Carter, Agnes, 21
Carter, William, 20–22, 37, 61, 136, 205
Cartwright, Thomas, 162–164, 179, 182, 191–192, 195
  Brief apologie ag. M. Sutcliffe, A, 191
  Christian letter... vnto Mr. R. Hoo[ker], 191
  Confvtation of the Rhemists translation, 196
  Replye to an answer made to Doctor Whitegift, 173–174
  Second Admonition to the Parliament, 162, 172–173, 175–176, 205
Casaubon, Isaac, 151
Castle for the soule, A, 175
Catechisms
  Brief Catechism, 57–58
  Catechisme... de la religion Chrestienne, 49
Catesby, Robert, 70
Catherine de' Medici, 139
Catholics, Catholicism & Recusancy, 3–4, 7–15, 18, 20, 22, 24–28, 31–39, 43–50, 53–63, 67–74, 78–82, 87, 90, 93–107, 111–120, 123–131, 135–144, 152, 157, 161, 163–166, 177, 180, 184, 186, 190, 202–204, 206–208
Catholic Books, see Missionary Program & Exportation & Importation of Books
Caumont, Jean de
  Advertissement des Advertissements, 140
  Foundation of the Catholic Religion, The, 62, 120
Cawood, Gabriel, 61–63
Cawood, John, 20, 61
Cecil, Sir Robert, First Earl of Salisbury, 78, 80, 87, 94, 97, 102, 105, 115, 118–119, 131, 143, 153, 162–163
Cecil, Sir William, Lord Burleigh, 9, 12–14, 33, 35–37, 39, 44–45, 47–48, 69, 135–138, 140–141, 173, 179, 184, 191
  Copy of a letter sent out of England to Don Bernardino Mendoza, Ambassa-

INDEX

dor to France for the King of Spain declaring the State of England, 13
Execution of justice in England, The, 138
Censorship, 15, 18, 78, 81–85, 87–90, 135–137, 152–153, 172, 191
Cerronio, Tomasso, 78
Chaderton, Laurence, 175
Chamberlain, Francis, 82
Chamberlain, John, 67, 72, 74, 78, 154, 166
Champny, Anthony
  Treatise of the vocation of bishops, 127
Chapman, George, 93, 101
Charles, Prince of Wales, later Charles I, King of England, 68, 73–74, 90, 143, 198
Charlewood, John, 57
Charlton, Geffrey, 71
Charnock, Robert
  Answere made by one of our brethren . . . to a fraudulent letter of M. George Blackwels, written to Cardinal Caietane, 56
  Reply to a notorious libell, 58
Charpentier, Pierre
  Lettre, 135–136
Charteris, Henry, 193
Chaulnes, Honoré d'Albert d'Ailly, Seigneur de Cadinet, Duc de, 143
Chepman, Walter, 31
Chettle, Henry, 60
Chetwyn, William, 97
Christopher, George, 81
Church of England, The, 3, 7–9, 124, 161, 165, 170, 177, 182, 202
Churchyard, Thomas, 59
Ciotto, Giovanni-Battista, 153
Clarke, William
  Letter of expostulation to Blackwell, A, 54
  Replie vnto a certaine libell, A, 58
Cleaver, Robert, 195
Clement VIII, Pope, 15, 53, 149
Clyfton, Richard
  Plea for the people, 194
Cobham, Sir Henry, 138, 196, 207
Coe, John & Helen, 104

Coffin, Edward, 72, 115
Coke, Sir Edward, 69, 72
Cole, 49
Colleton, John, 55
  Iust defence of the slandered priestes, A, 55
  Supplication, A, 141
Collyns, Mark, 182
Cologne, 150, 154–155
Comalada, Miguel de, 95, 114, 117
Confession of the true and Christian faith, The, 175, 179
Conincx, Arnout, 31, 131, 137
Contarini, Pietro, 73, 143
  Relation, 73
Conway, Edward, Viscount Conway, 119, 137, 198
Conyers, Mallory, 35
Cooper, Thomas, 177, 192
  Admonition to the people, 178
Copies of certaine discourses, 57
Copinger, Robert, 44
Copley, Anthony, 55
  Answere to a letter of a iesuited gentleman . . . Concerning the Appeale, State, Iesuits, 55–56, 58
Corkine, William, 101
Correr, Marc-Antonio, 105, 118–119, 141–143
Cosimo II de' Medici, Grand Duke of Tuscany, 153
Cotton, George, 87
Cotton, John, 87–88
Cotton, Robert
  Short History of Henry III, 101
Coventry, Thomas, First Baron Coventry, 198
Covert, 106
Cowell, John 85
  Interpreter, The, 85–86
Crab, William, 39
Crane, Mrs., 176–177, 180–181, 186
Creede, Thomas, 54, 56–57
Creswell, Joseph, 31, 33, 46, 117, 177, 207
  Copy of a letter . . . to his freind in England in refutation of sundry calumnies, 140

249

INDEX

Crosse, Humfrey, 80
Crowley, Robert, 170–172, 203
  Brief discourse against the outwarde apparell of the Popish Churche, 170–171
  Deliberat answer, 170
  Informacion . . . agaynst the oppressours of the pore Commons, An, 170
  One and thirty epigrams, 170
  Opening of the wordes of the prophet Joell, The, 171
  Pleasure and payne, 170
  Voyce of the last trumpet, The, 170
  Way to wealth, The, 170
Cuevas, Alfonso de
  Squitinio della liberta Veneta, 143
Cuffe, 84
Cushman, Robert, 198
Customs & Customs Officers, 36, 43, 73, 78, 81

Dabscot, John & Joan, 86, 104–105, 107, 114, 129, 204, 204N.
Dale, Jean van, 44
Dale, Dr. Valentine, 137
Dampmartin, Pierre
  De la connoissance et merveilles de l'homme, 118
Dandine, Louis, 81
Danett, Awdley, 191
Dante Alighieri
  Inferno, purgatorio e paradiso, 49
Danter, John, 60–61, 94
Darrell, John
  True narration of the . . . Vexation by the Deuil of seven Persons in Lancashire, A, 85
Davies, John
  Epigrammes and elegies, 84
Davies, Richard, 97
Davis, John, 38
Davison, Sir William, 195
Dawson, John, 84
Day, Angell
  Daphnis and Chloe, 175
  English Secretorie, The, 175
  Upon the life and death of Sir Philip Sidney, 175

Day, John, 60
De vera et genvina Iesv Christi . . . nostri Religione, 196–197
Defence of the old and true Christianitie against the newe and counterfaite secte of the Jesuits or feloship of Jesus, A, 9
Dekker, Thomas, 59, 93
Dering, Edmund, 184
Desserans, Jean, 55
Dexter, Robert, 181
Dialogue concerning the strife of our church, A, 175
Dieppe, 34–35
Diest, Aegidius Coppenius, 27, 37, 49, 135
Digby, Sir Everard, 87
Digby, Sir John, 154, 157, 207
Dighton, Thomas, 195
Dod, John, 181, 195
Doddeson, Robert, 182
Dolabella, Horatio, 86
Doleman, see Persons
Dolman brothers, 22, 38
Dones, 33
Dorman, Thomas, 28, 48
Dort, 183, 190, 193–194
Douai, 21, 26, 36–38, 45, 95, 97, 106, 115, 117–119, 123–124, 126–128, 130–131, 150, 204, 206
  College, 115–117, 126, 130, 142
Douce, "Widow," 101, 103, 105, 107, 182, 204
Doulye, George, known as William Warford
  Briefe instruction . . . concerninge the principall poyntes of Christian religion, 117, 131, 143
Douse, John, see Sweet
Dover, 23, 35–36, 81, 112, 119–120, 123, 144
Dowdaly, 45
Dowland, Robert, 101
Dowse, 80
Drayton, Michael
  Poly-Olbion, 101
Dublin, 80, 151
Duckett, James & Ann, 62–63, 94, 97, 100, 207

250

Du Moulin, Pierre, 151
Dunkirk, 102, 112, 118
Du Perron, Jacques, 151

East, Michael, 101
East, Thomas, 190
Ecclesiastical Commission, Court of, 173, 177, 185
Edinburgh, 31, 44, 179, 184, 193
Edmondes, Sir Thomas, 152
Edmonds, Father, alias Father Weston, 62
Edward VI, King of England, 20, 170–171
Egerton, Sir Thomas, Baron Ellesmere & Viscount Brackley, 98
Elizabeth I, Queen of England, 3, 7–15, 18–21, 31, 37, 45, 53, 55, 59, 61, 63, 67, 69–70, 72, 78, 81–86, 113, 118, 135–140, 149, 161–162, 164–165, 170–171, 173, 178, 185, 207
Elizabeth, Electress Palatinate, 68, 73
Elizabetha triumphans, 99
Elstrack, Renold, 83
Ely, Ferdinand, 87, 100–101, 104
Ely House, 79, 98
Emerson, Ralph, 34, 204
Engravings, 83
Epistle, The, see Martin Marprelate Controversy
Epitome, The, see Martin Marprelate Controversy.
Essex, Robert Devereux, Second Earl of, 35, 83–84
  Apologie, An, 84
Estella, Diego de, 27, 127, 130
  Contempte of the world, 130
Euring, William, 195
Evans, Lewis, 27
Exact discouerie of Romish doctrine in the case of conspiracie and rebellion, An, 71
Exportation & Importation of Books, 11, 19–21, 26–28, 31–39, 43–45, 48–50, 55, 61, 63, 79–81, 86, 93, 95, 98–100, 102–107, 112, 114–115, 117–120, 124, 126, 128–131, 137–141, 143–144, 150, 163, 183–185, 191–193, 196–197, 203–208
Extracte of the determinacion and censure of the doctours of the Vniversities of Salamanca and Valladolid, An, 117

Family of Love, 164
Fane, Sir Thomas, 35–36
Farnese, Alessandro, Duke of Parma, 12, 136–137, 140
Faunt, Nicholas, 11
Fawkes, Guy, 70
Feckenham, John, 20
Fenne, 164
Fenner, Dudley, 175, 184–185, 191–192
  Defence ... for maintenance of the Eldership, A, 192
  Defence of the godlie ministers, A, 192
  Groundes of religion, 192
  Song of Songs, transl., 192
Fenton, Sir Geoffrey, 79
Ferdinand II, Archduke of Styria, later H.R.E., 79, 144
Ferebrand, William, 85
Ferne, John, 47
Field, Henry, 55
Field, John & Wilcox, Thomas, 162, 171–172, 175
  Admonition to the Parliament, An, 162, 172, 180
  Caueat for Parsons Howlet, A, 175
  Certain articles collected by the byshops, 172–173
  Godly exhortation by occasion of the late judgement of God at Parris garden, 175
Field, Richard, 54–56, 60, 206
Fisher, Sir Clement, 116
Fisher, St. John, 20
Fitch, William, 61–62
Fitzherbert, Thomas, 11, 115–116, 119, 127, 130, 204
  Treatise of Pollicey and Religion, A, 118, 120, 128
Fitzsimon, Henry, 106, 129, 204
  Confutation of John Ryder, 118
  Iustification and exposition of the diuine sacrifice of the masse, The, 131

INDEX

Flavius, Christopher, 155
Fleetwood, William, 22, 39, 45
Fletcher, John, 93
Flinton, George, 27
  Golden Litany, 27
  Manual of Prayers including Jesus Psalter, 27–28, 49, 102, 114, 118, 120, 126, 130
Floyd, John, 115
Floyd, Richard, 117
Foigny, Jean, 28, 32, 130–131
Forbes, John & Patrick, 193
Foscarini, Antonio, 73, 143
Fowler, Alice, 26
Fowler, Anne, 101–103, 182, 204
Fowler, John, Sr., 24–26, 28, 37, 45, 49, 61, 126, 129, 135
Fowler, John, Jr., 26, 102, 141
Francis of Sales, St.
  Introduction to a deuoute life, An, 120, 127
Francklyn, Michael, 100–101
François, Duke of Alençon, 118
Frankfurt A/M, 57
  Book Fair, 143
Frarini, Pietro
  Oration against the vnlawfull insurrections of the Protestants of our time, vnder pretence to refourme religion, 25, 118
Fraser, John, 130
Frederick V, Elector of the Palatinate, 68, 73–74
Frisius, Gemma, 27
Fuchs, Leonhart, 27
Fulke, William, 36–37
  Briefe declaration concerning the desires of ... faithful ministers that ... do seeke for the discipline and reformation of the churche of Englande, A, 174–175
  "Catalogue of ... Popish Bookes," 28, 36–37
Fulwood, Richard, 128
Fysher or Fisher, William, 99–100

Gaillardi, Achilles
  Abridgement of Christian perfection, An, 120
Gardiner, Stephen
  Explication and assertion of the true Catholique fayth touching the most blessed sacrament of the aulter, An, 20
Garnet, Henry, 63, 67, 70, 96, 128, 152
Gee, John, 26, 93, 96–107, 112, 115–116, 124, 129, 131, 202, 205
  Foote out of the snare, The, 93, 105, 115
Gelke, William, 36
Gentle Jyrke for the Jesuits, A, 9
Gerard, John, 11, 14, 46–47, 69, 79, 96
  Memoirs, 112
Ghibbes, Jacques, 33
Gibbon, Richard, 38
Gibson, Thomas, 192
Giffard or Gifford, William, 12, 53–54
Gilby, Anthony, 184
Girardoni, Vincentio, 23
Giustiniani, Torzi, 141–142
Glepes, Thomas, 105
Gloucester, 23, 38–39
Godlie garden of Gethsemanie, The, 21
Godshall, 33, 204
Goodman, Christopher
  How superior powers ought to be obeyd, 185
Goodman, Gabriel, 183
Gordon, James, 44
Gouge, William, 181
Gravesend, 34, 36, 78–79
Gray, Sir & Lady Thomas, 105
Great Britayns great Delyuerance from the great danger of popish power, 71
Gregory, St.
  Dialogues, The, 142
Green, 194
Greene, Robert, 60
Greenfield, Sir Richard, 82
Greenham, Richard, 181, 184
  Works, 184
Greenstreet-East Ham Press, see Persons
Greenwood, John, 165, 182–183, 193
  Conference betwixt him and certayne ministers, 182
Gregory XIII, Pope, 9, 11
Grevinchovius, Nicholas, 197

Grindal, Edmund, 48, 185
Grismond, John, 88–90
Gryffith, William, 174
Gubbins, Thomas, 99–100
Guilpin, Edward
　Skialetheia or a shadow of truth, 84
Gunpowder Plot, 70, 79, 96, 104–105, 150
Guzman de Silva, 31, 207
Gylles, John, 140

Hales, John, 178
Hamburg, 44, 50
Hamillon, Cardin, 131
Hamilton, John
　Facile traictise, contenand . . . ane . . . reul to discerne trew from fals religion, 130
Hamlyn, Michael, 80
Hammond, John, 37
Hampton Court Conference, 166
Hanse, 183, 193
Harding, Thomas, 25, 27–28
Harlay, Christophe de, Comte de Beaumont, 118, 141
Harpsfield, Nicholas, 20
Harrison, John, Sr., & John, Jr., 48, 173
Harrison, John (apprentice), 175
Harrison, John, 194
Harrison, Robert, 163, 195
Harsnett, John, 83
Hart, Andro, 44, 184, 193
Hartly, William, 37
Harvey, Gabriel, 84
Hay any worke for Cooper, see Martin Marprelate Controversy
Hayward, John
　First parte of the life and raigne of King Henrie IIII, The, 83–84
Heigham, Marie-Boniface Bourgeois, 123, 129, 204
Heigham, John, known also as Roger, 105–106, 116, 120, 123–131, 135, 204–205, 208
　Devout exposition of the holie masse, A, 124–125, 208
　Via vere tuta, or the truly safe way, 125
Heigham, William, 123

Henry VIII, King of England, 18, 45, 86
Henry, Prince of Wales, 95–96, 98, 165
Henry III, King of France, formerly Henry, Duke of Anjou, 82–83, 139–140, 164
Henry IV, King of France, 71, 153
Henry, Duke of Guise, 140
Herbert, George, 93
Herbert, William, Third Earl of Pembroke, 97
Herle, William, 138
Heskyns, Thomas, 48
Hew, Nicholas de, 35
Heyrat, 155
Hide, Thomas, 23
High Commission, Court of, 11, 21, 78, 80–82, 89, 100–101, 144, 155, 175, 185
Hill, 119
Hill, Thomas, 97
Hill, Thomas
　Profitable arte of gardening, 175
Hilles, 34, 204
Hindlip Hall, 96
Hodgkins, John, 179–181, 185–186, 198, 203
Holinshed, Raphael
　Chronicles, 33
Holt, Henry, 32
Hooke, Henry, 192
Hooker, Richard, 93
Hopkins, Richard, 33
Hortulus anime, 26
Hosius, Cardinal Stanislaus, 34, 48
Hoskins, William, 60
Howard, Charles, Baron Howard of Effingham, Earl of Nottingham, 13
Howard, Henry, Earl of Northampton, 143, 153
Huicke, Dr. Robert, 70
Humble, George, 83
Hungerford, Sir Anthony, 88

Inquisoto, 106
Instructions and advertisements how to meditate the misteries of the rosarie of the most holy virigin, 21
Ioyfull entrie of the dukedome of Brabant The, 175

Ioyfull Tryumphes performed . . . beyond the seas for the happines of England and the overthrowe of the Spanishe barge, The, 13
Ireland & The Irish, 33, 44–45, 97, 112, 117, 136, 151
Irish Franciscan Press, see Louvain
Islip, Adam, 54, 56

Jackson, Jeremiah, 101
Jacob, Henry, 166, 192–193
 Defence of the churches and ministery of Englande, 192
 Reasons proving a necessitie of reforming our churches in England, 192
 Request to . . . James, 192
 Treatise of the sufferings & victory of Christ, A, 192
Jaey, Henry, 120, 131
James I, King of England, 3–4, 15, 26, 56, 59, 63, 67–75, 78–90, 93, 96, 106–107, 118–119, 131, 140–141, 143, 145, 149–157, 161, 165–166, 179, 186, 192–193, 197–198, 206–207
 Apologie for the oath of allegiance, An 119, 151–153, 157
 Basilicon Doron, 59, 149, 152, 165
 Concerning his proceedings in the cause of D. C. Vorstius, 155
 Declaration pour le droit des rois, 151
 Demonologie, 68
 Deus et Rex; Engl. trans., *God and the King*, 73, 144, 151, 206
 Essayes of a prentise in the diuine art of poesie, 149
 Poeticall exercises, 149
 Proclamation for the search of . . . John Cotton, A, 87
 Speech to Parliament (1610), 68–69
 Speech to Parliament (1612), 72
 Trew Law of Free Monarchies, The, 68, 149
 Triplici nodo, triplex cuneus: or an Apologie for the Oath of Allegiance, 128, 150
 Workes, 152
Jarrett, Edward, 94
Jenison, Robert

Christians apparelling Christ, The, 101
Jerome, St., 114
Jesuits & Jesuit Order, 8, 10–11, 14–15, 22, 24, 31–32, 34, 36, 45, 49, 53–59, 63–64, 69–74, 78, 80, 86, 105, 111–114, 116–117, 119, 128–130, 137–138, 144, 152, 155, 161, 203–204, 208
Jewel, John, 9
Jewel, Melanchthon, 182, 203, 205
John of Gaunt, 15
Johnson, Alexander, 44
Johnson, Francis, 47, 183, 195
Jones, William, 95, 97
Jonson, Ben, 93, 101
 Time Ridiculed, 89
Joyfull sonnet of the Rediness of the shires and nobilitie of England to her Maiesties service, A, 13

Keerberg, Jan, 131
Kellam, Lawrence, 106, 119–120, 128–131, 135
Kellam, Lawrence, the Younger, 131
Kellam, Widow, 131
Kellison, Matthew, 116
 Right and iurisdiction of the prelate and the prince, The, 106
 Suruey of the new religion, The, 118, 130
Kiene or Keene, Henry, 115
Killigrew, Sir Henry, 12, 136–138
King and the Prelate, The, 144
Kingston, Felix, 58
Kinsman, Edward & William, 106, 116, 119, 126, 204
Kirkham, Henry, 175
Knightley, Sir Richard, 4, 177–181, 186, 203
Knollys, Sir Francis, 164
Knowles, Peter, 32
Knox, John
 Exposition upon . . . Matthew, An, 175
 Godly letter, A, 175

La Boderie, Antoine Lefèvre de, 150
Lacon, Sir Francis, 86
Lacy, John, 173
Laet, Jan, 27, 37, 49, 135

Lake, Sir Thomas, 143, 156
Lambert, Peter, 87
Lamentation of Dickie for the death of his brother Jockey, The, 186
Lane, Sir Robert, 174
Langland, William
  Vision of Piers Plowman, 171
Lanson, Peter, 35
La Ramée, Pierre de, 175
La Sale, Antoine de
  Fyftene joyes of maryage, 85
Last Acts of Parliament, The, 33
Late wonderful dysastres whiche the Spanishe navye sustayned yn the late fighte in the sea, The, 13
Lawrence, 33
Lawson, Margaret, 182, 203, 205
Leech, Humphrey, 115, 130
Legate, John, 85, 181
Legislation, Anti-Catholic & Puritan, 8–12, 14, 19, 31, 45, 54, 70–72, 74, 78, 87, 117–118, 150, 162–165, 172–173, 178, 185–186, 191, 198
Leigh, Richard, 13
Lerma, Francesco de Sandoval Roxas, Marquis de Denia, 154
Leslie, John
  Defence of the honour of . . . princesse Marie quene of Scotland, 28, 102
  Treatise of treasons against Q. Elizabeth. and the croune of England, 26, 28, 49
Lessman, James, 10
Lewkenor, Lewis
  Discourse of the vsage of the English fugitiues, by the Spaniard, 33
Leyburne, James, 62
Leyden, 164, 190, 195–198, 203
L'Huillier, Pierre, 138
Licensing of the Press, 18–19, 81, 88–89, 185
Lichfield, Henry, 101
Lichfield, John, 96
Liége, 115, 117
Linde, Sir Humphrey, 125
Lion, John, 23
Lionello, Giovanni-Battista, 154
Loarte, Gaspare, 27–28, 114

Exercise of a Christian Life, 49
Lodge, Thomas, 60
London, 4, 19–20, 23–24, 31–34, 37–38, 43–44, 46, 48–49, 54–55, 57, 60, 62, 67, 71–72, 74, 78–79, 81, 85, 87, 93, 95–106, 111, 114–115, 123–124, 127, 130–131, 138, 141–144, 156–157, 164, 166, 171–173, 177, 180–183, 184, 186, 190–191, 196, 203–205, 208
Louvain, 23, 25–28, 31, 37, 45, 116–117, 126, 130, 154–155, 207
  Press of Irish Franciscans, 117, 131
  Seminary, 117
Lovett, Drugo, 100
Lowndes, Matthew, 89–90
L'Oyselet, George, 27, 49
Lucatelli, 106
Luis de Granada, 28, 49, 97, 114
  Memoriall of a Christian life, A, 127
  Spiritual doctrine, 130
  Treatise of consideration and prayer, 101, 127
  Treatise of the loue of God, A, 125
Lumley, John, Baron Lumley, 96
Lyly, John
  Euphues, 61

Madrid, 38, 44, 50, 154
Maihew, Edward
  Paradise & praiers, 131
Man, Thomas, 175, 181
Mandragon, Ambrosio, 137
Mangius, 120
Mann, William, 100
Manual of Prayers, see Flinton
Manual or Meditation, A, 23
Manyfest or a playne Dyscourse of a hole packefull of popyshhe knavery, A, 9
Marie de' Medici, Queen Mother of France, 154
Marlowe, Christopher, 59
Marnix, Philip van, Sieur de Aldegonde, 136–137
Marriott, John, 88–90
Marsham, 33, 204
Marston, John
  Metamorphosis of Pygmalion's image, 84

Scourge of villanie, The, 84
Martin, Gregory, 37
  Loue of the soule, 118, 131
  Treatyse of Christian peregrination, A, 22
  Treatise of Schisme, 21–22, 205
Martin Junior, see Martin Marprelate Controversy
Martin Marprelate Controversy, 23, 174, 176–182, 186, 192, 198, 203–205, 207
  Epistle, The, 23, 176–177, 181, 206
  Epitome, The, 178, 182, 192
  Hay any worke for Cooper, 178, 181, 205
  Martin Junior, 179–181
  Martin Senior, 179, 181, 205
  Minerall Conclusions, 178
  Protestation, The, 179
Martin, Sir Richard, 49, 172, 205
Martin, Lady Richard, 172, 205
Martin Senior, see Martin Marprelate Controversy
Marulic, Marko
  Dictorum factorumque memorabilium libri sex, 26
Mary I, Queen of England, 18, 20, 37, 61, 161, 171, 185
Mary Stuart, Queen of Scotland, 11, 21, 67, 106, 140
Mathias, Holy Roman Emperor, 153
Matthew, Tobias, 130
Maurice, William, 24
May of Shoe Lane, 101, 103
Mead, Joseph, 88, 90, 166
Meagh, Robert, 44
Mendoza, Bernardino da, 32
Mercurius Gallo-Belgicus, 87
Merye, Thomas, 171
Micro-cynicon, 84–85
Middleburg, 10, 138, 140, 183–184, 190, 192–193
Middleton, Thomas, 101
Minerall Conclusions, The, see Martin Marprelate Controversy
Mirkell, Henry, 44–45
Mirror to confesse well, A, 118
Missionary Program, 4, 10, 28, 32, 34, 36, 38, 115, 129–130, 137, 180, 202–203
  Conveyance of passengers, 10–11, 32, 34–35, 111–112, 115, 128, 130
  Conveyance of books, 8, 32, 37, 106, 113, 119, 142–143, 180
  "Letter of English Mission," 72, 113
  "News from England," 113
  "Relation of the English Mission in the State of Flanders," 117
Mocket, Richard, 151
Montagu, Richard, 150
Montague, Henry, First Earl of Manchester, 23, 105–106, 126
Moore, 33, 204
More, St. Thomas
  Dialogue of cumfort against tribulation, 25, 49, 102
More News from the Palatinate, 144
Moretus, Jean, 113
Most horrible murther committed at Mayfield, A, 60
Mount Calvary, 62
Murton, John, 166
Mush, John
  Declaratio motuum . . . ex controversiis inter Iesuitas . . . et sacerdotes seminariorum in Anglia, 56
  Dialogue betwixt a secular priest, and a lay gentleman, A, 56
Musket, George, 206
  Bishop of London his Legacy, The, 107
Myllar, Andrew, 31
Myrror for Magistrates, A, 33

Napier, John
  Discouerie of the conspiracie of the Scottish papists, A, 184
  Plaine discovery of the whole revelation of Saint John, A, 184
Nashe, Thomas, 60, 84
Naunton, Sir Robert, 196–197
Neville, Sir Henry, 24
New ballad of the glorious victory of Christ Jesus, as was seene by the overthrowe of the Spanyardes, A, 13
New Testament, (Rheims) The, 32, 35, 38, 99, 106, 115, 118, 143, 163, 205–206;

(Bèze Version), 193; (Barker Version), 194
Newberry, Ralph, 49
Newcastle on Tyne, 35, 80, 130
Newhaven, 33, 35
Newman, Humphrey "Brownbread," 181, 203, 204
Newman, Thomas, 99
News from Venice, 141
Nichols, Thomas, see Spencer
Niclaes, Henry, 164
Norris, Sylvester, 106, 115, 206
  Antidote against the pestiferous writings of all English sectaries, An, 107
  Guide of faith, 107
  Pseudo-Scripturist, 107, 120
Norton, John, 184, 193–194

Oath of Allegiance, 3, 7–8, 11, 71, 105, 112, 150
Okes, Nicholas, 88–90
Orwin, Thomas, 99
Osorio da Fonseca, Jeronimo, 87
Outreman, Philippe d'
  True Christian Catholique, The, 126
Owen, Henry, 62, 96–98, 107
Owen, Hugh, 33–34
Owen, Lewis, 86, 102, 113
  Rvnning Register. Recording a Trve Relation of the State of the English Colledges ... in all forraine parts, 111
Owen, Nicholas, 96
Oxford, 11, 19
  University of, 24–25, 81, 86, 96, 115, 151, 155, 157, 163, 170

Padilla y Manrique, Martin de, 14
Paeschen, Jan van
  Spiritual pilgrimage of Hierusalem, 126
Page, William, 82
Paget, John
  Arrow against separation, 194
Pagett, William, 191
Paine, Henry, 34
Paredes, Diego Gardia de, 44
Pareus, David, 156–157

Paris, 28, 32–33, 35, 39, 45, 102, 120, 129, 131, 139–140
Parish, Henry, 86, 105
Parker, Matthew, 173–174, 207
Parker, William, Fourth Baron Monteagle, 81, 86, 105
Parkins, Sir Christopher, 142
Parte of a register, contayninge sundrie ... matters, A, "Register," 184, 190
Pasquier, Estienne
  Iesuites Catechism, 58
Paul V, Pope, 71, 150, 152
  Breve, 71
Pauley, Simon, 97
Peacham, Henry
  Graphice, 101
Peele, George, 60
Pelletier, Jacques
  Religion Catholique ... contre le livre addresse aux Rois par ... Jacques I, 153
Penry, John, 165, 176, 181–182, 185–186, 193
  Appellation, 186
  Defence of that which hath bin written, 177
  Dialogue, A, 179
  Exhortation vnto the gouernours and people of Wales, The, 176
  M. Some laid open, 179
  Supplication, 181, 186, 205
Peralta, 33
Percy, John, 106, 115
  Answer to a pamphlet intituled: The Fisher catch'd in his owne net, 99, 106
  Treatise conteyning the true Catholike faith, 102
Percy, Thomas, 87
Perez, Francisco, 131, 143
Perkins, William
  Golden Chaine, A, 181
Persons, Robert, 10–11, 14–15, 23–24, 26–28, 31–34, 36, 44–45, 53–58, 63, 67, 70, 97, 111, 113–115, 118–119, 142, 149, 152, 165, 184, 208
  Answere to the fifth parte of Reportes lately set forth by Syr Edward Coke, An, 113

INDEX

Briefe apologie, or defence of the Catholike ecclesiastical hierarchie, 59
Brief discours conteyning certayne reasons why Catholiques refuse to goe to church, 23
Christian directory, The, 37, 102, 113, 130
Conference about the next succession to the Crown of Englande, A, 15, 28, 38, 54
Defence of the censure gyuen vpon two bookes of William Clarke and Meredith Hamner, Mynysters, A, 27
Discouerie of I. Nichols minister, 24
Epistle of the persecution of Catholickes in England, An, 27, 38
First booke of the christian exercise appartayning to resolution, The, 27
Greenstreet-East Ham Press, 23 –24
Iudgement of a Catholike Englishman, liuing in banishment for his religion, The, 129
Newes from Spayne and Holland, 31, 205
Relation of a triall between the bishop of Eureux and L. Plessis Mornay, A, 113
Review of Publike disputations, A, 113
Rouen Press, 26–27, 39, 49, 126, 139
Stonor Park Press, 4, 24
Treatise of three conversions of England, A, 113
Treatise tending to mitigation, A, 113, 118
Phelippes, Thomas, 165
Philip II, King of Spain, 7–8, 10, 12, 15, 31–33, 111, 117, 136
Philip III, King of Spain, 15, 69–70, 113, 153
Pickering, Lewis, 186
"Pilgrim Press" of Leyden, 195–198
Pilkington, Francis, 101
Pinart, Claude, Sieur de Cramailles, 139
Pinelli, Luca, 97
  Virgin Maries life, The, 130
Pius V, Pope, 8, 11
  "Regnans in Excelsis," 8, 11, 37
Plantin, Firm of, 26, 55, 113

Platus, Hieronymus
  De societate Jesu de bono statu religionis, 61
Ploughman's tale, The, 71
Plymouth, 43
Plymouth Colony, 198
Pointz, Robert, 48
Pole, Cardinal Reginald, 25
Popham, Sir John, 37, 62–63, 207
Ports & Port Patrol, 11, 14, 35, 43, 45–46, 50, 72, 78, 119, 206
Possevino, Antonio, 49
  Treatise of the holy sacrifice of the altar, 49
Preston, Thomas, 125
  Apologia, 56
  Responsio, 56
  Theologicall disputation concerning the oath of allegiance [Latin transl. *Disputatio theologica*], 56, 59
Prettyman, John, 81
Prevosteau, Etienne, 131
Price of books, 106–107, 114–115, 131, 182, 205–206
Primers, 20, 35–36, 49, 58, 120, 127, 194
Printing Regulations, 18–19, 46, 81
Prisons, 4, 47, 72–74, 143, 165
  Bridewell, 47, 74, 123, 180, 206
  Clink, The, 4, 10, 47, 74, 97, 165, 182–183, 206
  Compter in the Poultry, 4, 34, 47, 206
  Fleet, The, 22, 49, 106, 180
  Gatehouse, The, 21, 47, 79, 123
  Marshalsea, 10, 18, 47, 88, 165
  Newgate, 4, 10, 12, 18, 39, 47, 62, 95, 103–105, 107, 162, 165, 175, 206
  Queen's Bench, 47
  White Lion, 47, 97, 175, 182
Proclamation and edict of the Archbishop of Culleyn, 174
Prvrit-Anvs, 86–87, 94–96, 100, 104–105, 119, 129, 142, 204, 204n.
Psalters, 28, 49, 170, 181, 192–194
  Iesus Psalter, 21, 27, 61, 99, 127
  Ladies Psalter, 99
Puente, Luis de la, 116
  Meditations vppon the mysteries of our holy faith, 125

258

Purfoote, Thomas, 56
Puritans & Puritanism, 3–4, 69, 72–75, 87, 97, 140, 161–166, 170–186, 190–198, 202–209
Pursuivants, Intelligencers & Messengers of the Press, 4, 10–11, 19, 21, 24, 32, 43–44, 46–50, 56, 60, 62, 72, 78–80, 89, 116, 144, 177, 182, 184–186, 190, 203, 206
Putte, Henri de, 154
Pym, John, 75, 90

Questor, Matthew de, 72
Quinqué, Adrien, 117, 131

Ragazzoni, Girolamo, 139
Rainolds, William, 46, 131
   De iusta reip. Christianae in reges impios, 50
   Refutation of sundry apprehensions, A, 22
   Treatise conteyning the true Catholike . . . faith of the holy sacrifice, A, 33
Raleigh, Sir Walter
   History of the World, 88, 207
Ralston, Anthony, 33
Ramsey, James, 88
Randall, 36
Rastell, John, 28, 48
Rastell, William, 27
Ravaillac, François, 71
Ravenscroft, 90
Ravenscroft, Thomas (composer), 101
Rheims, 28, 32, 34–35, 38, 45, 53, 56, 115, 130–131, 138, 204
Rhiwledyn, 23
Riche, Allen, 171
Ridgely, Francis, 33
Ridley, Nicholas, 171
Rishton, Edward, 170
Rivers, Francis, 63
Robert, Griffith, 23
   Christiangawl, 23
   Dosparth byrr, (Welsh grammar), 23
   Ynglynion ar y Pader y Credo, 23
Roberts, James, 54, 57–58, 61, 84
Robinson, John, 195, 198
Robinson, Robert, 60
Robinson, Samuel, 44
Roels, 137
Rogers, Richard, 93, 164, 181
Rogers, William, 83
Rome, 8–9, 14, 38, 45, 55–56, 114, 136, 141, 150, 153, 164
   Venerabile Collegium Anglorum de urbe, 53, 117
Roper, Peter, 35
Rosier, Bernard du, 135
   Short Treatise about Ambassadors, A, 135
Ross, William, see Rainolds
Rouen, 20, 24, 26–27, 33–35, 44, 49–50, 56–57, 95, 97, 104, 130–131, 138–139, 142, 203
Rowlande, Richard, see Verstegan
Rowlands, Samuel
   Letting of humours blood in the headvaine, 85
Rule of the Friars Minor, 117
Rule of our holy mother S. Clare, The, 120
Ruyvot, 44

St. Omer, 27, 36, 80, 86, 101–102, 112–113, 116, 126–128
   Seminary, 111–113, 115–116, 127–129, 206
St. Omer English College Press, 86, 96, 104, 107, 111–115, 118–120, 127, 129, 142, 150, 204
St. Paul's Churchyard, 20, 54, 61, 105, 176, 181, 186, 202
Salesbury, William, 170
   Baterie of the pope's Botereulx, 171
Sander, Nicholas
   Supper of our Lord set foorth, The, 25
   Treatise of the images of Christ, A, 125
Sanderson, Henry, 80
Sandys, Edwin, Bishop of London, 162
Sandys, Sir Edwin
   Relation of the world, 85
Scandalum Magnatum, Decree of, 82
Schilders, Richard, 138, 184, 190–193, 196, 198, 205
Schoppe, Caspar, 154
   Corona Regia, 116–117, 154–155

INDEX

Scotland, 11, 31, 34, 53, 67, 117, 138, 184, 204–205
Scott, Thomas
  Vox populi, 144
Scupoli, Lorenzo, 97
  Spiritual conflict, The, 142
Search, Right of & Practise, 12, 14, 19, 21–22, 24, 43, 46–50, 60, 62, 74, 78, 82, 87, 89, 97, 139, 142, 173, 176–177, 182–186, 190, 197, 206
Seditious Literature, Catholic & Puritan, 8–9, 14, 21–23, 28, 38–39, 43, 45, 49, 56, 62, 78–90, 97, 100, 103–106, 118–120, 135–140, 154–157, 162–166, 171–180, 182, 185, 206–207
Seldenslach, Jacob, 131
Seminaries, Catholic, 11, 14, 32–33, 44–45 107, 111–118
Serlio, Sebastian, 27
Seville, 33, 117, 131, 143
Seymour, Sir Edward, First Earl of Hertford, 45
Shakespeare, John, 55
Shakespeare, William, 54–55, 93
  Comedies, histories & tragedies, 206
  Cronicle history of Henry the fift, The, 57
  Excellent conceited tragedie of Romeo and Juliet, 56, 60
  History of King Henrie the fourth, 180
  Midsomer nights dream, A, 57
  Most excellent historie of the Merchant of Venice, The, 57
  Most lamentable Romaine tragedie of Titus Andronicus, The, 60
  Most pleasant and excellent Comedie of Syr Iohn Falstaffe, and the merrie wives of Windsor, A, 57
  Much ado about nothing, 180
  Sonnets, 54, 206
  Tragedie of King Richard the Second, The, 180
  Tragedie of King Richard the third, The, 56, 180
  Tragicall historie of Hamlet, Prince of Denmark, The, 57
  Venus and Adonis, 56, 206
Sharpe, Henry, 179, 181

Shelton, Humphrey, 33, 203
Sidney, Sir Philip
  Arcadia, 59
Silvius, William, 37
Simons, see Fitzsimon
Simpson, Henry, 25
Singleton, Hugh, 82
Siroise, Abraham, 144
Six spirituall bookes, The, 118, 125–126
Sixtus IV, Pope, 12
  Declaration of the sentence and deposition of the vsvrped and pretensed qvene of England, A, 12, 137
Skinner, Anthony, 35
Sledd, John, 45
Sleeps, John & Catherine, 104
Smith, Peter, 98–99, 106
Smith, Richard, 106, 115, 130, 206
  Of the author and substance of the Protestant church and religion, 107
Smith, Stephen, 114
Smits, Gerard, 26
Smythe, John, 194
Snape, Edmund
  Defensive of the ecclesiastical discipline, 186
Snode, Giles, 44
Snowden, John, 14
South Shields, 35, 112, 130, 204
Southwell, Robert, 12, 14, 35, 44, 46, 57, 61, 95, 97, 127
  Humble supplication to her maiestie, 62–63
  Mary Magdalene's teares, 61
  Saint Peter's Complaint, 61–62
  Short rule of good life, A, 118, 142
Spanish Influence on England, 7–8, 10, 12–15, 26, 32–35, 38, 45, 48, 59, 68–71, 73–74, 106, 138, 141–145, 207
"Spanish John," 112
Sparke, Michael, 97
Speed, John, 49, 172
Spencer, Sir John, 174
Spencer, William, 105
Spiegel des Howelicks, Den, 190
Spinola, Ambrogio, 74
Stafford, Sir Edward, 138–140, 196, 207
Stafford, William, 71

INDEX

Stanley, William, 14
Stansby, William, 88, 99
Stapleton, Thomas, 25, 27, 45, 49
   Didimus, 38
Star Chamber, Court of, 8, 45, 73, 81–82, 89, 182, 185
Stationers, Company of, 4, 13, 19, 43, 46–49, 54, 57–61, 63, 81, 83–85, 89–90, 94, 98–99, 102, 107, 151–152, 171, 173, 175–176, 179–180, 183–184, 186, 194, 205–206
   Records, 47, 58, 61, 94, 173
Stepney, 58, 89
Stewart, James, Earl of Moray, Regent of Scotland, 68
Stinter, 139
Stock, Stephen, 72
Stokes, Robert, 183, 193
Stonor Park Press, see Persons
Stowe, John, 48
   "Cataloguy of ... vnlawfulle bookes," 48
   Summarie of Englyshe Chronicles, The, 48–49
   Strange sightes seene in the ayre ... about the cittye of Rosenberghe, 60
Strowd, John, 172–174, 185, 192, 208
Strype, John, 192
Stuart, Esmé, First Duke of Lennox, 68
Stubbs, John, 82–83
   Discouerie of a gaping gulf where into England is like to be swallowed, 82
Studley, Daniel, 183
Stuteville, Martin, 88
Sudbury, John, 83
Surius, Laurentius
   History of the Dominican Order, A, 50
Suso, Henry
   Certain sweet prayers of the glorious name of Jesus, 21
Sutcliffe, Matthew
   A treatise of ecclesiastical discipline, 33
Sweet, John, 115, 119
Symmes, Valentine, 179–180, 186

Talpin, Jean
   Pollicie Chrestien, La, 49

Taurinus, Jacob
   Weegh Schael ... over weghen de Oratie van ... Dudley Carleton, 156
Taverner, John, 88
Tavernier, Artus, 117
Taylor, Henry, 116, 155, 206
Taylor, Robert, 26
Taylor, Ursula, 112, 130
Teak, 105
Tendring, John, 74
Thackwell, 23, 176
Thevet, André, 27
Thomas a Becket, 70
Thomas a Kempis, 114, 127
   Following of Christ, The, 33, 120
Thorp, Giles, 194–195
   Hunting of the foxe, The, Part I, 194
Tomkins, Nicholas, 181–182
Tomlyn, Arthur, 179–180, 186
Topcliffe, Richard, 35, 47
Torsellino, Orazio
   History of our B. Lady of Loreto, 143
Tournai, 117, 131
Tower, The, 21, 24, 38–39, 47, 87–88, 96, 180
Tracy, Bryan, 35
Travers, Walter, 195
   Declaration of ecclesiastical discipline, A, 163, 174
Tresham, Francis, 70
Tresham, Sir Thomas, 49
Trial of trueth, The, 33
Trognaesius, Joachim, 140
Tuck, Mother, 101
Turnbull, 117
Turner, 79
Turner, Robert, pseud, Barnestapolius, Obertus
   Maria Stuarta Regina, 136
Tyburn Hill, 4, 10, 18, 22, 39, 63, 72, 103
Tyrell, Anthony, 33

Udall, John, 99, 164, 176, 184
   Amendment of life, The, 176
   Combate betwixt Christ and the Devill, The, 176

INDEX

Demonstration of discipline, The, 177, 192
State of the Churche of Englande laid open in a conference between Diotrephes a bishop, Tertullus a papist, The, known as "Diotrephes," 176
True remedie against famine and warres, The, 176
Udall, William, 78–80, 86, 94–98, 102–107, 114–115, 118–119, 128–129, 141, 150, 204, 206
Udall, Mrs. William, 101, 103, 182, 204
Underground Press, 3–4, 18, 22, 48, 63, 93–98, 107, 116, 119, 203, and *passim*
   Bunhill, 99, 106
   Greenstreet – East Ham, 23–24, 26
   Lancashire, 4, 79, 95, 98, 203
   Marprelate
      Coventry, 178
      East Moseley, 176–177
      Fawsley, 177–178
      Walston Priory, 179
   Northamptonshire, 4, 97, 174, 203
   Pilgrim, 195–198
   Smithfield, 22
   Staffordshire, 4, 62, 79, 86, 94–98, 102, 203
   Stepney, 38, 89
   Stonor Park, 24, 26
   Thackwell, 23
   Warwickshire, 4, 94
   Worcestershire, 94, 203
Ungle, Edward, 175
Unmaskinge of murder, The, 71

Vachel, 44
Vallenger, Stephen
   True reporte of the death and martyrdome of M. Campion Iesuite and priest M. Sherwin and M. Bryan priests, A, 22, 140
Vautrollier, Thomas & Jacqueline, 55
Vaux, Laurence, 28, 97
   Catechisme, 35, 120, 126
Venetian Republic, 73, 141–143, 153
Venge, Edward or Walter, 58, 63
Verstegan, Richard, 10, 14, 22, 32–34, 36, 38, 44, 140, 165, 182–184

Briefve description des diuers cruautez que les Catholiques endurent . . . pour la foi, 139
Speculum pro Christianis seductis, 33
Theatrum crudelitatum haereticorum nostri temporis, 32
Vervliet, Daniel, 131
Villegas, Alfonso
   Flos sanctorum The lives of saints, 106, 116, 118, 126–128, 204
Villeroy, Nicolas de Neufville, Seigneur de, 154
Villiers, George, Duke of Buckingham, 74
Vincent, John, 38
Vincent, John (book scout), 97
Vincent (St.) of Lerins, 20
   Pro Catholicae Fidei, 27
Vineis, Raymundus de
   Life of Catherine of Siena, The, 126
Vorst, Conrad, 155–157
   Tractatus theologicus de deo, 155

Waad, Sir William, 80, 97, 100, 129
Wadsworth, James, 127
   English Spanish Pilgrime, The, 123
Waldegrave, Robert, 23, 149, 174–181, 184–186, 192, 198, 203
Waller, 73
Walley, John, 99
Walpole, Richard, 33, 35, 112, 114
Walsingham, Francis, 119
Walsingham, Sir Francis, 11–12, 22, 37, 43, 135–140, 163
Walton, Richard, 185–186
Wandsworth, 171–173
Ward, Roger, 56
Warford, William, see Doulye
Warren, Laurence, 86, 95–97, 104
Waters, George, 194
Waterson, James, see Warren
Watson, Thomas, 20, 55, 58, 171
   Decacordon of ten quodlibeticall questions, 55
   Holsome and Catholyke doctryne concerning the seven Sacraments, The, 20
Watts, 48

Weaver, Edmund, 71
Webley, Thomas, 38–39, 43
Westenholme, John, 118
Weston, William, 34, 38
Whitelocke, Sir James, 68
Whites lamentacion, 60
Whitgift, John, 56, 162, 177–178, 182, 185
Wiclif, John
   True copy of a prolog . . . The, 171
Widdrington, John, see Preston
Wiggington, Giles, 182
Wigston, Roger, 179
Wilcox, Thomas, see Field
Williamson, William, 123
Wilson, John, 86, 96, 104, 114, 118
   English Martyrologe, The, 114
   Key of paradise, 120
   Treasury of devotion, 114
Winslow, Edward, 195
Winter, Thomas, 70
Winwood, Sir Ralph, 155, 157
Wisbeach Castle, 53, 57, 62
Wiseman, William, see Fitch
Wither, George, 88–90, 93
   Letter in answere to a late Pamphlet, 89–90
   Hymnes and Songs, 89
   Motto, 88, 205
   Schollers Purgatory, 89
Wolfe, John, 83, 176
Wollaston, William, 33
Wood, George, 89

Wood, William, 123
Woodcock, Thomas, 175–176, 180
Woodhouse, William
   Almanac, 84
Woodward, Philip, 143
   Dolefull knell of Thomas Bell, The, 130
Worthington, Thomas, 99, 128, 131, 204, 206
   Anker of Christian doctrine, The, 106, 131
   Catalogue of martyrs in England, 130, 143
   Relation of sixtene martyrs, 116
Wotton, Sir Henry, 73, 142, 152–155, 157
Wowtenel, Hans, 36
Wrench, Margaret, 95
Wrench, William, 62, 86, 94–98, 105, 107, 123
Wright, Thomas & William, 86, 95, 97
   Certaine articles . . . discouering the . . . absurdities . . . of the Protestant religion, 97
Wriothesley, Henry, Third Earl of Southampton, 87

York, 47
Young, Peter, 149
Young, Richard, 47

Zouch, Edward la, Lord, 144
Zuñiga, Pedro de, 143